Folklore and Social Media

Folklore and Social Media

Edited by
Andrew Peck and Trevor J. Blank

Utah State University Press
Logan

© 2020 by University Press of Colorado

Published by Utah State University Press
An imprint of University Press of Colorado
245 Century Circle, Suite 202
Louisville, Colorado 80027

All rights reserved

 The University Press of Colorado is a proud member of the Association of University Presses.

The University Press of Colorado is a cooperative publishing enterprise supported, in part, by Adams State University, Colorado State University, Fort Lewis College, Metropolitan State University of Denver, Regis University, University of Colorado, University of Northern Colorado, University of Wyoming, Utah State University, and Western Colorado University.

ISBN: 978-1-64642-058-2 (paperback)
ISBN: 978-1-64642-059-9 (ebook)
https://doi.org/10.7330/9781646420599

Library of Congress Cataloging-in-Publication Data

Names: Blank, Trevor J., editor. | Peck, Andrew, 1985– editor.
Title: Folklore and social media / edited by Andrew Peck & Trevor J. Blank.
Description: Louisville : University Press of Colorado, [2020] | Includes bibliographical references and index.
Identifiers: LCCN 2020028068 (print) | LCCN 2020028069 (ebook) | ISBN 9781646420582 (paperback) | ISBN 9781646420599 (ebook)
Subjects: LCSH: Folklore and the Internet. | Communication in folklore. | Social media. | Digital media.
Classification: LCC GR44.E43 F64 2020 (print) | LCC GR44.E43 (ebook) | DDC 398.20285—dc23
LC record available at https://lccn.loc.gov/2020028068
LC ebook record available at https://lccn.loc.gov/2020028069

Cover illustration © latenter/Shutterstock.

To Robert Glenn Howard

Contents

Acknowledgments ix

Introduction: Old Practices, New Media
    Andrew Peck 3

1 #LatinxGradCaps, Cultural Citizenship, and the "American Dream"
    Sheila Bock 24

2 Bridges, Sex Slaves, Tweets, and Guns: A Multi-Domain Model of Conspiracy Theory
    Timothy R. Tangherlini, Vwani Roychowdhury, and Peter M. Broadwell 39

3 The Vernacular Vortex: Analyzing the Endless Churn of Donald Trump's Twitter Orbit
    Whitney Phillips and Ryan M. Milner 67

4 The Death of Doge: Institutional Appropriations of Internet Memes
    Andrew Peck 83

5 "Zero Is Our Quota": Folkloric Narratives of the Other in Online Forum Comments
    Liisi Laineste 108

6 Trickster Remakes This White House: Booby Traps and Bawdy/Body Humor in Post-Election Prankster Biden Memes
    Jeana Jorgensen and Linda J. Lee 129

7 Dear David: Affect and Belief in Twitter Horror
    Kristiana Willsey 145

8 The Beauty, the Beast, and the Fanon: The Vernacularization of the Literary Canon and an Epilogue to Modernity
    Tok Thompson 161

9 Classifying #BlackLivesMatter: Genre and Form in Digital Folklore
    Lynne S. McNeill 179

10 The Clown Legend Cascade of 2016
      John Laudun   188

11 The Blue Whale Suicide Challenge: Hypermodern Ostension on a Global Scale
      Elizabeth Tucker   209

12 Overt and Covert Aspects of Virtual Play
      Bill Ellis   226

About the Contributors   251

Index   255

Acknowledgments

FIRST AND FOREMOST, WE WOULD LIKE TO THANK the editorial and production staff at Utah State University Press and the University Press of Colorado, especially Rachael Levay for her diligent work and guidance in bringing this volume together. We would also like to thank our reviewers for their excellent feedback, which was instrumental in honing this volume for publication. Additionally, we would like to recognize the hard work and insightful scholarship of our contributors, without whom this volume would not have been possible.

We would also like to thank our friends and colleagues for their moral support and advice throughout this process. Specifically, we would like to thank Tracy Cox, Jim Donahue, Kathleen German, Ashley Hinck, Robert Glenn Howard, Mike Jadlos, Andrea Kitta, Rosemary Pennington, Casey Schmitt, Chris Strebendt, and Jeff Tolbert.

Finally, we would like to offer special thanks to our families: to Nicky Kurtzweil for her keen copyediting eye and brilliant editorial insight and to Angelina, Louis, and Elliott Blank for their love and support.

Folklore and Social Media

Introduction
Old Practices, New Media

Andrew Peck

GAYLE KING STOPPED LAUGHING AND TURNED SERIOUS. With gravitas, the *CBS This Morning* news anchor relayed an important and timely warning to her viewers. With Halloween only a few weeks away, police in states ranging from Pennsylvania to Washington and Colorado were urging parents to check their children's trick-or-treat bags for tainted candy. The danger, the report suggested, came in the form of marijuana-laced candy, which was barely distinguishable in taste from an unadulterated treat. After a short pretaped segment featuring video from the Denver Police Department and interviews with a local family and a doctor, the camera returned to the studio, where King quipped, "Remember when you were little you just wanted to avoid the house that had the apple and the raisins. Now . . . an apple or raisin seems like a good thing compared to what kids have to worry about today. That's scary" (Garrand 2019).

This perennial worry about contaminated Halloween candy should be familiar to any folklorist. King's off-the-cuff recollection was based on oral legends about Halloween candy being tampered with that were prevalent during her youth in the 1950s and '60s and have received mass media attention for almost as long (Grider 1984, 131–133). In the 1980s, Sylvia Grider observed the role media played in propagating and reinforcing this legend, writing that such reports "pass quickly into oral tradition and thus reinforce the syndrome" (133). Even though the phenomenon—which Grider calls "Razor Blades in the Apples Syndrome"—has its nebulous roots in oral tradition, the mediation of the phenomenon demonstrates an ongoing reciprocal relationship between institutional agents, mass media, and folk practice.

Worries about marijuana-laced candy in 2019 exhibited all these traits with one important addition–the panic started because of a post on social media. A few days before the report on CBS's morning news program, the police department in a small town in Pennsylvania seized various THC-laced edibles while executing a search warrant. Although there was no evidence that the owner had planned to give them out to children on Halloween, the police department—likely inspired by similar existing legends—posted pictures and a PSA to Facebook, advising parents to "be ever vigilant in checking their children's candy before allowing them to consume those treats" (Dickson 2019).[1] Although many commenters mocked this post by suggesting naiveté on the part of police (e.g., "No one is giving away their weed to your kids. Shits expensive and you're trying to scare people"), the story received coverage from a variety of local news outlets that took the warning seriously. A few days later, these local reports were picked up by national news media, and worrying about the dangers of marijuana-laced candy became a national news item. From there, just as Grider suggests, the reports (as well as the rumors they inspired) found their way back onto social networks, feeding further vernacular expression (this time much more sincere) and reinforcing the syndrome.

For scholars of digital media and folklore, this example may be unsurprising. After all, the internet's role as a conduit for folk practice has been well documented by a variety of scholarship over the last several decades. Early work on internet folklore by scholars like John Dorst (1990), Robert Glenn Howard (1997, 2005), Barbara Kirshenblatt-Gimblett (1998), Bill Ellis (2001, 2002), Giselinde Kuipers (2002, 2005), Lajos Csaszi (2003), Jan Fernback (2003), Jeannie Banks Thomas (2003, 158–170), Russel Frank (2004), Alan Dundes (2005), Rosemary Hathaway (2005), Marjorie Kibby (2005), and Trevor J. Blank (2007) often looked at how pre-digital folk practices, like joke cycles or chain letters, were being extended and changed by the affordances of this new digital medium. Taken as a whole, this scholarship suggested that not only did folklore exist on the internet but also that digital media represented both an opportunity and a challenge for the future of folkloristics. Digital networks, Alan Dundes argued, were helping folklore flourish through increased transmission (2005, 405); but at the same time, as Barbara Kirshenblatt-Gimblett (1998) noted, this new form of digital transmission complicated our basic understanding of folk groups and their practices.

In 2008, Robert Glenn Howard critiqued some of these early approaches for being too centered around discrete media texts. The goal of digital folklore scholarship, Howard argued, was to treat these communication events discursively and to attend to the "community processes that create, maintain, and re-create these expectations" (194). Such an approach, Howard suggested, reveals the fundamentally hybrid nature of vernacular expression. In 2009's *Folklore and the Internet* Trevor J. Blank built on Howard's perspective, adding that "the Internet is new territory for the folklore discipline, and while we might be late to the dialogue, our perspectives and methodologies should not only broaden the scope of Internet studies but provide important insights into the process of everyday life in the modern technological world" (17).

In many ways, scholars like Blank and Howard (2013b) were at the forefront of the current digital turn in folklore scholarship. In the last ten years, this corpus of digital folklore scholarship has grown to include studies of vernacular religion (Howard 2011), contemporary legends (Tucker 2012; Tolbert 2013; Peck 2015; Blank and McNeill 2018), legend trips (Kinsella 2011; Tucker 2018), ostension (Peck 2016; Tolbert 2018), humor (Blank 2013, 2015; Peck 2015; Rezaei 2016), memes (Phillips and Milner 2017; Blank 2018; Peck 2019), tradition (Blank and Howard 2013b; Szpila 2017), performance (Buccitelli 2012), curation (Kaplan 2013), fan communities (Ellis 2012, 2015), virtual worlds (Gillis 2011; Lau 2010), blogging (Glass 2016), fake news (Frank 2011, 2015; Mould 2018; Peck 2020), health and medicine (Kitta 2012, 2019), computational methods (Tangherlini 2013, 2016), indigenous voices (Cocq 2015; Dubois and Cocq 2020), race (González-Martin 2016; Bock 2017; Buccitelli 2018b), disability (Blank and Kitta 2015; Milbrodt 2019), social movements (Thomas 2018), posthumanism (Thompson 2019), and intersections between folk and popular culture (Foster and Tolbert 2016; Blank 2018).[2] In other words, despite Blank's well-founded worry that the field was "late to the [digital] dialogue" (2009, 17), it appears that folkloristics has spent the better part of the last ten years making up for lost time.

However, the internet has been changing over the course of this decade of study. Digital communication technologies have become inextricably integrated into the everyday lives of millions of Americans (Buccitelli 2018a, 1), and devices like smartphones have drastically increased on-the-go access as well as access across the globe (Tsetsi and Rains 2017). In addition, web traffic has become highly centralized among a few major social media sites and social networks (Tufekci 2017, 134). Social media platforms like Facebook, Instagram, Snapchat, Twitter, and YouTube focus on supplying users with the tools to create their own content while also providing users with a steady stream of content created by others. The vernacular expression that takes place in these web locations is highly visible not only to other users but also to a variety of institutions, including politicians, journalists, advertisers, and the corporate ownership of the platforms themselves. In short, we are living in an age of constant connectedness that is defined by social media.

Much like the opportunities and challenges noted near the turn of the twenty-first century, the centrality of social media in our current cultural moment raises new questions and complicates existing answers regarding the nature of digitally mediated folklore. What happens, for instance, when informal transmission becomes subject to a proprietary algorithm? How does increased social media interactivity from a variety of institutional agents, ranging from journalists and advertisers to the president of the United States, complicate our understanding of vernacular hybridity? How does social media function as an intermediary between folk practice and mass media, and what happens when mass media covers a social media folk behavior that never actually existed? These are just some of the fundamental questions about contemporary folk practice in the age of social media that the chapters in this book strive to answer.

This book, *Folklore and Social Media*, is meant to reflect a decade of strides in the study of digital folklore while also considering the opportunities and challenges facing the next decade of scholarship. Our central premise is that digital folklore scholarship needs to take both the "digital" and "folklore" elements seriously because social media fundamentally changes folk practices in new, often invisible ways. In some respects, social media makes digital folklore look more familiar than ever. The affordances built into social media platforms encourage hybrid performances that appear informal and everyday while also offering significant space to obfuscate backstage behaviors through editing and retakes. The result is that expression online becomes increasingly reminiscent of traditional forms of face-to-face interaction while also hiding its fundamental differences.

Although a folk practice like the "Razor Blades in the Apples Syndrome" may look similar in 1984 and 2019, the affordances of social media affected nearly every aspect of the 2019 panic—how it emerged, how people initially reacted to it, how it got institutional attention, and how that institutional attention fed back into the network as a self-fulfilling prophecy. Digital folklore scholarship needs to be careful not to simply reduce our encounters with social media to their seemingly equivalent forms of unmediated everyday communication. The affordances of social media mean that we folklorists can't just apply our existing tools uncritically in this new space; instead, we must continually develop new tools and consciously adapt old ones if we are to remain viable experts of contemporary culture in this emerging media environment. The scholarship contained in this anthology is meant to demonstrate various ways in which we might refine our methods and analyses in order to develop a more complete view of the vast and complex informal and traditional dynamics that define an era of folklore and social media.

In the introductory sections that follow, I offer a brief explanation of some of the affordances that structure social media as well as digital communication more broadly. I suggest that the reciprocal relationship between these affordances and the proliferation of social media has encouraged the emergence of everyday behaviors that express new forms of (1) connection, (2) fluidity, (3) visuality, and (4) visibility. These traits, I argue, serve as an entry point for understanding how the contemporary digital folklore differs from pre-digital and pre-social media. Having established this foundation, I then provide an outline of the chapters contained in this volume and suggest how this scholarship extends our understanding of the relationship between folklore and social media.

THE CHANGING NATURE OF EVERYDAY COMMUNICATION IN AN AGE OF SOCIAL MEDIA

Networked digital communication technologies offer the potential to decouple interpersonal connection from geography and locality (Lee and Lee 2010; Blank and Howard 2013b). *Connection* in the digital age enables interaction between groups and individuals who would not otherwise meet in the course of their everyday lives. As a result, digital communities tend to form based around mutual interests or similar values (Birch and Weitkamp 2010, 905). Early work by Nancy Baym (1993), for instance, demonstrated the utility of digital communication for connecting geographically diverse soap opera fans. Similar dynamics of connectivity form the basis for a diverse range of digital communities, including the Black Lives Matter movement (Thomas 2018), Christian fundamentalists (Howard 2011), vaccination skeptics (Kitta 2012), trolls (Phillips 2015), anime fans (Ellis 2012), fans of the supernatural (Kinsella 2011; Blank and McNeill 2018; McNeill and Tucker 2018), and sleep-deprived nursing mothers (Cooper-Rompato 2013). These communities may emerge in their own discrete web spaces, but in the age of social media, these connections often emerge as a subset of linked interactions that exist on a larger website.

Social media builds on these connective affordances by also strengthening our connections to those we see every day (Blank 2013, 101–102). In her study of networked media use among adolescents, danah boyd (2014), notes that teens tend to use the internet as a social space to hang out with their friends—occupying a similar role to the mall, movie theater, or arcade in decades past (see also Hundley and Shyles 2010; Winocur 2009). For young people, these technologies enable connections that allow them to circumvent limitations and continue maintaining their face-to-face friendships, even after curfew or without a car. Adults, despite working under different sets of constraints, often use social media similarly—Facebook's chat function might help a couple stay connected during their workday, or a group chat might help sustain casual conversation among a group of friends even after one has moved to a different city and another has a newborn to look after.

The connections enabled by digital communication are always on, offering the potential for users to "feel emotionally close and connected to others even when they are physically apart from them" at all hours of the day (Patchin and Hinduja 2010, 199). This creates an expectation for constant connectedness. At 3:00 in the morning, a user can reach out to her Instagram followers or text a friend for advice. Often, this communication is faster and more frequent than pre-digital communication, even when interaction is asynchronous (Baym 2010, 8). As media scholar Henry Jenkins observes, this increased speed and frequency may intensify the social bonds between individuals or within a community (2006, 142).

Ongoing connection fosters community, and in the digital age, community membership tends to be defined by a sense of *fluidity*. Users are presented with many more options for where to engage and how to define themselves. At the same time, users are also better enabled to easily shift between those spaces and identities (Giddens 1991; Bauman 2007). Even the platforms themselves are constantly updating and changing their digital architecture (Neff and Stark 2004). Many scholars have referred to this aspect of digital communication as demonstrating "weak ties" or exhibiting "loose connections" (Green-Hamann et al. 2011, 464; Li 2011; Baym 2010, 125); however, digital communication scholar Ashley Hinck offers a compelling case for viewing these relationships in terms of fluidity. Whereas the idea of "weak ties" suggests an inferior way of associating, fluidity is meant to suggest a larger cultural shift, one in which "the agent chooses and constructs their own lifeworld from the vast array of options available in an increasingly globalized information society" (2019, 26). Fluidity, then, focuses attention on the simultaneously transient and inclusive role of choice among a multiplicity of connections (Castells 2012; Rainie and Wellman 2012). "Fluidity" denotes ease of shifting between typing an email to one's mother, upvoting a new post on Reddit, watching a livestream on Twitch, and posting a new story on Snapchat almost instantaneously (Blank 2018).

The fluid nature of digital group membership among individuals means that every network location maintains a unique set of shared expectations derived from the product of ongoing group interactions yet belonging to no specific individual. Users only ever see a small, personalized slice of the network. Even on a major social networking site like Facebook users see *their*

Facebook, not *the* Facebook (although users commonly mistake the former for the latter). The shared expectations that emerge in these localized digital spaces on social media are "displayed, reinforced, negotiated, and taught through members' shared behaviors" (Baym 2010, 80), and "any newcomer to an Internet chat room, or a Facebook page, or even a back-and-forth mobile phone texting scenario, will know that there exists a certain shared body of knowledge about how to behave in such settings" (McNeill 2009, 82). These shared expectations, in turn, affect how individuals manage and perform within their social and group identities. Since users imagine each other within the confines of these shared expectations when communicating online (Blank and Howard 2013a, 12), these shared expectations guide and delimit the emergent possibilities for interaction (Pentzold 2011, 706).

Everyday communication in the digital age is also increasingly *visual*. Networked and mobile digital communication technologies allow users to easily capture and circulate media in the course of their everyday lives. Smartphones, for instance, make it easy to record a video or snap a photograph at a moment's notice. These devices have become ubiquitous, meaning that cameras are always on our person and easy to use. The result, as sociologist Martin Hand argues, is that "digital imaging and photography have become thoroughly ordinary accompaniments to communication and connection practices in daily life" (2012, 11).

While these technologies make it easy to document the everyday, it is the social networks they connect to that enable the circulation of this documented media via the click of a button. This novel landscape is aided by the prevalence of digital locations that forefront or integrate the visual. Social media sites like Instagram, Snapchat, Facebook, and YouTube make uploading media and finding content widely accessible. Social networking sites make it easy to curate one's everyday life via media and to share that media with other users.

Social norms have embraced the affordances provided by these technologies and platforms in ways that make the visual documentation and circulation of everyday life not only possible but also expected. As Hand writes, the unprecedented levels of visual mediation in Western culture have led to social norms that support "the visual publicization of ordinary life in a ubiquitous photoscape" (2012, 1–3). Several other scholars have also noted this convergence between everyday life, digital media, and visual communication. Aaron Hess (2009), Christina Smith and Kelly McDonald (2011), Lei Guo and Lorin Lee (2013), and Kari Andén-Papadopoulos (2009) have argued that user videos posted to the popular social media website YouTube constitute forms of everyday argument. Similarly, scholars such as Blank

(2012), Milner (2013), and Peck (2014) have noted the popularity of image manipulation ("photoshopping") as a form of everyday argument on social media and as a resource for vernacular resistance of institutional narratives. Therefore, whether uploading pictures of a fancy meal or sharing a picture of oneself at a major tourist attraction, every image, Susan Murray notes, "becomes something that even the amateur can create and comment on with relative authority and ease" (2008, 151).

The resulting expressions integrate elements of visual, textual, and oral communication, but rarely fit wholly into any single category. "The devices," Hand writes, "enable and are enabled by new visual rhetorics and techniques, all of which are producing a novel landscape of screens and images" (2012, 3). Since digital communication often bears the signs of both written and spoken language, Nancy Baym suggests that it is best viewed as a mixed modality (2010, 63–64; see also Peck 2015). More than just remediation, digital technologies allow users to blend and extend written, oral, and visual communication in novel ways. The result, as Barbara Kirshenblatt-Gimblett eloquently writes, "is neither speech nor writing as we have known it, but something in between, and, increasingly, with the convergence of technologies, it is multimedia" (1998, 284). Therefore, regarding digital communication as a mixed oral/visual/textual modality is fundamental to understanding the multi- and cross-mediated ways individuals choose to engage in acts of everyday expression in digital spaces.

By allowing users to more easily capture and circulate the details of their everyday lives across networks, the affordances of digital media make the practice of everyday life more *visible* (Peck 2016). A user might live-tweet his reactions to the latest episode of *The Bachelor*, interacting with other users as if they were present on the living room couch and hailing them into his Monday night viewing routine. Another user might be reminded by Facebook to send birthday wishes to a friend and is enabled to do so via a few button presses from 600 miles away. Other users engage in intense arguments with friends, acquaintances, and strangers on topics ranging from the personal to the political, which play out in myriad forms across status updates, tweets, and comment sections. Vacation and baby photos are expected forms of public self-documentation. Mobile applications allow users to check in at a concert, share a photograph of a meal at a trendy restaurant, or post a map of that day's jogging route, notifying their social networks of their location while also publicly displaying their movement through everyday life.

These public displays of connection are vital to personal identity work on social networking sites (Van Doorn 2010, 585; Toma and Hancock

2013, 322) and, as Howard notes, "if the vernacular process of public self-imagining were to stop, no geographic location would be there to bind the individuals together" (2008, 202). As a result, sharing these quotidian details forms the backbone of social media and the Web 2.0 era. This can create a legitimating effect, allowing fringe or subcultural behaviors to transcend from the periphery toward the mainstream (Jenkins 2006, 142). Through these public displays on a mass scale, a silly trend like planking can become a full-blown cultural fad. These trends point toward the emergence of a culture of sharing, through which connection and expression create new potential for visibility and awareness of everyday practices (Peck 2016).

The visibility of everyday life enabled by new media creates an awareness that individual actions exist as part of a larger body of practice. As everyday acts circulate across networks and become more visible, users begin to recognize them not only as distinct actions but also as parts of a larger practice. Digital communication scholar Limor Shifman (2014) observes that by documenting and sharing everyday actions across networks, users make these formerly ephemeral and interpersonal communication events more visible across space and more persistent over time. The sum total of these interactions is catalogued on a variety of web locations, allowing previously uninitiated users to quickly learn about the myriad variations at play (Kaplan 2013). This mass sharing inadvertently results in a widely accessible archive of everyday practice where "it only takes a couple of mouse clicks to see hundreds of versions" (Shifman 2014, 30). The outcome of these changes in visibility, Shifman argues, is an increase in user awareness of the overall sum of these actions (29). The affordances of the digital age enable users to see their individual actions not only as discrete forms of everyday expression but also as connected to a larger body of everyday practice. In other words, the visibility created by digital communication makes users more aware of genres of expression in their everyday lives.

This increased visibility carries implications not only for vernacular expression but also for institutional influence. The visibility created by networked communication hails the attention of a variety of institutional agents looking to report on popular trends, to capitalize on the next "big thing," or to communicate in a vernacular mode for the purpose of strategic communication. A political campaign, for instance, might harvest publicly available demographic information to micro-target individual users by promoting appealing features while concealing less appealing ones (Howard 2006, 179), and a corporation can monitor large-scale social media trends as well as individual users crowdsourced to prominence (Uldam 2016). A major news network might spend part of its newscast covering a hashtag trending on Twitter or allow web users to respond to a story by using a certain hashtag. Similarly, users may circulate a bystander video or a blog post that provides initial or timely coverage to an event not yet covered by local news, creating visibility and possibly even setting the agenda for subsequent coverage by major news outlets (Meraz and Papacharissi, 2013, 139; Zelizer 2010, 245; Howard and Hussain 2011, 36). Conversely, when mass media coverage of digital trends feeds back into the network, it might reify and spread those trends, occasionally turning viral hoaxes into widely practiced reality (Peck 2020). Visibility, then, should be construed as a mixed blessing. It can give everyday users some influence over institutional narratives, but it also creates new opportunities for institutional influence and appropriation of everyday communication.

FOLKLORE AND SOCIAL MEDIA

As this introduction makes clear, the affordances built into devices like smartphones and into platforms like Facebook, Tumblr, Twitter, Instagram, and Snapchat have created new possibilities and expectations for everyday expression. Folk behaviors, practices, expressions, and creativity are similarly extended by the affordances of contemporary digital media, creating an environment that looks both familiar and uncanny. But, at the same time, social media offers new opportunities for institutions looking to sell products, bypass fact checkers, harvest data, or influence people. Increasingly, various institutional agents are adopting a vernacular mode and engaging in forms of influence that are increasingly hard to separate from everyday interactions. In other words, social media complicates our understanding not only of how folklore is expressed and transmitted but also of how folk practices can be deployed as a resource to reinscribe or resist dominant power structures.

The chapters in this volume are dedicated to teasing out the ways in which social media extends existing folk dynamics while also creating new possibilities, challenges, and power relations for vernacular and institutional interaction online. Our authors take a variety of approaches to addressing these issues, ranging from participant observation and digital ethnography to computational approaches and close textual analysis. Similarly, the studies in this volume approach folklore and social media from a variety of angles—some chapters are centered on the digital folk while others focus on institutions that adopt digital folk practices or on the relationship between mass and social media. But consistent among all of these perspectives is a recognition that a folkloric approach is crucial to understanding the increasingly central role that social media plays in our culture.

Folklore and Social Media begins with Sheila Bock's chapter, "#LatinxGradCaps, Cultural Citizenship, and the 'American Dream.'" Bock examines social media posts marked with the hashtag #LatinxGradCaps and addresses how the aesthetic and narrative framing of immigrant identities in these online displays work to problematize and reframe prevalent cultural narratives about Latinx immigrants in the United States. Bock highlights how cultural forms of expression take on heightened significance and become powerful modes of communication as Latinx individuals and communities navigate the discursive terrain of belonging and exclusion in the United States. Social media, Bock argues, is a powerful tool for reorienting dominant discourses of belonging and exclusion and for creating emergent publics that recognize the value of a more inclusive vision of the American Dream.

Chapter 2 looks at how networks create visibility for a very different type of narrative. In "Bridges, Sex Slaves, Tweets, and Guns: A Multi-Domain Model of Conspiracy Theory," Timothy R. Tangherlini, Vwani Roychowdhury, and Peter M. Broadwell outline a method for determining the structural features of conspiracy theories as well as distinguishing those theories from actual conspiracies. To do this, the authors show how conspiracy theories, from early legend complexes about witchcraft to modern-day narratives circulating on and across social media, often rely on hidden knowledge to align otherwise unlinked domains of human interaction. The authors apply this method to a variety of cases, including the Pizzagate conspiracy theory that thrived on sites like 4chan and Reddit and proposed that Democratic Party politicians were running a child sex-trafficking ring out of a Washington, DC, pizza parlor. The affordances of social media, they conclude, are uniquely situated to aid the emergence, circulation, and persistence of conspiracy theories, especially those that align with and confirm existing group biases.

Chapter 3, "The Vernacular Vortex: Analyzing the Endless Churn of Donald Trump's Twitter Orbit," by Whitney Phillips and Ryan M. Milner, builds on the previous chapters by looking at the increasingly blurry relationship between vernacular expression and institutional agents. Phillips and Milner focus on the Twitter account of the president of the United States to demonstrate how social media frustrates how we think about not only vernacular hybridity online but also the inter-relationship between the complex systems that enable it. Phillips and Milner suggest that Trump's prolific and prominent tweets are a multifaceted fusion of vernacular and institutional expression that tie together state, corporate, and folk entities as well as the affordances of social media and its users. The result, they argue, is that scholars must account more completely for these complex systems; focusing on just one element gives an incomplete picture and forestalls any discussion of what should be done in response.

In chapter 4, "The Death of Doge: Institutional Appropriations of Internet Memes," Andrew Peck examines a different way that institutional agents have tried to co-opt digital vernacular practices by looking at how institutions attempt to construct a sense of vernacular authority by integrating internet memes into their strategic communication on social media. Peck argues that the problem for institutions is that their attempts to leverage memetic practice frequently express a contradictory sense of hybridity—neither fully institutional nor fully vernacular but trying to be both. As these conflicting qualities emerge, they create a breach in expectations for vernacular memetic practice, which hails users to respond in order to reconcile the vernacular/institutional contradiction with which they are presented. The result, Peck argues, is that successful attempts by institutions to appropriate meme culture tend to be referential and concerned with affect, whereas contentious attempts try to exert too much singular control over memetic practice.

In chapter 5, "'Zero Is Our Quota': Folkloric Narratives of the Other in Online Forum Comments," Liisi Laineste looks at the role of digital humor and play in acts of Othering on Estonian social media. Laineste's chapter focuses on reactions to a sketch in a televised Estonian comedy show whose authors rewrote a popular patriotic song from the 1990s to parody xenophobic ideas regarding refugees in contemporary Estonian culture. By looking at the responses to this sketch on social media, Laineste describes how online forums simultaneously communicate approval of and opposition to such humor, sometimes within the same post. The result, Laineste argues, is that investigating humorous texts and their public reception on social media offers an entry point into describing the practices of Othering and the role of folklore, figurative speech, and grand narratives in the process.

Chapter 6, Jeana Jorgensen and Linda J. Lee's "Trickster Remakes This White House: Booby Traps and Bawdy/Body Humor in Post-Election Prankster Biden Memes" builds on the previous chapters' focus on humor, memes, politics, and play. Jorgensen and Lee look at how users transformed outgoing Vice President Joe Biden into a memetic trickster figure in the wake of the 2016 US presidential election. These memes, they argue, draw on users' cultural inventories to make critiques of President-elect Donald Trump, often by using language and imagery of the body to suggest that Trump is unsuitable for the presidency. Although these memetic critiques can be seen as problematically reinforcing hegemonic ideas of gender and power, Jorgensen and Lee suggest that these memes might also offer a resistive space to present alternative interpretations of male relationships and caring.

Chapter 7, Kristiana Willsey's "Dear David: Affect and Belief in Twitter Horror," considers vernacular hybridity through the relationship between social media and the commercialization of digital folklore. Willsey argues that it is the folkloric (collaboratively created, open-ended, and "free") quality of the web that makes a story believable, and paradoxically also what must be discarded for a story to be commercially viable (single-authored, closed, copyrighted). To make this argument Willsey examines the viral life of a Twitter ghost story through the emotional engagement of its audience. The story's creator treads a difficult line, she argues, orchestrating a dialogic and collaborative viral ghost story that thrives on uncertainty, while still holding the reins on what eventually becomes a commercial project.

Chapter 8 looks at the relationship between commercial media and folk practice from the other direction, considering the power of social media to appropriate and reimagine meaning in mass media texts. In "The Beauty, the Beast, and the Fanon: The Vernacularization of the Literary Canon and an Epilogue to Modernity," Tok Thompson historicizes the concept of the "fan-canon," or *fanon*, explaining how the aggregate volition of fans poaching elements of mass media texts creates something analogous to a canon, yet without the canon's singular (and often copyrighted) status. The fanon, Thompson argues, emerges from the idea of literary canons in order to invert the process of authorial control and institute a vernacular authority in shaping guidelines for creative copying and further storytelling. The result of this process, Thompson suggests, can be seen as a bookend to the "Gutenberg parenthesis" or as an epilogue to modernity.

Chapter 9 is a short commentary chapter by Lynne S. McNeill based on her work with the Digital Folklore Project. In "Classifying #BlackLivesMatter: Genre and Form in Digital Folklore," McNeill argues for the value of looking at a hashtag as a form of folklore, rather than (or at least as well as) seeing it as a word or phrase. Although the classification of emergent forms of vernacular digital practice represents an ongoing challenge for scholars and archivists, McNeill observes that folkloristics is uniquely suited to handle this challenge. Ultimately, McNeill argues that understanding a hashtag as folklore—that is, as culture that is both repeated and variable—is important because it offers a more holistic perspective on digital trends that other disciplines lack. Adopting a folkloric perspective, McNeill suggests, highlights how the diverse forms of related trends, both online and off, are a central, inextricable part of the phenomenon itself.

In chapter 10, "The Clown Legend Cascade of 2016," John Laudun considers the relationship between social and mass media in spreading a legend-based panic centered around sightings of creepy clowns across the United States. As Laudun observes, legend cascades have long occurred across multiple media, often leaping from one speech community to the next via either oral or media conduits. This suggests that social media not only extends familiar communities and conduits in new ways but also opens up new opportunities for data collection and analysis. By combining computational methods with close textual analysis, Laudun demonstrates how mass media reports and social media discussions fed into each other, developing and propagating the 2016 version of this perennial Halloween legend in novel ways. The result of this analysis, Laudun suggests, shows an extraordinary spike in activity that occurred far earlier than in previous years, revealing social media as not only a vehicle for legend transmission but also as a topic of contemporary concern.

Chapter 11, Elizabeth Tucker's "The Blue Whale Suicide Challenge: Hypermodern Ostension on a Global Scale," also considers how the internet can spread misinformation, especially when ostensibly "real" social media trends are picked up and disseminated by mass media. Tucker explores adolescents' interpretation of the "Blue Whale Suicide Challenge," in which evil adult curators allegedly gave vulnerable adolescents fifty tasks culminating in suicide. On YouTube many adolescents responded to rumors of this challenge with outrageous "Blue Whale" prank videos, which victimized their peers and irritated adults. Tucker notes the similarities between this social media trend and the "Satanic panic" of the 1980s and suggests that many of these pranks are based on ostension, which brought legends of the "Blue Whale Suicide Challenge" to life. While adolescents' pranks usually do not get much attention from adults, Tucker argues, their study can offer significant insights into youth culture and social problems.

Finally, in chapter 12, "Overt and Covert Aspects of Virtual Play," Bill Ellis explores one of the overarching themes of this volume—the value and significance of play on social media. Building on the work of scholars like Brian Sutton-Smith, Ellis argues that seemingly trivial forms of virtual play offer important insight not only into individuals' personalities and cultural roles but also regarding how institutions cultivate user information. Surveying examples from email, forums, and Facebook, Ellis proposes that play on social media is most engaging when enabled by six aspects, three overt (or plainly visible to observers) and three covert (subjectively sensed by the person playing). This type of virtual play results in communal processes that encourage users to share their personal information and agree to abstruse permissions in third-party applications. Such sharing and authorizing—while seemingly trivial—are invaluable to corporations that data-mine or sell the information generated by virtual play to help manipulate the public's choices.

Ellis's conclusion regarding virtual play echoes the overall conclusion of this volume. "If we choose not to study such a 'trivial' pursuit," he writes, "there are many other interest groups that already understand its value to individuals and are ready to observe and covertly exploit it for their own purposes." Everyday communication on social media may look straightforward or, at times, even trivial. But there are many stakeholders paying attention and seeking to exploit these new media environments in increasingly hidden or subtle ways.

Our authors differ in their methods, their perspectives, and even in their answers to many of the questions raised in this introduction. Which elements of the folklorist's tool kit are best suited for the study of social media? How should we update those tools? What cases necessitate the development of new tools? As our authors' varied answers to these questions (and others) suggest, this book is not meant as the final word on folklore and social media; instead, we hope to guide a rapidly growing conversation about the changing nature of vernacular communication that is taking place both inside and outside the field of folklore. Returning to Ellis's conclusion, other disciplines and interest groups already understand the value of folklore and social media (even if they do not use those terms directly), so if we choose not to participate in this conversation, then we only disempower ourselves.

Actively contributing to this conversation is crucial because while our authors may differ on many points, they all agree on one fundamental idea: that folklore is one of the best-suited disciplines for understanding how new forms of media are extending traditional dynamics like orality, vernacular expression, and the informal circulation of culture in new ways. As editors, Trevor and I hope that the ideas contained in this volume will spark a multitude of cross-disciplinary conversations and mark the beginning of another decade of insightful and incisive scholarship on folklore and the internet.

NOTES

1. In a piece fact-checking the panic for *Rolling Stone*, writer E. J. Dickson (2019) asked the Johnstown Police Department why the post implied these candies might be given to trick-or-treaters. The police department denied this was the intention of the post, though it is difficult to deny that many journalists took this unintended meaning seriously.

2. This list of digital folklore scholarship is meant to be representative and not comprehensive.

REFERENCES

Andén-Papadopoulos, Kari. 2009. "US Soldiers Imaging the Iraq War on YouTube." *Popular Communication* 7 (1): 17–27. https://doi.org/10.1080/15405700802584304.

Bauman, Zygmunt. 2007. *Liquid Times: Living in an Age of Uncertainty*. Cambridge: Polity.

Baym, Nancy K. 1993. "Interpreting Soap Operas and Creating Community: Inside a Computer-Mediated Fan Culture." *Journal of Folklore Research* 30 (2/3): 143–176.

Baym, Nancy K. 2010. *Personal Connections in the Digital Age*. Cambridge: Polity.

Birch, H., and E. Weitkamp. 2010. "Podologues: Conversations Created by Science Podcasts." *New Media and Society* 12 (6): 889–909. https://doi.org/10.1177/1461444 809356333.

Blank, Trevor J. 2007. "Examining the Transmission of Urban Legends: Making the Case for Folklore Fieldwork on the Internet." *Folklore Forum* 37 (1). http://hdl.handle.net/2022/3231.

Blank, Trevor J. 2009. "Toward a Conceptual Framework for the Study of Folklore and the Internet." In *Folklore and the Internet: Vernacular Expression in a Digital World*, edited by Trevor J. Blank, 1–20. Logan: Utah State University Press.

Blank, Trevor J. 2012. "Pattern in the Virtual Folk Culture of Computer-Mediated Communication." In *Folk Culture in the Digital Age: The Emergent Dynamics of Human Interaction*, edited by Trevor J. Blank, 1–24. Logan: Utah State University Press.

Blank, Trevor J. 2013. *The Last Laugh: Folk Humor, Celebrity Culture, and Mass-Mediated Disasters in the Digital Age*. Madison: University of Wisconsin Press.

Blank, Trevor J. 2015. "Faux Your Entertainment: Amazon.com Product Reviews as a Locus of Digital Performance." *Journal of American Folklore* 128 (509): 286–297.

Blank, Trevor J. 2018. "Folklore and the Internet: The Challenge of an Ephemeral Landscape." *Humanities* 7 (2): 50. https://doi.org/10.3390/h7020050.

Blank, Trevor J., and Robert Glenn Howard. 2013a. "Living Traditions in a Modern World." In *Tradition in the Twenty-First Century: Locating the Role of the Past in the Present*, edited by Trevor J. Blank and Robert Glenn Howard, 1–21. Logan: Utah State University Press.

Blank, Trevor J., and Robert Glenn Howard, eds. 2013b. *Tradition in the Twenty-First Century: Locating the Role of the Past in the Present*. Logan: Utah State University Press.

Blank, Trevor J., and Andrea Kitta, eds. 2015. *Diagnosing Folklore: Perspectives on Disability, Health, and Trauma*. Jackson: University Press of Mississippi.

Blank, Trevor J., and Lynne S. McNeill. 2018. "Introduction: Fear Has No Face: Creepypasta as Digital Legendry." In *Slender Man Is Coming: Creepypasta and Contemporary Legends on the Internet*, edited by Trevor J. Blank and Lynne S. McNeill, 2–23. Logan: Utah State University Press.

Bock, Sheila. 2017. "Ku Klux Kasserole and Strange Fruit Pies: A Shouting Match at the Border in Cyberspace." *Journal of American Folklore* 130 (516): 142–165.

boyd, danah. 2014. *It's Complicated: The Social Lives of Networked Teens*. New Haven: Yale University Press.

Buccitelli, Anthony Bak. 2012. "Performance 2.0: Observations toward a Theory of the Digital Performance of Folklore." In *Folk Culture in the Digital Age: The Emergent Dynamics of Human Interaction*, edited by Trevor J. Blank, 60–84. Logan: Utah State University Press.

Buccitelli, Anthony Bak. 2018a. "Introduction: Race, Ethnicity, Tradition, and Digital Technology." In *Race and Ethnicity in Digital Culture: Our Changing Traditions, Impressions, and Expressions in a Mediated World*, edited by Anthony Bak Buccitelli, 1–13. Santa Barbara: Praeger.

Buccitelli, Anthony Bak, ed. 2018b. *Race and Ethnicity in Digital Culture: Our Changing Traditions, Impressions, and Expressions in a Mediated World*. Santa Barbara: Praeger.
Castells, Manuel. 2012. *Networks of Outrage and Hope: Social Movements in the Internet Age*. Malden, MA: Polity.
Csaszi, Lajos. 2003. "World Trade Center Jokes and Their Hungarian Reception." *Journal of Folklore Research* 40 (2): 175–210.
Cocq, Coppélie. 2015. "Indigenous Voices on the Web: Folksonomies and Endangered Languages." *Journal of American Folklore* 128 (509): 273–285.
Cooper-Rompato, Christine. 2013. "The Talking Breast Pump." *Western Folklore* 72 (2): 181.
Dickson, E. J. 2019. "Are THC Edibles Being Given out as Halloween Candy? What Do You Think?" *Rolling Stone* (blog), October 14, 2019. https://www.rollingstone.com/culture/culture-features/thc-edibles-halloween-candy-urban-legend-898517/.
Dorst, John. 1990. "Tags and Burners, Cycles and Networks: Folklore in the Telectronic Age." *Journal of Folklore Research* 27 (3): 179–191.
DuBois, Thomas A., and Coppélie Cocq. 2019. *Sámi Media and Indigenous Agency in the Arctic North*. Seattle: University of Washington Press.
Dundes, Alan. 2005. "Folkloristics in the Twenty-First Century (AFS Invited Presidential Plenary Address, 2004)." *Journal of American Folklore* 118 (470): 385–408.
Ellis, Bill. 2001. "A Model for Collecting and Interpreting World Trade Center Disaster Jokes." *New Directions in Folklore* 5.
Ellis, Bill. 2002. "Making a Big Apple Crumble: The Role of Humor in Constructing a Global Response to Disaster." *New Directions in Folklore* 6.
Ellis, Bill. 2012. "Love and War and Anime Art: An Ethnographic Look at a Virtual Community of Collectors." In *Folk Culture in the Digital Age: The Emergent Dynamics of Human Interaction*, edited by Trevor J. Blank, 166–211. Logan: Utah State University Press.
Ellis, Bill. 2015. "What Bronies See When They Brohoof: Queering Animation on the Dark and Evil Internet." *Journal of American Folklore* 128 (509): 298–314. https://doi.org/10.5406/jamerfolk.128.509.0298.
Fernback, Jan. 2003. "Legends on the Net: An Examination of Computer-Mediated Communication as a Locus of Oral Culture." *New Media and Society* 5 (1): 29–45. https://doi.org/10.1177/1461444803005001902.
Foster, Michael Dylan, and Jeffrey A. Tolbert, eds. 2016. *The Folkloresque: Reframing Folklore in a Popular Culture World*. Logan: Utah State University Press.
Frank, Russell. 2004. "When the Going Gets Tough, the Tough Go Photoshopping: September 11 and the Newslore of Vengeance and Victimization." *New Media and Society* 6 (5): 633–658. https://doi.org/10.1177/146144804047084.
Frank, Russell. 2011. *Newslore: Contemporary Folklore on the Internet*. Jackson: University Press of Mississippi.
Frank, Russell. 2015. "Caveat Lector: Fake News as Folklore." *Journal of American Folklore* 128 (509): 315–332.
Garrand, Danielle. 2019. "Police Urge Parents to Check Halloween Candy After THC-Laced 'Nerds Rope' Edibles Found." *CBS This Morning*, October 13, 2019. https://www.cbsnews.com/news/nerds-rope-thc-police-urge-parents-to-check-halloween-candy-after-thc-laced-nerds-rope-edibles-found/.
Giddens, Anthony. 1991. *Modernity and Self-Identity: Self and Society in the Late Modern Age*. Stanford: Stanford University Press.
Gillis, Ben. 2011. "An Unexpected Font of Folklore: Online Gaming as Occupational Lore." *Western Folklore* 70 (2): 147–170.
Glass, Andrea. 2016. "'I Want to Be a Witness': Blogging for Urban Authenticity and Cultural Authority in the East Village." *New Directions in Folklore* 14 (1/2): 3–39.

Gonzalez-Martin, Rachel V. 2016. "Digitizing Cultural Economies: 'Personalization' and U.S. Quinceanera Practice Online." *Cultural Analysis* 15 (1): 57–77.

Green-Hamann, Sara, Kristen Campbell Eichhorn, and John C. Sherblom. 2011. "An Exploration of Why People Participate in Second Life Social Support Groups." *Journal of Computer-Mediated Communication* 16 (4): 465–491. https://doi.org/10.1111/j.1083-6101.2011.01543.x.

Grider, Sylvia. 1984. "The Razor Blades in the Apples Syndrome." In *Perspectives on Contemporary Legend: Proceedings of the Conference of Contemporary Legend*, edited by Paul Smith, 128–140. Sheffield: CECTAL.

Guo, Lei, and Lorin Lee. 2013. "The Critique of YouTube-Based Vernacular Discourse: A Case Study of YouTube's Asian Community." *Critical Studies in Media Communication* 30 (5): 1–16. https://doi.org/10.1080/15295036.2012.755048.

Hand, Martin. 2012. *Ubiquitous Photography*. Cambridge: Polity.

Hathaway, Rosemary V. 2005. "'Life in the TV': The Visual Nature of 9/11 Lore and Its Impact on Vernacular Response." *Journal of Folklore Research* 42 (1): 33–56.

Hess, Aaron. 2009. "Resistance Up in Smoke: Analyzing the Limitations of Deliberation on YouTube." *Critical Studies in Media Communication* 26 (5): 411–434. https://doi.org/10.1080/15295030903325347.

Hinck, Ashley. 2019. *Politics for the Love of Fandom: Fan-Based Citizenship in a Digital World*. Baton Rouge: Louisiana State University Press.

Howard, Philip N. 2006. *New Media Campaigns and the Managed Citizen*. Cambridge: Cambridge University Press.

Howard, Philip N., and Muzammil M. Hussain. 2011. "The Upheavals in Egypt and Tunisia: The Role of Digital Media." *Journal of Democracy* 22 (3): 35–48. https://doi.org/10.1353/jod.2011.0041.

Howard, Robert Glenn. 1997. "Apocalypse in Your In-Box: End-Times Communication on the Internet." *Western Folklore* 56 (3/4): 295–315.

Howard, Robert Glenn. 2005. "Toward a Theory of World Wide Web Vernacular: The Case for Pet Cloning." *Journal of Folklore Research* 42 (3): 323–360.

Howard, Robert Glenn. 2008. "Electronic Hybridity: The Persistent Processes of the Vernacular Web." *Journal of American Folklore* 121 (480): 192–218.

Howard, Robert Glenn. 2011. *Digital Jesus: The Making of a New Christian Fundamentalist Community on the Internet*. New York: New York University Press.

Hundley, H. L., and L. Shyles. 2010. "US Teenagers' Perceptions and Awareness of Digital Technology: A Focus Group Approach." *New Media and Society* 12 (3): 417–433. https://doi.org/10.1177/1461444809342558.

Jenkins, Henry. 2006. *Fans, Bloggers, and Gamers: Exploring Participatory Culture*. New York: New York University Press.

Kaplan, Merrill. 2013. "Curation and Tradition on Web 2.0." In *Tradition in the Twenty-First Century: Locating the Role of the Past in the Present*, edited by Trevor J. Blank and Robert Glenn Howard, 123–148. Logan: Utah State University Press.

Kibby, M. D. 2005. "Email Forwardables: Folklore in the Age of the Internet." *New Media and Society* 7 (6): 770–790. https://doi.org/10.1177/1461444805058161.

Kinsella, Michael. 2011. *Legend-Tripping Online: Supernatural Folklore and the Search for Ong's Hat*. Jackson: University Press of Mississippi.

Kirshenblatt-Gimblett, Barbara. 1998. "Folklore's Crisis." *Journal of American Folklore* 111 (441): 281–327.

Kitta, Andrea. 2012. *Vaccinations and Public Concern in History: Legend, Rumor, and Risk Perception*. New York: Routledge.

Kitta, Andrea. 2019. *The Kiss of Death: Contagion, Contamination, and Folklore*. Logan: Utah State University Press.

Kuipers, Giselinde. 2002. "Media Culture and Internet Disaster Jokes: Bin Laden and the Attack on the World Trade Center." *European Journal of Cultural Studies* 5 (4): 450–470.

Kuipers, Giselinde. 2005. "'Where Was King Kong When We Needed Him?' Public Discourse, Digital Disaster Jokes, and the Functions of Laughter After 9/11." *Journal of American Culture* 28 (1): 70–84. https://doi.org/10.1111/j.1542-734X.2005.00155.x.

Lau, Kimberly J. 2010. "The Political Lives of Avatars: Play and Democracy in Virtual Worlds." *Western Folklore* 69 (3/4): 369–394.

Lee, Junghee, and Hyunjoo Lee. 2010. "The Computer-Mediated Communication Network: Exploring the Linkage between the Online Community and Social Capital." *New Media and Society* 12 (5): 711–727. https://doi.org/10.1177/1461444809343568.

Li, Xigen. 2011. "Factors Influencing the Willingness to Contribute Information to Online Communities." *New Media & Society* 13 (2): 279–296. https://doi.org/10.1177/1461444810372164.

McNeill, Lynne S. 2009. "The End of the Internet: A Folk Response to the Provision of Infinite Choice." In *Folklore and the Internet: Vernacular Expression in a Digital World*, edited by Trevor J. Blank, 80–97. Logan: Utah State University Press.

McNeill, Lynne S., and Elizabeth Tucker. 2018. *Legend Tripping: A Contemporary Legend Casebook*. Logan: Utah State University Press.

Meraz, S., and Z. Papacharissi. 2013. "Networked Gatekeeping and Networked Framing on #Egypt." *International Journal of Press/Politics* 18 (2): 138–166. https://doi.org/10.1177/1940161212474472.

Milbrodt, Teresa. 2019. "Dating Websites and Disability Identity: Presentations of the Disabled Self in Online Dating Profiles." *Western Folklore* 78 (1): 66–100.

Milner, Ryan M. 2013. "Pop Polyvocality: Internet Memes, Public Participation, and the Occupy Wall Street Movement." *International Journal of Communication* 7: 2357–2390.

Mould, Tom, ed. 2018. "Fake News: Definitions and Approaches." *Journal of American Folklore* 131 (522). http://muse.jhu.edu/article/707441.

Murray, S. 2008. "Digital Images, Photo-Sharing, and Our Shifting Notions of Everyday Aesthetics." *Journal of Visual Culture* 7 (2): 147–163. https://doi.org/10.1177/1470412908091935.

Neff, Gina, and David Stark. 2004. "Permanently Beta: Responsive Organization in the Internet Era." In *Society Online: The Internet in Context*, edited by Philip N. Howard and Steve Jones, 173–188. Thousand Oaks, CA: Sage.

Patchin, J. W., and S. Hinduja. 2010. "Trends in Online Social Networking: Adolescent Use of MySpace over Time." *New Media and Society* 12 (2): 197–216. https://doi.org/10.1177/1461444809341857.

Peck, Andrew. 2014. "A Laugh Riot: Photoshopping as Vernacular Discursive Practice." *International Journal of Communication* 8: 1638–1662.

Peck, Andrew. 2015. "Tall, Dark, and Loathsome: The Emergence of a Legend Cycle in the Digital Age." *Journal of American Folklore* 128 (509): 333–348.

Peck, Andrew. 2016. "At the Modems of Madness: The Slender Man, Ostension, and the Digital Age." *Contemporary Legend* 3 (5): 14–37.

Peck, Andrew. 2019. "Beautiful Human Sweater Memes: Internet Memes as Vernacular Responses to Presidential Debates." In *Televised Presidential Debates in a Changing Media Environment*. Vol. 2: *The Citizens Talk Back*, edited by Edward A. Hinck, 179–202. Santa Barbara: Praeger.

Peck, Andrew. 2020. "A Problem of Amplification: Folklore and Fake News in the Age of Social Media." *Journal of American Folklore* 133 (529): 329–351.

Pentzold, C. 2011. "Imagining the Wikipedia Community: What Do Wikipedia Authors Mean When They Write about Their 'Community'?" *New Media and Society* 13 (5): 704–721. https://doi.org/10.1177/1461444810378364.
Phillips, Whitney. 2015. *This Is Why We Can't Have Nice Things: Mapping the Relationship between Online Trolling and Mainstream Culture.* Cambridge, MA: MIT Press.
Phillips, Whitney, and Ryan M. Milner. 2017. *The Ambivalent Internet: Mischief, Oddity, and Antagonism Online.* Cambridge: Polity.
Rainie, Harrison, and Barry Wellman. 2012. *Networked: The New Social Operating System.* Cambridge, MA: MIT Press.
Rezaei, Afsane. 2016. "'The Superman in a Turban': Political Jokes in the Iranian Social Media." *New Directions in Folklore* 14 (1/2): 89–132.
Shifman, Limor. 2014. *Memes in Digital Culture.* Cambridge, MA: MIT Press.
Smith, Christina M., and Kelly M. McDonald. 2011. "The Mundane to the Memorial: Circulating and Deliberating the War in Iraq through Vernacular Soldier-Produced Videos." *Critical Studies in Media Communication* 28 (4): 292–313. https://doi.org/10.1080/15295036.2011.589031.
Szpila, Grzegorz. 2017. "Polish Paremic Demotivators: Tradition in an Internet Genre." *Journal of American Folklore* 130 (517): 305–334.
Tangherlini, Timothy R. 2013. "The Folklore Macroscope: Challenges for a Computational Folkloristics." *Western Folklore* 72 (1): 7–27.
Tangherlini, Timothy R. 2016. "Big Folklore: A Special Issue on Computational Folkloristics." *Journal of American Folklore* 129 (511): 5–13. https://doi.org/10.5406/jamerfolk.129.511.0005.
Thomas, Jeannie B. 2003. *Naked Barbies, Warrior Joes, and Other Forms of Visible Gender.* Urbana: University of Illinois Press.
Thomas, Jeannie Banks. 2018. "#BlackLivesMatter: Galvanizing and Oppositional Narratives." In *Race and Ethnicity in Digital Culture: Our Changing Traditions, Impressions, and Expressions in a Mediated World*, edited by Anthony Bak Buccitelli, 95–114. Santa Barbara: Praeger.
Thompson, Tok. 2019. "Ghost Stories from the Uncanny Valley: Androids, Souls, and the Future of Being Haunted." *Western Folklore* 78 (1): 39–65.
Tolbert, Jeffrey A. 2013. "'The Sort of Story That Has You Covering Your Mirrors': The Case of Slender Man." *Semiotic Review*, no. 2 (November): 1–23.
Tolbert, Jeffrey A. 2018. "'The Sort of Story That Has You Covering Your Mirrors': The Case of Slender Man." In *Slender Man Is Coming: Creepypasta and Contemporary Legends on the Internet*, edited by Trevor J. Blank and Lynne S. McNeill, 25–50. Logan: Utah State University Press.
Toma, C. L., and J. T. Hancock. 2013. "Self-Affirmation Underlies Facebook Use." *Personality and Social Psychology Bulletin* 39 (3): 321–331. https://doi.org/10.1177/0146167212474694.
Tsetsi, Eric, and Stephen A. Rains. 2017. "Smartphone Internet Access and Use: Extending the Digital Divide and Usage Gap." *Mobile Media and Communication* 5 (3): 239–255. https://doi.org/10.1177/2050157917708329.
Tucker, Elizabeth. 2012. "From Oral Tradition to Cyberspace: Tapeworm Diet Rumors and Legends." In *Folk Culture in the Digital Age: The Emergent Dynamics of Human Interaction*, edited by Trevor J. Blank, 150–165. Logan: Utah State University Press.
Tucker, Elizabeth. 2018. "'There's an App for That': Ghost Hunting with Smartphones." In *Legend Tripping: A Contemporary Legend Casebook*, edited by Lynne S. McNeill and Elizabeth Tucker, 192–206. Logan: Utah State University Press.
Tufekci, Zeynep. 2017. *Twitter and Tear Gas: The Power and Fragility of Networked Protest.* New Haven: Yale University Press.

Uldam, J. 2016. "Corporate Management of Visibility and the Fantasy of the Post-political: Social Media and Surveillance." *New Media and Society* 18 (2): 201–219. https://doi.org/10.1177/1461444814541526.

Van Doorn, N. 2010. "The Ties That Bind: The Networked Performance of Gender, Sexuality and Friendship on MySpace." *New Media and Society* 12 (4): 583–602. https://doi.org/10.1177/1461444809342766.

Winocur, Rosalía. 2009. "Digital Convergence as the Symbolic Medium of New Practices and Meanings in Young People's Lives." Translated by Margaret Schwartz. *Popular Communication* 7 (3): 179–187. https://doi.org/10.1080/15405700903023285.

Xigen, Li. 2011. "Factors Influencing the Willingness to Contribute Information to Online Communities." *New Media and Society* 13 (2): 279–296. https://doi.org/10.1177/1461444810372164.

Zelizer, Barbie. 2010. *About to Die: How News Images Move the Public*. New York: Oxford University Press.

1

#LatinxGradCaps, Cultural Citizenship, and the "American Dream"

Sheila Bock

DECORATING MORTARBOARDS HAS BECOME an increasingly common practice among graduating students. Within the context of commencement ceremonies, participating in this practice can serve multiple functions for graduates, ranging from the practical—specifically, helping friends and family members to spot them in the crowd—to the expressive, such as making visible individual personality traits, personal experiences, strongly held beliefs, aesthetic preferences, and personalized messages of appreciation, pride, or frustration (Bock 2014, 2017a). In other words, decorating their mortarboards allows graduates to highlight aspects of the self that are often rendered invisible by the ceremonial dress of the commencement ritual.[1]

The practice of embellishing mortarboards is certainly not new. In the 1960s, for example, some graduates would place peace signs on the tops of their mortarboards to protest the Vietnam War. Using the blank canvas of the mortarboard as a site of material expression has become increasingly more common over time, particularly as a way to personalize a typically impersonal ritual event. The widespread popularity of the practice in the present day can be attributed, at least in part, to social media. Indeed, the majority of the recent graduates I have interviewed identified social media platforms as the sites where they first learned about the practice of decorating mortarboards. The mortarboards themselves, to quote one interviewee, are very "Instagrammable," meaning that they are visually appealing, easy to photograph, and easy to share. Understood as spaces of personal expression, they also fit in well with the goals of social media platforms like Instagram, a social networking application typically used for curating one's digital self through sharing with friends and followers photos representing personal perspectives and experiences. As more and more people have posted photos of their decorated mortarboards online, and as these photos have been shared by others, individual decorated mortarboards have found much larger audiences than they have had in the past, which in turn has inspired others to decorate their own.

Aside from contributing to more widespread participation in the practice of decorating mortarboards, social media platforms also provide opportunities for new contexts of display, beyond the ceremony itself, that engage with different and more extensive audiences. These new contexts of display become sites of both amplified personal performances and community enactments. This chapter focuses on the interplay between personal performances and community enactments in online posts marked with the hashtag #LatinxGradCaps. This hashtag, which began in spring 2016 and has reemerged during subsequent graduation seasons, was initiated by Prisca Dorcas Mojica Rodriguez, founder of Latina Rebels, a social media platform that extends across multiple sites, including Facebook, Instagram, Tumblr, and Twitter. The purpose of Latina Rebels, according to its mission statement, is to empower "fully present Latinidad, one Latina at a time, by disrupting the binary expectations that are placed on Latinas' bodies and minds," and "to f*ck with your colonized expectations of 'acceptability.'"[2] The description on the Facebook page at the time the #LatinxGradCaps hashtag launched in 2016 offers further explanation: "We, as Latinas, are passionate about unveiling the injustices that exist when gender and race (or ethnicity) collide in Latinas' embodied realities. We function to disrupt the 'good' girl versus 'bad' girl binary that is a product of white colonization, which functions to police the bodies and mind of womxn of color—thus by voicing our contextual realities as mostly Latina immigrants, we hope to further the perspective of Latinidad in America."[3]

The #LatinxGradCaps hashtag itself uses the term *Latinx* as an alternative signifier to the *Latina/o* gender binary, similarly to how the term *womxn* above works to be more inclusive of a broader range of gender identities.[4] While many of the images posted online with this hashtag feature decorated mortarboards that illustrate more widespread trends I have observed and documented in the tradition more broadly—including, for example, the use of inspirational quotes, popular culture references, expressions of gratitude to parents, and large amounts of flowers and other colorful embellishments to help stand out in the crowd—the feminist activist imperative driving this online community is clearly visible in the mortarboards featured in the posts. Assertions of Latinx feminist identities take many forms, ranging from proclamations like "Soy Capaz So Fuerte Soy Incencible Soy Mujer" (I

Am Capable I Am Strong I Am Invincible I Am a Woman) to visual and textual references to the Mexican artist and queer feminist icon Frida Kahlo to quotes from the Chicana queer feminist scholar, writer, and activist Gloria Anzaldúa. Working to disrupt the "good girl"/"bad girl" binary, other mortarboards make proud claims to gender-, ethnic-, and class-based identities that often carry negative connotations, such as "educated Chingona" and "you can't spell scholar without Chola."[5]

Many of the mortarboards posted with the #LatinxGradCaps hashtag also engage with the theme of immigration, for example, by marking the graduate as an immigrant or by situating the achievement of graduation as part of an ongoing family immigration story. The remainder of this chapter will address how the aesthetic and narrative framings of immigrant identities in these online displays individually and collectively work to problematize and reframe prevalent cultural narratives about Latinx immigrants in the United States and their relationship to the "American Dream."[6]

The popularization of the phrase the "American Dream" can be traced back to author James Truslow Adams's book *The Epic of America*. According to Adams, the American Dream is one "of social order in which each man and each woman shall be able to attain to the fullest stature of which they are innately capable, and be recognized by others for what they are, regardless of the fortuitous circumstances of birth or position" (1931, 404). This idea has been a prevalent force in the history of the United States. Some of the core values that have consistently shaped the idea of the American Dream in both the past and the present include freedom, equality of opportunity, and individual rights, along with hard work, perseverance, and an enduring optimism that eventual success is possible (Cullen 2003; Terkel 1980; White 2016).

Critiques of the American Dream have called attention to the ways in which the concept relies on a conflation between citizenship and whiteness, particularly middle-class whiteness (Dick 2011; Hanson and White 2016; Martínez et al. 2016). Within this framing, assimilation to the white middle-class ideal is a key prerequisite for immigrants to gain access to the dream, a prerequisite that works to exclude people of color from its promises. In the words of Carola and Marcelo Suárez-Orozco: "Today's immigrants of color are seen by many as possessing traits that make them 'unmeltable' and incompatible with modern American culture. Like other minority groups (such as African Americans and Puerto Ricans), some new immigrants have been characterized as being culturally inferior, lazy, and prone to crime and therefore less deserving of sharing in the dreams of dominant mainstream society" (2001, 8).

This framing constructs immigrants of color and their children as standing in the way of others who are considered "more deserving" of achieving the benefits of the American Dream. Anthropologist Leo R. Chavez has looked extensively at how the white-centered framings of the American Dream affect Latino immigrants and their US-born counterparts in particular through the construction of what he terms the "Latino Threat Narrative": "According to the assumptions and taken-for-granted 'truths' inherent in this narrative," Chavez explains, "Latinos are unwilling or incapable of integrating, of becoming part of the national community" (2013, 3). This pervasive narrative both homogenizes and pathologizes Latinx communities, framing them as "other" regardless of official citizenship status.

Within this hostile discursive context of marginalization, citizenship is not just a legal site of negotiation but also a cultural one. Expanding the scope of inquiry beyond the legal categories of citizenship, scholars have increasingly turned attention to the idea of cultural citizenship, which refers to "how Latinos are incorporating themselves into US society, while simultaneously developing specifically Latino cultural forms of expression that not only keep identity and heritage alive but significantly enrich the cultural whole of the country" (Flores and Benmayor 1997, 2). Cultural forms of expression, in other words, take on heightened significance and become powerful modes of communication as Latinx individuals and communities navigate the discursive terrain of belonging and exclusion in the United States.

Attending to this discursive terrain of belonging and exclusion, my analysis here takes as its starting point the perspective of what Rachel González-Martin terms Critical Latinx Folkloristics, one that foregrounds "the inter-subjective experiences of people of color in the United States, in particular Latinx communities" by examining "communities and individuals at the interstices between that which is understood as the public sphere and the recognized personal or private sphere" (forthcoming). According to González-Martin, recognizing the interplay between these two domains in the study of expressive culture is crucial for understanding how Latinx individuals and communities create spaces of creative expression within discursive contexts of marginalization and contingent citizenship. Such an approach moves away from prioritizing ethno-nationalist identities (e.g., Mexican American) as modes of orienting people's relationships to the expressive practices under study and instead turns attention to the shared experiences of the Latinidad in the United States and the ways in which cultural expressions create emergent *publics*.

Building upon Michael Warner's understanding of *publics* as being constituted through discourse (2002), Critical Latinx Folkloristics brings attention to how cultural expressions are shaped by intersectional identities and work as "self-conscious forms of self-documentation that simultaneously refuse outsider judgment to validate the process of public self-creation, while also benefitting from legibility to outsider gaze to circulate political dissent" (González-Martin, forthcoming). In short, studying cultural expressions through the framework of Critical Latinx Folkloristics opens up opportunities to examine not only how people navigate, but also how they actively seek to reorient, dominant discourses of belonging and exclusion.

Attaining an education is widely understood to be one important way of opening up opportunities for achieving the upward mobility promised by the American Dream. As a result, academic dress and mortarboards have served as potent symbols used by activists fighting for the Development, Relief, and Education for Alien Minors Act, more commonly known by its acronym the DREAM Act, a legislative proposal providing undocumented immigrants who came to the United States as children with a pathway to citizenship. Immigrant rights activists have used images of students in graduation robes and mortarboards on T-shirts, posters, and websites to illuminate the contradictory plight of undocumented college students who exemplify the values of hard work and perseverance central to the American Dream without having access to the potential rewards due to their circumstances of birth. They have also worn robes and mortarboards in mock graduations at the local and national level, holding banners touting messages such as "Now What?" and "It is not my fault my parents brought me here 4 a better future" (Chavez 2013, 187).

Turning attention now to the images posted with the #LatinxGradCaps hashtag, it is clear that the mortarboard itself serves as more than a blank canvas on which people are presenting their personal and political messages. The mortarboard serves as a potent symbol itself. As a recognizable marker of the achievement it signifies, the mortarboard becomes a visible way to rhetorically claim a sense of value and belonging. Within this rhetorical framing, assertions of Latinx and/or immigrant identities (both through the use of the hashtag and through the way the mortarboards are decorated) become forms of resistance to and rearticulations of dominant narratives excluding these identities from claims to the benefits of citizenship.

Many of the mortarboards make reference to the immigrant status of the graduates or their family members. These references take both visual form—for example, by including images of butterflies, a prevalent symbol of the immigrant rights movement—and textual form, through phrases like "HIJA DE INMINGRANTES" (daughter of immigrants), "WE MIGRATED SO I GRADUATED," and "undocumented unafraid unapologetic." Many of the mortarboards also make explicit reference to the DREAM Act, using the multiple meanings of the word *dream* to situate DREAMers, individuals who arrived in the United States as minors and consequently do not have American citizenship, as belonging within the narrative of the American Dream:

> TURNING MY DREAMS INTO REALITY—Undocumented Student!
> DREAMS WITHOUT BORDERS GRACIAS MAMI Y PAPÁ [Thank you, Mom and Dad]
> Dreamers can do it too!
> Every Dream Begins with a Dreamer
> Create opportunities NOT Walls—1st GEN DREAMer
> AMERICAN DREAM

Other mortarboards tout messages of optimism and opportunity—for example, "Y Seguiré Volando" (And I Will Continue Flying)—that exemplify some of the core values of the American Dream. At the same time, the use of the Spanish language in this example and so many others works also to problematize and resist the assimilation narrative associated with the dream. The prevalence of flag images in these mortarboards, or the colors and imagery associated with specific flags, does similar work.[7] Some of these caps include imagery from both the US flag and other flags, communicating alignment with different national identities and cultural heritages. A good number, however, notably make visible the graduates' connections to countries of origin only, not just through flag imagery but also through folk speech (e.g., "PURA VIDA" [Pure Life]).[8]

One image posted with the hashtag features a mortarboard that reads, "I CARRY RESILIENCE EN LA FRENTE" (on the forehead), an adaptation of a folk saying—"con el nopal en la frente" (with a cactus on the forehead)—used in reference to people who try to deny their Mexican identity.[9] On Instagram, the photo of this mortarboard is accompanied by a caption that offers some additional context for the experiences and perspectives of the graduate who wore it: "I used to hate my skin tone & I used to hate being 'just Mexican,' but college changed that. I am proud to be Mexican, I am in love with my perfectly imperfect brown skin, but more than anything I am proud of my struggle because it makes this moment mean so much more."

Struggle and resilience, in fact, are recurring themes in the mortarboard images posted with this hashtag. Several, for example, made textual or visual reference to the phrase "They tried to bury us. They didn't know we were seeds." Originally written by gay Greek poet Dinos Christianopoulos, these words were adopted by the Zapatista movement and have come into common use by Mexican and Mexican American activists, often labeled in online memes as a Mexican proverb. One mortarboard featuring this quote was accompanied by the following caption: "My papi was on his death bed on April 11, 2015 due to a traumatic brain injury. The doctors told us he had a slim chance. I was angry. Why did I take so long in school? He is supposed to be there to see his little girl receive her bachelor's degree. Here we are a year later and my papi will be in the stands like a seed who has risen with new life. Like all of us, the children of immigrants, la raza . . . we rise against all odds. My papi taught me that. This is political. This is personal. This is all of us." This caption exemplifies two key trends in the body of posts as a whole marked by the hashtag #LatinxGradCaps: the clear situating of struggle as a family (not just a personal) affair and the linking of the personal and the political.

Many of the mortarboards feature text that explicitly situates the accomplishment of attaining a college degree as part of an ongoing family immigration story, through phrases like "PARA MI MAMI QUIEN CRUZO FRONTERAS PARA QUE YO ESTE AQUI" (For my mama, who crossed borders for me to be here) and "SUS SACRIFICIOS NO FUERON EN VANO" (Your sacrifices were not in vain). Further illustrating this theme, many of the mortarboards feature names and photographs of family members. One even includes material from the graduate's grandmother's work dress, which is explained with the following caption: "As I wrapped my grandmother's work dress around my cap I could not help but feel overwhelmed with tears as I channeled her strength to be where I am today. I could not have done it without her, my mother or my daughters. 'Here's to strong women, may we know them. May we be them. May we raise them.'"

Notably, given Latina Rebels's goals of "voicing our contextual realities as mostly Latina immigrants," many of the posts featuring decorated mortarboards foreground female gender identities as key dimensions of graduates' contextual realities. These posts often highlight these identities as key parts of the ongoing family stories being shared, as in the accompanying explanation above, as well as through mortarboards proclaiming "PARA LAS MUJERES FUERTES EN MI FAMILIA" (For the strong women in my family), "CHINGONA COMO MI MADRE" (Badass like my mother), and "Here b/c of Mujeres Chingonas como mi mama" (Here because of Badass Women like my mom).

Within the online context of display, numerous photos feature the graduates standing proudly with family members, and many are accompanied by specific family narratives of hard work and overcoming adversity. To offer one example:

My parents came to this country back in 1993 from Zacatecas, Mexico to give their future children a better future. It took my father 20 years to get his residency and we are still fighting for my mom. Today I made them proud by walking that stage. I do everything for them and without their help and support I wouldn't have done it alone. Those long hours they worked when I was a child I remember. My father working from different restaurants to my mother busting her ass in 12 hour shifts as a housekeeper and in dry cleaners. It's all for us. Immigrants truly work harder than anyone else and they do it for us! Their children! Gracias mama y papa for todo lo que han hecho por mi y mis hermanos [Thank you, Mom and Dad, for everything you have done for me and my siblings].

Of course, as I have already noted, a key theme in so many of these mortarboards is the undeniable connection between the personal and the political, an idea foregrounded in the graduation caps themselves through phrases like "¡Sí Se Puede!" (Yes, it can be done!) and "¡Sí se pudo!" (I did it!), phrases *both* infused with personal hope and accomplishment *and* connected to the struggle of working-class Latinx communities and the quest for pro-immigrant rights.[10] We also see other explicit references to specific immigrant rights activist movements both visually (e.g., the "Migration is Beautiful" butterfly) and textually (e.g., "Sin Papeles Sin Miedo" [No Papers No Fear]).

Other graduates posting with the #LatinxGradCaps hashtag feature raised fists, a gestural tradition of political resistance and solidarity with oppressed groups, either in the visual designs of the mortarboards themselves, as emojis in the captions accompanying the images, or in their poses within the photographs shared on social media.[11] In one post featuring a photo of a graduate raising her fist with her back to the camera, showing a mortarboard adorned with an image of a Day of the Dead skull laid over the colors of the Mexican flag, the accompanying caption reads: "Shout out to the white guy who yelled that I was stupid Mexican when I was 8 years old while doing chalk art. I graduate mañana [tomorrow] and you've never been more wrong." In fact, many of the images posted with the #LatinxGradCaps hashtag are accompanied by personal narratives or references to formative experiences of racism.

Some of the mortarboards posted with the hashtag reference the pervasive narrative that immigrants steal jobs from American-born citizens, proclaiming, "JOB STEALING IMMIGRANT" and "TRUCHA, I'm here to steal your job!"[12] Others make direct reference to President Donald Trump and his anti-immigrant rhetoric, as in "This LATINA TRUMPed the STEREOTYPE" (with the word "Trump" crossed out) and "MEXICO DOES SEND ITS BEST

Gracias a mis padres!" (Thank you to my parents), with a caption that reads, "Nunca me olvidare de mis raíces" (I will never forget my roots). These examples of mortarboard displays, in recontextualizing and reframing the rhetoric of Donald Trump, align with the observations of Stephanie Slaughter that productions of this kind work to construct counternarratives through social media and create ways "to claim discursive spaces for Latinx political perspectives in a media landscape and political process that silence those perspectives" (2016, 543).

Clearly, the posts marked with the #LatinxGradCaps hashtag are shaped in response to the homogenizing and pathologizing dominant narratives circulating about Latinx immigrants and their families. Leo Chavez explains: "How newcomers imagine themselves and are imagined by the larger society in relation to the nation is mediated through the representations of immigrants' lives in media coverage. Media spectacles transform immigrants' lives into virtual lives, which are typically devoid of the nuances and subtleties of real lived lives" (2013, 6). Posts using the #LatinxGradCaps hashtag, particularly those that focus on the experiences of immigration, work actively to problematize mediated representations of Latinx communities and foreground the nuances and subtleties of the real lived lives of the graduates and their families. During an interview, Prisca Dorcas Mojica Rodriguez, the founder of Latina Rebels who initiated the #LatinxGradCaps hashtag, further called attention to the visibility politics grounding people's choices to post with this hashtag, explaining: "I think to be seen is really important for people . . . the 'undocumented and unafraid' movement highlighted that. So . . . being seen and being brown is becoming really important, and it's only going to get more important in . . . these next few years" (Rodriguez 2017).

Decorating one's mortarboard is an act of personal expression within the ritualized setting of the commencement ceremony, and the #LatinxGradCaps hashtag works performatively within the digital public sphere to mark the meanings of the decorated mortarboards as *both* personal *and* larger than personal. In other words, these material enactments of creative expression become, to borrow the language of González-Martin, forms of self-documentation that "exist in between autobiography and auto-ethnography, and in this way are neither wholly personal nor wholly communal" (forthcoming).

Material and customary folkloric practices are often indexed in the process of self-documentation, and mortarboards embellished with fresh pupusas, lotería cards, and artwork associated with Day of the Dead altars take on heightened meaning as "blended symbols of cultural heritage and personal politics" (González-Martin, forthcoming). Popular cultural references do similar work. Mortarboards proclaiming "HE DICHO CASO CERRADO!" (I said, case closed!) and "[Graduates in Spanish] 2016,"[13] for example, reference Spanish-language television shows and the popular internet memes they inspired, indexing a humorous shared frame of reference that is marked as distinct from mainstream American culture. Many mortarboards marked with this hashtag also reference Selena Quintanilla Pérez, the Tejana recording artist who posthumously became a transnational Latina icon as collective mourning after her untimely death shaped shifting articulations of Latinidad in the 1990s (Parédez 2009). These references not only demonstrate personal appreciation of her artistry as a musician and performer but also invoke her role as a unifying symbol of "transnational Latin/o American success" (24). The unifying and recognizable force of Selena as symbol can then be instrumentalized in the service of sharing personal sentiments and experiences, as in the case of one mortarboard featuring the text "COMO LA FLOR" (Like the Flower), the title of one of Selena's hit songs, accompanied by this caption:

> it's not what you think; this isn't a tribute to Selena Quintanilla. The lyrics do come from one of her greatest hits, if not her greatest hit to ever grace the world of music, but this isn't about her. this is about my mom. her name is Flor. my mom has always been my greatest motivator, inspiration, and hero. Flor defied all the odds. as a single mother who emigrated from Mexico, she at times worked two jobs so that she could provide for me and my siblings. Flor fought tooth and nail against the world to protect her children. Flor has stayed the course and has remained resilient in the face of adversity. when you see me know that i come from the ribs of a boss, that i'm elevated on the shoulders of a giant, and ready to make today happen como la Flor. many doubted Flor and did not believe she could raise her kids on her own. well look at us now mom.
> you did it. I love you

This post shares a story that is at once personal and communal, intimate and political. The individual family's immigration story of sacrifice and resilience resonates with many similar stories attached to this hashtag, and the use of the phrase "como la Flor" in both the design of the mortarboard and the written explanation invokes a shared frame of reference that transcends ethno-national identities. Indeed, what draws together the diverse individuals who choose to post images of their decorated mortarboards with the #LatinxGradCaps hashtag is not necessarily shared geographic origins or ethno-national identities but the shared experiences of marginalization and contingent citizenship in the United States.

Direct references to recognizable cultural forms and traditions work not only to foreground pride in identity and heritage but also to resist the conflation of assimilation and belonging. Many of the #LatinxGradCaps exemplify some of the core values associated with the American Dream, including optimism and resilience, while at the same time refusing to disentangle them from explicitly Latinx identities. Social media platforms like Instagram further allow individuals to contextualize their caps by sharing individual stories of family hardships and experiences with racism that make visible the convergence of the personal and the political in the graduates' lives and direct how the decorated mortarboards (and by extension the meaning of the achievement they signify) should be interpreted by others.

Put on display in social media contexts, the individual performances of activism, solidarity, and resistance to the assimilation narrative within the context of individual ceremonies become *amplified* as they are connected to other, similar types of performances through the hashtag, an aesthetic feature that provides a framework for interpreting individual posts and visibly marking a sense of "groupness" in online performances (Bock 2017b). Through this amplification, the collection of posts using the #LatinxGradCaps hashtag makes visible a large and diverse activist community.

Of course, the reliance on the visual currency of higher education to articulate the value of immigrants and their families creates its own exclusions. One graduate chose to bring attention to this issue by posting a photo of a mortarboard embellished with the text "HYPERDOCUMENTED #SISEEPUDO." This text references the idea of *hyperdocumentation*—the effort to collect awards, accolades, and academic degrees to compensate for undocumented status (Chang 2011). Marking herself as hyperdocumented, this graduate is notably using this moment of personal achievement to call into question the perceived links between education and legitimacy and acceptance in the United States that in turn perpetuate the good versus bad immigrant narrative. She is also bringing attention to those who do not have mortarboards to post—those who have not pursued or completed their degrees, those who do not fit within this articulation of value and belonging.

Despite these exclusions, academic dress and mortarboards have served as potent symbols in activists' fights for immigrant rights. The circulation of posts marked by the #LatinxGradCaps hashtag on social media is carrying on this tradition, as personal experiences encoded into the caps take on meanings of collective political dissent. Take, for example, one image of a decorated mortarboard marked by the hashtag shared by Latina Rebels in March 2017, almost a year after it was initially posted. "My parents crossed the border so I could cross the stage," it reads, and it features a Mexican flag, an American flag, a monarch butterfly, a red rose, and a graduation gown with a diploma. The accompanying text reads: "white people's president keeps wanting to make us feel like shit. making our parents efforts feel like theft. remind them who we are. and how important our people are, no matter. Love this cap! #latinxgradcaps." In a hostile political climate, the collective presentation of personalized mortarboards linked by the #LatinxGradCaps hashtag serves as one such reminder, explicitly valuing the individual, family, and community stories and experiences so often rendered invisible or problematic within broader discourses of the American Dream.

Importantly, the analytical lens of Critical Latinx Folkloristics helps us recognize that the posts circulating on social media with the #LatinxGradCaps hashtag are not addressing stable, preexisting communities. For example, the "we" referenced in the post quoted above is not referencing a discrete group of individuals who share ethno-nationalist identities; rather, it is envisioning a diverse and politically active audience with a desire to disrupt the dominant discourses working to devalue and marginalize Latinx communities, an audience with the potential to grow as the post is shared by others via online media and individual reposts. The language choices in the captions accompanying the images of the decorated mortarboards (e.g., English only, Spanish only, English and Spanish, English and Portuguese) also do significant work in envisioning and creating the publics that form around the visual texts circulating online, both the individual posts and the collection of posts linked together through the hashtag. In short, instead of addressing preexisting communities, the posts marked with the #LatinxGradCaps hashtag are simultaneously imagining and creating emergent publics that question, resist, and re-envision the dynamics of belonging and exclusion embedded in the American Dream.

NOTES

1. I have been studying the tradition of decorating mortarboards since 2014, attending to both the forms and meanings of people's participation in the practice, as well as to how individuals use these acts of creative expression to publicly fashion their personal engagement with notions of self, community, and the purpose and value of higher education. I initially tracked examples graduates posted online, and in 2016, I began collecting survey and interview data and documenting mortarboards at commencement ceremonies at the University of Nevada, Las Vegas. Many of the materials collected for this ongoing study have been digitally archived in the Folklore Archives of the Ohio State University Center for Folklore Studies: https://cfs.osu.edu/archives/collections/gradcaptraditions. I presented

earlier versions of this chapter at the Western States Folklore Society Annual Meeting and the American Folklore Society Annual Meeting in 2017, where I received valuable feedback that helped me refine the key arguments presented here.

2. The term *Latinidad* refers to the geopolitical experience of being Latina/o/x that transcends national and geographic borders. Beyond the shared nature of this experience, the term "also contains within it the complexities and contradictions of immigration, (post) (neo)colonialism, race, color, legal status, class, nation, language, and the politics of location" (Rodríguez 2003, 9–10).

3. Although this text is no longer posted on the Latina Rebels Facebook page, it can still be found in the Remezcla article "9 Young Central American Creatives and Thought Leaders You Should Be Following" (Simón 2016).

4. Originating in the online queer Latinx community, use of the term *Latinx* has become more widespread, though it remains contentious. As Catalina (Kathleen) M. De Onís notes in "What's in an 'X'? An Exchange about the Politics of 'Latinx,'" "Some individuals and communities readily adopt and advocate for increased usage of 'Latinx,' arguing for its transgressive sexual, gender, and language politics. Meanwhile, others express hesitancy or reject usages of "x" altogether, maintaining that the signifier symbolizes linguistic imperialism, poses pronunciation problems, and alienates non-English-speaking im/migrants (2017, 79).

5. The term *chingona* is often used to refer to a "badass woman" (Aguirre 2017). Mexican American writer Sandra Cisneros has played a significant role is rearticulating the meaning of the term, which loosely translates to "fucker" in English. The masculine version of the term describes someone who dominates through sexual penetration. According to Cisneros, "I had to take that word back [because] I felt that that word was a word that's used against women and gays . . . I wanted to find a positive way to say 'a woman who is on her path and who is powerful and is not being defined by a man but is being defined as a woman on her own path, on her own direction, on her own intuitive powers" (quoted in Moreno 2017). See also Gloria Anzaldúa (2007) and Octavio Paz's (1961) writings on "la Chingada." As sociologist Julie Bettie explains, the term *chola/o* "describes a Mexican-American street style that sometimes marks identification with gangs, but it also can mark merely racial/ethnic belonging" (2000, 9). It has historically carried negative associations with criminality and being lower class. See also Castro 2001.

6. In spring 2017, UndocuMedia and Define American—a nonprofit media and culture organization that seeks to use the power of storytelling to shift conversations about immigrants and citizenship in the United States—launched the #ImmiGrad hashtag, with the express purpose of "giving immigrants and the children of immigrants a platform to break down harmful stereotypes and to celebrate their accomplishments" (Remezcla EStaff 2017). Many posts tagged with this hashtag, along with the #undocugrad hashtag, featured decorated mortarboards, and the themes found in these posts overlap greatly with posts marked by the #LatinxGradCaps hashtag. In many cases, both hashtags were included in the same posts. Acknowledging these overlaps, for the purposes of this chapter, I am focusing particularly on the posts shared using the #LatinxGradCaps hashtag.

7. Pineda and Sowards (2007) offer a more in-depth examination of the visual rhetorics of flag waving within contexts of immigration protests and rallies in the United States. See also Martínez's analysis of the symbolic role flags play in collective performances of Puerto Rican culture (2017).

8. This phrase is used often in Costa Rica and carries many meanings, including "hello," "good-bye," "thank you," and "it's all good," among others (Maney 2016).

9. See Chumakov 2016.
10. "¡Sí Se Puede!" was the rallying cry of the United Farmworkers Union in the 1970s, and since that time it has been adopted by many groups and movements fighting for Latina/o/x rights in the United States. The English equivalent, "Yes We Can," served as the slogan for presidential candidate Barack Obama's campaign in 2008.
11. Penial E. Joseph (2016) offers an overview of the powerful historical resonance of the raised fist in the United States.
12. Literally translated as "trout," *trucha* is also slang for "Be careful" or "Watch out."
13. See, for example, https://knowyourmeme.com/memes/soraya-montenegro.

REFERENCES

Adams, James Truslow. 1931. *The Epic of America*. Boston: Little, Brown.
Aguirre, Angela. 2017. "How I Define My Chingona Fire." *Huffington Post*, updated January 25, 2017. https://www.huffingtonpost.com/entry/how-i-define-my-chingona-fire_us_5887de69e4b0a53ed60c6a35.
Anzaldúa, Gloria. 2007. *Borderlands/La Frontera: The New Mestiza*. 3rd ed. San Francisco: Aunt Lute.
Bettie, Julie. 2000. "Women without Class: Cholas, Trash, and the Presence/Absence of Class Identity." *Signs* 26 (1): 1–35.
Bock, Sheila. 2014. "Performing the Personal in a State of Transition: Decorated Mortarboards." *Journal of Folklore and Education* 1 (1): 34–38.
Bock, Sheila. 2017a. "Decorated Mortarboards: An Introduction." Center for Folklore Studies. Accessed June 15, 2018. https://cfs.osu.edu/archives/collections/grad captraditions/decorated-mortarboards-introduction.
Bock, Sheila. 2017b. "Ku Klux Kasserole and Strange Fruit Pies: A Shouting Match at the Border in Cyberspace." *Journal of American Folklore* 130 (516): 142–165.
Castro, Rafaela G. 2001. "Cholos (-as)." In *Chicano Folklore: A Guide to the Folktales, Traditions, Rituals, and Religious Practices of Mexican Americans*, 54–55. Oxford: Oxford University Press.
Chang, Aurora. 2011. "Undocumented to Hyperdocumented: A Jornada of Protection, Papers, and PhD Status." *Harvard Educational Review* 81 (3): 508–521.
Chavez, Leo R. 2013. The Latino Threat: Constructing Immigrants, Citizens, and the Nation. 2nd ed. Stanford: Stanford University Press.
Chumakov. 2016. "Con el nopal en la Frente." *USC Digital Folklore Archives*. May 12, 2016. http://folklore.usc.edu/?p=33460.
Cullen, Jim. 2003. *The American Dream: A Short History of the Idea That Shaped a Nation*. Oxford: Oxford University Press.
De Onís, Catalina (Kathleen) M. 2017. "What's in an 'X'? An Exchange about the Politics of 'Latinx.'" *Chiricù Journal: Latina/o Literature, Art, and Culture* 1 (2): 78–91.
Dick, Hilary Parsons. 2011. "Language and Migration in the United States." *Annual Review of Anthropology* 40: 227–240.
Flores, William Vincent, and Rina Benmayor, eds. 1997. *Latino Cultural Citizenship: Claiming Identity, Space, and Rights*. Boston: Beacon.
González-Martin, Rachel. Forthcoming. "Latinx Publics: Self-Documentation and Latina Youth Activists." *Journal of American Folklore*.
Hanson, Sandra L., and John Kenneth White. 2016. Introduction to *The Latino/a American Dream*, edited by Sandra L. Hanson and John Kenneth White, 1–17. College Station: Texas A&M University Press.

Joseph, Penial E. 2016 "The Many Meanings of a Fist." *Chronicle Review.* May 18, 2016. https://www.chronicle.com/article/The-Many-Meanings-of-a-Fist/236509.

Maney, Andrew. 2016. "Pura Vida." *USC Digital Folklore Archives.* May 12, 2016. http://folklore.usc.edu/?p=34094.

Martínez, Daniel E., Jeremy Slack, Alex E. Chávez, and Scott Whiteford. 2016. "'The American Dream': Walking toward and Deporting It." In *The Latino/a American Dream*, edited by Sandra L. Hanson and John Kenneth White, 88–98. College Station: Texas A&M University Press.

Martínez, Elena. 2017. "¡Que Bonita Bandera! Place, Space, and Identity as Expressed with the Puerto Rican Flag." In *Public Performances: Studies in the Carnivalesque and Ritualesque*, edited by Jack Santino, 113–132. Logan: Utah State University Press.

Moreno, Carolina. 2017. "Sandra Cisneros Defines What It Means to Be a Chingona." *Huffington Post.* September 6, 2017. https://www.huffingtonpost.com/entry/sandra-cisneros-chingona-definition_us_59ae10ade4b0dfaafcf2030b.

Paredez, Deborah. 2009. *Selenidad: Selena, Latinos, and the Performance of Memory.* Durham: Duke University Press.

Paz, Octavio. 1961. *The Labyrinth of Solitude.* Translated by Lysander Kemp. New York: Grove.

Pineda, Richard D., and Stacey K. Sowards. 2007. "Flag Waving as Visual Argument: 2006 Immigration Demonstrations and Cultural Citizenship." *Argumentation and Advocacy* 43: 164–174.

Remezcla EStaff. 2017. "The #ImmiGrad Hashtag Is a Testament to the Sacrifices Parents Make for Their Children." *Remezcla.* May 22, 2017. http://remezcla.com/lists/culture/immigrad-parents-sacrifice/.

Rodríguez, Juana María. 2003. *Queer Latinidad: Identity Practices, Discursive Spaces.* New York: NYU Press.

Rodríguez, Prisca Dorcas Mojica. 2017. Recorded phone interview with Sheila Bock. February 5, 2017.

Simón, Yara. 2016. "9 Young Central American Creatives and Thought Leaders You Should Be Following." *Remezcla.* September 15, 2016. http://remezcla.com/lists/culture/central-american-creatives-and-thought-leaders-you-should-be-following/.

Slaughter, Stephany. 2016. "#TrumpEffects: Creating Rhetorical Spaces for Latinx Political Engagement." *Latin Americanist* 60 (4): 541–576.

Suárez-Orozco, Carola, and Marcelo M. Suárez-Orozco. 2001. *Children of Immigration.* Cambridge, MA: Harvard University Press.

Terkel, Studs. 1980. *American Dreams: Lost and Found.* New York: Pantheon Books.

Warner, Michael. 2002. "Publics and Counter Publics." *Public Culture* 14 (1): 49–90.

White, John Kenneth. 2016. "Whose Dream? US Presidents, Hispanics, and the Struggle for the American Future." In *The Latino/a American Dream*, edited by Sandra L. Hanson and John Kenneth White, 18–41. College Station: Texas A&M University Press.

2

Bridges, Sex Slaves, Tweets, and Guns
A Multi-Domain Model of Conspiracy Theory

Timothy R. Tangherlini, Vwani Roychowdhury,
and Peter M. Broadwell

> *The single greatest Witch Hunt in American history continues.*
> —Donald Trump, January 10, 2018

> *This vast right-wing conspiracy . . . has been conspiring against my husband.*
> —Hillary Clinton, January 27, 1998

ON SEPTEMBER 9, 2013, SEVERAL LANES AT THE main toll plaza of the George Washington Bridge in Fort Lee, New Jersey, were closed without warning, leading to massive traffic jams. The inexplicable closures and the ensuing week-long traffic chaos led many to speculate that there was an underlying conspiracy concocted by New Jersey state government officials to punish the Democratic mayor of Fort Lee, who had not endorsed Governor Chris Christie in his reelection bid. While social media initially focused on the traffic chaos itself, Twittizens soon adopted the hashtag #bridgegate as they began to follow news stories investigating the reasons for the lane closures. In early December 2013, Twitter exploded in a frenzy of memes and commentary that continued unabated for several months once it became clear that the closures were a deliberate political act and not part of a traffic study, as initially reported. Subsequent investigations over the course of the following year charted the emerging conspiracy, revealing a pattern of deliberate moves by the governor's aides and appointees that were designed to cause the traffic problems as part of a political payback operation. Furthermore, criminal investigations detailed a pattern of lying and deception by the conspirators as they attempted to cover up their

DOI: 10.7330/9781646420599.c002

actions and protect their powerful boss. The investigation ultimately led to convictions of several of Christie's aides and staffers and essentially ended his aspirations for a run for the presidency.

Although the conspiracy was far reaching and replete with baroque twists and turns, leading at least one pundit to remark, "You can't make this stuff up," there is in fact no reason to believe that one could not "make this stuff up" (Moran 2017). Indeed, "making up" stories to explain the seemingly inexplicable is something that people have been doing for millennia (Niles [1999] 2010). And telling stories to explain the nefarious and malicious intent of powerful individuals, whether those stories are true or made up, has been documented for centuries (Knight 2003). That said, there are features of social media narratives detailing conspiracy theories that set them apart from the retrospective journalistic narratives of conspiracy. This short investigation outlines a method for determining the structural features of conspiracy theories that, in the long term, could be useful in distinguishing conspiracy theory from conspiracy.

Critics of American politics have remarked on the long-standing propensity of people to think in terms of conspiracies and cover-ups as explanatory devices for understanding social, political, and economic developments. Richard Hofstadter traces conspiracies in American history back to the founding of the nation, characterizing this "paranoid style of thinking" as marked by a "sense of heated exaggeration, suspiciousness, and conspiratorial fantasy" (1964, 1). He links the increasing ability of this conspiratorial thinking to capture the imaginations of people to greater access to the mass media, noting, "Events since 1939 have given the contemporary... paranoid a vast theatre for his imagination, full of rich and proliferating detail, replete with realistic cues and undeniable proofs of the validity of his suspicions" (4).

If the Second World War and the attendant technological developments in media and communications widened the scope of the "theatre [of] imagination" undergirding conspiratorial thinking, the internet revolution and the concomitant growth of social media have provided two additional supports: amplification and velocity.[1] With social media, individuals or groups of individuals now have the ability to vastly amplify their messages, reaching more people, by orders of magnitude, than they could in their earlier face-to-face social interactions.[2] Similarly, the speed with which messages can propagate across groups is almost instantaneous, with one-to-many technologies such as Twitter, Snapchat, and Facebook creating the opportunity for messages to reach huge numbers of people in a matter of seconds, while the direction of these signals can be highly targeted to reach specific communities. Importantly, many social media platforms can be manipulated by skilled individuals, substantially increasing these two effects while simultaneously increasing the level of distrust people have toward their sources of information (Shao et al. 2018; Ferrara et al. 2016).

The fact that certain conspiracies, such as Bridgegate and Watergate before it, were actual conspiracies provides an important basis for the elaborate conspiracy theories that Hofstadter identifies as a consistent yet dangerous feature of the American political landscape, and that folklorists recognize as an established genre in many storytelling traditions.[3] Peter Knight provides a helpful distinction between "conspiracy" and "conspiracy theory": conspiracy is "a small group of powerful people [who] combine together in secret to plan and carry out an illegal or improper action"—a near-perfect description of what occurred in Bridgegate—while "conspiracy theory" is "an interpretation of history that claims things aren't always what they seem, and that things haven't just tumbled out by coincidence . . . but that they have only got like this because someone with evil intentions planned it this way" (2003, 15–16). Knight suggests that conspiracy theories are "symptomatic of larger fears that circulate through the culture at particular moments of stress" (21). Véronique Campion-Vincent expands on this idea, writing, "Conspiracy theories try to explain a complex and seemingly random environment through the adoption of a simple model of causality" (2005, 107).[4] Implicitly, for these theorists, the distinction between "conspiracy" and "conspiracy theory" is one predicated on narrative. While the former emerges (or remains hidden) through the messy process of legal and journalistic investigation, the latter emerges in performance. Yet the mere existence of conspiracy provides motivation for narrators to develop conspiracy theories. Ralph Rosnow and Gary Alan Fine, in their examination of rumor, highlight that the discoveries of the Watergate investigation, for example, which traced a conspiracy all the way to the Oval Office, fed a "pervasive atmosphere of mistrust and suspicion," providing a fertile environment beginning in the 1970s for the propagation of conspiracy theories (1976, 58). A broadly reported event such as Watergate primes social networks to be open to similar stories, creating a receptive environment not only for conspiracies but also for conspiracy theories (Pennycook et al. 2018).

Mark Fenster, in his study of conspiracy theories, emphasizes this narrative aspect, pointing out that "the gripping, dramatic story is, ultimately, at the heart of conspiracy theory" (1999, 106). In his formulation, "Conspiracy narrative is compelling in its rapid, global movement . . . and its attempt to explain a wide range of seemingly disparate, past and present events and structures within a relatively coherent framework" (106). This concept of a "coherent [narrative] framework" is an important one, even though Fenster leaves it undefined. In earlier work, we explored how narrative frameworks can quickly emerge as embedded features in domains of knowledge, and used this concept to develop a generative model of the legend based on the study of millions of blog posts on social media sites (Tangherlini 2017; Tangherlini et al. 2016). In this context, legends are characterized as largely mono-episodic stories, presented as true in a highly historicized and localized way, and circulated largely in conversational forums, such as online chat rooms and discussion boards.[5] In our approach, a narrative framework, grounded in a modification of Greimas's actantial model, is derived by aggregating the actants and the interactant relationships that appear in all the stories, story parts, and story allusions that constitute a particular topic within a tradition group (Greimas 1966a, 1966b; Tangherlini 2017). In this context, actants are conceptualized as an aggregation of characters or objects into classes, so that references to Chris Christie, Christie, and the governor, are all aggregated into the single entity of Christie. Interactant relationships either describe the condition of a relationship, such as "is the boss of," or some interaction, such as "directed"; these are also aggregated into a higher grouping to avoid a proliferation of similar relationships. Instead of concentrating solely on complete stories, we follow the lead of John Laudun (2001), who points out that people rarely tell complete stories. This incompleteness is a common feature of social media posts, where people allude to other stories, recount parts of experiences, or provide their own incomplete personal experiences as commentary on other people's posts.

Taking a cue from the nineteenth-century philosopher George Boole, topics can be characterized as domains of discourse, with the domain placing certain limits on what is admissible within that discourse: "In every discourse, whether of the mind conversing with its own thoughts, or of the individual in his intercourse with others, there is an assumed or expressed limit within which the subjects of its operation are confined" (1854, 42). Folklorists will be quick to recognize this type of limitation, formalized in Alan Dundes's work (1964) on the allomotif and motifeme in Native American tales. For any group, we recognize that multiple domains exist, and that the narrative frameworks embedded in these domains can be derived from the expressive forms circulating in that group. While the boundaries of these domains are in constant flux, reflecting the dynamic yet productive tension that exists between individuals and the groups to which they belong, the overall frameworks converge on stable boundaries fairly quickly.⁶ Our initial task, then, is to discover the actants and their relationships from the observed discourse in a particular domain, which in turn allows us to discover the underlying narrative framework.

A narrative framework delimits what is admissible in that domain. In the domain of politics, for example, space aliens are not admissible as actants in normal discourse. Instead, the appearance of space aliens would constitute the intrusion of one domain (space aliens) into another domain, violating Boole's "assumed or expressed limits" on discourse. In our work on legend, we have shown how legends focus on these moments of intrusion, where actants from an "outside" domain intrude, usually in a threatening manner, on another, often more quotidian, "inside" domain (Tangherlini 2017). In legend, therefore, the limitations on discourse are relaxed from the realm of normal discourse, allowing these inadmissible actants entry into an otherwise separate domain.⁷ Legends can be characterized by this intersection of two domains, and the response of the insiders to that unexpected intrusion.⁸ For instance, Bridgegate would be very different if the cause of the traffic jams was the appearance of an alien spacecraft, and the discourse would veer from political news reporting into legend.

Limitations on what is allowed in a particular discourse, already destabilized by the legend, are fundamentally challenged by conspiracy theories. Unlike the legend, which focuses on the limited intrusion of actants from one domain into another, conspiracy theories, in their narrative voraciousness, attempt to concatenate all of these intrusions in multiple domains through the alignment of actants or interactant relationships across those domains. Ellis suggests that conspiracy theories are "scenarios made up of many beliefs and narratives which are accepted on faith and used to link and give meaning to stressful events" (2000, 5). With this insight, Ellis identifies two important features of the underlying mechanics of conspiracy theories: first, the ability of conspiracy theories to link and integrate seemingly disconnected realms of discourse, and second, their totalizing nature, aiming to concatenate disparate domains of knowledge into a single domain through the intervention of an explanatory meta-story. The alignment of multiple domains, rather than the intersection of domains, is the main invention of the conspiracy theory, in effect eliding the previous limits separating discourses. Instead of challenging the existing cultural ideology of the group within which the conspiracy narrative circulates by breaking through domain boundaries, as the legend does, the conspiracy theory attempts a grand unifying gesture by aligning all of the different domains, developing an overarching meta-narrative as a means for normalizing the otherwise jarring intrusions of legends. For example, if the space aliens that caused the traffic jams in Fort Lee, New Jersey, in the above fictional example had been released from a military research center that the government had kept secret as part of an ongoing program related to eugenics, our series of linked narratives would have veered into the world of conspiracy theory. In the model presented below, conspiracy theory is conceptualized as a meta-narrative framework, providing a linking mechanism for otherwise disparate narrative frameworks, whether those frameworks are journalistic (such as Bridgegate) or folkloristic (such as legends about alien invasions and secret government programs). The results of these alignments are conspiracy theories such as Pizzagate, QAnon or, to reach back into history, the apparent collusion between Danish Lutheran ministers, local women, wealthy landowners, witches, and Satan.

TOWARD A GENERATIVE MODEL OF CONSPIRACY THEORIES

In the work described below, we outline a method for mapping conspiracy theory meta-narrative frameworks (Tangherlini et al. 2020). The model is predicated on the notion that conspiracy theories rely on the alignment of multiple domains of knowledge through the identification of actants that play different roles across these domains. Whereas normal discourse is constrained to a single domain ($D=1$), and legend focuses on the clash of two domains ($D=2$), conspiracy theories work with many domains ($D > 2$). In a conspiracy theory, domain alignment is part of the meta-narrative framework, and is usually carried out by the narrator or narrators of the conspiracy theory; the alignment thus exists in an extra-diegetic frame (Genette [1969] 1982, 1983; Bal and Tavor 1981). The conceit of the conspiracy theory narrator is the ability to see these alignments, which are only visible if you "know where to look" (Clarke 2007, 170).

In earlier work, we found that a sequenced actant-relation representation of thousands of stories in a single domain could provide the necessary limits to generate new legends that would be classified as admissible stories (Tangherlini 2017; Tangherlini et al. 2016). In that model, potential actants were limited by the existing group of stories within a specific topic, while domains were limited by the tradition as a whole. We extend that model for the conspiracy theory model outlined here. As we show below, conspiracy theories consist of the alignment of multiple narrative frameworks, where an actant (or actants) in one narrative framework fulfills a different role in a separate narrative framework. The conspiracy theory resides not in the independent narrative frameworks, but rather in the story that explains the linking. Through this multi-dimensional alignment, the conspiracy theory can easily be expanded to a totalizing meta-narrative, potentially encompassing all domains of knowledge for a particular tradition group.

The disparate historic scope and source material we employ to model our conspiracy theory narrative framework is deliberate, as it helps confirm the consistency of the model across time and transmission media. At the same time, it underscores the importance of social media as an ongoing experiment in self-archiving folklore, providing us with an enormous volume of cultural expressive forms that overlap and intersect while providing insight into the messy dynamic process of negotiating cultural ideologies.

A BRIEF METHODOLOGICAL OVERVIEW

In developing our methodology, we have intentionally focused on developing the least complex approach to ensure its broad applicability. While the processing pipeline is fully automated, one can, for small datasets, apply parts or all of the pipeline manually.[9] The pipeline consists of five steps: a data-harvesting step, a domain-discovery step, an entity-relationship and sequence-extraction step, an actant-aggregation step, and a framework-discovery step. For conspiracy theories, the pipeline adds a sixth step, the framework-alignment step. Graphical representations of the frameworks and their alignment are used to illustrate the results. Earlier work on Bridgegate confirms that this pipeline approach to narrative framework discovery produces results similar to manual coding of news stories (Tangherlini 2017) (figure 2.1).[10]

A difficult yet necessary first step for any of this work is the discovery of suitable resources and the preprocessing and cleaning of the data. For historical archives, it is often best to work with digitized resources although, as mentioned, with enough patience, this approach can be applied manually. Once machine actionable, we coarsely sort the material by topic domain. As described in our work on anti-vaccination narratives, we identify the topic domains in an online community by applying a hierarchical topic-modeling algorithm to the concatenated posts on all of the forums (Tangherlini et al. 2016; Falahi 2017). The hierarchical model allows us to identify the posts associated with a domain of discourse irrespective of the forum in which the post appears. For the archival material considered here, we take an even more straightforward approach, concentrating on the preexisting topic classifications presented in the archive, and finding associated stories through the use of a multi-modal network classifier described in earlier work (Abello et al. 2012).

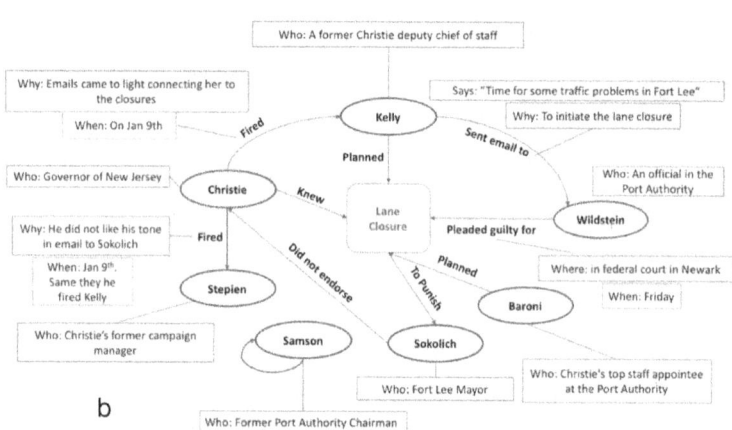

Figure 2.1. *A*, a manually coded network of the actants and their relationships in the Bridgegate conspiracy as mapped by the *New York Times* (Marsh and Zernike 2015) and captured by our pipeline. (We have reduced the complexity of the original graphic to show only nodes and relationships.) The ranking of actants in order of importance to the conspiracy as determined by our algorithms is indicated by the darkness of the node border, while the affiliation of the actant is represented by color: gray for Governor Chris Christie and his staff, white for Port Authority staff, dots for Mark Sokolich and his staff and associates, vertical stripes for attorneys, black for Governor Cuomo, and gray for developers. *B*, a subgraph of actants and relationships discovered by our pipeline from a corpus of news articles from the *Huffington Post* and the news aggregator site, NorthJersey.com. Our data collection stops prior to the *New York Times* graphic, and consequently additional discoveries shown in the *New York Times* graph are not present in our graph.

Once we have the candidate stories (and story parts or story allusions) for a particular domain, we extract all entities and their pairwise relationships. For most datasets, we accomplish this through the use of natural language-processing tools, with actants largely being represented by nouns, and interactant relationships largely being represented by verbs. Since there can be a great deal of variation in both references to and spelling of entities, we apply stemming and lemmatization to reduce this variation. Once we have entities and inter-entity relationships, we aggregate entities into single actant classes so, for example, references to "Katie Reilly," "Katie," and "Reilly" in the Pizzagate corpus are aggregated into the single actant "Katie Reilly" in the Pizzagate narrative framework.[11]

Once we have all of the actants for a given domain, we discover all of the interactant relationships by examining sentences that include any two actants. In an aggregation step similar to the one that we use to create actant classes, verbs that function in the same manner in interactant contexts are aggregated to relationship classes. We derive sequencing from the stories by examining which relationships appear before and after any given relationship. This step is particularly difficult for social media posts, where temporal ordering is often obscured by the partial and noisy nature of many posts. The result of these steps is an ordered narrative framework graph, where the nodes are actants, the edges are relationships, and the sequence of relationships is represented by ordinal numbers as labels on the edges.

A final step for conspiracy theories explores how different narrative frameworks are aligned through shared actants across narrative-framework graphs or, less commonly, through shared relationships. The meta-narrative is determined by those statements that make the alignment explicit and, as in the case in Pizzagate or QAnon, the information source that provides a basis for that alignment. In our graphical representations, this meta-narrative is represented by dashed lines connecting the various narrative frameworks.

A CONSPIRACY OF WITCHES AND MINISTERS

In Evald Tang Kristensen's Danish legend collections (1892–1901), there are over two thousand stories detailing the activities of witches. Witches in Danish tradition are always disruptive, often larcenous, and very hard to catch and punish. In many stories, they receive their powers directly from Satan. In the same tradition, there are hundreds of stories that detail the collusion between local priests, their wives, and Satan. Although priests often work to protect their communities against spiritual threats, such as revenants, a few are accused of being in league with the devil, either directly

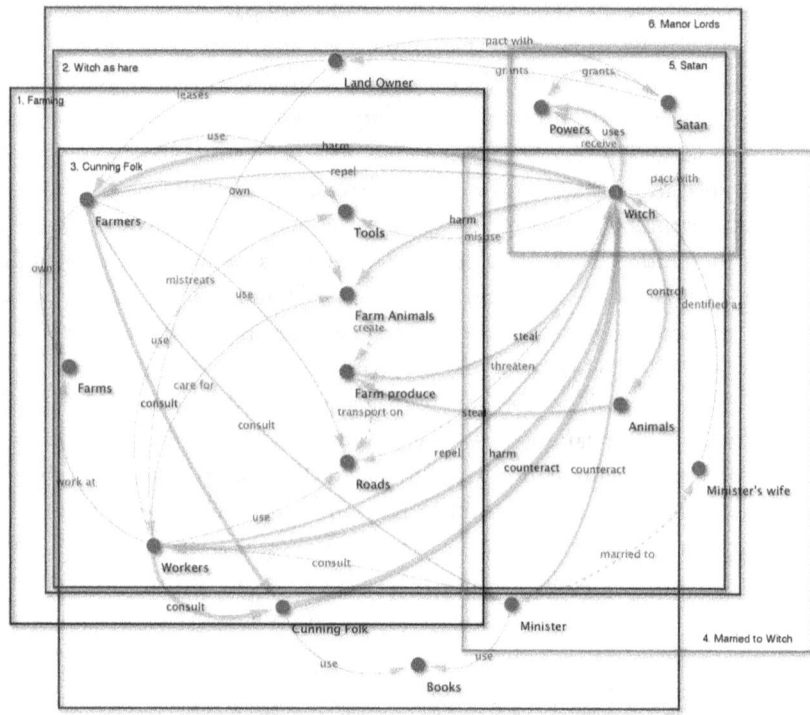

Figure 2.2. Six overlapping domains with their corresponding narrative frameworks from the Danish legend collection: (1) stories of farming, (2) witch as hare, (3) witches defeated by minister or cunning person, (4) priests married to witches, (5) witches in league with the devil, (6) manor lords' pacts with the devil (Kristensen 1892–1901). Each domain is presented as a separate story plane, outlined by a border and numbered as noted above in parentheses; the immanent conspiracy theory is presented by overlapping nodes (actants) that play linking roles in multiple domains.

or, more often, through their wives, who turn out to be witches.[12] There are, in addition, many stories that explore the close connection between wealthy landowners, who frequently abuse their tenants, and Satan, who has provided them with or allowed them to keep their wealth as the result of a pact.

A series of narrative frameworks created from a semi-supervised coding of stories of witches, stories of priests married to witches, and stories of manor lords who have sold their soul to the devil identify these actants, who occur across multiple narrative frameworks, and provide obvious points for alignment (figure 2.2).

Intriguingly, there are no overt conspiracy meta-narratives in Tang Kristensen's collection that make this alignment explicit.[13] While this lack of an overt linkage may be an artifact of collecting and editing practices, there are several other possible explanations. First, the connections may be so clear to the tradition participants that they do not feel the need to mention it. Arguing in favor of this position is a very small number of stories that tell of Satan riding off with manor lords and priests in tow, thereby confirming at least a latent awareness of these connections on the part of tradition participants. These stories support the idea that storytellers and their audiences had a mental model of what Carol Clover (1986) has labeled "immanent" narratives or, in this case, "immanent conspiracy theories." Consequently, they never gave voice to it—everyone already knew about it. Alternatively, Danish farmers and smallholders in the nineteenth century may not have been given to conspiratorial thinking and failed to make the connection between witches, priests, and large landholders who had sold their souls to the devil. This latter explanation seems unlikely, particularly since many storytellers told stories from each of these different domains as part of their individual repertoires (Tangherlini 2014). Along with the concept of the immanent conspiracy theory, another likely explanation for the lack of explicitly narrated conspiracy theories in nineteenth-century Danish legend tradition was that storytellers, already suspicious of the outside collector, Tang Kristensen, were reluctant to connect the dots in an overt manner for him, leaving the conspiracy theory as a latent meta-narrative. Of course, the age of witch hunts in Denmark was long over by the time that Tang Kristensen was collecting, and so there may have been no need for such meta-narratives. Indeed, by the time that he was collecting, the power of the minister had waned considerably, the manorial system was an artifact of the past, and many accusations of witchcraft were closely tied to the market behavior of cunning folk (Tangherlini 2000).

PIZZAS AND PEDOPHILES

Unlike immanent conspiracy theories such as those from nineteenth-century Denmark, social media provides numerous examples of explicit conspiracy theories presented as such. Perhaps the most notorious recent such conspiracy theory is Pizzagate, which exploded into public consciousness in the weeks after the 2016 presidential election (figure 2.3).

The meta-narrative, which developed over the course of several months on the social media sites 4chan and Reddit, relied for primary evidence on the hacked emails of John Podesta, the chair of Hillary Clinton's presidential campaign in 2016, that were released by Wikileaks in October and November 2016.[14]

The meta-narrative links a series of seemingly independent stories from different domains—Democratic Party politics, casual family dining,

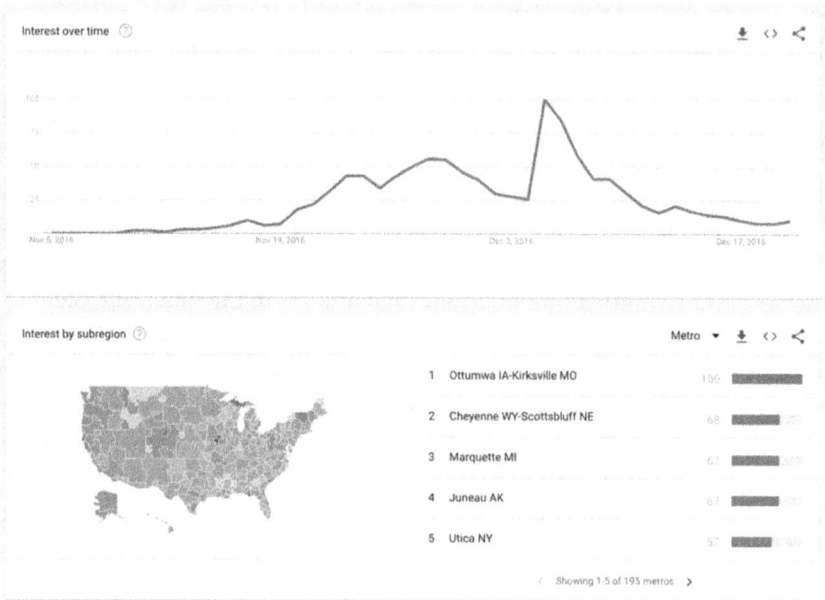

Figure 2.3. Google trends chart and map for the term *Pizzagate* during the period November 5–December 20, 2016.

Satanism, pedophilia, and sex trafficking—into a single, coherent conspiracy theory. In short, it posits that highly placed Democratic officials and members of Hillary Clinton's inner circle used a family pizza parlor in the Washington, DC, area as a front for a large-scale child abuse and trafficking ring as part of their occult practices. The conspiracy theory gained numerous followers on Reddit who deployed Twitter as one of many social media channels to propagate and attract new followers who could in turn help "uncover" the hidden links between these domains. Through a series of linked hashtags, mentions, and retweets, for example, it is possible to capture the development of the underlying propagation network, as well as to discover the hashtags most frequently co-occurring with the Pizzagate hashtag (figure 2.4).

Of particular note in the Twitter network is the prominence of active conspiracy theorists such as David Seaman, a former *Jezebel* intern at *Gawker*, and alt-right activists such as Brittany Pettibone.[15] The co-occurrence network identifies a series of related hashtags, while also highlighting some of the main actants in the Pizzagate network: Hillary Clinton, John Podesta, James Alefantis, Barack Obama, Comet Ping Pong, and practices such as pedophilia and Satanic ritual (figure 2.5).

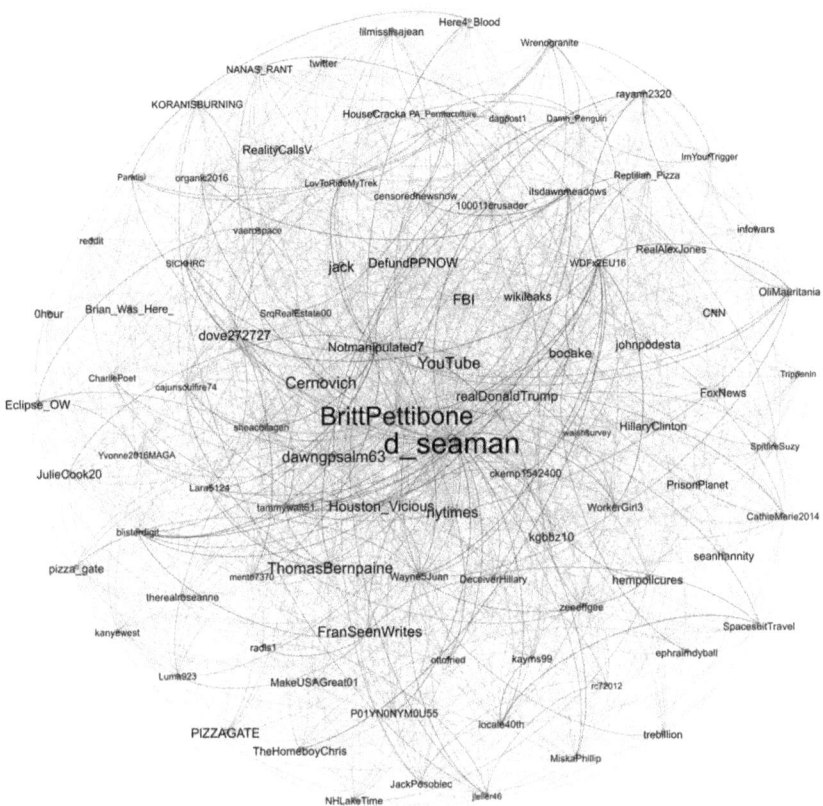

Figure 2.4. Twitter network describing the #Pizzagate hashtag, focusing on tweets (black edges), retweets (gray edges), and mentions (light gray edges), for the month of November 2016.

Conveniently, as is the case for many conspiracy theories that have taken root on social media, the people involved in developing the conspiracy theory have archived all of their materials in a single place, offering a clear corpus for study. Equally conveniently, the *New York Times*, in a move reminiscent of its detailing of the Bridgegate conspiracy, developed a graphic to detail the convoluted connections described in the rapidly expanding Pizzagate meta-narrative. Accordingly, we used the curated collection of Pizzagate materials as our study corpus, and the *New York Times*'s hand-coded representation of the meta-narrative framework to test the ability of our approach to automatically discover actants and relationships present in the conspiracy theory (figure 2.6).

In addition to discovering the entire group of actants and their relationships as detailed by the *New York Times*, we were also able to create weights

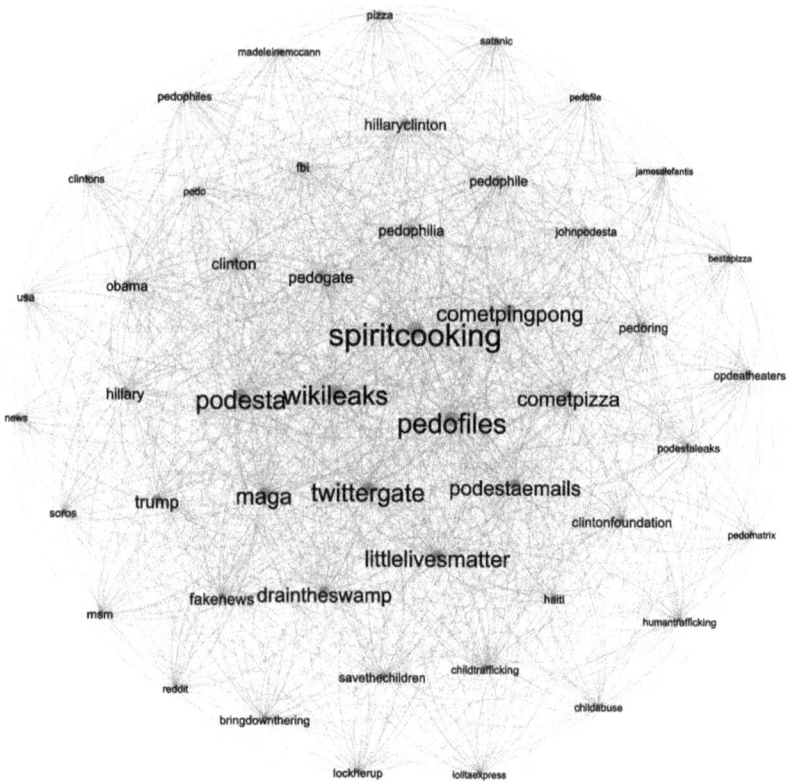

Figure 2.5. The most prevalent hashtags co-occurring with the hashtag #Pizzagate. To reduce the initial network "hairball," we present only the K-core of that graph showing nodes with degree > 45 (see Seidman 1983).

based on the normalized mention frequencies, allowing us to identify key actants and relationships that might serve as linchpins for the alignment of disparate domains. Since the alignment of domains is carried out by Reddit contributors, we can remove Wikileaks from the narrative framework graphs, allowing it to serve as the source for the alignment of actants across the otherwise separate story domains of Democratic Party politics, casual dining, occult practices, pedophilia, and child trafficking (figure 2.7).

In an unsettling twist, the addition of the domain of Satanism to the Pizzagate meta-narrative creates a link between Hillary Clinton and the Satanic, much like the connection made between Satan and witches in the Danish immanent witchcraft conspiracy theory described above. The chants of Michael Flynn, the former, subsequently indicted national security

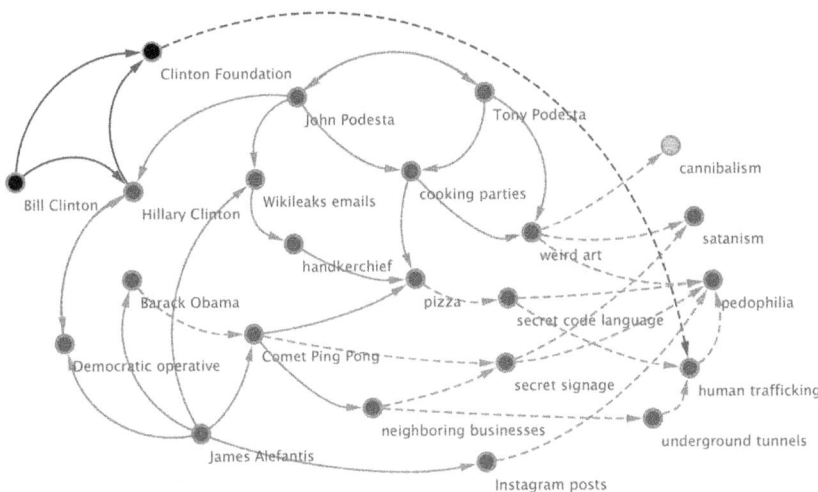

Figure 2.6. A comparison network graph of those nodes and edges present in the *New York Times* graph for Pizzagate (dark gray nodes) (Aisch et al. 2016). "Cannibalism" is shown in the *Times* graph but is poorly represented in our corpus (dots). Bill Clinton and the Clinton Foundation, in contrast, are ranked highly in our corpus (added in black with darker edges). Dashed edges match the newspaper's visual vocabulary and align with those edges added by the Wikileaks domain, constituting "hidden knowledge."

advisor to President Trump, to "lock her up" present a chilling echo to the centuries-old shouts of "Burn her!" at witchcraft trials. In contrast, Trump's repeated dismissals of Robert Mueller's increasingly productive investigation into possible Russian interference in his election as a "witch-hunt" attempt to cast the Russia conspiracy into the realm of conspiracy theory (even though, with its single domain, it is quite clearly a conspiracy), while implicitly suggesting, through the conspiracy theory of Pizzagate, that Clinton was involved in some sort of conspiracy.

An important implication of the cross-domain meta-narrative alignments is the potential for conspiracy theorists to generate entirely new narrative frameworks that cut across domains, violating Boole's limits in an expansive manner. As new narrative frameworks are added to the conspiracy theory, those actants become available to all of the domains covered by the conspiracy theory. This totalizing feature of the conspiracy theory consequently allows for a normalization of otherwise inadmissible actants, allowing one to say and imagine things that were previously unimaginable.

These conspiracy theories are not without real-world impact. While Pizzagate struck many observers as paranoid, delusional, and divorced from reality, the fringe became very real when Edgar Welch, a twenty-eight-year-old

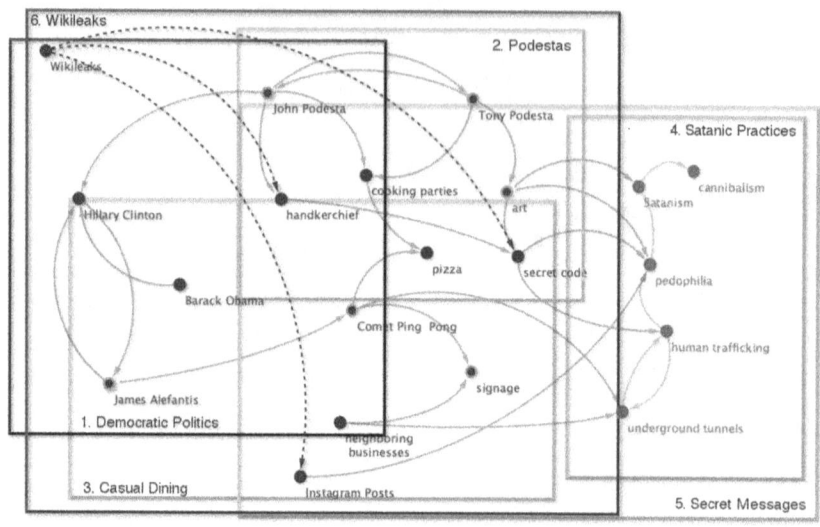

Figure 2.7. Five story domains in Pizzagate that are aligned through particular nodes: (1) Democratic politics is linked to the private life of (2) John Podesta and his brother. It is also linked to (3) James Alefantis, the owner of Comet Ping Pong. These domains are linked to (4) the Satanic practices (in gray) domain through a series of (5) secret messages that rely on a handkerchief, Instagram posts, and a secret code. The meta-narrative links for these special nodes are denoted by (6) Wikileaks. The nodes of the aligned actants are outlined in gray, with Alefantis playing a special role, appearing in all but one of these linked domains (private life of the Podestas).

Pizzagate follower, drove from his home in North Carolina to Washington, DC, to "self-investigate" what he had learned. His intention was to release the children he believed were being held in the restaurant's dungeons. After firing several shots both inside and outside the restaurant, and realizing that the restaurant lacked a basement (let alone dungeons), he surrendered to police. Even though the event ended relatively peacefully (in that no one was killed), his actions reveal the very real danger that these meta-narratives can pose when they spill over into real-world actions (Ellis 2000).

QANON AND THE STORM: THE CONSPIRACY OF ALL CONSPIRACIES

The addition of the Satanic/occult practices domain to Pizzagate occurred late in the lifespan of the conspiracy theory.[16] Yet the ability of conspiracy theory followers to make this type of late addition, in effect growing the meta-narrative to encompass yet one more domain, confirms that conspiracy theories can not only accommodate additional domains, but also that such accommodation is a fundamental feature of these meta-narrative frameworks. Once Pizzagate began to lose followers, the inclusion of the domains of Satanism and occult practices paved the way for the development of the far more elaborate "Calm before the storm" conspiracy theory, as social networks were already primed for such stories and beliefs.[17]

The first salvo in the Gathering Storm conspiracy theory came on 4chan's /pol/ (shorthand for "politically incorrect") forum on October 28, 2017, when a person using the default "Anonymous" identifier posted a series of questions under the title "Mockingbird."[18] Two days later, the same person, now identifying as "Q Clearance Patriot," posted: "HRC extradition already in motion effective yesterday with several countries in case of cross-border run. Passport approved to be flagged effective 10/30 @ 12:01 a.m. Expect massive riots organized in defiance and others fleeing United States to occur. US M's will conduct the operation while NG activated. Proof check: locate a NG member and ask if activated for duty 10/30 across major cities." Several days later, the poster, now referred to by most followers simply as "Q," began posting a series of "breadcrumbs."[19] The first of these posts, similar in format to the initial post, presented a series of clues about a broad conspiracy posed as questions.[20] Taken together, these questions present an initial list of actants and possible relationships that can be easily matched to domains in the news, in rumors and legends, and in other conspiracy theories (table 2.1).[21] Numerous archives along with complex comment threads sprouted up not only on Reddit, 4chan, and 8chan, but also on various elaborate websites created to concatenate the growing information about the conspiracy theory.

A novel feature of QAnon is its inclusion of already existing conspiracy theories in its meta-narrative linking. Foremost among these linked conspiracy theories is Pizzagate, as revealed in a Twitter co-occurrence network from the month beginning on November 1, 2017 (figure 2.8).

In subsequent posts, Q has continued to release increasingly cryptic breadcrumbs interlaced with pronouncements and predictions, creating a cottage industry among the followers, who call themselves "bakers," in deciphering and fitting these crumbs into the expanding meta-narrative. This process is referred to as "baking" the "dough," with Justin Caffer of *Vice* amusingly opining, "Some bakers, clearly not catching on to the Hansel and Gretel symbolism, have been known to refer to this dough as 'batter'" (2018).

Another striking aspect of the QAnon conspiracy theory is the large penetration of bots and other untrustworthy communicators in the overall propagation graph for Twitter (figure 2.9).

Table 2.1. A list of the actants and relationships extracted from the first post by "Anonymous" on October 28, 2017, along with the possible domains in which narrative frameworks that include those actants might appear

Actant	Potential domains
Hillary Clinton (HRC)	Democratic politics
Huma Abedin	Democratic politics
Russia	Global politics
Trump (POTUS)	US politics, Republican politics
Military intelligence	Military, global politics, spying
NSA, CIA, FBI	US politics, global politics, spying
Supreme Court	US politics
Congress	US politics
Anthony Weiner (AW)	Democratic politics
Prince Al-Waleed Bin Talal (AW)	Global politics, global finance
The media	Media
Classified material	Spying
Soros	Global finance
Obama	US politics, Democratic politics
Criminals	Crime, global finance, spying
United States	US politics, global politics
Republicans	US politics, Republican politics
Democrats	US politics, Democratic politics
Money	Global finance, crime, US politics, global politics
God	US politics
Patriots	US politics
Mockingbird	Spying, media, US politics
Registered charity (RC)	Global finance

Although the "bakers" present themselves as "true patriots," implying a degree of independence and dedication to protection of the United States, it is worth noting that the signal appears to be amplified by a relatively large number of Twitterbots. Similarly, the number of followers of the conspiracy seems to be inflated by the participation in the networks of these agents.

The QAnon conspiracy theory is impressive in its scope, not only because it includes many domains, spanning everything from politics to Christian belief to popular film to the Covid-19 pandemic, but also because it incorporates a series of conspiracy theories as subdomains. Here, a conspiracy theory and its attendant meta-narrative become domains in themselves, as noted above. Consequently, QAnon subsumes not only the

Bridges, Sex Slaves, Tweets, and Guns 57

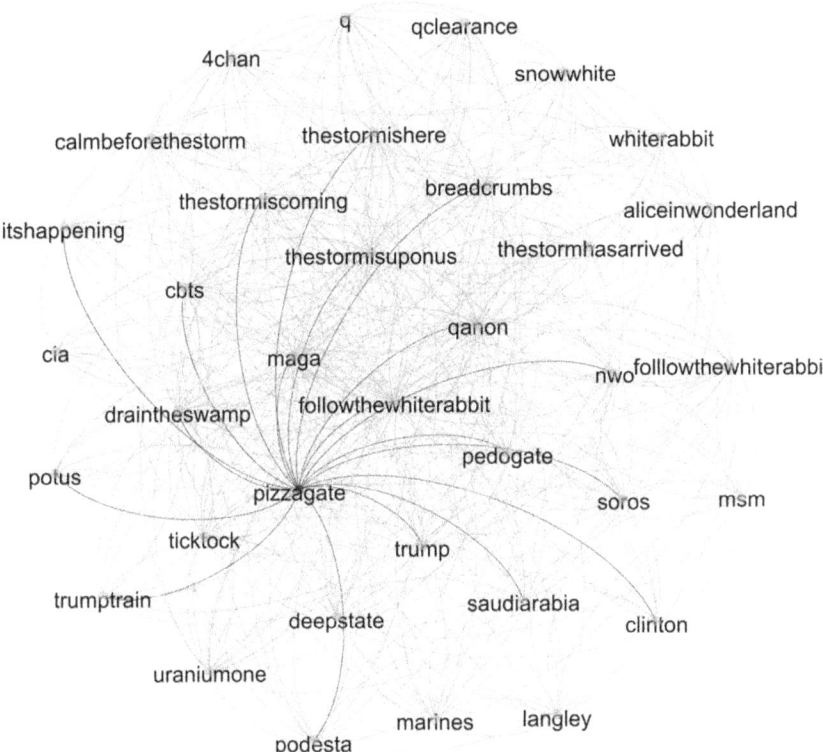

Figure 2.8. A Twitter co-occurrence graph showing the most prevalent co-occurring hashtags with the #TheStorm hashtag. For clarity's sake, the graph is reduced to a K-core of 25. The Pizzagate node is highlighted in black and the edges directed out from the node are in black.

narrative frameworks of news stories, as well as legends and rumors, but also the meta-narrative frameworks of other conspiracy theories and, in that manner, creates a single totalizing meta-narrative. A small sampling of the conspiracy theories that are embraced by QAnon include a conspiracy of computer manufacturers whose super-computers may run the country, if not the world (Snow White and the Seven Dwarves); a CIA plot to control the mass media (Operation Mockingbird); the collusion of the three wealthy families—the Soros family, the Rothschilds, and the House of Saud (the Triangle)—whose infighting led them to eliminate a fourth family (Family Y); J. P. Morgan's role in sinking the *Titanic* (*Titanic* and *Olympic* switch); involvement of the papacy in a global pedophile ring (Godfather III); crisis actors posing as student victims after the shooting at Marjory Stoneman Douglas High School (Florida crisis actors); and, of

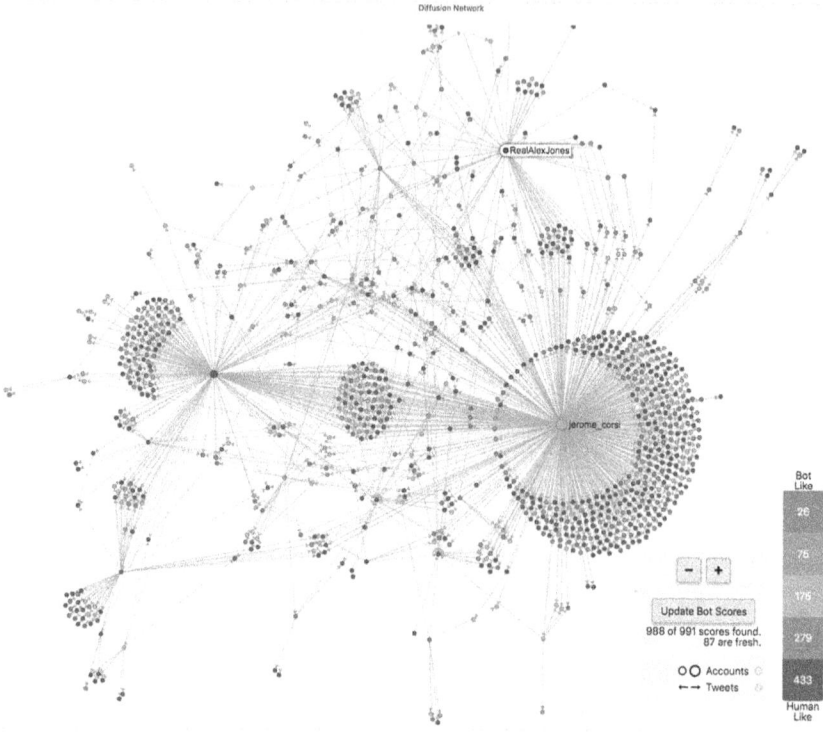

Figure 2.9. Propagation network of QAnon on Twitter, February through April 2018, created using tools from OSoMe at Indiana University (Davis et al. 2016). Two of the largest nodes are the accounts of Jerome Corsi and Alex Jones, both affiliated with the conspiracy theory website InfoWars. It is worth noting that Corsi's account behaves more like a Twitterbot than an actual person. The other prominent node in the star pattern on the left is someone using the Twitter name "followerrr," the account of a 9/11 conspiracy theorist.

course, Pizzagate. As Caffer (2018) points out, the process of generating the conspiracy theory allows the "bakers" an opportunity for diegetic imaginings, projecting themselves as analogues of Neo in the film *The Matrix*, thereby justifying their work on the conspiracy theory as heroes chosen to save humanity.

Unfortunately, the QAnon followers, much like the self-proclaimed child rescuer Welch from the Pizzagate narrative, are not content to do their sleuthing online. Instead, in a noteworthy echo of the "legend tripping" studied by Ellis and others, QAnon conspiracy theorists are now engaged in activities that spill over into the real world, such as excursions that act out parts of the conspiracy theory or otherwise mark the landscape—for example, QAnon billboards in Oklahoma (Ellis 1989; Kasprak 2018). These activities might be amusing if they were not dangerous, including Lewis Arthur's "Veterans on Patrol" group's armed searches of homeless encampments in Arizona for physical evidence of pedophilic sex-trafficking rings linked to the Democratic Party and Satanic cults, and another man's armed stand-off with police at the Hoover Dam (Gault 2018; Baer 2018). As Gault points out, "So far, no one has been harmed, but what's happening in Tucson right now is a good reminder that the tentacles of crazy internet conspiracies reach into the real world."

FUTURE WORK

The research presented here points to several clear areas for future work. While the exploration of Pizzagate made use of a preexisting, well-curated set of data generated by the conspiracy theorists themselves, developing a system that can discover possible target corpuses as they emerge on social media for further investigation would be a worthwhile extension. Another worthwhile extension would be to integrate our approach more closely with tools such as those from Indiana University's Observatory on Social Media (OSoMe), which track the propagation of specific signals on social media networks, and highlight whether nodes in the networks are compromised or artificial (Davis et al. 2016). Such a combined system would not only provide information about emerging topics, it would also yield data about underlying narrative frameworks driving storytelling in those domains and, in the case of conspiracy theories, the identity of the actants who serve as the links between frameworks. Community detection methods on these social networks could in turn help us understand which communities are engaged in these discussions, ultimately providing insight into how ideologies emerge and become entrenched in various communities (Bandari et al. 2017).

The multi-layered feature of the conspiracy theory detailed in the model could also be used to support methods for determining whether a story is actual news or whether it is an elaborate fiction, a growing concern in recent years, given the rise of "fake news." Such a system would identify stories that rely on multi-domain meta-narrative frameworks and flag them as potentially fictitious, providing a series of candidate stories for additional scrutiny. These methods for flagging potentially fictitious stories are important in a time marked by increasing instability of and distrust in our information sources (Allcott and Gentzkow 2017).

In the field of folkloristics, the model could be used to help develop a sophisticated multi-feature typology of conspiracy theories. Currently, most classifications of conspiracy theories are based on categorizing the underlying topics of the stories. For example, *Conspiracy Theories in American History: An Encyclopedia* provides an alphabetized catalogue of hundreds of conspiracy theories organized primarily according to content and the evidence on which the theory rests (Knight 2003). Other typologies trace the movement of conspiracy theories across separate media, with a considerable emphasis on the depiction of conspiracy theories in film (Arnold 2008). The meta-narrative model allows for additional dimensions of classification, such as by class of conspiracy theorist. As Steve Clarke points out, in the age of the internet, "the construction of the vast majority of conspiracy theories is a social enterprise—particularly nowadays, given the widespread use of the internet—with different people transmitting different versions of conspiracy theories to one another, adding to these and revising them in the face of new evidence and in the face of challenges from rival theories" (2007, 169). This consensus approach to conspiracy theorizing differs radically from the "lone wolf" conspiracy theorist working alone to uncover the hidden machinations of powerful elites, a common trope of popular film. The QAnon conspiracy theory offers an interesting example of a different type of conspiracy theory: the "lone wolf" figure of Q's cryptic pronouncements must be deciphered by the members of the social media groups who then construct the overarching meta-narrative by consensus. Another dimension for classification could be the number and type of linked domains in a given conspiracy theory, as well as the types of linking actants between domains.

Ultimately, whether or not a conspiracy theory gains traction in a community is dependent on the interaction of several processes, including confirmation bias and network effects such as preferential attachment, network priming, and homophily. A conspiracy theory can be broadcast on various social media channels; whether or not it spreads and, once it spreads, whether or not it persists, can be attributed to these network effects. It is well established that mere exposure to an idea, no matter how outlandish, primes people to be more receptive to that idea the next time they encounter it (Collins and Loftus 1975; Pennycook et al. 2018). Even a negating statement such as "John Podesta was not involved in a child-trafficking ring centered in a Washington, DC, pizza parlor," predisposes people to the idea that Podesta has some relationship to child trafficking and pizza parlors. Subsequent stories that include this idea are likely to gain some traction, as the network is already primed to be receptive to that idea. Preferential attachment relies on a desire of people to associate with high-status people in social networks. If a person of high status in a network begins to propagate a particular story, the process of preferential attachment kicks in, resulting in an amplification of that signal, a phenomenon illustrated in the Pizzagate

Twitter graph above (Newman 2001). Since people often sort themselves into communities according to common viewpoints, social media quickly becomes populated with "echo chambers," where people are exposed only to ideas that are shared by people with similar values (McPherson et al. 2001). The circulation of QAnon on 8chan is an excellent example of this type of self-reinforcing mechanism, a mechanism that the conspiracy theorists are themselves aware of, referring to themselves as "anons" and those outside the community as "normies" who can be potentially converted to the movement by "redpill[ing]," the latter a direct reference to the film *The Matrix*.[22] Finally, the well-documented phenomenon of confirmation bias tells us that people are more receptive to stories that confirm, rather than challenge, their existing beliefs, an effect that seems to be amplified in groups brought together by a common belief in conspiracy theories (Nickerson 1998). Social media is uniquely situated to take advantage of all these phenomena, ensuring an additional arena for the emergence, circulation, and persistence of conspiracy theories that align with and confirm group biases. More detailed studies could elucidate the interdependence of these processes, while also identifying possible methods for interrupting the emergence of potentially harmful conspiracy theories.

CONCLUSION

Conspiracy theories are part of the narrative landscape and have been for centuries. Instead of viewing conspiracy theories as a singular narrative, we take a cue from numerous folklorists, such as Ellis and Campion-Vincent, and model conspiracy theories as meta-narratives that align a series of narratives that already have validity in their communities as confirmed by their circulation in the tradition group. Unlike the news, which is messy and hard to contain, with new actants and new relationships entering and exiting the framework as the investigations progress, conspiracy theories are characterized by their neatness, aligning narrative frameworks from many disparate domains in an efficient and compact manner. In the examples presented here, we highlight the linking mechanism between narrative frameworks, illustrating the process through which a conspiracy theory forms. Quite possibly part of the excitement of engaging in the construction of a conspiracy theory resides in this alignment, providing clear motivation for people to engage with these theories.

The goal of a conspiracy theory is to tie up all loose ends, thereby providing a hermetically sealed narrative that explains the current state of affairs, while aligning itself with the cultural ideology of the group in which it circulates. The model presented here is generative, and consequently offers a clear method for creating additional meta-narrative frameworks linking otherwise disconnected narrative frameworks. Because of the generative nature of the model, there is no reason that it could not be deployed to create additional conspiracy theories. Although Hofstadter and others, in an act of wishful thinking, have attempted to confine conspiracy theories to the fringes of civil society, the eruption of genocidal regimes and populist governments that deploy conspiracy theories as part of their rhetoric reveal the potential danger posed by conspiracy theories to democratic institutions. Consequently, while one could criticize the model we present here for contributing to the weaponizing of storytelling, the evidence suggests that stories have already been weaponized. QAnon will likely fade into obscurity in the near future, as many conspiracy theories have in the past. But there will be countless others to replace it. The rise of social media and the concomitant ability of people to overwhelm channels with stories and conspiracy theories now make it possible to influence tens if not hundreds of thousands of people in a very short time. It is then of considerable ethical urgency that we work to understand the emergence of conspiracy theories, their structure, how they circulate on social media, and how they take root in various communities.

NOTES

1. The term *velocity* here is used to describe the propagation of a story through a network, with a specific speed through the network (on Twitter measured between tweet-retweet) and a specific direction (on Twitter through the mention of additional hashtags or particular users). This definition of velocity departs from Fenster's concept of narrative velocity as "the geographic, geopolitical, and cognitive aspects of the conspiracy narrative's movement" (1999, 122).

2. It should be noted that not all individuals can take advantage of the possibilities afforded by the internet for the amplification and targeting of their messages.

3. For example, see Fine et al. 2005; Fine and Ellis 2013; Renard 2006; Fine and Turner 2001; and the special issue of *Folklore: The Electronic Journal of Folklore* (Kalmre 2017). In our experiments, we focus on conspiracy theories about witchcraft, the devil, and religious figures mined from nineteenth-century folklore archives; the Pizzagate conspiracy theory; and QAnon, a developing conspiracy theory mined from social media sites.

4. Functionalist approaches such as these delineate narrators' motivations for telling these stories, thereby removing the stories and their narrators from the dark realm of psychopathology to which Hofstadter and his acolytes had banished them.

5. We base this characterization of the genre on Tangherlini 1990.

6. Albert Eskeröd's concept of "tradition dominants" coupled with Walter Anderson's "law of self correction" anticipate this process of convergence on stable forms and the

culturally determined limits on admissible actants or relationships within a particular narrative framework (Eskeröd 1947; Anderson 1923).

7. This instantiates in an indirect manner Dell Hymes's notion of "breakthrough into performance" (1975), where the performance discourse is marked and separate from everyday discourse. What is permissible in performance is often not permissible in everyday discourse, just as what is admissible in legend is not admissible in everyday reporting.

8. There are some indications that the reportability of the story relies entirely on that intrusion (Robinson 1981).

9. A fully manual approach would require the use of preexisting classifiers to determine the domains in a larger archive.

10. Our current pipeline is also able to make use of linked open data to provide additional information about nodes, and to provide additional confirmation of the validity of nodes and edges.

11. We also aggregate all noncapitalized versions of these strings as well as misspellings with low Levenshtein edit distance scores. Katie Reilly was a reporter for *Fortune* magazine who wrote stories about the Pizzagate conspiracy theory and subsequently was drawn into the overarching meta-narrative herself.

12. In some of these stories, the priest is taken by surprise by the revelation that his wife is a witch who travels to the Black Mass once a year to pay homage to Satan, and at other times he appears entirely complicit in her activities.

13. At least, there are no meta-narrative conspiracy theories that we can find. The collection is quite large, and searching for these meta-narrative alignments is a difficult process.

14. On July 13, 2018, a grand jury in Washington, DC, looking into Russian meddling in the 2016 presidential election, handed down indictments of twelve Russian military officers, as part of Robert Mueller's investigations, who were involved in hacking these emails and providing them to Wikileaks.

15. *Jezebel* and *Gawker* are two well-known social media sites for gossip about celebrities. *Gawker* shut down in 2016 after a protracted legal battle over the release of sex tapes of Hulk Hogan and a subsequent judgment against the site bankrupted it.

16. The addition was promoted in part by Michael Flynn Jr., the son of Donald Trump's disgraced national security advisor, and David Seaman, who played a central role in the Pizzagate Twitter network.

17. The conspiracy theory is also referred to as "the Gathering Storm," "the Storm," or simply QAnon.

18. The default identifier on 4chan for posters is "Anonymous" and so this user identifier has no particular meaning. The user apparently adopts the new user ID "Q Clearance Patriot" several days later.

19. Q identifies himself as a high-level government employee with a top-secret, sensitive compartmentalized information clearance (TS-SCI) known as "Q clearance." Q is a compartment that deals primarily with nuclear secrets and is often used for Department of Energy employees who work on nuclear weapons.

20. As the posts continued, and more posters joined in offering support to Q, the discussion eventually moved to 8chan. A great deal of the QAnon discussion has been archived by members of the group and is available at https://archive.fo/aaWPu. An annotated version of the posts can also be found at https://web.archive.org/web/20181121170747/https://genius.com/13518082.

21. Although we have not yet applied our pipeline to the increasing volume of QAnon material, the success of the approach with the Pizzagate materials provides grounds for optimism.

22. Referring to other posters as "anons" is standard practice on 4chan and 8chan irrespective of the topic of the discussion.

REFERENCES

Abello, James, Peter Broadwell, and Timothy R. Tangherlini. 2012. "Computational Folkloristics." *Communications of the ACM* 55 (7): 60–70.

Aisch, Gregor, Jon Huang, and Cecilia Kang. 2016. "Dissecting the #PizzaGate Conspiracy Theories." *New York Times*, December 10, 2016. https://www.nytimes.com/interactive/2016/12/10/business/media/pizzagate.html.

Allcott, Hunt, and Matthew Gentzkow. 2017. "Social Media and Fake News in the 2016 Election." *Journal of Economic Perspectives* 31 (2): 211–236.

Anderson, Walter. 1923. *Kaiser und Abt: Die Geschichte eines Schwanks*. FF Communications 42. Helsinki: Suomalainen Tiedeakatemia.

Arnold, Gordon B. 2008. *Conspiracy Theory in Film, Television, and Politics*. Westport, CT: Praeger Publications.

Baer, Stephanie K. 2018. "An Armed Man Spouting a Bizarre Right-Wing Conspiracy Theory Was Arrested After a Standoff at the Hoover Dam." *Buzzfeed*, June 16, 2018. https://www.buzzfeednews.com/article/skbaer/qanon-believer-arrested-hoover-dam.

Bal, Mieke, and Eve Tavor. 1981. "Notes on Narrative Embedding." *Poetics Today* 2 (2): 41–59.

Bandari, Roja, Zicong Zhou, Hai Qian, Timothy R. Tangherlini, and Vwani P. Roychowdhury. 2017. "A Resistant Strain: Revealing the Online Grassroots Rise of the Antivaccination Movement." *Computer* 50 (11): 60–67.

Boole, George. 1854. *An Investigation of the Laws of Thought: On Which Are Founded the Mathematical Theories of Logic and Probabilities*. London: Walton and Mayberley.

Caffer, Justin. 2018. "A Guide to QAnon, the New King of Right-Wing Conspiracy Theories." *Vice*, June 12, 2018. https://www.vice.com/en_us/article/ywex8v/what-is-qanon-conspiracy-theory.

Campion-Vincent, Véronique. 2005. "From Evil Others to Evil Elites." In *Rumor Mills: The Social Impact of Rumor and Legend*, edited by Gary Alan Fine, Véronique Campion-Vincent, and Chip Heath, 103–122. New Brunswick: Aldine.

Clarke, Steve. 2007. "Conspiracy Theories and the Internet: Controlled Demolition and Arrested Development." *Episteme* 4 (2): 167–180.

Clover, Carol. 1986. "The Long Prose Poem," *Arkiv for nordisk filologi* 101: 11–39.

Collins, Allan M., and Elizabeth F. Loftus. 1975. "A Spreading-Activation Theory of Semantic Processing." *Psychological Review* 82 (6): 407.

Davis, Clayton A., Giovanni Luca Ciampaglia, Luca Maria Aiello, Keychul Chung, Michael D. Conover, Emilio Ferrara, Alessandro Flammini, Geoffrey C. Fox, Xiaoming Gao, Bruno Gonçalves, et al. 2016. "OSoMe: The IUNI Observatory on Social Media." *PeerJ Computer Science* 2: e87.

Dundes, Alan. 1964. *The Morphology of North American Indian Folktales*. FF Communications 195. Helsinki: Suomalainen Tiedeakatemia.

Ellis, Bill. 1989. "Death by Folklore: Ostension, Contemporary Legend, and Murder." *Western Folklore* 48 (3): 201–220.

Ellis, Bill. 2000. *Raising the Devil: Satanism, New Religions and the Media*. Lexington: University Press of Kentucky.
Eskeröd, Albert. 1947. "Årets äring: Etnologiska studier i skördens och julens tro och sed." PhD diss., Nordiska museet.
Falahi, Misagh. 2017. "A Cognition-Driven Approach to Modeling Document Generation and Learning Underlying Contexts from Documents." PhD diss., University of California, Los Angeles.
Fenster, Mark. 1999. *Conspiracy Theories: Secrecy and Power in American Culture*. Minneapolis: University of Minnesota Press.
Ferrara, Emilio, Onur Varol, Clayton Davis, Filippo Menczer, and Alessandro Flammini. 2016. "The Rise of Social Bots." *Communications of the ACM* 59 (7): 96–104.
Fine, Gary Alan, Véronique Campion-Vincent, and Chip Heath. 2005. *Rumor Mills: The Social Impact of Rumor and Legend*. New Brunswick: Aldine Transaction.
Fine, Gary Alan, and Bill Ellis. 2013. *The Global Grapevine: Why Rumors of Terrorism, Immigration, and Trade Matter*. Oxford: Oxford University Press.
Fine, Gary Alan, and Patricia A. Turner. 2001. *Whispers on the Color Line: Rumor and Race in America*. Berkeley: University of California Press.
Gault, Matthew. 2018. "#QANON Conspiracy Theorists Are Hunting for 'Child Sex Camps' in the Arizona Desert." *Motherboard*, June 7, 2018.
Genette, Gérard. (1969) 1982. "Frontiers of Narrative." In *Figures of Literary Discourse*. Translated by Alan Sheridan, 127–144. New York: Columbia University Press.
Genette, Gérard. 1983. *Narrative Discourse: An Essay in Method*. Translated by Jane E. Lewin. Ithaca: Cornell University Press. First published 1972.
Greimas, Algirdas J. 1966a. "Eléments pour une théorie de l'interprétation du récit mythique." *Communications* 8 (1): 28–59.
Greimas, Algirdas J. 1966b. *Sémantique structurale*. Paris: Larousse.
Hofstadter, Richard. 1964. "The Paranoid Style in American Politics." *Harper's*, November 1964.
Hymes, Dell. 1975. "Breakthrough into Performance." In *Folklore: Performance and Communication*, edited by Daniel Ben-Amos and Kenneth Goldstein, 11–74. New York: Routledge.
Kalmre, Eda. 2017. "Introduction: The Social and Political Dynamic of Conspiracy Theories, Rumours, Fake News, and Belief Narratives." *Folklore: The Electronic Journal of Folklore* 69: 7–14.
Kasprak, Alex. 2018. "Billboards Promoting 4chan Conspiracy Theory 'QAnon' Pop Up across America." Snopes, June 29, 2018. https://www.snopes.com/news/2018/06/29/billboards-promoting-4chan-conspiracy-theory/.
Knight, Peter, ed. 2003. *Conspiracy Theories in American History: An Encyclopedia*. Vol. 1. New York: ABC-CLIO.
Kristensen, Evald Tang. 1892–1901. *Danske sagn som de har lydt i folkemunde*. Silkeborg and Århus: Jacob Zeuner.
Laudun, John. 2001. "Talk about the Past in a Midwestern Town: 'It Was There at That Time.'" *Midwestern Folklore* 27 (2): 41–54.
Marsh, Bill, and Katie Zernike. 2015. "Chris Christie and the Lane Closings: A Spectator's Guide." *New York Times*, April 8, 2015. https://www.nytimes.com/interactive/2015/04/08/nyregion/chris-christie-and-bridgegate-guide.html.
McPherson, Miller, Lynn Smith-Lovin, and James M. Cook. 2001, "Birds of a Feather: Homophily in Social Networks." *Annual Review of Sociology* 27 (1): 415–444.
Moran, Tom. 2017. "Bridgegate Judge's Smack Down of Christie Hits a Nerve." *New Jersey Opinion*. March 31, 2017. https://www.nj.com/opinion/index.ssf/2017/03/bridgegate_judges_smack_down_of_christie_hits_a_ne.html.

Newman, Mark E. J. 2001. "Clustering and Preferential Attachment in Growing Networks." *Physical Review E* 64 (2): 025102.

Nickerson, Raymond S. 1998. "Confirmation Bias: A Ubiquitous Phenomenon in Many Guises." *Review of General Psychology* 2 (2): 175–220. https://doi.org/10.1037/1089-2680.2.2.175.

Niles, John D. (1999) 2010. *Homo Narrans: The Poetics and Anthropology of Oral Literature.* Philadelphia: University of Pennsylvania Press.

Pennycook, Gordon, Tyrone Cannon, and David G. Rand. 2018. "Prior Exposure Increases Perceived Accuracy of Fake News." *Journal of Experimental Psychology: General.* 147 (12): 1865–1880.

Renard, Jean-Bruno. 2006. "Les rumeurs négatrices." *Diogène* 1: 54–73.

Robinson, John A. 1981. "Personal Narratives Reconsidered." *Journal of American Folklore* 94 (371): 58–85.

Rosnow, Ralph L., and Gary A. Fine. 1976. *Rumor and Gossip: The Social Psychology of Hearsay.* New York: Elsevier.

Seidman, Stephen B. 1983. "Network Structure and Minimum Degree." *Social Networks* 5 (3): 269–287.

Shao, Chengcheng, Pik-Mai Hui, Lei Wang, Xinwen Jiang, Alessandro Flammini, Filippo Menczer, and Giovanni Luca Ciampaglia. 2018. "Anatomy of an Online Misinformation Network." *PLoS One* 13 (4): e0196087.

Tangherlini, Timothy R. 1990. "'It Happened Not Too Far from Here . . .': A Survey of Legend Theory and Characterization." *Western Folklore* 49 (4): 371–390.

Tangherlini, Timothy R. 2000. "'How Do You Know She's a Witch?' Witches, Cunning Folk, and Competition in Denmark." *Western Folklore* 59 (3/4): 279–303.

Tangherlini, Timothy R., ed. 2014. *Danish Folktales, Legends, and Other Stories.* Seattle: University of Washington Press.

Tangherlini, Timothy R. 2017. "Toward a Generative Model of Legend: Pizzas, Bridges, Vaccines, and Witches." *Humanities* 7 (1). https://doi.org/10.3390/h7010001.

Tangherlini, Timothy R., Vwani Roychowdhury, Beth Glenn, Catherine M. Crespi, Roja Bandari, Akshay Wadia, Misagh Falahi, Ehsan Ebrahimzadeh, and Roshan Bastani. 2016. "'Mommy Blogs' and the Vaccination Exemption Narrative: Results from a Machine-Learning Approach for Story Aggregation on Parenting Social Media Sites." *JMIR Public Health and Surveillance* 2 (2). https://doi.org/10.2196/publichealth.6586.

Tangherlini, Timothy R., Shadi Shahsavari, Behnam Shahbazi, Ehsan Ebrahimzadeh, and Vwani Roychowdhury. 2020. "An Automated Pipeline for the Discovery of Conspiracy and Conspiracy Theory Narrative Frameworks: Bridgegate, Pizzagate and Storytelling on the Web." *PloS one* 15(6): e0233879.

3

The Vernacular Vortex
Analyzing the Endless Churn of Donald Trump's Twitter Orbit

Whitney Phillips and Ryan M. Milner

HURRICANES, ALSO KNOWN AS TROPICAL CYCLONES, form along the equator. As the bright sun heats the ocean water, some evaporates, creating a band of warm rising mist. Surrounding higher-pressure air flows in, warms up, evaporates, and pushes upward, allowing even more air to flow in, warm up, evaporate, and push upward, again and again. Clouds form and expand, like someone blowing air into a balloon. Because the Earth rotates on an axis, the clouds begin to rotate as well. An eye forms at the center as even more air flows down the chute, warms up, rises, and further bulks out the clouds. Then it becomes a question of winds. If they are strong enough, and carry the storm over water warm enough for a long enough time, and suddenly there is land, the storm will hit with catastrophic force. When it does, its impact won't be the result of just the wind, or just the Earth's axis, or just the descending or ascending air; it would make little sense to separate any of those elements out, point, and say, "That's a hurricane."

This chapter will take a similar approach to the vernacular vortex that is the Twitter account of US president Donald J. Trump. Just as a hurricane is the interconnection of its constituent parts, Trump's prolific and prominent tweets are a fusion of inseparable components. His role as a private citizen and his role as commander in chief; his behavior on social media and the behavior of the millions of people who react to that behavior; his own thumbs and the digital tools that allow him, and all those in his Twitter orbit, to ricochet messages across social media—all are integral, overlapping aspects of the story. To make sense of Trump's orbit—to make sense of any content, community, or practice online—digital scholars, regardless of discipline, must account for ever-expanding digitally mediated weather systems.

CAUGHT BETWEEN VERNACULAR AND INSTITUTIONAL WINDS

Trump's favorite microblogging platform, Twitter, allows him to sidestep more formal channels of communication, including White House press releases, prepared speeches, and interviews with journalists. He is able, instead, to directly reach his tens of millions of followers, along with the tens of millions of nonfollowers who are exposed to his tweets through social media sharing and news coverage. Trump's use of Twitter as a daily (and sometimes hourly, and sometimes even more than that) public address system represents a fundamental breakdown between *vernacular* and *institutional* communication: that is, between the informal, everyday expression of everyday people, and the expressions emanating from corporate entities, news outlets, state agencies, and other formal seats of sociopolitical power. This breakdown is the first and most conspicuous gust fueling Trump's vernacular vortex.

The crux of the issue is that Trump chooses to tweet from @realDonaldTrump, a personal account that predates his presidency, rather than from @POTUS, the official White House account.[1] Tweets sent from @realDonaldTrump fall outside of the formal White House communications purview. They represent, on the one hand, Trump's informal commentary about the news of the day—regardless of whether Trump tweets the messages with his own fingers or if they're written and/or sent by members of his staff. In either case, the act of tweeting from that account brands them, essentially, as Trump properties, not formal White House communications. This is a position the White House itself has affirmed. For example, in an August 1, 2018, tweet, Trump admonished the FBI to end its investigation of possible collusion between his campaign and the Russian government during the 2016 election. When asked about the tweet at a White House press briefing, Press Secretary Sarah Huckabee Sanders explained that Trump was expressing an opinion as a citizen, not making an order as president.[2] On the other hand, no matter how Trump and his administration frame his tweets, he is still the president of the United States when he sends them. All his speech, regardless of where the communication might take place, through what medium, or to what effect, is spoken as commander in chief. President is not a hat one can choose to take off.

Whether Donald Trump tweets as a citizen or as a head of state isn't solely a question of classification. It's also an unresolved First Amendment issue. For instance, in March 2018 a group of American Twitter users whose accounts were blocked by @realDonaldTrump sued the Trump administration. They argued that Twitter is akin to a mediated town hall and that being blocked by the president's account undermined their right to public participation (Toobin 2018). The court agreed, and Trump was ordered to unblock all blocked users. The Trump administration appealed the decision, however, on the grounds that @realDonaldTrump "belongs to Donald Trump in his personal capacity and is subject to his personal control, not the control of the government" (Shepardson 2018). According to this argument, Trump tweets as a citizen, but according to Trump's own @realDonaldTrump Twitter bio, he tweets as the "45th President of the United States of America." In the case of Trump's Twitter, the vernacular and the institutional unfold simultaneously.

HYBRID VERNACULAR STORM CHASING

This point matters, most pressingly, because of who Trump is and the political impact his expression has. The underlying question, however, about where one can or should draw the line between vernacularity and institutionality online, is much bigger than Trump himself. For decades, a range of academic disciplines has contended with the hybridity of media: the fact that mass media systems and texts, and audience participation with those systems and texts, are fundamentally intertwined.

Our area of specialization, media and communication studies, is replete with conversations about, for example, how news organizations influence what the public sees, what the public discusses, and therefore what the public does in response (see McCombs and Shaw 1972; Postman 1985). Other common foci include how mass media messages around race, gender, and sexuality impact identity performance and communication practices (see Mulvey 1975; Dyer 1997; Adams-Bass et al. 2014).

The discipline of folklore explores similar themes, particularly in analyses of ostension. In an influential essay on the subject, Linda Dégh and Andrew Vázsonyi describe ostension as the process by which "fact can become narrative, and narrative can become fact" (1983, 29), one that unfolds through a complex intertwining of folklore, mediated messages, and other cultural signs. Foundational studies like Jan Brunvand's (1981) examination of multi-modal urban legends (and legend tripping, the act of living out aspects of particular legends) and Bill Ellis's (2003) exploration of 1980s "Satanic Panics" also highlight the entanglement of mass media and folk participation.

Folklorists studying computer-mediated communication have been even more pointed in their foregrounding of how the vernacular overlaps with, or at least butts up against, the institutional. In 1990, John Dorst argued that the "telectronic age," ushered in by emerging communication technologies, posed a direct challenge to "the discursive practice which sustains the distinction between the vernacular, the folk, the marginal, and so on, on the one hand, and the dominant, the mainstream, the official, the mass, on the other" (189). Building on Dorst's observations, Robert Glenn Howard highlighted the "inextricably intertwined nature" (2008a, 195) of publicity and privacy, personal expression and commercial culture, and individual identity and group norms on the vernacular web. Trevor Blank (2013), Andrew Peck (2017), and Sheila Bock (2017) similarly emphasize the reciprocal influence between the digital and the corporeal, between the mediated and the experiential, and between platforms and sociocultural practices more broadly.

Although the above scholars blur the boundaries between the vernacular and the institutional, there are, according to these schemas, still boundaries to be drawn. Writing about the vernacular web, for instance, Howard argues that even the most hybrid vernacularity functions dialectically as an "authority *alternate* to that of any institution" (2008b, 491; emphasis added). Drawing from Howard, Blank (2013) affirms this distinction in his study of the hybridization of embodied discursive practices and digitally mediated discursive practices; through hybridization, the vernacular may replicate, adapt to, or fill in the gaps of the institutional, but it is still distinguishable from the institutional. Similar boundaries are maintained in any study that focuses on what the folk are doing as opposed to what institutions are doing.

It makes good empirical sense to establish such boundaries. The complication, however, is that in the contemporary hyper-mediated, hyper-networked and, frankly, just hyper-social media landscape, such boundaries—even the most basic distinctions between folklore and *not*-folklore—are often impossible to demarcate. This difficulty stems, first, from the ease with which everyday folk networks can plug into corporate, state, and other institutional entities through networked media, and corporate, state, and other institutional entities can plug into everyday folk networks. It also stems from the rise of algorithms and other technological tools for social sharing, which help to amplify all those plug-ins. Perhaps most ambivalently, boundaries between vernacular and institutional expression are eroded by the frequent collapse and reconstitution of novel audiences across social media. Any given post to any given platform has the potential to move far beyond its initial, intended audience; regardless of why or with whom something was originally shared, messages can spread across a range of platforms for a range of reasons with a range of effects on whole new participants, who begin the process anew through further sharing.

As a consequence of all this hybridity, much is often *not* known, and in fact remains unknowable, about vernacular expression on social media, particularly as networks of participants expand. This complicates a number of methodological approaches that under more controlled circumstances would reliably yield valuable insight—for example, when particular behaviors, texts, or traditions are confined to bounded, relatively small communities, or when participants are already well known to researchers. Bock provides an example of this tension in her study of collective performance of racial (and racist) discourse on Twitter (2017). She argues that analyzing online vernacular demands identifying the complex social dynamics at play in a social scene, with a particular focus on how embodied power dynamics and structural inequities manifest in digital spaces. Bock further maintains that these analyses demand exploring participants' construction and maintenance of differential identity, the complex intermingling of conflicting perspectives centered around the same object (in Bock's case, a specific hashtag).

Both objectives are, without a doubt, critical to strong analyses. The problem is that online, as we'll demonstrate below in relation to Trump's vernacular vortex, participating voices can become so cacophonous, information networks so tangled, and chains of amplification so ambivalent that it is often impossible to verify what exactly is differential from what. Identity performances might *appear* to be sincere; participation might *appear* to be organic; vernacular and institutional expressions might *appear* to be distinct. On the internet, however, observation is not the same as confirmation, a point we have previously explored (Phillips and Milner 2017). The constant chaos and churn of social media—much of which unfolds through private back channels or otherwise out of view of the researcher—also undermines efforts to account for all the technological and social variables that have precipitated a particular social scene. It can, in short, be difficult for researchers to know what they're even looking at online, let alone to accurately assess the political and ethical stakes of specific behaviors, groups, and texts. All the more reason to not lose the storm for its winds.

HURRICANE TWITTER FINGERS

The following case studies will track these analytic storms by charting Trump's quasi-personal, quasi-official @realDonaldTrump Twitter persona. The first case study will zero in on a particular tweet—the equivalent of one news cycle hurricane—and the broader energies that fueled it forward. The second can be likened to the meteorological phenomenon known as the

Fujiwhara Effect, in which coexisting storms impact each other's strength and trajectory. Both cases will highlight the endless churn between the vernacular and the institutional online. Both will also underscore the fact that online, a lone gust of wind does not an entire storm make.

M Is for Maelstrom

On June 16, 2015, Trump kicked off his presidential campaign with the following remarks about immigrants to the United States from Mexico:

> When Mexico sends its people, they're not sending their best. They're not sending you. They're not sending you. They're sending people that have lots of problems, and they're bringing those problems with us.[3] They're bringing drugs. They're bringing crime. They're rapists. And some, I assume, are good people. (*Washington Post* 2015)

That last little caveat only served to underscore Trump's primary claim, as it implied that he had never personally met any Mexican immigrants whom he would consider to be "good people." As his presidency has worn on, Trump has followed through on his explicitly stated racial animus. His staunchly anti-immigrant measures include putting renewed emphasis on Immigration and Customs Enforcement (ICE) raids, arrests, and deportations (Leonard 2018); rescinding the Obama-era Deferred Action for Childhood Arrivals (DACA) program (Kopan 2017); and forcibly separating thousands of immigrant children from their parents, many of whom were seeking political asylum, at the US-Mexico border (Rizzo 2018).

No policy has resonated as broadly, however, as what Trump has described as an "impenetrable, physical, tall, powerful, beautiful, southern border wall" (McCaskill 2016), the illusive crown jewel in his anti-immigrant platform. From the earliest days of his campaign, audiences at Trump's rallies frequently chanted, "Build the Wall!" and Trump frequently promised to do so, along with the promise that he would strong-arm Mexico into paying for its construction. The popularity of calls to "Build the Wall" also translated to the spread of countless pro-wall memes across social media, including one embodied iteration in which an attendee at one of Trump's Orlando, Florida, campaign rallies dressed up as the wall, complete with the lettered message "MEXICO WILL PAY" (Griffin 2016).

But Mexico has not paid, and convincing Congress to approve other sources of funding has proven to be a challenge. Trump's public frustrations over his idling wall prompted him to tweet a novel solution to the problem on May 25, 2018:

> Because of the $700 & $716 Billion Dollars gotten to rebuild our Military, many jobs are created and our Military is again rich. Building a great Border Wall, with drugs (poison) and enemy combatants pouring into our Country, is all about National Defense. Build WALL through M!

The last line of the tweet in particular drew public attention. On Twitter, folk participants reacting to Trump's cryptic imperative floated guesses as to what *M* might mean. Could it mean Michael Cohen, Trump's then personal attorney and financial fixer? Could it mean Money, which one certainly needs to build a wall? Could it mean Mexico, Miracles, or 'Merica itself? Maybe it stood for Michigan (to keep the Canadians out), MENSA (the genius IQ society), MI6 (Britain's intelligence agency), or Marmaduke (the cartoon dog). Perhaps *M* was for Monday, and then take the rest of the week off. In the end, the consensus view from journalists—one ultimately confirmed by two sources within the administration (Watkins et al. 2018)—was that *M* was short for military. Still, Trump's tweet certainly left room for speculation.

This was not the first time Trump had employed cryptic Twitter abbreviations. Nor was this the first time these abbreviations had spurred a cavalcade of social media speculation, mockery, and memes. In one well-publicized tweet from February 8, 2017, Trump lamented in a tweet ostensibly about traffic problems that "our people are far more vulnerable as we wait for what should be Easy D"—promptly "melting Twitter," according to *Vanity Fair*'s Maya Kosoff (2017). While *D* likely stood for "defense" or "decision," Kosoff notes, many participants took a more creative approach, suggesting, for example, that "Easy D" was the name of a musician (genres varied), or had something to do with the gay dating app Grindr. Trump's odd Twitter abbreviations inspired a similarly raucous response on May 7, 2018, when he described the FBI's Russia investigation as a "witch hunt"—by then his default descriptor for it. "There is no O," Trump wrote; "it's called fighting back." While *O* apparently referred to "obstruction of justice," that didn't stop countless Twitter participants from making a range of crude sex jokes (see Covucci 2018).

Trump's "Build WALL through M" tweet speaks to more than his particular brand of vernacular expressiveness, however. While it was Trump's own declaration, it was also opaquely tangled up with external institutional messaging. As Dina Radtke (2018) of the media watchdog group Media Matters for America noted, Trump's tweet came just hours after hyperconservative pundit Ann Coulter argued that the military should fund the border wall during an appearance on one of Trump's favorite Fox News shows, *Justice with Judge Jeanine*.

The president's obsession with cable news and his habit of tweeting about the things he watches on television are well documented. Trump himself affirmed this pattern soon after he announced his presidential candidacy during an interview with Chuck Todd, host of NBC's *Meet the Press* (2015). Todd asked Trump whom he talked to for military advice. "Well I watch the shows," Trump answered. Once he was elected, Trump's advisors and other officials catered to his media diet by frequently booking themselves on cable shows in the hopes of getting his ear (Borchers 2018). During an April 2018 Fox News appearance, for instance, South Carolina senator Lindsey Graham turned directly to the camera, breaking the fourth wall with a plaintive "Mr. President, if you're watching . . ." (Feldman 2018).

Politico's Matthew Gertz—who spent months comparing Trump's tweets to Fox News's programming—painted an even more striking portrait of the president's television habits. He noted that Trump spends so much time live-tweeting Fox News in particular that his Twitter feed essentially functions as a "Trump–Fox News feedback loop" (2018) between what Fox says on cable TV, what Trump says on Twitter, and what is then reupped as Fox News talking points.

The Trump-Fox feedback loop illustrates the profound ambiguity highlighted at the outset of the chapter. Trump's tweets are the social media equivalent to someone watching TV, shaking their fist, and repeating what their show said. Simultaneously, these comments are made in the name of the Office of the President—at least to the extent that Trump uses Twitter to make his thoughts as president known to the world. In the case of Trump's "Build Wall through M" tweet, Trump's call to build the wall using military funding resulted in no subsequent policy talks to that effect. The idea appears to be nothing more than something Trump saw on television, tweeted out, and then forgot about.

In addition to highlighting the vernacular institutionality of Trump's tweets, the "Build Wall through M" case also blurs the lines between corporate news, especially Fox News, the state, and vernacular responses to both. As Trump is president of the United States and is therefore, by default, the most powerful person in the country, it would seem reasonable to assume that his particular institution would trump, so to speak, all other institutions. In the case of Trump's tweets, however, a corporate news and entertainment media tail has been wagging the president's dog by shaping the president's musings about policy through television programming. This interplay has spurred a great deal of vernacular social media commentary in response to Trump's tweets, in turn spurring a great deal of journalistic coverage of the tweets and their social media reactions, followed by even more public commentary, more journalistic coverage, and often more tweets from the president, raising the question of which category, actually, is which.

The final point of hybridity in this case is the profound influence of social media platforms on unfolding public discourse. Looping back to the broader "Build the Wall" meme (to which Trump's "Build Wall through M" tweet was directly responding), vernacular expression—which served to champion, remix, mock, or analyze the meme—hinged on a range of technological affordances. Without them, the meme could not have spread as it did.

On Twitter, these affordances include, most conspicuously, hashtags, which index and archive conversations, allowing people to engage asynchronously with unfolding stories and trends. In the process, they bring countless additional participants into the narrative. The most notable hashtags in this case are, of course, #BuildTheWall, as well as #FuckingWall, which was inspired by former Mexican president Vicente Fox's use of the hashtag in a tweet @-mentioning Trump and affirming that Mexico would never pay for "that fucking wall" (Chen 2017).

A second Twitter affordance is the ability to interact with particular messages through retweets, likes, captions, and replies, all of which amplify those messages by inserting them into others' timelines, again ensuring that more people are brought to the story. Trump's "Build Wall through M" tweet, for instance, has garnered hundreds of thousands of replies, retweets, and likes, each individual action increasing the chances that the message will be seen by someone new. A third affordance is trending topic algorithms, which are triggered when a particular phrase (a category that includes individual hashtags) experiences an uptick in engagement. When the phrase spreads fast enough, it is featured in Twitter's "Trending Topics" window, thus pushing the phrase to additional networks of participants—precisely the outcome of Vicente Fox's #FuckingWall tweet, which immediately topped Twitter's global trending topics.

These affordances are complicated by a number of other factors that employ, and sometimes exploit, Twitter's platform functionality, in turn impacting the vernacular participation that unfolds. These include bots, individual programs designed to automate platform participation, often by liking, retweeting, or even replying to selected tweets to boost their apparent popularity; disinformation agents, individual human actors impersonating sincere participants in the hopes of sowing discord and confusion; and computational propaganda efforts, which seek to artificially trigger Twitter's trending algorithms by establishing retweet networks, whether enacted by bots or actual users (either disinformation agents or unwitting users retweeting sincerely). Under the right conditions, catalyzed by the right people, these networks can take what otherwise would be the tiniest narrative and make that narrative a global trending topic with shocking rapidity, a point technologist Renee DiRista underscored when she observed—in an article by the *New York Times*'s Farhad Manjoo—that "if you can make something trend, you can almost make it come true" (2017).

The impact of the "Build Wall through M" tweet, like the impact of any hurricane, was the result of a host of interdependent factors. It wasn't just that Trump said a particular thing, or that reporters responded to that thing, or that everyday people reacted to that thing, or that social media platforms provided tools for amplifying that thing. It was all of it: temperature, pressure, speed, rotation. As these components churned together, tens of millions of people were drawn into discourses around the wall, even if they didn't themselves seek out information about the wall—in turn ensuring further journalistic fodder, further penetration of the ideas, and further incentive for Trump to push his hybrid, dizzying, tweet-from-the-blue agenda, around and around the eye of the storm.

Superstorm Fake News

In this vernacular vortex, the storms are ceaseless, with tweet after tweet flying from Trump's fingers in rapid succession. If Trump's presidency is hurricane season, it's an especially active one. And, as is true of every hurricane season, storms don't exist in a vacuum. Instead, when multiple storms simultaneously swirl in the same vicinity, they influence each other. If the storms are about equal in size, each will alter the others' course. If one storm is stronger, it will pull fledgling storms into its orbit. This is the Fujiwhara Effect at work, and Trump's Twitter cyclones exhibit similar behaviors.

In the meteorological world, merging hurricanes are relatively rare, but in Trump's vortex, they are all too common. One bombastic tweet, one inscrutable abbreviation, one act of off-the-cuff xenophobia is always bashing into others in kind. Every tweet, every controversy, every meme—from any number of the endless sources constantly interacting with Trump—is a potential storm with its own specific speed, size, and pressure. When these storms collide, the Fujiwhara Effect dictates that they'll have compounding complications with compounding scope.

One such collision was set in motion on July 2, 2017, when Trump tweeted an animated GIF of him pummeling an anthropomorphized version of the CNN logo. The GIF, captioned by Trump with the hashtags "#FraudNewsCNN" and "#FNN," was crafted from footage of the 2007

World Wrestling Entertainment (WWE) event Wrestlemania 23. In the source footage, Trump, at the time a reality TV star in a scripted feud with WWE CEO Vince McMahon, sneaks up on McMahon during a match, body slams him to the ground, and elbows him about the face before walking away victorious. In the Trumpian remix, McMahon's head has been replaced with the CNN logo in an act of folkloric political commentary that apparently resonated with the president. The individual who took credit for that commentary (and later apologized for it, as well as their overall online behavior) was a Redditor going by the handle HanAssholeSolo, who, according to a piece published by CNN's Andrew Kaczynski (2017), frequently posted racist, misogynistic, and Islamophobic content to Reddit's notorious pro-Trump Subreddit, /r/The_Donald.

This certainly wasn't the first time a journalist had called attention to dehumanizing content emerging from /r/The_Donald (see Koebler 2016; Romano 2017b). What set this story apart, first, was that Donald Trump himself had retweeted that content, and second, that a line had been added to Kaczynski's story—reportedly by a CNN executive during the editing process (Perlberg 2017)—that stated CNN reserved the right to reveal HanAssholeSolo's identity if they continued posting hateful content. The most generous reading of this line was that it deviated from established journalistic norms. The most *un*generous reading was that it was tantamount to blackmail. Right-wing outlets like Fox News and other far-right personalities, including Donald Trump Jr., descended on the resulting controversy, more than happy to sling additional arrows at Trump's long-standing media adversary. Using a range of network propaganda efforts, notably the hashtag #CNNBlackmail, participants decried Kaczynski's report and CNN as an organization. Many spread the false narrative that CNN was endangering the life of a child, claiming that HanAssholeSolo was a fifteen-year-old (according to the information uncovered by Kaczynski, HanAssholeSolo is an adult man). Far-right extremists with a range of inscrutable motives also fabricated damaging allegations against Kaczynski, personally and persistently attacked him on social media, and posted the contact information of—as well as made physical threats against—several of his family members (Romano 2017a; Tani 2017).

Because these attacks were so publicly visible, and because they were accruing increasing momentum as they pinged back and forth between right-wing media outlets like Fox News and the *National Review* and extremist spaces like the Daily Stormer, 4chan, 8chan, and parts of Reddit, the establishment news media mobilized in kind. Journalists at CNN and other outlets formally published and informally tweeted countless responses to the unfolding story. This attention only spurred further reaction, ensuring that the story—along with the damaging falsehoods being spread about Kaczynski—persisted into subsequent news cycles.

As the reaction to it evidences, Trump's tweet of the CNN GIF was a hurricane all on its own. It was also—as the Fujiwhara Effect would predict—simultaneously energized by and absorbed into a bigger storm, one that has sucked up much of Trump's attention since he began his campaign: the supercell meme that is Trump's obsession with what he calls "fake news." This term first came into public consciousness early in the election cycle as a way to describe deliberately false articles designed to commoditize partisan eyeballs for advertisements. From there, it became a catchall classification for disinformation and misinformation spread across social media. Trump, however, took "fake news" in a different direction, twisting it into a pejorative dismissal of perceived conspiratorial journalistic bias against him.

Of course, it is not the case that Trump distrusts the news media wholesale; as evidenced by the fact that he relies on them for policy advice, Trump holds Fox News, along with other sympathetic outlets, in very high regard. The classification of "fake news" instead hinges on whether any given coverage is pro-Trump enough, a point Trump himself admitted in a May 9, 2018, tweet where he claimed that "despite the tremendous success we are having with the economy & all things else, 91% of the Network News about me is negative (Fake)." According to Leslie Stahl of *60 Minutes*, Trump made an even more illustrative comment during the filming of his first post-election interview. While Trump and Stahl were chatting off camera, she asked why he so frequently accused media outlets of propagating "fake news." Trump explained he did it to discredit and demean reporters, with the goal of preemptively undermining any subsequent negative coverage of him (Hernandez 2018). In this way, Trump's "fake news" label represents more than just a (selective) attack against the news media. It also serves as epistemic boundary-policing, in which positive coverage is framed as fact and negative coverage is framed as falsehood, thus giving Trump, at least within his own orbit, empirical veto power over things like approval ratings, unemployment numbers, and even the size of his inauguration crowd.

Trump's highly publicized war against "fake news" reached a high-water mark in what he hailed as the "2017 Fake News Awards," yet another storm primed to collide with those already swirling. It started, like so many things in the Trump administration, with a tweet. On January 2, 2018, Trump declared the following:

> I will be announcing THE MOST DISHONEST & CORRUPT MEDIA AWARDS OF THE YEAR on Monday at 5:00 o'clock. Subjects will cover Dishonesty & Bad Reporting in various categories from the Fake News Media. Stay tuned!

On January 7, the day before the awards were scheduled to air, Trump tweeted out a slight change of plans:

> The Fake News Awards, those going to the most corrupt & biased of the Mainstream Media, will be presented to the losers on Wednesday, January 17th, rather than this coming Monday. The interest in, and importance of, these awards is far greater than anyone could have anticipated!

As promised, on January 17, Trump tweeted, "And the FAKE NEWS winners are..." along with a link to GOP.com, the RNC site. The Twitter-generated preview of that link featured a headline that read, "The Highly Anticipated 2017 Fake News Awards: 2017 has been a year of unrelenting bias, unfair news coverage, and even downright fake news." Once clicked, however, the link directed many readers to a 404 page-not-found message. The lucky few who were able to access the site were greeted by a short listicle of errors made by news publications—errors that had already been publicly corrected or retracted by the outlets in question.

The Fake News Awards, Trump's retweet of the #FraudNewsCNN wrestling GIF, and the broader "fake news" meme all embody the tensions animating Trump's "Build Wall through M" tweet. They are also part of a full-scale Fujiwhara Effect; each grows increasingly powerful as it collides with all the others. The resulting energy, roaring across platforms, across media, across dining room tables, is attributable to the everyday expression of everyday citizens (the president very much included), the actions of the state (the president very much included), amplification by corporate news media, the corporate inner workings of social media platforms, and the attention-directing power of algorithms, bots, and other forms of networked propaganda. Making sense of any one storm—to say nothing of one particular component of one particular storm—requires contending with an ocean of storms, and the various interactions and collisions these hurricanes generate.

TRACKING THE COMING STORMS

As Trump's Twitter orbit evidences, the lines between seemingly distinct categories online—between vernacular and institutional expression, between state, corporate, and folk entities, and between the affordances of digital tools and the people who use those tools—become so blurred so quickly that they are, very often, effectively moot. It's not that those lines never existed or cannot logically exist. It's that in a large number of cases across social media, they simply cannot be demarcated, restricting what a scholar is able to see. When tracking a social media hurricane, understanding winds individually or pressure individually or rotation individually is not enough to understand that hurricane, and understanding a singular storm on its own is not enough to understand how it churns reciprocally with others.

It's not only that media scholars, folklorists, and others exploring the vernacular dimensions of online interaction will have less of an analytic foothold by focusing on just the wind or just the air pressure or just the earth's rotation. This precarity holds significant policy, media literacy, and ethical implications as well. Not being able to map a storm, wherever in its life cycle it might be, forestalls discussion of what can or should be done in response.

The stakes are especially high when studying vernacular expression that's part of a coordinated media manipulation campaign, like white supremacists' attacks against CNN reporter Andrew Kaczynski; or that dehumanizes, like racist calls to "Build the Wall"; or that undermines faith in democratic institutions, like the ceaseless pillorying of a free and open press. In these cases, cordoning *this* network from *that* network, *this* institution from *that* institution risks not saying enough about a particular unfolding narrative and saying too much about the wrong thing. Given how easily vernacular expression in the Trump era is harnessed toward corporate and state-sponsored manipulation, looped into cycles of media amplification, and exploited to undermine democracy, there has, in short, never been a more critical time to take up storm chasing.

NOTES

1. These accounts can be found at https://twitter.com/realDonaldTrump and https://twitter.com/potus, respectively.

2. Sanders's emphasis on this distinction should come as no surprise; an order from Trump to end the Russia probe would constitute criminal obstruction of justice. Opinions expressed by private citizens are constitutionally protected speech.

3. "With us" appears to be a linguistic misfire, meant either to be "with them" or "to us."

REFERENCES

Adams-Bass, Valerie N., Howard C. Stevenson, and Diana Slaughter Kotzin. 2014. "Measuring the Meaning of Black Media Stereotypes and Their Relationship to the Racial Identity, Black History Knowledge, and Racial Socialization of African American Youth." *Journal of Black Studies* 45 (5): 367–395.

Blank, Trevor J. 2013. "Hybridizing Folk Culture: Toward a Theory of New Media and Vernacular Discourse." *Western Folklore* 72 (2): 105–130.

Bock, Sheila. 2017. "Ku Klux Kasserole and Strange Fruit Pies: A Shouting Match at the Border in Cyberspace." *Journal of American Folklore* 130 (516): 142–165.

Borchers, Callum. 2018. "More Evidence That Trump's Advisors Talk to Him through the Television." *Washington Post*, January 23, 2018. http://wapo.st/2DFb81g.

Brunvand, Jan Harold. 1981. *The Vanishing Hitchhiker: Urban Legends and Their Meanings*. New York: Norton.

Chen, Tanya. 2017. "The Former President of Mexico Has Inspired the Hashtag #FuckingWall and People Are Running with It." *BuzzFeed*, January 25, 2017. https://www.buzzfeednews.com/article/tanyachen/fucking-wall.

Covucci, David. 2018. "Everyone Is Cracking Sex Jokes After Trump's Latest Tweet." *Daily Dot*, May 7, 2018. https://www.dailydot.com/layer8/trump-no-o-tweet/.

Dégh, Linda, and Andrew Vázsonyi. 1983. "Does the Word 'Dog' Bite? Ostensive Action: A Means of Legend-Telling." *Journal of Folklore Research* 20 (1): 5–34.

Dorst, John. 1990. "Tags and Burners, Cycles and Networks: Folklore in the Telectronic Age." *Journal of Folklore Research* 27 (3): 179–191.

Dyer, Richard. 1997. *White: Essays on Race and Culture*. New York: Routledge.

Ellis, Bill. 2003. *Aliens, Ghosts, and Cults: Legends We Live*. Jackson: University Press of Mississippi.

Feldman, Josh. 2018. "Lindsey Graham on Fox News Directly Appeals to Trump Not to Fire Mueller: 'Mr. President, if You're Watching . . .'." *Mediaite*, April 11, 2018. https://www.mediaite.com/tv/lindsey-graham-on-fox-news-directly-appeals-to-trump-not-to-fire-mueller-mr-president-if-youre-watching/.

Gertz, Matthew. 2018. "I've Studied the Trump-Fox Feedback Loop for Months. It's Crazier Than You Think." *Politico*, January 5, 2018. https://www.politico.com/magazine/story/2018/01/05/trump-media-feedback-loop-216248.

Griffin, Tamerra. 2016. "Someone Showed Up to a Trump Rally Dressed as the Wall He's Proposing to Build." *BuzzFeed*, March 5, 2016. https://www.buzzfeed.com/tamerragriffin/trump-wall-at-the-trump-rally.

Hernandez, Salvador. 2018. "Trump Revealed Why He Continues to Attack the 'Fake News' Media." *BuzzFeed*, May 22, 2018. https://www.buzzfeed.com/salvadorhernandez/trump-fake-news-leslie-stahl.

Howard, Robert Glenn. 2008a. "Electronic Hybridity: The Persistent Processes of the Vernacular Web." *Journal of American Folklore* 121 (480): 192–218.

Howard, Robert Glenn. 2008b. "The Vernacular Web of Participatory Media." *Critical Studies of Media Communication* 25 (5): 490–513.

Kaczynski, Andrew. 2017. "How CNN Found the Reddit User behind the Trump Wrestling GIF." *CNN*, July 5, 2017. http://cnn.it/2teY9xj.

Koebler, Jason. 2016. "How /r/The_Donald Became a Melting Pot of Frustration and Hate." *Motherboard*, July 12, 2016. https://motherboard.vice.com/en_us/article/53d5xb/what-is-rthedonald-donald-trump-subreddit.

Kopan, Tal. 2017. "Trump Ends DACA but Gives Congress Window to Save It." *CNN*, September 5, 2017. http://cnn.it/2wDZzS3.

Kosoff, Maya. 2017. "Twitter Melts Down After Trump Tweets about 'Easy D.'" *Vanity Fair*, February 8, 2017. https://www.vanityfair.com/news/2017/02/twitter-melts-down-after-trump-tweets-about-easy-d.

Leonard, Ben. 2018. "Numbers Show ICE Is Using Tougher Tactics in New York under Trump, Says Report." *NBC News*, July 25, 2018. https://www.nbcnews.com/politics/immigration/numbers-show-ice-using-tougher-tactics-new-york-under-trump-n893671.

Manjoo, Farhad. 2017. "How Twitter Is Being Gamed to Feed Misinformation." *New York Times*, May 31, 2017. https://nyti.ms/2rqcCG3.

McCaskill, Nolan D. 2016. "Trump Promises Wall and Massive Deportation Program." *Politico*, August 31, 2016. https://www.politico.com/story/2016/08/donald-trump-immigration-address-arizona-227612.

McCombs, Maxwell E., and Donald L. Shaw. 1972. "The Agenda-Setting Function of Mass Media." *Public Opinion Quarterly* 36 (2): 176–187.

Meet the Press. 2015. "Meet the Press Transcript—August 16, 2015." August 16, 2015. https://www.nbcnews.com/meet-the-press/meet-press-transcript-august-16-2015-n412636.

Mulvey, Laura. 1975. "Visual Pleasure and Narrative Cinema." *Screen* 16 (3): 6–18.

Peck, Andrew. 2017. "Capturing the Slender Man: Online and Offline Vernacular Practice in the Digital Age." *Cultural Analysis* 16 (1): 30–48.

Perlberg, Steven. 2017. "CNN Is Standing by Its Controversial Reddit User Story." *BuzzFeed*, July 5, 2017. https://www.buzzfeed.com/stevenperlberg/cnn-is-standing-by-its-controversial-reddit-user-story.

Phillips, Whitney, and Ryan M. Milner. 2017. *The Ambivalent Internet: Mischief, Oddity, and Antagonism Online*. Cambridge: Polity.

Postman, Neil. 1985. *Amusing Ourselves to Death: Public Discourse in the Age of Show Business*. New York: Penguin Books.

Radtke, Dina. 2018. "Trump's Border Wall Proposal Is Exactly What Ann Coulter Pitched on Fox News Saturday Night." *Media Matters for America*, March 26, 2018. https://www.mediamatters.org/blog/2018/03/26/trumps-border-wall-proposal-exactly-what-ann-coulter-pitched-fox-news-saturday-night/219737.

Rizzo, Salvador. 2018. "The Facts about Trump's Policy of Separating Families at the Border." *Washington Post*, June 19, 2018. https://wapo.st/2I0rQGr.

Romano, Aja. 2017a. "#CNNBlackmail: How Trump's Wrestling GIF Sparked a Debate about CNN and Doxxing." *Vox*, July 5, 2017. https://www.vox.com/culture/2017/7/5/15922224/cnn-blackmail-doxxing-hanassholesolo-reddit-wrestling-gif.

Romano, Aja. 2017b. "Reddit Just Banned One of Its Most Toxic Forums. But It Won't Touch The_Donald." *Vox*, November 13, 2017. https://www.vox.com/culture/2017/11/13/16624688/reddit-bans-incels-the-donald-controversy.

Shepardson, David. 2018. "Group Asks Trump to Unblock 41 Twitter Users After Court Ruling." *Reuters*, August 10, 2018. https://reut.rs/2Me0gLY.

Tani, Maxwell. 2017. "The Far Right Is Floating Conspiracy Theories about a CNN Reporter Who Profiled a Pro-Trump Reddit User." *Business Insider*, July 10, 2017. http://www.businessinsider.com/conspiracy-theories-andrew-kaczynski-2017-7.

Toobin, Jeffrey. 2018. "Trump's Twitter Blockees Go to Court." *New Yorker*, March 26, 2018. https://www.newyorker.com/magazine/2018/03/26/trumps-twitter-blockees-go-to-court.

Washington Post. 2015. "Donald Trump Announces a Presidential Bid." June 16, 2015. https://wapo.st/1HPABjR.

Watkins, Eli, Jeremy Diamond, and Elizabeth Landers. 2018. "Trump Suggests US Military Foot the Bill for Border Wall." *CNN*, March 27, 2018. https://cnn.it/2Gx9qR4.

4

The Death of Doge
Institutional Appropriations of Internet Memes

Andrew Peck

IN OCTOBER 2015, PRESIDENT BARACK OBAMA SPOKE AT the Democratic National Committee Women's Leadership Forum. During the talk, meant to rally his party's base, Obama touched on the often negative rhetoric put forth by the opposing party. "It does make you wonder," Obama said, addressing his audience directly. "Why is it that Republican politicians are so down on America? Have you noticed that? I mean they are . . ." Obama paused, briefly considering his words, "they are *gloomy*." He paused again and, suppressing a smirk, added, "They're like grumpy cat."

This reference to a popular internet meme was met with cheers and applause from his audience. To drive the point home, Obama contorted his face into an exaggerated frown, replicating the popular grumpy cat meme (figure 4.1). Cheers and applause from the audience crescendoed as Obama milked the moment for all it was worth. This act of memetic reference brought an otherwise unremarkable speech into the limelight. Videos of the speech went viral and stories about Obama's appropriation of an internet meme appeared in several news outlets: *ABC News*, *Time*, *CNN*, *BBC News*, and the *Guardian* (BBC News 2015; Begley 2015; Koran 2015; Saenz 2015; Guardian 2015).

Of course, not all institutional attempts to appropriate meme culture are this successful. In late 2013, Republican Texas state representative Steve Stockman was locked in a tough, uphill race for his party's 2014 senatorial nomination against incumbent senator John Cornyn. Looking to gain any edge they could for their candidate, Stockman's campaign managers turned to social media. On the morning of December 23, 2013, Stockman's team posted a memetic image on Twitter (figure 4.2), a riff on the popular

DOI: 10.7330/9781646420599.c004

Figure 4.1. The image that formed the basis for the popular Grumpy Cat meme and President Barack Obama's imitation of the meme during a 2015 speech.

"doge" internet meme (figure 4.3). The doge meme features a picture of a Shiba Inu dog to which text is added to represent the dog's internal monologue. The text is typically written in the Comic Sans font, displayed in multiple colors, and generally involves short phrases that are grammatically dubious, such as "much fear," "very fashion" and "so scare." These images almost always include the character's trademark exclamation—"Wow." The Stockman campaign's doge image was accompanied by a tweeted message written in the same style of memetic speech, "wow. such obamacare funding. oppose ted cruz" (StockmanSenate 2013).

In contrast to the Obama example, Stockman's attempt to appropriate vernacular digital culture failed. The tweet received coverage from many of the same news organizations that would also report on the Obama event in 2015. However, coverage of Stockman was decidedly less favorable, focusing on the extensive negative reactions by internet users, who mocked the ad for reeking of a room full of PR professionals trying to help a middle-aged member of the GOP seem hip. These users lamented that their beloved meme—a large-scale inside joke in many web communities—had been co-opted and ruined by institutional forces. This mainstream institutional appropriation led many to declare "doge" a dead meme. As one blogger for the *Daily Dot* concluded, "RIP, doge. And thank you for your short—but never forgotten—brilliance" (McHugh 2013).

Despite many users giving doge up for dead, a variety of institutions continued to try to capitalize on the meme well into 2014. In February,

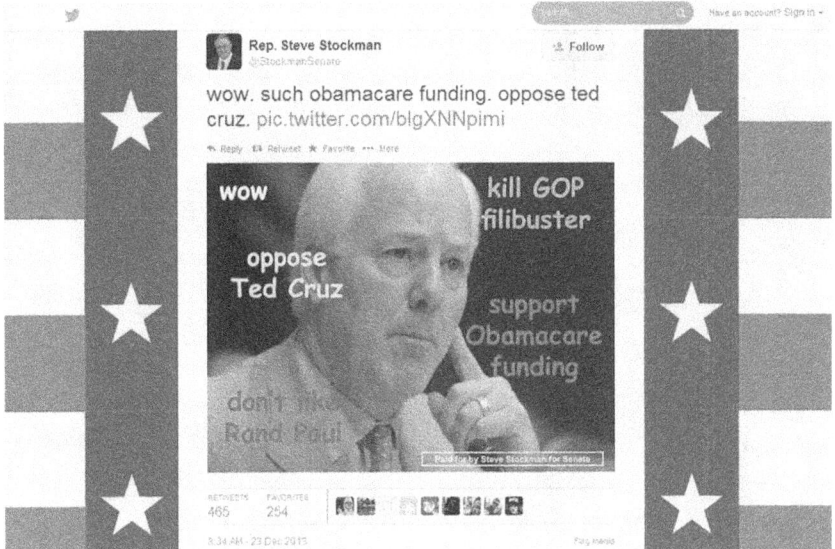

Figure 4.2. A Stockman congressional campaign image appropriates the popular "doge" meme to attack his opponent. Stockman would ultimately lose the Republican primary, coming in second (behind Cornyn) with 20 percent of the vote.

Figure 4.3. A typical example of the doge internet meme.

Figure 4.4. Campus organizations and local restaurants demonstrate the surge in popularity of doge-based advertising. (Photos by Nicky Kurtzweil.)

a London-based business ran a doge-based advertisement in the *Guardian* (Cook 2014). That spring, campus organizations and local restaurants at the University of Wisconsin–Madison used doge in their advertisements (figure 4.4). In June 2014, the official Twitter account of the Republican National Committee tweeted an image mocking Bill and Hillary Clinton using doge speak (GOP 2014).

The success of Obama and the failure of Stockman represent divergent outcomes of an increasingly prevalent phenomenon: institutional use of internet memes to seek empowerment through vernacular authority. On the surface, Obama's and Stockman's attempts seem quite similar—each involves a politician using a popular pet-based memetic practice to cultivate a sense of vernacular authority in service of making a political argument. But whereas Barack Obama succeeded in appropriating meme culture, Stockman became the target of widespread derision. While the ethos (or "brand") of the communicator may be partially responsible for the differences in each message's reception, focusing exclusively on the performer obfuscates many of the most salient elements of meme culture, crowdsourced folklore, and digital vernacular practice. Instead, we might begin with a more holistic approach, asking: why do some institutional attempts to appropriate memetic practice fail while others succeed? Why do institutions choose to speak in the vernacular when attempts to do so are so frequently derided by users? What are the limits of vernacular appropriation and empowerment?

To answer these questions, scholars of digital folklore must understand not only how these images seek to speak in a memetic vernacular but also how users speak back. As Robert Glenn Howard notes in his study of the official Kerry/Edwards campaign blog, institutional attempts to leverage vernacular practice create a sense of vernacular/institutional hybridity and open those institutions to vernacular criticism (2008a, 212). In this chapter, I extend this view by arguing that the problem for institutions is that their attempts to leverage the memetic vernacular frequently express a contradictory sense of hybridity—neither fully institutional nor fully vernacular but trying to be both. This contradictory hybridity creates a breach in user expectations that hails everyday individuals to reassert their primacy over vernacular communication—both by challenging the institution's construction of vernacular authority and by reaffirming their own vernacular authority through performances of vernacular knowledge. The result is that these communications tend to fail when their vernacularity and institutionality come into conflict.

I begin this chapter by demonstrating that internet memes are vernacular folk practices made possible by the affordances of contemporary digital participatory media. Next, I build on the work of Linda Dégh to suggest that these digital vernacular practices are appealing to advertisers because they tap into "commonness" and construct vernacular authority (1994). In the following section, I analyze a Facebook post made by the United States Department of Health and Human Services that used doge to advertise HealthCare.gov. Unlike the Stockman ad (which missed the mark significantly), the doge image posted by Health and Human Services initially appears as a much more typical example of the memetic practice; however, it was still met with harsh assessments by Facebook users. I assert that even though the institution correctly copied the form, it was unsuccessful in its attempt to reproduce the sense of alterity that enables vernacular practice. Ultimately, I argue that the failure of this communication event offers valuable insight into vernacular discourse that goes beyond Obama, Stockman, and doge. Whereas institutional messages thrive on centralized control and careful construction, memetic practices succeed by ceding control to a nebulous digital crowd. Therefore, successful institutional appropriations of internet memes need to demonstrate an awareness of memetic practice—an understanding that vernacularity emerges from ongoing and communal (not singular) actions.

THE INSTITUTIONAL APPEAL OF VERNACULAR PRACTICES IN ADVERTISING AND SOCIAL MEDIA

Internet memes are digital vernacular practices extended by the affordances of contemporary participatory media (Blank 2013, 2018; Foote 2007; Kaplan 2013; McNeill 2009, 2013a, 2013b; Milner 2016; Peck 2014, 2015a, 2015b, 2016; Rezaei 2016; Shifman 2014). Around the turn of the millennium, users conveyed similar expressive dynamics via chain emails (Blank 2007; Hathaway 2005; Kibby 2005; Thomas 2003), discussion boards (Fernback 2003; Howard 1997), image-based hoaxes (Frank 2004), digital joke cycles (Csaszi 2003; Ellis 2001, 2002; Kuipers 2002, 2005), and other forms of "netlore." The Web 2.0 era put this sort of user-generated content at the forefront of the World Wide Web (Baym 2010), building in new affordances that have made everyday networked communication more rapid, connected, visual, mobile, fluid, and multimedia. Folk forms and practices continued to evolve and embrace these new affordances, and the resulting practices—which users commonly call "memes"—are expressed in a variety of emergent, hybridized forms that frequently mix written, oral, and visual modalities (Peck 2015b). As media scholar Limor Shifman writes, "The meme concept is not only useful for understanding cultural trends: it epitomizes the very essence of the so-called Web 2.0 era" (2014, 15).

Ryan M. Milner observes that internet memes are, at their heart, recurring online vernacular practices (2016; see also Peck 2014). Calling something a practice emphasizes the role of social and structural dynamics in the creation of individual artifacts and in individual acts of volition (Giddens 1984). A practice-driven framework is inclusive. It still values the importance of individual artifacts and content, but it also understands that these fragments are not created in a vacuum. Digital communication practices emerge as part of a greater whole that includes not only acts of individual volition, communal norms, and traditions of behavior but also the underlying structure and affordances of the technology itself (Buccitelli 2016; see also Schmitt 2016). These facets may seem discrete, but they are constantly influencing each other in a mutually constitutive feedback loop that is simultaneously individual, collective, and structural (Giddens 1984).[1] Individual acts of memetic creation emerge both in concert and in tension with the community's rules for sharing (both formal and informal) and the technological affordances (the options for communication made available [and preferred] by the underlying platform) present in any and every given scenario. Put more simply, these facets work together to structure the modes of engagement users often find themselves engaging (and playing) with.

The visibility of memetic communication enabled by digital media creates an awareness that individual actions exist as part of a larger body of practice. As Anthony Bak Buccitelli notes, "Digital technologies are increasingly commonly aggregating, multiplying, and layering both practices and performances both at a single temporal point (the initial temporally extended discursive event) and across time (the durable trace)" (2016, 91). Limor Shifman offers a similar perspective directed more specifically at memetic practice (2014). She observes that by documenting and sharing everyday actions across networks, users make formerly ephemeral and interpersonal communication events more visible across space and more persistent over time. The sum total of these interactions is catalogued on a variety of web locations, allowing previously uninitiated users to quickly learn about the myriad variations at play (Kaplan 2013). This mass sharing inadvertently results in a widely accessible archive of everyday practice where "it only takes a couple of mouse clicks to see hundreds of versions" (Shifman 2014, 30).

The outcome of these changes in visibility, Shifman argues, is an increase in user awareness of the overall sum of these actions (2014, 29). In other words, as memetic acts begin to circulate across networks and become more visible, users begin to recognize them not only as distinct actions but also as parts of a larger vernacular practice. However, the increased visibility afforded by digital media has another major implication for memetic practice—while it may make users more aware of the aggregated continuities between their acts of everyday self-expression, it also makes those practices much more visible to cultural outsiders and institutional agents.

Institutional appropriations of vernacular practice seek empowerment by appealing to vernacular authority. As Linda Dégh writes in *American Folklore and the Mass Media*, by combining the magical or folkloric with the banal and everyday, advertisers repackage belief and practice in order to sell products or ideas back to the folk, constituted as consumers (1994, 37, 53). Dégh's work, which focuses on folklore and television advertising, suggests that the cavalcade of *märchen*-like helpers across commercials are welcomed much more readily into living rooms than the "traveling salesperson" (43). By appropriating these folkloric helpers, advertisements hide their commercial intentions behind a trusted, authentic, familiar, and affective face.

These appropriations of vernacular practice traffic heavily in allusion and reference (Dégh 1994, 44–45). To understand them, the viewer must access their personal cultural inventory (Blank 2013, 2018, 4–5). This serves as part of the advertisement's appeal. By asking the audience members to tap into their personal vernacular or folk knowledge in order to gain understanding, a moment of identification occurs (Burke 1950). In this moment, the institution reaches out to the consumer and conveys the idea of a shared sense of the common.[2] By drawing on the tacit knowledge represented by these shared vernacular practices (González-Martin 2016), it is as if the institution is hailing its audience by saying "Hey, look, we're just like you!"

The potential for vernacular authority is available to institutions because vernacularity emerges discursively from a diffuse process and not from any specific individual's identity or social position (Howard 2008b, 509). As Robert Glenn Howard writes, "The defining characteristic of an institution is that it has been instituted or founded by some formal act" (2013, 78). Many different organizations in contemporary society might fall under this label, including corporations, nonprofits, mass media outlets, and government agencies. Institutional agents (that is, individuals working in an official capacity representing an institution) have the ability to speak both in formal, institutionally prescribed ways as well as in a vernacular mode (Howard 2010).[3] As Howard has noted, the distinction between the vernacular and institutional grows increasingly blurry online (see also Phillips and Milner, this volume).

Vernacular expression can support or oppose institutions but, as Howard observes, it often does a little of both (2008a, 205). This disparity reflects the pitfalls of construing the vernacular and institutional as absolutes. To circumvent this problem, Howard suggests a reconfiguration that imagines a dialectical vernacular. This dialectical vernacular locates vernacularity in a process that "imagines a web of intentions moving along vectors of structural power that emerge as vernacular whenever they assert their alterity from the institutional" (2008b, 497). At the most basic level, calling something vernacular means it expresses alterity from institutions, even when it is simultaneously enabled by existing hegemonic ideas or institutional structures. Hence, the vernacular is not a material state of being (it is not something that one either has or does not have), it is a quality that emerges through practice in various levels of hybridity.[4]

Understanding vernacularity as fundamentally hybrid and discursive allows us to better consider the complex relationship between vernacular and institutional in mediated communication. For example, when Barack Obama (acting as president and quintessential institutional agent) imitates Grumpy Cat, strikes a meme-referencing pose for a photograph, or uses the popular memetic phrase "Thanks, Obama" in a promotional video, he is engaging with meme culture and vernacular practice. Conversely, an everyday user may use vernacular memetic practices to support hegemonic or institutional ideas. Calling something vernacular acknowledges how a communication or practice works; it is not a value judgment.

Vernacular memetic practices serve as markers of group competence and membership. Memes are akin to inside jokes—being aware of the joke not only shows an ongoing relationship but also offers a generic baseline to play with the shared practice. However, instead of being shared only by a dyad or small group, these specific practices are shared by individuals who belong to and transition between various digital communities. Because of this amorphous flow, memes seemingly manifest paradoxically—they are simultaneously localizations based on larger bodies of memetic practice and the instantiations of the genre that set expectations for larger bodies of memetic practice (Miltner 2014).

Communication scholar Eric S. Jenkins recognizes that memes exist in this state of liminality, as both individual artifacts and as modes of communication (2014). This relationship between virality and community makes the practice seem like a public resource that belongs to no specific individual or community. Instead, such expressions are specific instances that inherit from larger bodies of practice. This suggests that underlying any memetic communication is an expectation that the event inherits from the force of a larger, broadly defined set of vernacular internet communicators, drawing on a larger reserve of vernacular authority existing independently from the specific communication event where these expectations may be invoked. This is more than suggesting that memes are vernacular because they are everyday or "common;" instead, I am arguing that "commonness" functions as a tacit argumentative resource in memetic communication.

This ability to tap into "commonness" and construct vernacular authority is why appropriating memetic practice is so appealing for institutional communicators and commercial organizations seeking to extend their existing institutional authority onto social media (see González-Martín 2016, 62). As Dégh argues, the specific element of folk culture that is appropriated for an advertisement is frequently inessential to the actual message. What matters here is not what folkloric character is used in an advertisement (whether it be a fairy or doge), but instead what the inclusion of folkloric qualities *does* for the institution that uses it (1994, 47). In television advertising, Dégh suggests, a good scriptwriter can make the audience suspend disbelief and accept the fantastic (or the folkloric or folkloresque) to lower message scrutiny and make the appeal seem more magical, familiar, or palatable (47).[5] In strategic communication on social media, a skilled institution or influencer can use memetic practice to make an idea go viral or to raise publicity for a cause.[6]

The most effective institutional appropriations of memetic practice obfuscate their roots and intentions and can even convince users to adopt new memetic practices and continue spreading the institution's message for them. Take, for instance, a low-budget commercial for a small-town business that went viral after someone posted it to Reddit in September 2011. The ad for Ojai Valley Taxidermy showed a variety of individuals fooled into thinking obviously taxidermized animals were alive, only to be corrected by the taxidermist himself, using the commercial's recurring catchphrase "Nope! Chuck Testa" (Testa 2011). The ad subsequently accrued over 16 million views on YouTube and sparked a meme based on the catchphrase. The meme become so popular with web users that "Nope! Chuck Testa" was included in *Time* magazine's top ten memes of 2011 (Carbone 2011).

This advertisement's memetic and viral success was no accident. It was created by a pair of successful YouTube content producers as part of their television show *Commercial Kings* on the IFC Network. The idea was to create a viral video with the appearance of a low-budget local television commercial in order to garner social media buzz for Testa's taxidermy business (Locker 2011). The video likely resonated with users because it appeared to strike a balance between sincerity and playfulness (Marwick and boyd 2011, 149). However, these values were purposely coded into the video as part of the advertisement's overall "social media friendly" design, which sought to influence everyday users to forward, share, or remix portions of the video as a meme on social networks. The video doesn't reveal the creators' intentions—users aren't asked to "like" it, share it, or turn it into a meme. By not revealing their intentions to go viral, the creators made it seem like the choice to "meme" the Ojai Valley Taxidermy ad was an everyday act that emerged organically from users. Yet the viral video is constructed in such a way that to make subsequent allusion and reference recognizable, users had to adopt the central catchphrase as the memetic element. By controlling the key points of memetic articulation in this way, the creators provided a blueprint for the ensuing memetic practice. The result was that for several weeks in 2011 users created and circulated "Chuck Testa" memes across social media, and in doing so generated free publicity for the advertiser's client and his business.

Few institutional appropriations of meme culture are this successful. The problem for institutions is that their attempts to leverage meme culture frequently express a contradictory sense of hybridity, where the vernacular and institutional elements emerge in direct contention with one another.

When an institution is too blatant, misjudges, or misuses vernacular digital culture in this way, the result is a sense of uncanniness that breaches users' generic expectations for vernacular practice and exposes the institution's inauthenticity and intent. This understanding illuminates why some institutional appropriations of meme culture are more effective at constructing vernacular authority than others. The breach of generic expectations hails users not only to reassert their primacy over vernacular communication but also to engage in acts that critique institutional authority in order to reconcile the vernacular/institutional contradiction with which they are presented.

THE DEATH OF DOGE

Nearly two months after the massive memetic missteps of the Stockman campaign, the United States Department of Health and Human Services turned to doge to advertise HealthCare.gov. On February 20, 2014, the organization posted an image on its Facebook page that used the doge meme to advertise enrolling for health coverage under the Affordable Care Act (figure 4.5).

The post got an uncharacteristically large number of responses from Facebook users. In February 2014, Health and Human Services made fifty-five Facebook posts. The doge post attracted approximately 3,000 "likes," 8,000 shares, and 1,350 comments. In comparison, the other fifty-four posts each averaged about 240 "likes," 100 shares, and 40 comments. Roughly 40 percent of the total comments made that month were directed at the doge image (the remaining 60 percent was split across the other fifty-four posts), and the image was shared 50 percent more times than all other content posted to the page that month *combined*. This post is notable not only for attracting user attention but also because it received a huge proportion of comments and shares compared to "likes." Considering how much more effort goes into writing a comment versus hitting the "like" button, user response to this image is particularly striking, suggesting two things. First, the misuse of vernacular practice drew a huge crowd of responses beyond the usual small group of users who used the page to air their grievances with the Obama administration and the Affordable Care Act. Second, something about this post drove users to respond in ways that were more active and engaged than simply hitting the "like" button or scrolling past the image.

In many ways, the image posted to Facebook by Health and Human Services accurately replicates and adheres to the form of a typical a doge meme. Unlike the Stockman image, a picture of a cute Shiba Inu is used for the background. The text is written in various colors and Comic Sans font.

Figure 4.5. The US Department of Health and Human Services advertised HealthCare.gov by posting its own variation of the doge meme to its Facebook page.

The messages are kept simple, with doge's trademark "Wow" appearing in large text on the top left side of the image. The image post is accompanied by a short hashtag (#GetCovered) and the URL for HealthCare.gov. Although seemingly insignificant details, these small choices tap into an existing matrix of knowledge much more effectively than many other institutional attempts to appropriate memetic practice. Including these elements of memetic practice displays a sort of competency that serves to tap into an ongoing vernacular practice to create a sense of vernacular authority. In addition to using a meme, several other choices (such as adding a hashtag and sharing via Facebook) strive to show awareness of vernacular digital practices, inviting users to aid in the construction of crowdsourced authority for this communication.

However, while the form of this image adheres to the generic conventions of this memetic practice, the message conveyed by the text frustrates this communication's construction of vernacular authority. The text overlaying the image combines doge-speak with advertising buzzwords, creating messages like "Very benefits" and "Much affordable." With the exception of doge's trademark "Wow," all of these short phrases involve directing people to HealthCare.gov. The failure here is that this communication comes off as prescriptive, not interactive.[7] It doesn't invite users to create their own versions or collaborate. It encourages sharing, but only exactly as it is. It also solicits a different form of action from users, one that is in service to the institution. More successful institutional attempts at appropriating memetic practice tend to avoid this problem by acknowledging the meme in a more tongue-in-cheek fashion instead of using it to directly ask for institutional action or engagement. The result is that this communication mixes institutional authority (and a call for institutional action) with an appeal to vernacular authority and crowdsourced circulation, undercutting both forms of authority. In other words, the form of the meme is at odds with the message, and the message is at odds with itself.

In this image, we see form and content working together to appeal to vernacular authority, and at the same time, we also see how that appeal confounds itself. If invoking separation from the institutional is what defines the vernacular, then this communication emerges in hybridity, deeply at odds with itself. Hence, an unreconciled tension between vernacular and institutional exists in this image. In responding to it, users—by and large—pick up on this tension. As one commenter put it, "This makes no sense with doge meme. There is not even relation from the pic and text" (Ulises 2014).[8] It is the reconciliation of this contradiction between vernacular and institutional that users seek to navigate in their responses.

Challenging Vernacular Authority

The form of the Health and Human Services doge image was so typical that, to some users, its institutional roots weren't readily apparent. Many users who stumbled across the image because it popped up in their Facebook news feed initially thought the image was a vernacular joke meant to humorously mock the very institution that had been the one to post it. One commenter discussed this realization, expressing how amusement quickly gave way to disappointment:

> So, when this first popped up in my feed, I laughed because I thought it was a picture making fun of healthcare.gov.
>
> Then I realized it was made to support healthcare.gov, by my own government.
>
> Now I am just sad. (Kelly 2014)

Responses and comments by other users suggest this was not an isolated reaction to the image. Such reactions denote a shift in decoding the image based on changing perceptions of vernacularity. Initially, these users recognize the image as belonging to a vernacular memetic practice with which they are familiar, and they make certain assumptions that tacitly support the image's vernacular authority. Under this interpretation, users appreciate the image because of its alterity—it works as an effective piece of humor because it mocks institutions as well as institutional attempts to appropriate memetic practice. Here the hybrid institutional/vernacular contradiction presented by the image is reconciled into a punch line that is almost antithetical to Health and Human Services' intent.

As users came to understand the image as it was intended—as an advertisement for HealthCare.gov—this sense of alterity shifted, creating the occasion for users to challenge these constructions of vernacular authority. As an advertisement, the image no longer represents a playful self-awareness or a vernacular critique of the state. The contradiction between vernacular and institutional is revealed not as part of a joke but as an attempt by the institution to appeal via a constructed sense of alterity using memetic practice. Hence, instead of being in on the joke, Health and Human Services *becomes* the joke.

This ridicule represents an awareness among users that generic expectations for engaging with memetic practice have been violated. Much of the resulting discourse attempts to navigate this violation and reclaim vernacular authority from institutional agents. In other words, moments where the vernacular and institutional come together in messy ways serve as occasions that hail users to reassert their primacy over vernacular authority. In this case, users challenged the attempts of the institution to appropriate memetic practice by disputing its efforts to construct a sense of vernacular authority.

To many participants in the Facebook post's comments section, Health and Human Services' post demonstrated an awareness of vernacular practice, but it lacked an understanding of it. As one user put his critique, "Doge is fun when it's used correctly. When pages try to use memes like this, however, it comes off the same way as parents trying to 'be hip' towards their kids" (Sebastian 2014). This assessment distanced the greater vernacular memetic practice from this specific instance, suggesting that doge still had merit and authenticity, even if this specific communication did not. Differentiating this case as a facsimile allowed users to reject institutional appeals to vernacular authority while still maintaining authority and value for the greater vernacular memetic practice.

Many other commenters suggested that the institution had invested significant time and resources in constructing a sense of vernacular authority. Instead of the meme emerging naturally (as it would from everyday speech), the institution is said to have expended large amounts of power and resources to produce this attempt at vernacular speech. Here, users position this communication as coming from an institutional chimera—the result of focus groups, marketing meetings, and notes from management. Despite the significant institutional resources invested, the resulting communication is perceived as little more than a simulacrum of authentic vernacular discourse. In effect, the ways in which users decried this communication are very similar to the challenges to vernacular authority levied by the "trying too hard to be hip" comments. Both sets of users are challenging this institutional attempt to appropriate memetic practice by suggesting that even though Health and Human Services may get the memetic form right, this communication fails because it lacks a deeper or more genuine understanding of the practice.

While most users denied Health and Human Services the vernacular authority it sought, several others challenged the institution to follow through on its appeals to vernacularity, calling on it to prove its sincerity by embracing wider vernacular practice. The implication is that vernacular authority is available to the institution, but this communication was insufficient to garner it.

Many commenters, for example, challenged the institution to continue building its vernacular authority by accepting a doge-based cryptocurrency as payment.[9] By suggesting that the US government could attain vernacular authority by accepting an established user-created digital cryptocurrency, these claims (made with varying levels of sincerity) enact a double-bind scenario that redirects the impetus for further action back on the institution. Either the institution ignores this suggestion, proving correct the assertions that it was merely appropriating (instead of engaging with) vernacular authority for short-term gains, or the institution engages further with the vernacular in a more comprehensive way that threatens its own institutional authority. This rhetorically constructs a situation in which these users remain in a position to deny Health and Human Services vernacular authority—either the organization admits defeat or it continues to play while lacking its home field advantage.

When viewed this way, a pattern begins to emerge. The cryptocurrency enthusiasts, as well as those users making the "un-hip" or "focus group" comments, are all reasserting their primacy over vernacular speech by undercutting the attempts of the institution to establish a sense of vernacular authority. To do this, users repeatedly suggest that the institution has failed to understand the vernacular because it has seen only the trees and not the forest. The specific nature of the challenge may vary by individual, but consistent across all efforts is a sense that the institution lacks vernacular authority because it confuses vernacular artifact for vernacular practice.

These challenges to the institution's vernacular authority suggest that institutions *can* successfully engage with meme culture, but they need to demonstrate a more comprehensive awareness of memetic practice—an understanding that vernacularity emerges from ongoing and communal (not singular) action.[10]

PERFORMING VERNACULAR KNOWLEDGE

While some users handled this contradiction between vernacular and institutional speech by challenging the institution's claims to vernacular authority, others responded with performances of their own vernacular knowledge. These performances do more than repeat irreverent memes or bemoan the death of doge, they reinforce a sense of shared identity and knowledge that the institutional attempt at appropriation has challenged. The comments that perform vernacular knowledge suggest that users not only speak the same memetic language, they do so with more eloquence and skill than Health and Human Services.

Many of the initial responses to Health and Human Services' Facebook post lamented that the institution's appropriation of the memetic practice had rendered doge a dead meme.

> *Adam*: You just killed doge, in a similar manner to how you killed many people's health insurance plans.
>
> *Wyatt*: i liked the doge. but now it's dead. thanks obama[11]
>
> *Meg*: how long will it take for you to realize this was a terrible idea, person in charge of US Health facebook page? the healthcare plan is bad enough without having to ruin perfectly good memes in the process.

As this last comment suggests, many users feel strong and personal affective ties to memetic practices. As a result, when acts of institutional appropriation feel inauthentic, they spark a sense of disappointment and negative affect for users. To these users, this instance of institutional appropriation has destroyed any future potential for doge as vernacular expression. In this view, the Health and Human Services post not only failed to provide the institution with vernacular authority but also threatened the credibility of the larger memetic practice. Consequently, some individuals saw this moment of institutional appropriation as the death of the doge meme.

Other commenters, however, were adamant that this moment changed nothing—doge was dead long before this incident. When user Griffin commented that "rarely do you get to actually pinpoint the moment when something stops being funny, but now is that moment for doge," several other commenters were quick to point out that the memetic practice was already well past its prime:

> *Oni*: You know a meme is dead when it starts being picked up for viral marketing campaigns . . . well, that and Doge is so 2014 . . .
>
> *Douglas*: it stopped being funny like almost a year ago
>
> *Matt*: Doge died when it was born 2 and a half years ago

Unlike the "dead" posts (which saw this moment as the pivot point in doge's lifespan), these "outdated" posts suggest that the meme's pivot point was much earlier. In fact, users disagree on exactly how much earlier the meme started to fade, positing earlier and earlier dates. This act of deliberative hipsterism serves as an occasion for these users to establish that they were aware of the meme before it garnered mainstream popularity (and, subsequently, institutional attention). In effect, an institution like Health and Human Services was only able to find and appropriate doge because the meme had long since surged past an implied saturation point. This mainstream popularity threatens the cool factor of memetic practice, and as a result is positioned in opposition to vernacular authority.

This disparity on doge's expiration date represents a struggle between users trying to outdo each other in deploying their knowledge of vernacular memetic practice. Hence, these arguments serve as moments in which users rhetorically reassert their primacy over vernacular authority. Take the following exchange for example:

> *Reed*: once a 4chan joke becomes popular it immediately stops being funny
> *Adam*: ^Doge was originally a tumblr meme.
> *Joseph*: No, Adam. All Tumblr stuff is either made up or comes from 4chan.
> *Stuart*: yeah but doge actually originated from Tumblr

Here four users are arguing as part of a larger comment chain. Each is invested in correcting another user as to the exact origin of doge. Such arguments regarding ideas like origin and evolution of the memetic practice were common responses to the Health and Human Services image. Strictly speaking, none of these users are exactly right or wrong, but the exact truth here is secondary to what these performances are doing. These moments serve less as critiques of the institution and more as occasions for users to perform their competency and understanding of memetic practice. In the exchange above, for instance, each user is invested in showing that the practice originated from a specific web community (likely one they are invested in). Such a defense suggests that they are reasserting control of the meme as belonging to their community. In such acts of performance, these users reject the institution through assertions of vernacular knowledge that establish both legitimacy and superiority for their own sense of vernacular authority over the institution's.

Such performances of vernacular knowledge frequently invoked meme culture itself to assert vernacular authority and reject Health and Human Services. For many commenters, this meant reappropriating doge-speak back against the institution, writing things like "Such failure. Much desperation. Very cognitive dissonance. Wow." (Charles 2014). Other users responded to Health and Human Services by referencing other memes, sarcastically thanking Barack Obama, commenting that they no longer wanted to live on this planet, or claiming that this post was so bad it had given them cancer. Several users peppered their comments with memetic language (like ermagherd speech) or terminology (anon, kek, dank).[12]

These performances of the memetic knowledge build credibility into the act of rejection, establishing a sense of vernacular knowledge and identity through which users are enabled to dismiss Health and Human Services as less knowledgeable and less authentic. Such tactics redirect memetic practice back against the institution, reasserting the sense of alterity missing from Health and Human Services' attempt. This creates a rhetorical distinction that allows these users to discount this attempt at using doge as too institutional while still reaffirming the vernacular legitimacy of the larger body of memetic practice.

The same mechanisms that enable the appropriation of meme culture also enable reclaiming it as a form of resistance. Users engage in such acts of appropriation by displaying their knowledge and competency with vernacular memetic practice. By launching these critiques through displays of vernacular knowledge, these users are invoking the fundamentally crowd-sourced nature of memetic practice (which the Health and Human Services image ignores) and reasserting their control over vernacular speech. Whether arguing over the origin of the memetic practice or invoking the memetic practice to resist the attempt at institutional appropriation, these performances of vernacular knowledge enable users to resist Health and Human Services' appeal by reasserting and reaffirming their primacy over vernacular authority.

THE ALLURE OF MEMETIC SUCCESS AND THE COST OF FAILURE

Health and Human Services' attempt to advertise on social media using an internet meme illustrates why institutional attempts to appropriate vernacular practices frequently fail as well as the possible risks for the institution in making such attempts. Although Health and Human Services accurately mimicked the form of the meme, the institutionality of its message revealed the image as separate from the greater vernacular practice. And whereas advertising thrives on the circulation of messages, meme culture is about the circulation of practice. Because of this crossing of institutional messages with vernacular practice, users' generic expectations were breached. This resulted in a sense of contradictory hybridity that made the image appear inauthentic, which hailed users to respond in ways that reasserted their own authority while also diminishing the authority of the institution.

Since institutional messages (especially those conveyed via mass media) thrive on centralized control and careful construction, institutional agents are often reluctant to embrace the crowdsourced nature of memetic practice. By sharing control with everyday users—as is necessary when engaging with a memetic practice—much of the power involved is diffused through networks. And if the institutional attempt is not perceived as authentic enough, the diffuse process that enables memetic practice may also enable users to channel the power of meme culture back against the institution itself.

Successful attempts by institutions to appropriate the memetic vernacular tend to be referential and concerned with affect; contentious attempts tend to encourage specific action in service of the institution. The former engage *with* the practice, the latter attempt to appropriate it for institutional goals. Memetic communication may be good for creating awareness or conveying simple messages, but it is poor at maintaining intentionality and specificity. Effective appropriation of memetic practice, then, means spreading awareness and reframing conversations about a brand.[13]

The most effective memetic ads hide their institutionality behind a veil of vernacular aesthetics and alterity, intervening into vernacular practice without making their intentions known. Such communications invite further participation by everyday users, giving them the tools or template to engage in their own subsequent acts of cultural remix. By allowing these users to believe that the emerging memetic practice was their own idea, the institution not only spreads its message but also insulates the idea from critique. It creates an affective tie to the practice among users who adopt and circulate it as part of their networked selves and locates the institution's authority in that same diffuse crowd of vernacular communicators, making backlash seem like a reaction against vernacular culture itself.

This potential suggests why, despite the possible costs, appropriating vernacular practice continues to appeal to institutions. Institutional appropriation of vernacular culture is not new, and it is unlikely that institutions will cease their attempts to appropriate vernacular practices going forward. The allure of hipness, coolness, authenticity, and virality are simply too strong. Instead, an expanding array of institutions will continue to refine their methods, learning from the mistakes and successes of others. This trend further reinforces the need to focus on how vernacular digital practices might be used, or misused, in strategic communication because as institutions continue to improve their methods, elements like institutional affiliation and intention will become increasingly obfuscated behind a constructed veneer of vernacular authenticity.

NOTES

1. For a more in-depth discussion of how Giddens's structuration theory might be integrated into (or expanded upon by) studies of practice in folkloristics, see Bronner 2012.

2. This play at consubstantiality is evident from a popular memetic response frequently levied by everyday users to reject intuitional appropriations of vernacular practice. In a clip from the television show *30 Rock*, an aging Steve Buscemi, decked out in a baseball cap worn backward and carrying a skateboard, tries to blend in with a group of high school students, casually asking the group, "How do you do, fellow kids?" The phrase has become a popular cultural shorthand for users to mock out-of-touch or inauthentic ads, especially those that appropriate vernacular practices in inappropriate ways. "How do you do, fellow kids?" is one of many ways that users acknowledge the institutional intent driving these messages but patently reject their attempts at constructing consubstantiality and vernacular authenticity as forced and insincere.

3. Examples of institutionally prescribed ways of communicating include speaking to the media via a press release, adhering to a series of institutionally developed talking points, or addressing political constituents with a sense of official decorum.

4. Since the vernacular must define itself as alternate from the institutional that enables it, the two are never truly separate but exist in degrees of hybridity. This is especially important to acknowledge in digital communication, which—from individual websites to the network itself—are the result of a cascade of institutional structures and choices (Howard 2009).

5. My use of "folkloresque" draws on the work of Foster and Tolbert (2016) to suggest that these advertisements may give the impression that they derive from a specific folk tradition or practice while, in actuality, they are closer to folklore-inspired *bricolage*. By giving consumers the impression that they derive from folk traditions, these popular culture artifacts are constructed to draw on the power of vernacular expression and to a convey sense of continuity to existing vernacular practices (Foster 2016, 5).

6. Perhaps the most well-known example of this is the "Ice Bucket Challenge" meme, created to raise money for ALS research (Reinwald 2017).

7. It should be noted that from a pure visibility standpoint, the word *failure* here might be overly reductive. As I've written elsewhere, intentionally constructing a controversy can be an effective tool for circulating messages across both social and mass media (Peck 2020). Still, while the post may have received significant visibility, it is hard to divorce that visibility from the extremely high percentage of oppositional responses it received.

8. Although these posts are available publicly, I identify users by first name in this chapter to preserve some of their anonymity. All original comments may be found at https://www.facebook.com/HHS/photos/a.577318915631772.1073741828.573990992631231/711923322171330/.

9. Based on the popularity of the doge meme, in 2013 Jackson Palmer created "dogecoin" as a satire of the popular digital cryptocurrency "bitcoin." Dogecoin went on to gain a life of its own as a digital cryptocurrency, eventually hitting a market value of $400 million (Roose 2017).

10. Health and Human Services actually posted a much less divisive meme only a week prior to posting the doge image. A February 14, 2014, post by the institution used the "Success Kid" image macro format. The "Success Kid" meme involves posting text describing a personal success above and below a specific picture of a determined-looking, fist-pumping infant (Julien 2015). Health and Human Services' post read, "Has a pre-existing condition / still covered." The post received 531 "likes," 141 shares, and 20 comments. Although the post attracted only a fraction of the attention devoted to the doge image, it received a high number of "likes" compared to most of the other content posted to the page that month. Of the 20 user comments, virtually none mention the meme and the few that do tend to be positive, mentioning the baby's cuteness. It is likely that the relative success of this meme (compared to both doge and other content posted by Health and Human Services to social media) was influential in the decision to post the doge meme the following week.

11. This user is referencing the popular "Thanks, Obama!" meme. Although this phrasal meme originated on conservative social media early in Obama's first term, it quickly became a way for moderate and progressive users to ironically mock what they saw as conservative overblaming of President Barack Obama by adding the phrase to small, inconsequential frustrations or failures (Rezaei 2016, 114; Schwarz 2015).

12. "Ermagherd" speak (referencing a memetic image macro of the same name) is meant to emulate a nerdy manner of speaking, as if the individual had a strong retainer lisp (e.g., "Ermagherd" means "Oh my God!") (King 2015). "Anon" and "kek" are popular slang terms on 4Chan, an anonymous image board responsible for significant memetic creation

and circulation. Anon (short for "anonymous") is a common way for users to refer to each other on the site, and kek is a way of expressing laughter or amusement (a derivation of "lol," or "laughing out loud"). Internet users often jokingly apply the term "dank" (meaning "quality" in marijuana enthusiast subcultures) to describe memetic content that is deemed to be high quality (Dewey 2016).

13. Tide laundry detergent engaged in a particularly effective example of memetic reframing in early 2018. Following several news reports that teenagers were eating Tide laundry pods in January 2018 (which gave birth to its own meme cycle on social media), the company ran a series of Super Bowl ads designed to fake out viewers. Each commercial segment initially appeared to be for another popular genre of advertisement before ultimately revealing the fake out—"It's a Tide ad." The commercials were constructed in such a way as to control the possible memetic aspects—users who adopted the form had to include the fake-out phrase "It's a Tide ad" or risk that the cultural reference would be unintelligible. Much like the Chuck Testa commercial discussed earlier, the "It's a Tide ad" fake-out template quickly was adopted by users as a meme. This new meme helped overshadow the Tide pod meme and course-correct the way the brand was shared in many social media locations.

REFERENCES

Obama, Barack. 2015. "President Obama at Democratic Women's Leadership Forum." *C-SPAN*. October 23, 2015. http://www.c-span.org/video/?328919-2/president-obama-remarks-dnc-womens-leadership-forum.

Baym, Nancy K. 2010. *Personal Connections in the Digital Age*. Cambridge: Polity.

BBC News. 2015. "Barack Obama Mocks 'Grumpy Cat' Republicans." October 23, 2015. http://www.bbc.com/news/world-us-canada-34622866.

Begley, Sarah. 2015. "Watch President Obama Make a Grumpy Cat Face to Mock Republicans." *Time*, October 24, 2015. http://time.com/4086015/obama-grumpy-cat-republicans/.

Blank, Trevor J. 2007. "Examining the Transmission of Urban Legends: Making the Case for Folklore Fieldwork on the Internet." *Folklore Forum* 37 (1): 15–26. http://hdl.handle.net/2022/3231.

Blank, Trevor J. 2013. *The Last Laugh: Folk Humor, Celebrity Culture, and Mass-Mediated Disasters in the Digital Age*. Madison: University of Wisconsin Press.

Blank, Trevor J. 2018. "Folklore and the Internet: The Challenge of an Ephemeral Landscape." *Humanities* 7 (2): 50. https://doi.org/10.3390/h7020050.

Bronner, Simon J. 2012. "Practice Theory in Folklore and Folklife." *Folklore* 123: 23–47.

Buccitelli, Anthony Bak. 2016. "Hybrid Tactics and Locative Legends: Re-reading de Certeau for the Future of Folkloristics." *Cultural Analysis* 15 (1): 78–98.

Burke, Kenneth. 1950. *A Rhetoric of Motives*. Berkeley: University of California Press.

Carbone, Nick. 2011. "Top 10 Memes: 10. Chuck Testa." *Time*, December 7, 2011. http://content.time.com/time/specials/packages/article/0,28804,2101344_2100875_2100876,00.html.

Cook, James. 2014. "Meet the CEO Who Put a Doge Meme in the Guardian." *Daily Dot* (blog), February 7, 2014. http://www.dailydot.com/business/guardian-doge-meme-ceo/.

Csaszi, Lajos. 2003. "World Trade Center Jokes and Their Hungarian Reception." *Journal of Folklore Research* 40 (2): 175–210. https://doi.org/10.1353/jfr.2003.0010.

Dégh, Linda. 1994. *American Folklore and the Mass Media*. Bloomington: Indiana University Press.

Dewey, Caitlin. 2016. "How Bernie Sanders Became the Lord of 'Dank Memes.'" *Washington Post*, February 23, 2016. https://www.washingtonpost.com/news/the-intersect/wp/2016/02/23/how-bernie-sanders-became-the-lord-of-dank-memes/?utm_term=.72b588365065.

Ellis, Bill. 2001. "A Model for Collecting and Interpreting World Trade Center Disaster Jokes." *New Directions in Folklore* 5. https://scholarworks.iu.edu/journals/index.php/ndif/article/view/19881/25963.

Ellis, Bill. 2002. "Making a Big Apple Crumble: The Role of Humor in Constructing a Global Response to Disaster." *New Directions in Folklore* 6. https://scholarworks.iu.edu/journals/index.php/ndif/article/view/19883/25953.

Fernback, Jan. 2003. "Legends on the Net: An Examination of Computer-Mediated Communication as a Locus of Oral Culture." *New Media and Society* 5 (1): 29–45. https://doi.org/10.1177/1461444803005001902.

Foote, Monica. 2007. "Userpicks: Cyber Folk Art in the Early 21st Century." *Folklore Forum* 37 (1): 27–38. http://hdl.handle.net/2022/3251.

Foster, Michael Dylan. 2016. "Introduction: The Challenge of the Folkloresque." In *The Folkloresque: Reframing Folklore in a Popular Culture World*, edited by Michael Dylan Foster and Jeffrey A. Tolbert, 3–35. Logan: Utah State University Press.

Foster, Michael Dylan, and Jeffrey A. Tolbert, ed. 2016. *The Folkloresque: Reframing Folklore in a Popular Culture World*. Logan: Utah State University Press.

Frank, Russell. 2004. "When the Going Gets Tough, the Tough Go Photoshopping: September 11 and the Newslore of Vengeance and Victimization." *New Media and Society* 6 (5): 633–658.

Giddens, Anthony. 1984. *The Constitution of Society: Outline of the Theory of Structuration*. Berkeley: University of California Press.

González-Martín, Rachel V. 2016. "Digitizing Cultural Economies: 'Personalization' and U.S. Quinceañera Practice Online." *Cultural Analysis* 15 (1): 57–77.

GOP. 2014. "@HillaryClinton's Out-of-Touch Idea of 'Dead Broke' Is Some Mansions & $200,00 for a Few Hours Work." Twitter, June 9, 2014, 4:44 p.m. https://twitter.com/GOP/status/476102578116501504.

Guardian. 2015. "Obama Does 'Grumpy Cat' Face to Imitate 'Gloomy' Republican Candidates—Video," October 24, 2015. https://www.theguardian.com/us-news/video/2015/oct/24/obama-does-grumpy-cat-face-to-imitate-gloomy-republican-candidates-video.

Hathaway, Rosemary V. 2005. "'Life in the TV': The Visual Nature of 9/11 Lore and Its Impact on Vernacular Response." *Journal of Folklore Research* 42 (1): 33–56.

Howard, Robert Glenn. 1997. "Apocalypse in Your In-box: End-times Communication on the Internet." *Western Folklore* 56 (3/4): 295–315.

Howard, Robert Glenn. 2008a. "Electronic Hybridity: The Persistent Processes of the Vernacular Web." *Journal of American Folklore* 121 (480): 192–218.

Howard, Robert Glenn. 2008b. "The Vernacular Web of Participatory Media." *Critical Studies in Media Communication* 25 (5): 490–513. https://doi.org/10.1080/15295030802468065.

Howard, Robert Glenn. 2009. "Enacting a Virtual 'Ekklesia': Online Christian Fundamentalism as Vernacular Religion." *New Media and Society* 12 (5): 729–744. https://doi.org/10.1177/1461444809342765.

Howard, Robert Glenn. 2010. "The Vernacular Mode: Locating the Non-institutional in the Practice of Citizenship." In *Public Modalities: Rhetoric, Culture, Media, and the Shape of Public Life*, edited by Daniel C Brouwer and Robert Asen, 240–261. Tuscaloosa: University of Alabama Press.

Howard, Robert Glenn. 2013. "Vernacular Authority: Critically Engaging 'Tradition.'" In *Tradition in the Twenty-First Century: Locating the Role of the Past in the Present*, edited by Trevor J Blank and Robert Glenn Howard, 72–99. Logan: Utah State University Press.

Jenkins, Eric S. 2014. "The Modes of Visual Rhetoric: Circulating Memes as Expressions." *Quarterly Journal of Speech* 100 (4): 442–466. https://doi.org/10.1080/00335630.2014.989258.

Julien, Chris. 2015. "Bourdieu, Social Capital and Online Interaction." *Sociology* 49 (2): 356–373.

Kaplan, Merrill. 2013. "Curation and Tradition on Web 2.0." In *Tradition in the Twenty-First Century: Locating the Role of the Past in the Present*, edited by Trevor J. Blank and Robert Glenn Howard, 123–148. Logan: Utah State University Press.

Kibby, Marjorie D. 2005. "Email Forwardables: Folklore in the Age of the Internet." *New Media and Society* 7 (6): 770–790. https://doi.org/10.1177/1461444805058161.

King, Darryn. 2015. "Ermahgerddon: The Untold Story of the Ermahgerd Girl." *Vanity Fair*, October 15, 2015. https://www.vanityfair.com/culture/2015/10/ermahgerd-girl-true-story.

Koran, Laura. 2015. "Obama Compares Republicans to 'Grumpy Cat.'" *CNN*, October 23, 2015. http://www.cnn.com/2015/10/23/politics/grumpy-cat-obama-republicans/.

Kuipers, Giselinde. 2002. "Media Culture and Internet Disaster Jokes: Bin Laden and the Attack on the World Trade Center." *European Journal of Cultural Studies* 5 (4): 450–470.

Kuipers, Giselinde. 2005. "'Where Was King Kong When We Needed Him?' Public Discourse, Digital Disaster Jokes, and the Functions of Laughter After 9/11." *Journal of American Culture* 28 (1): 70–84. https://doi.org/10.1111/j.1542-734X.2005.00155.x.

Locker, Melissa. 2011. "Rhett and Link: The Making of a Viral Video." *IFC*, September 20, 2011. https://www.ifc.com/2011/09/rhett-link-the-making-of-a-viral-video-nope-chuck-testa.

Marwick, Alice, and danah boyd. 2011. "To See and Be Seen: Celebrity Practice on Twitter." *Convergence: The International Journal of Research into New Media Technologies* 17 (2): 139–158.

McHugh, Molly. 2013. "The Life and Death of Doge, 2013's Greatest Meme." *Daily Dot* (blog), December 23, 2013. http://www.dailydot.com/unclick/doge-is-dead-long-live-doge/.

McNeill, Lynne S. 2009. "The End of the Internet: A Folk Response to the Provision of Infinite Choice." In *Folklore and the Internet: Vernacular Expression in a Digital World*, edited by Trevor J. Blank, 80–97. Logan: Utah State University Press.

McNeill, Lynne S. 2013a. "And the Greatest of These Is Tradition: The Folklorist's Toolbox in the Twenty-First Century." In *Tradition in the Twenty-First Century: Locating the Role of the Past in the Present*, edited by Trevor J. Blank and Robert Glenn Howard, 174–185. Logan: Utah State University Press.

McNeill, Lynne S. 2013b. *Folklore Rules*. Logan: Utah State University Press.

Milner, Ryan M. 2016. *The World Made Meme: Public Conversations and Participatory Media*. Cambridge, MA: MIT Press.

Miltner, Kate M. 2014. "'There's No Place for Lulz on LOLCats': The Role of Genre, Gender, and Group Identity in the Interpretation and Enjoyment of an Internet Meme." *First Monday* 19 (8). https://doi.org/10.5210/fm.v19i8.5391.

Peck, Andrew. 2014. "A Laugh Riot: Photoshopping as Vernacular Discursive Practice." *International Journal of Communication* 8: 1638–1662.

Peck, Andrew. 2015a. "Jokin' in the First World: Appropriate Incongruity and the #first-worldproblems Controversy." In *Hashtag Publics: The Power and Politics of Discursive Networks*, edited by Nathan Rambukkana, 179–188. New York: Peter Lang.

Peck, Andrew. 2015b. "Tall, Dark, and Loathsome: The Emergence of a Legend Cycle in the Digital Age." *Journal of American Folklore* 128 (509): 333–348.

Peck, Andrew. 2016. "At the Modems of Madness: The Slender Man, Ostension, and the Digital Age." *Contemporary Legend* 3 (5): 14–37.

Peck, Andrew. 2020. "A Problem of Amplification: Folklore and Fake News in the Age of Social Media." *Journal of American Folklore* 133 (529): 329–351.

Reinwald, Jennifer. 2017. "Hashtags and Attention through the Tetrad: The Rhetorical Circulation of #ALSIceBucketChallenge." In *Theorizing Digital Rhetoric*, edited by Aaron Hess and Amber L. Davisson, 184–195. New York: Routledge.

RepThomasMassie. 2013. "Much Bipartisanship. Very Spending. Wow. #doge http://reut.rs/1bml7Pf." Twitter, December 23, 2013, 10:43 a.m. https://twitter.com/RepThomasMassie/status/415145732661059584.

Rezaei, Afsane. 2016. "'The Superman in a Turban': Political Jokes in the Iranian Social Media." *New Directions in Folklore* 14 (1/2): 89–132.

Roose, Kevin. 2017. "Is There a Cryptocurrency Bubble? Just Ask Doge." *New York Times*, September 15, 2017. https://www.nytimes.com/2017/09/15/business/cryptocurrency-bubble-doge.html.

Saenz, Arlette. 2015. "Obama Makes 'Grumpy Cat' Face Talking about Republicans." *ABC News*, October 23, 2015. http://abcnews.go.com/Politics/obama-makes-grumpy-cat-face-talking-republicans/story?id=34688936.

Schmitt, Casey R. 2016. "The Tactical Trail: Sense of Place and Place of Practice." *Cultural Analysis* 15 (1): 128–144.

Schwarz, Hunter. 2015. "'Thanks Obama.' The Evolution of a Meme That Defined a Presidency." *Washington Post*, February 13, 2015. https://www.washingtonpost.com/news/the-fix/wp/2015/02/13/thanks-obama-the-evolution-of-a-meme-that-defined-a-presidency/?utm_term=.1f70f49f6942.

Shifman, Limor. 2014. *Memes in Digital Culture*. Cambridge, MA: MIT Press.

StockmanSenate. 2013. "Wow. Such Obamacare Funding. Oppose Ted Cruz." Twitter, December 23, 2013, 11:34 a.m. https://twitter.com/StockmanSenate/status/415158586101080064.

Testa, Chuck. 2011. *Official Ojai Valley Taxidermy TV Commercial*. YouTube. August 14, 2011. https://www.youtube.com/watch?v=LJP1DphOWPs.

Thomas, Jeannie Banks. 2003. *Naked Barbies, Warrior Joes, and Other Forms of Visible Gender*. Champaign: University of Illinois Press.

5

"Zero Is Our Quota"
Folkloric Narratives of the Other in Online Forum Comments

Liisi Laineste

STRAIGHT FROM THE HEART: INTERNET FOLKLORE, HUMOR AND INSULT

THE INTERNET HAS BECOME A VIGOROUS medium for all kinds of interaction, including the folkloric. The online environment offers a burgeoning site for cultural expression (Blank 2013, 110); it's a hotbed for creating, reframing, and disseminating folklore. Among other features, the asynchronic nature (Crystal 2001) of the internet encourages the "pouring out" of emotions. Studies have shown that not only has the emotional climate of the internet become harsher but people have also become more emboldened to post under their own names, taking pride in exercising their freedom of speech (Sandell 2018; Rost et al. 2016). At the same time, how safe it is to express your opinion in online communities may be deceptive. Online discussions expose the participants, who are actually seeking like-minded partners in communication, to wide audiences, including people who advocate different or even frightening ideas.[1] This leads to a conflict of opinions and causes emotions to erupt, sometimes displaying hostility and humor at the same time. Humor is, after all, regardless of its appeal, not just about positive feelings and functions; it is an ambiguous phenomenon quite often tied to negative notions such as xenophobia, exclusion, ridicule, and othering. The excuse of "just joking" (Pickering and Lockyer 2005; Bell 2015) is often offered to mitigate or camouflage insults. Social media only increases the chances of (mis)interpreting humor and responses of unlaughter (Billig 2005), a reaction of nonamusement explicitly following a recognized humorous intent.

The ambivalent internet creates a folkloric arena full of playful images, texts, and videos (as well as combinations of these mediated modalities;

see Phillips and Milner 2017). Humor plays an important part in facilitating communication and grabbing the attention of people (da Silva and Garcia 2012), but because of the characteristics of internet communication it can also be misunderstood more frequently and on a bigger scale than in other venues (Lewis et al. 2008). Moira Marsh (Smith 2009) describes the failure of humor as an important antipode to the laughter reaction that brings about important social consequences and reveals power relations within society. Unlaughter thus becomes a tool in the power struggle between different online voices, opinions, and definitions of humor. It is a downplayed feature of humor, but an indispensable outcome of humorous communication. The fact that some people don't agree to recognize, understand, or appreciate the humor they encounter stirs more intensive reverberations, more opposite reactions, and may help the humor eventually to reach wider audiences.[2] The concept of unlaughter, I argue, has become more central and its scope wider in the digital age because the online environment brings together bigger audiences and a greater selection of humorous texts.

In this chapter, I look at the European refugee crisis of recent years, focusing on a specific incident in early 2016 that heightened emotional engagement of both pro- and anti-refugee groups in Estonia. Within the anti-refugee groups offensive rhetoric and humor often existed side by side, and reactions ranged from direct insults to satirical criticism. This included humor based on phraseology, that is, playful and humorous use (e.g., remixing) and adaptation of known phrases. In these instances, humor stems from an unexpected collocation of phraseological items, punning, exaggerative and/or cumulative use of phrases.

Othering, as I will demonstrate, relies on traditional, revitalized ideas and beliefs about "us" and "them." Trying to draw the lines between these (rather fuzzy) categories, people refer to ideas that have passed from generation to generation to justify their claims of who has the right to live in Estonia. People aim to make their voice reach further using the affordances of social media by combining their xenophobic convictions with colorful and creative use of the phraseology of fixed expressions (idioms, metaphorical utterances, sayings, proverbs, and other types of phrases). It's the witty, the exaggerated, and the humorous (or, perhaps, the satirical and critical, depending on the audience) that guarantee a victory in the "battle of the fittest" in the digital jungle. This study sets out to describe and analyze the use of phraseology in offensive speech on the internet, giving an account of its patterns of usage. Notions of moral panic, cultural trauma, conspiracy theories, rumors, myths, and known motifs from age-old debates about nationalism are revived and pertinent in the context of the online discussion of the refugee crisis that, since 2014, has seen more than a million people cross into Europe seeking asylum (Miles 2015). Through examples of responses found in the online discussion forum delfi .ee, this chapter investigates how humorous texts and their public reception (including unlaughter) relate to the practices of othering. The chapter draws conclusions from content analysis of online newsreaders' comments that followed the airing of the controversial Estonian New Year's Eve television program *Mood Spoiler* in 2015/2016.

SPITTING ON 700 YEARS OF SERFDOM: PARODY AND RESPONSES

Refugee Crisis in Estonia

In line with the European Union's July 2015 plan to distribute new asylum seekers across the union, Estonia agreed to eventually take in up to 500 refugees. The public debate before and after this decision was announced, together with freshly actualized vernacular ideas about immigration, has been emotional and so far quite ineffective (Veebel 2015; see also Makarychev and Yatsyk 2017). It has also powered the popularity of the country's right-wing movement (as evident in the results of the March 2019 parliamentary election; for a commentary, see Tuch 2019). Discussions are characterized by the reappearance of folk beliefs and conspiracy stories (Laineste 2017), false information, and a growing support of conservative parties such as the Eesti Kristlik Rahvaerakond (EKRE, the Estonian Christian Nationalist Party). Grim chapters in Estonian history, above all the Soviet occupation from 1944 to 1991, have kept national myths and images of the vulnerability of the Estonian culture and language alive, and newer trends in politics support the (re)appearance of such narratives.[3] Estonians have seen their nation as the victim of countless invasions, waves of migration, and cultural domination by bigger nations. Not only immigration but also emigration has been perceived as damaging to the nation. During World War II (a time of mass migrations even more severe than the ones witnessed since 2014, even though the two have often been compared in scale; see Alfred 2015), it is estimated that between 70,000 and 90,000 Estonian refugees (7 to 8 percent of the population) left for the United States, Canada, Sweden, and elsewhere (Faure and Mensing 2012, 253–54; Miljan 2004). Adding to these fears is the fact that Estonians have had limited contact with people from geographically faraway regions, such as the Middle East or Africa, where many current refugees are coming from. The local inhabitants are afraid that the refugees will overburden the Estonian social system, increase unemployment and conflict, and pose a threat to Estonian language and culture (Pagulasuuring 2014). This reasoning, based on resilient grand narratives, cultural traumas, and deep-rooted beliefs, has given rise to increased sentiments of nationalism. Conflicting emotions and opinions intensified after September 2015, when the media was overrun with news (and even more notably, images) about Syrian refugees looking for a better life in Europe. Gradually, the tensions grew to such a level that a refugee center in Vao in northeastern Estonia was set on fire (Laineste 2017). After this incident, which fortunately resulted in no casualties, the xenophobic tendencies of the small nation became a daily topic.

At the same time, Estonia's national policy shows a strikingly different rhetoric, which is disseminated in the mainstream media. It stresses that Estonia, as part of Europe, has a moral duty to help the refugees and suggests that the country is strong enough to contribute to solving the crisis. Mainstream news websites and articles work to convince Estonians that because the nation's population is in decline, its citizens need to welcome refugees, helping them integrate quickly into society. These two conflicting—and coinciding—opinions have been called the "black and pink discourse" (Lotman 2018), referring to the colors as emblematic of the views: black as critical, oppositional, and conservative and pink (perhaps a bit ironically) as allowing, tolerant, and liberal.

Mood Spoiler 2015: "No Country Stands Alone"

Mood Spoiler (*Tujurikkuja* in Estonian) was a (in)famous television program that aired annually on New Year's Eve from 2008 to 2015. It frequently displayed provocative satirical content and thus elicited polarized responses from viewers. The controversy it engendered was especially acute in online commentaries. The show's name, *Mood Spoiler*, is a reference to the feelings of social awkwardness that people experience when everybody is in a good mood (appropriately enough during New Year's Eve celebrations), only to have someone spoil the mood by making failed attempts at humor that evoke unlaughter or uncomfortable silence from the audience.[4] In a way, the name predicted the negative comments that the show's creators received from audiences every year the program aired (Külmoja 2016). The frequent uproars the show ignited on social media also show that the satirists often hit sore but important points regarding social issues.

In its heyday, *Mood Spoiler* was the true flagship of Estonian humor.[5] The creative team behind the scenes, Õ Fraktsioon and Catapult Films together with the comedians Märt Avandi and Ott Sepp, became widely known after the very first show.[6] The team was influenced by the 1970s *Monty Python's Flying Circus* and the comedy show *Big Train*. *Mood Spoiler* and its creators had a controversial reputation, recognized and appreciated by audiences and at the same time scolded and condemned by them. *Mood Spoiler* has a history of mastering the art of absurd and dark humor while producing socially biting satire.[7]

In the first sketches of 2008 and 2009, *Mood Spoiler* was more tuned to the absurdity of its characters—showcasing a failed public speech or awkward musical performance, for instance. In the following years, the practice of mood spoiling acquired a more symbolic character—it was no longer about characters who failed to act in a socially normative way; instead, the show addressed more painful social and political topics. In the last installments of the show, the jokes became more complicated, requiring deeper intertextual knowledge of Estonia's cultural and social background (Taaniel 2015). *Mood Spoiler*'s sketches also became more self-directed: the negativistic, whining nature of the whole Estonian nation was the target of the comedy as well as parodies of bad Estonian movies or television series. In 2012 the show was awarded a renowned prize, the Kultuurivedur (Cultural Engine) because it has brought to the national table a number of important questions that are otherwise often forcefully silenced in political discussions. Additionally, both main actors in the show, Ott Sepp and Märt Avandi, have received a renowned prize for humorists, in 2011 and 2013 respectively. The 2015 New Year's Eve show was supposed to be their final episode.[8]

It is no surprise that the comedians behind the 2015 *Mood Spoiler* used the topic of immigration in their sketch "Ei ole üksi ükski maa" ("No Country Stands Alone"). While the sketch was appreciated by some of their audience, it was greeted indignantly by many others. The sketch made fun of Estonians's reluctance to accept refugees, parodying a song created by legendary Estonian songwriters Alo Mattiisen and Jüri Leesment, important public figures in Estonia's quest for independence in the 1990s[9] The original version protested expeditionary forces and immigration from Russia, more specifically resisting the plan to open new phosphorite mines in Estonia.[10] The song praises different regions in Estonia (Läänemaa, Saaremaa, etc.) for fighting for the unity and independence of the country. It quickly became an influential song, uniting the country. It is frequently performed in Estonian song festivals.[11] It is precisely the central idea of this song—the unity of the separate regions of an entire nation against a foreign threat—that *Mood Spoiler* turned upside down to express criticism of xenophobic Estonians. In the parody, the setting of the video for the original song is retained (a studio that has been used by many well-known and loved contemporary artists) and so is the structure of the song, naming all the regions in turn and highlighting their share in the struggle (in this case against the immigrants, not the phosphorite mines). The text itself is full of phraseological elements and references (highlighted in bold in the original and translation below). In the final punch line, the song points at the negativism and criticism Estonians show not only toward immigrants but also toward each other (in a way predicting—and dismissing—the aggressive reactions of the audience):

Jääb ikka nii, et Saaremaal,
ei toimu eales lõimumist.
Ta kõrval tunneb Hiiumaa,
et liiga vähe vihkab vist.
Paar **nõginägu** Läänemaal,
on leitud rannaroost.
Nad sinna peksis Harjumaa,
sest **null on meie kvoot**.

[REF] Ei taha, ei või, ei saa
piir kinni Virumaal!
Teab loodus vaid, teab isamaa,
et neegri koht on Aafrikas.
Seal kaugel võime neid sallida,
ja kõiki teisi loomaliike ka.

Ei ole jännis Järvamaa,
seal pole **muldki kuigi must**.
Veel südikam on Pärnumaa,
ka **mustal leival näitab ust**.
Teab **tarkust toitev** Tartumaa,
et islam on vist . . . seen?
Mis teha siis, vaeb Võrumaa,
kui murjan on tšetšeen?

Ei tahagi teada kah,
ah, **kõik üks mooramaa**!

Teab loodus vaid, teab isamaa,
neil meeldib ennast õhata.
Me rass on ohus, Kristiina ka,
see pole rassism, puhas loogika.

Ei jää see nii, et Mulgimaa,
vaid jälestab võõrast keelt!
Ka teatab vapralt Valgamaa,
et suudab raevuda mitmekesiselt.
Kui russofoobia Virumaal,
käib käsi-käes homofoobiaga,
siis julgen ütelda,
et elan omal maal!

So be it that no multiculturalism
Ever occurs in Saaremaa.
Next to it, Hiiumaa feels
That it doesn't hate enough.
A few **Negros** have been found
In the reeds in Läänemaa.
They were beaten there by Harjumaa,
Because **zero is our quota**!

Don't want to, won't and can't.
Close the borders in Virumaa!
Nature knows, fatherland knows,
A Negro belongs to Africa!
Far away over there we can tolerate them
And all the **other animals** as well.

Järvamaa **is not in a pickle**,
Over there even the **soil isn't very black**.
Pärnumaa is braver than that
They even **show the door to black bread**.
Educated Tartumaa knows
that Islam is . . . maybe a **mushroom**?
What to do, wonders Võrumaa,
if the black guy is a **Chechen**?

I don't even care,
It's all **the same**.

Nature knows, fatherland knows
they like **blowing themselves up**.
Our **race is in danger**, **Kristiina** [Ojuland] too,
it's not racism, it's just logic.

It wont stay like this that only Mulgimaa
Despises a foreign language!
Valgamaa as well announces
That it can hate in various ways.
Once Russophobia in Virumaa
Goes hand in hand with homophobia,
Only then I can proudly say
That this is my country!

Teab loodus vaid, teab isamaa,	Nature knows, fatherland knows,
meil meeldib kõike vihata.	We like to hate everything!
Kui keegi naerab, kui vesi keeb,	When someone laughs, when the water boils
või kui üldse keegi midagigi teeb.	Or whenever anyone does anything!
On vaid üks isend jälgim veel . . .	There is only one creature even worse . . .
Teab loodus vaid, teab isamaa,	Nature knows, fatherland knows,
teist eestlast me ei või seedida.	**We can't tolerate other Estonians.**
Meid on küll vähe, kuid ühtsena,	There may be few of us, but in unison
kõik **kargame külakuhja kaklema.**	We will **jump on top of each other and fight!**
Ei ole üksi ükski maa . . .	No country stands alone
Või kui siis ainult Süüria . . .	Except maybe Syria

This is the ultimate satire of the original version, which emotionally repeats, "No country stands alone—we need to help each other." The parody points out that Estonians don't help immigrants—and, moreover, they don't even help their fellow Estonians; instead, they choose to attack them out of envy and anger whenever they have a chance. With its 1.3 million views on YouTube, the song became hugely popular (according to Estonian standards) at least in part because of both the positive and the negative feedback—including unlaughter—it got. The controversy caused by the New Year's Eve parody sketch can also be seen as representing the opposition between official and nonofficial voices regarding immigration: on the one hand, the sketch was aired on the national state-owned television channel ETV and satirized xenophobic compatriots (thus voicing the "official position"), and on the other hand, there were audience members who saw tolerance toward immigrants as a threat to the nation and its independence, expressing the "unofficial" vernacular opinions heard especially loudly on social media and in other online settings.

MOOD SPOILER RECEPTION ON delfi.ee INTERNET FORUM

The material for the analysis is collected from the Estonian delfi.ee news forum, an anonymous online commenting environment dubbed the "toilet wall of Estonian Internet" (Laineste 2008, 35), and covers the period of the most intense public response, January 1–15, 2016. The collected data (2,782 comments altogether, in Estonian and translated into English by the author) published on delfi.ee were posted in reaction to twelve online articles about *Mood Spoiler*: discussions of its reasons and justifications, opinions from celebrities and other involved people, both pro and against the show. The comedians had to explain to an enraged audience why they had parodied a highly patriotic cultural text and used it to criticize Estonians.

Mixed qualitative and quantitative analysis software, QDA Miner, was used to tease out the reasoning behind the attacks against the authors of the parody and to point toward the main types of phraseological expressions used.

Dividing the texts into the broad categories of pro- and anti-parody showed that delfi.ee news comments were mostly negative (53 percent of the total number of comments). Positive ones (18.2 percent) were considerably less frequent, with the remainder of comments (28.8 percent) either neutral or irrelevant to the main topic. Negative comments were also longer and more detailed than positive and neutral ones. This finding is further supported by the fact that there was more figurative speech in negative comments (31.8 percent) and less phraseology in supportive/positive ones (5 percent). The negative posts are not just more verbose but also more creative in seeking different, more colorful ways of showing their indignation with the parody; one of the most vivid images used was that of spitting in the face of the nation/people/Estonians (see the "Hostile Comments" section below for examples).

Quantitative analysis of the frequency of pronouns shows that an "us"-"them" opposition emerges in the posts. While "I" is very frequent in online comments in general (Crystal 2001; see also the post examples below), the high frequency of both "us" and "them" (see figure 5.1) indicates that the question divides people into opposing sides. Upon closer analysis, this division is backed by references in the comments to a generation gap—members of the older generation who remember the difficult history of Estonia, those who "sang the country free," (in this distinction, "us"), don't consider the parody funny versus the inexperienced, inconsiderate younger generation ("them"), perceived as making tasteless jokes about anything.[12] Additionally, "them" is also often used to refer to migrants, whom these hostile commenters see as threatening the independence and culture of the nation.

Supportive Comments

Examples of positive reactions to the sketch show—laughing with the satirists—were present in the form of simple and short comments like "10 points!" and "Great show, you didn't disappoint me once again!" There were not many figurative expressions to enliven the statements apart from a few like "hitting the bull's-eye" or "hats off." A few of the positive comments were more elaborate: "Well they really did spoil my mood! And precisely with that being the last show. Please, don't stop!!! You are the best! I adore that black irony. . . . Thank you and a deep bow for all those years!" (fänn, January 1, 2016, 1:59 a.m.).

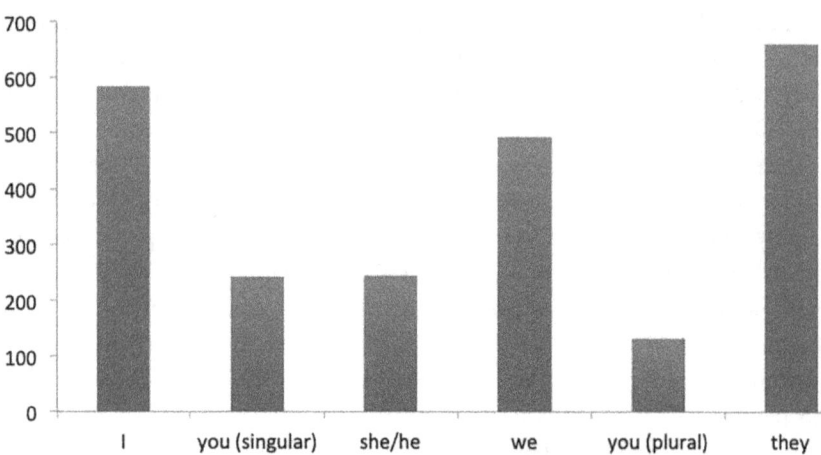

Figure 5.1. Frequency of pronoun usage in the data (total of 2,782 comments)

The comments supporting the show claim that *Mood Spoiler* creates excellent humor: "Not everyone can produce humor—some can master it, some can't. For me, *Mood Spoiler* always offers sarcasm and makes me smile . . . I will be sorry if this will be the last show. Happy New Year and don't be so malicious" (Märtson, January 1, 2016, 3:16 a.m.). Some commenters try to characterize the humor: "Satire has always been something not everyone understands. I think it was 100% success. There was both humor and a realization—yes, this is how life is in this country. Anyway, I wish the boys good luck! There are only few brave ones who dare and want to parody and ridicule our society . . . I feel ashamed of the people who don't understand humor or satire, or how deep we've sunk with our attitudes and views" (KT, January 1, 2016, 5:37 a.m.).

When supporters were attacked by commenters who did not agree with their positive evaluation of the humor, they retorted by stating that only those who lack a sense of humor (Marsh 2016) would find the parody unfunny or insulting: "I am not saying I am sinless (in hating everything and everyone and whining) but at least I am able to laugh at myself" (N, January 1, 2016, 12:23 a.m.). The positive commenters see those who oppose the sketch as lacking knowledge or being narrow-minded: "This last year was the best one. The final song was the best sketch that they have ever made. It hit the nail on the head. But well, who doesn't understand it or who doesn't like it, maybe they are unfamiliar with present-day politics and life or they don't see past the nose on their face" (asd, January 1, 2016, 1:56 a.m.). In these comments, the supporters clearly distance themselves from the audience members who disliked the show and didn't appreciate the satire and ridicule. By referring to "them" as people with no sense of humor, they assign them other features that allegedly go together with this (like lack of intelligence).

The ones displaying unlaughter are laughed at as grouchy people who dislike everything: "I hate Savisaar [Estonian politician], Putin, Merkel, Soviet Union, European Union, roubles, euros, New Year's Eve programme, lesbians, blacks, gays, Russians, work, bosses, rules of anonymous commenting, prices in shops, refugees, and everyone who doesn't hate the same things! Year of tolerance begins—down with everyone who doesn't think that way!!!" (JM, January 1, 2016, 12:57 a.m.).

Hostile Comments

Various ways of expressing unlaughter (e.g., verbal displays of hate, indignation, and umbrage) dominate in the comments culled from the delfi.ee online news forum. The prevailing element in these hostile comments is pointing out the inappropriateness of the form of the parody. Commenters show that they are feeling angry and insulted because a sacred cultural text (the original song) has been violated: "There are some songs that should never be parodied and this is one of them. If the songwriter was still alive and they had his permission, maybe then . . . Sorry but for me it seems that this bunch simply showed their unintelligence" (Uitaja, January 1, 2016, 5:09 a.m.). Many commenters stress that the song is very significant for the nation: "It was a nightmare to listen to befouling the song that is almost an anthem to the Estonians" (Maite, January 1, 2016, 11:56 a.m.). The original song stands for more than just the fight for freedom in the 1990s; for them, it captures the essence of the country's difficult history and addresses the most sacred beliefs and feelings: "To disgrace one's own nation, their most sacred feelings—this is awful!" (tugitoolifilosoof, January 1, 2016, 12:11 a.m.). These examples take the form of very serious messages and only rarely do the commenters joke back at the comedians, trying to reply in line with the initial humorous communication, for instance: "Everyone who took part in creating this sketch should get a refugee family as a present" (tissidega elajas, January 2, 2016, 10:20 a.m.). The tone of these few joking retorts is sarcastic and ironic, trying to exaggerate further the intention of the comedians: "Very good! More of such songs! Actually all Estonian songs should be rewritten! Especially those that speak about Estonia and Estonians . . . Without this [the parody] the whole Estonian song heritage would be like a mud puddle!" (MancunianPicker, January 1, 2016, 2:47 a.m.).

The most common way of expressing indignation in a figurative and symbolic way in the analyzed comments is to describe the sketch as an act of spitting into the face/heart/eyes of the nation or on the beliefs and opinions Estonians hold. The comments read, for example: "Especially unpleasant was the final song that spat on the opinions and fears of the majority" (Hääd teed teil minna! January 1, 2016, 12:15 a.m.). It was not just the source text itself but everything associated with it in a vernacular belief system— the grand narratives important to the identity of the nation (e.g., fighting for independence in the 1990s, the difficult Soviet times, living under the rule of occupants during different periods in history). The references are present in comments like "Your parents have worn T-shirts that read 'Phosphorite? No, thank you!'—and now you spit in their faces! Will they forgive you? Will the by now deceased songwriter Alo Matiisen forgive you? . . . You have insulted with your parody the contemporaries of your mothers and fathers, who have fought with the help of this song against the Soviet Union and its attempts at mining phosphorite in Virumaa" (Loodetavasti jõuab lauljateni, January 6, 2016, 9:51 p.m.). Not only the recent quest for independence is referenced but also earlier times during which the country's forefathers built the foundation for the nation: "Those people behind the microphones are ridiculing and booing at our ancestors' wisdom and values, collected grain by grain during the centuries under foreign rulers" (aivo Peterson, January 6, 2016, 9:51 p.m.). Even the hatred that the song and the discussion brought up (either against one's own nation and the state, as the "unlaughers" argue, or against each other) is said to have its roots in the difficult history of the country: "700 years of serfdom must be the reason why Estonians hate themselves and each other" (Arvan, January 1, 2016, 2:06 a.m.).

The symbolic image of spitting is a powerful one. It is simultaneously an ultimate insult (originating from the Bible, e.g., Matthew 26:67) as well as an act of protection against the evil power of the spirits known from folklore. It is difficult to determine the origins of spit-related phrases in Estonian, but what strikes the eye are the ample references to the Slavic cultural space in older material (Dal 1863–1866; Reitsak 1975; Vakk 1970). At the same time, its connections to the Bible (translated into Estonian from German in 1739) indicate that the much wider base of the image comes from many parallel sources, including Germanic ones. The Slavic phrase more commonly uses "spitting in the soul" rather than in the face or heart, as was usual in the comments analyzed in the delfi.ee comments section. Side by side with the image of spitting, we find other equally strong metaphors, all connected to waste and bodily excretions in one way or another.

Thus, several strong images are blended in the following comments: "[The song was like] a social democrat Marxist splash of spit that came from the mouths of clowns into the face and soul of the old folks" (Kuldar Pärt, January 6, 2016, 4:43 p.m.) and "If the author [of the original song] would have known how the *kulturniks* [a reference to the Soviet Union's cultural workers] ridicule the song and piss on it, he would have been sorry. I am ashamed. Very much so. A very personal and important piece of work has been thrown into garbage" (Moneylaundery1, January 1, 2016, 5:41 p.m.). Taking the figurativeness one level up, online commenters mix and match conventional phraseology and create pastiches of figurative expressions, resulting in powerful images like these, where spitting has been replaced with defecation: "During 1990s people took freedom to their hearts and sang this song from their hearts—such things happen very rarely. And then [Märt] Avandi came . . . and shitted in their souls! Avandi, would you like if someone made fun of or taunted your deceased child?!" (Avandile, January 6, 2016, 6:50 p.m.). Similar is this comment, only now the target is not the soul but the face: "At the moment you have defecated into the faces of your funders, but ok, now try to clean yourselves, you hating tolerasts" (olen senini veel roojane, January 1, 2016, 00:23 a.m.).[13] Following up with the image of targeting the face (with implicit allusions to impoliteness as "attacking the face"), another comment reads, "This was one of the many times that the official broadcast media has fucked the nation in the face [*näkku panema*; literally, 'put in the face']" (TE, January 1, 2016, 00:31 a.m.).

Conjunctions and disclaimers (*but, although, however*, etc.) trying to divert possible accusations concerning the lack of a sense of humor are frequently used, such as "I like satire, black humor, and people who can laugh at themselves. But these singing traitors were serving the propaganda machine and jeering at their nation, spitting into its face" (ei, January 2, 2016, 12:23 a.m.). A milder statement from a commenter tries to find reasons for such an explosive public response: "Generally I like [Märt] Avandi, I understand humor . . . but this time, yes, they probably chose a slightly wrong joke and a wrong topic to laugh at" (mxpx, January 6, 2016, 9:38 p.m.).

The tension between the official and vernacular lines of thinking (the blurred relationship of these in online contexts is described in Howard 2008) leads to conspiracy theories that draw a connection between the Soviet Union (and censorship, whereby one is not allowed to say what one thinks about the country's leaders or the immigrants from the east) and the European Union: "The final song was as if made to the order by political clowns. Attack the Estonians; praise the multicultural, niggers and gays. Then you are cute. Keep on bleating" (oss, January 1, 2016, 7:39 a.m.). This line of thought leads easily to the conclusion that the European Union is even worse than the Soviet one and that the regulations of political correctness have grown out of bounds, which is why those in power have to pay lip service to the European officials: "Even in Soviet times there weren't so many ass-lickers as there are now!" (alt, January 1, 2016, 8:10 a.m.). Censorship (both in society as a whole as well as in the forum where the commenters express their opinion) is often pointed out: "Comments keep disappearing. You have to praise the song! Otherwise your comments will not be published!" (MancunianPicker, January 1, 2016, 1:46 a.m.). Such commenters claim vehemently that their posts are being censored (while in fact, at least in this forum, the negative and anti-parody voices are statistically in the majority) and blame the other discussants for being in opposition: "When I wrote yesterday that they [the singers] flushed themselves down with their last song—may their path be slippery—my comment was erased. Did I incite hate? Insulted someone? Wounded someone? Or maybe somebody read something obscene into my comment, according to their spoiled minds affected by 'European values'? Isn't my opinion (different from Brussels, our government or ETV) enriching and different?" (väga hea, January 1, 2016, 9:20 a.m.).

The Soviet Union–European Union comparisons extend to pointing at a generation gap between those who have witnessed difficult Soviet times and participated in freeing Estonia and those who were too young at the time. They have, according to the commenters, different beliefs, experiences, and also a different sense of humor. On the whole, discussions about what is humor abound in the analyzed comments. Commenters mention old classics as examples of the best kind of humor.[14] The classics from Soviet times are referred to as idols still worthy of praise: "Today we watched some sketches made by [Eino] Baskin in 1977/78 . . . It was really good. Sharp human-centred satire!" (free estonia, January 1, 2016, 2:25 a.m.).[15] These humor classics are then contrasted with the comedians of the *Mood Spoiler* show, with the latter—as well as their audience—portrayed as unintelligent: "Present-day youth seems to be unicellular, and their only cell is not a humor cell" (eid_15068491b3ff0d, January 1, 2016, 4:52 p.m.). Such humor is labeled as "bad" and the comedians are described as "#clowns": "I don't want to watch these clowns for some time already. Cheap banal humor" (ahh, January 1, 2016, 3:54 a.m.).

Time and again, the critics point at the intangible limits within humor that are always present: "There is a difference between a joke and a joke . . . When your brains are defective, look into your hearts, go and sit on the graves of your close ones and meditate" (aivo Peterson, January 6, 2016, 9:51 p.m.).

There is not much dialogue between the commenters. In the few cases that commenters react to each other, attack follows as a reaction to praising the parody: "It was fun, bon voyage, guys!" (Heino, December 31, 2015, 11:28 p.m.) and the reply "Fun? No. Bon voyage? Yes" (Olen vapustatud, January 1, 2016, 3:02 a.m.). The tension between commenters can also intensify to mutual accusations and insults: "You can put exactly as many minuses as you wish but this will not change my views or those of other intelligent people. Most of delfi.ee commenters are clowns with only primary education who should educate themselves instead of posting here" (Mõistuse hääl, January 1, 2016, 5:35 a.m.), with the reply "Typical, that someone like that uses the nickname 'Mõistuse hääl' ['Voice of reason'] . . . If there was no possibility for anonymous commenting, the voice of reason would sit quietly in the corner and suck its thumb" (lugu, January 1, 2016, 8:30 a.m.) and a follow-up: "The fact that you think you are so intelligent tells everything about your intelligence" (Mõistuse hääl, January 1, 2016, 10:32 a.m.). All kinds of comments—positive or hateful—can lead to hateful reactions, including threats of violence toward the commenters or threats to the singers who took part in the sketch. In the later comments (after January 5, 2016), the commenters attack the positive comments (by then less frequent) even more fiercely, accusing their writers of treason and insolence, among other rhetorical jabs, and threatening the comedians with physical assault.

There are also comments that show support and indignation at the same time. Such polyvocal statements reveal well the inherent complexity of the topic of the discussion: "The song was very good and will be in my playlist. Self-irony is a good expression of a sound mind, as is being against refugees" (pagulasvastane, January 1, 2016, 12:04 a.m.). However, polyvocality of opinions within and between posts doesn't necessarily mean that people who are able to represent different positions would also be more open and tolerant toward immigrants or their fellow Estonians who accept the refugees, which is evident in the large overall proportion of negative comments.

SHOWING THE DOOR: FINISHING NOTES

In recent years, the use of humor in genres where it has usually been kept at bay has flourished, especially on the internet, constituting a gold mine for folkloristic studies. Social media—with its exaggerated emotionality, ambiguity, asynchronicity, "just for lulz policy" (Milner 2013; Phillips and Milner 2017)—favors the battle of wits; any fresh reference, new connection, or intertextual element is welcome. Early studies of internet humor stressed that new media has extended humor conduits and increased accessibility to humorous material. Paul Smith, writing about jokes on the early World Wide Web, calls the personal computer "a joke machine" (1991) to underline the internet's disposition to engage in humor. Since then, humor has become one of the prime constituents of communication on the internet (Shifman 2014; Blank 2013; Milner 2013; Vandergriff and Fuchs 2009; Tsakona 2018; Laineste 2016). Due to the ambiguity of humor, its potential meanings may easily get mixed up in the communication, depending on if and how people recognize, understand, and appreciate it (Hay 2001). Whether it is understood or misunderstood, humor does create a discursive space that allows for open discussion about matters that are otherwise silenced or tabooed (Goldstein 2003; see also Kuipers 2008, 370) because it regularly targets the controversial, forbidden, or odd. In an online context, the emerging discussions can be even more emotional than in face-to-face situations, as the internet operates as an open agora for a collision of opposite opinions.

The humor we encounter on the internet often uses the tools of satire, parody, and irony to merge topics, formats, popular culture, and stereotypes into a potentially entertaining medley (Tay 2012; Denith 2000; Palmer 2005; Malmqvist 2015; Blank 2016). Parody targets order, and thus the part of the audience unappreciative of the humorous sketch by *Mood Spoiler* is consequently seen as dry, humorless, and conservative—but also as unintelligent. The higher concentration of figurative speech and otherwise colorful rhetoric in the negative comments displaying unlaughter might have been because the commenters tried to create memorable, attention-catching statements that would dispute such accusations of being dry and unintelligent (see Roberts and Kreuz 1994). Too much pathos and seriousness can frighten readers away (Milner 2013), as can sentimentality, earnestness, and seriousness; instead, frivolity, verbal word play, ambiguity, and wit are essential. Jamie Warner (2008) maintains that stressful societal events (taking 9/11 in the United States as a case in point) bring about excessive irony that feeds on the dominant serious discourse, which rigidly labels all interpretations deviating from the official ones as suspect, unpatriotic, or even treasonous, arguing against those who see such events as the end of irony.

One of the more common choices of retaliation in the discussion concerning the parody of "No Country Stands Alone" was to say that it wasn't funny and blame the other party for having a bad sense of humor. This underlined the "us" and "them" division and led to particular understandings about certain individuals and groups lacking a sense of humor, with the underlying belief that having a sense of humor is generally a character strength (Ruch 2008, 42, 52). The hostile commenters claimed that the sketch was not humor and brought examples of "real" humor from the past to prove it, while the fans of *Mood Spoiler* criticized the negative posters for faults like narrow-mindedness, aggressiveness, and lack of a sense of humor. In more extreme cases, such a controversy regarding humor can also lead to legal action being taken against satirists when the polemics constitute, as Giselinde Kuipers points out, not just academic, but also moral, political, practical, and legal issues (2015, 31).[16] Laughter and other expressions of amusement are rhetorical; social actors use them as tools for boundary maintenance, to communicate meanings, and to position themselves in conversations (Billig 2005, 189–192). Laughter intensifies about the polarization of opposing statements and makes dialogue more complicated. The sensitive topic of the sketch touched upon "them" endangering "us," involving important concepts like national identity, narratives from the past, and sacred symbols of the nation. The reverberations made the sketch even more popular and led many people to (re)watch it on social media. As Marsh posits, "Risk is part of the challenge and appeal of jokes; the louder the unlaughter, the more credit goes to the jokers for having risked it" (2016, 39). Serious and heated arguments may cause further alienation between the conflicting sides, but the final verdict most likely depends on the power lines and status of the parties involved (see Kuipers 2015). In the case of the parody discussed here, it was the politically incorrect, nationalist voice of the unlaughing audience that was heard the loudest—the unofficial medium of the internet forum reinforced and increased the volume of their governing points of view, as perhaps did their ample use of rhetorical devices.

Emotional reactions can be studied by focusing on phraseology (Ahmed 2004, 11–13), as metaphors, ethnonyms, paroemia, and other kinds of figurative language indicate what the audience is feeling. This can be especially useful in online environments. Figurative speech occurs frequently in posts that make a negative statement or argue against something. For example, a milder way to indicate that someone is not to be taken seriously, lacks responsibility for his actions, and shows low intelligence is to compare that person to a clown, meaning someone whose only aim or function is to entertain. In the data studied here, "clown" is employed as an insult in both directions: the comedians are called clowns and so are the commenters who are against the parody.

The comments analyzed in this chapter show also that conflicting opinions do not always oppose one another in a nice sequence; sometimes, the audience communicates appreciation and indignation even within the same post (separated only by the use of conjunctions like "but"). The debate brought together different opinions, often merging and melting them into fuzzy sets of ideas. Boundaries of "us" and "them" and also of laughter and indignation are not as straightforward as we would perhaps like them to be. The functionality of humor depends on if and how people recognize, understand, and appreciate humor: all three of these levels must be passed in order for the audience to fully enjoy something as humorous. As Moira Marsh argues, "Some joke performances are meant to elicit differential responses—laughter from some, and unlaughter from salient others" (Smith 2009, 148). Hence, the possibility that something as ambiguous as humor will be understood in a similar way by everyone is unlikely, to say the least.

I have previously suggested that reactions to mediated humor differ from those that are experienced face-to-face (Laineste 2013, 41–43). The social cues that would normally inform the recipient(s) about the intentions of the sender are missing and thus the meanings of a statement can be manifold, escaping the control of the sender, and the message is understood depending on the varied interpretations of the (global) audience. Computer-mediated communication, it has been claimed, enhances the ambiguity of statements (Vandegriff and Fuchs 2009). Playfulness, which magnifies ambiguity, has been amply documented in online interactions (see Danet et al. 1997). Of course, misunderstandings due to ambiguity are not unique to online interactions only, research suggests they might be more prevalent in that medium (Hancock 2004). Giselinde Kuipers notes that it is easier to ignore mediated satire that is televised or on the internet—one is not put directly to the test (2015, 23). This study offers proof that internet users eagerly engage in a battle of wits on controversial subjects, using humor and playful remix of figurative speech, and do it more often to criticize than to praise the object of discussion.

Folkloric communication flourishes in the virtual arena when emotional topics are being discussed. Grand narratives—such as ideas about identity and nationality—surge; myths and folk beliefs are reintroduced. The polyvocal internet allows for multiple, sometimes conflicting opinions to be voiced at once. Othering occurs on both sides, and this opens up a public discussion about the definition of "humor" (see Kuipers 2006). Due to increasingly unpredictable audience choice, the thin line between humor and insult gets stepped on, redrawn, and pushed about in these online discussions, with the excuse "I was only joking" making it even more difficult to spot and define. These complicated but meaningful patterns of folkloric expression in online controversies like the one following the *Mood Spoiler* sketch of 2015 need to be studied to document the folkloric means of expressing emotions and discussing the limits of humor online in order to yield a generally more detailed insight into this kind of communication on social media.

NOTES

1. For echo chamber theories, see Jamieson and Cappella 2008.
2. See Hay's model of failed humor (2001).
3. For example, the metaphor of 700 years of serfdom (Boldane and Šņitņikovs 2006; Jõesalu 2010). For a brief overview of Estonian history, see an article published as part of the 100 years of independence celebrations: Estonian World 2018.
4. For an example of style, see one of the first sketches from 2008'a *Mood Spoiler*: https://www.youtube.com/watch?v=nQ59WMRjC1o.
5. The show even attracted academic interest (see Taaniel 2015).
6. See http://www.catapult.ee/kontakt.html for a list of people engaged in the creative team.
7. See examples of some of the more controversial ones: on Nazis (*Estonia Is Looking for the Neo-Nazi*, a parody of the program *Estonia Is Looking for a Superstar*, similar to *American Idol*, ERR archive, http://arhiiv.err.ee/guid/201005120050552010010002081001517C41A040000005020B00000D0F066767, 4:00); on hospitals (a mockumentary of coma patients struggling for survival, one being voted out every week), ERR archive, http://arhiiv.err.ee/guid/201005120050552010010002081001517C41A040000005020B00000D0F066767, 21:00; on the sinking of the ferry *Estonia* (a fake ad of an exhibition depicting the sinking, https://www.youtube.com/watch?v=PaABXCWQ2Mg); and on Estonian history (a sketch about deportations of Estonians to Siberia after the end of World War II), https://www.youtube.com/watch?v=IWLKiLXBGhg.
8. Although the comedians and their creative team promised to finish performing on New Year's Eve program after a particularly controversial clip was aired, both Avandi and Sepp were featured on the 2016 program as well. The short sketch presented a dark self-ironical take on humorists and their role in present-day Estonia (if not in the entire world). In a parody of Tarantino's *The Hateful Eight* (2015), the most prominent Estonian comedians and entertainers performed a mock collective suicide, justifying it by how impossible it is to please everyone. "This is something that will not spoil your mood," the introduction to the sketch promised.
9. The original song was recorded in 1987 in the studio of ETV, the Estonian national television channel: https://www.youtube.com/watch?v=-FNKJGBtmM8.
10. For details about the so-called phosphorite war, see Oll 2004.
11. For example, in the 2013 night song festival, where some of the artists who later sang the parody sang the original of the song. https://www.youtube.com/watch?v=Qvnp0Y0EOew.
12. The Singing Revolution is a commonly used term for events between 1987 and 1991 that led to the restoration of the independence of Estonia and other Baltic countries. See the trailer of a 2006 documentary *The Singing Revolution* at https://singingrevolution.com/; and Smidchens 2014.
13. *Tolerast* is a Russian loan word mixing the neutral term for a tolerant person with an offensive word for a homosexual, pederast. It is customarily used to allude to a tolerant person who openly and completely favors refugees as well as gay marriage. Use of the word is meant to criticize people who are too tolerant and at the same time subservient to the government, especially the European Union rules and regulations.
14. Most of the classic examples of old humor mentioned in the comments belonged to the period of Soviet Estrada; see Laineste 2012. Russian Estrada, a stage genre very popular in Estonia from the 1970s onward, provided commentary on the shortcomings of the regime and daily life in a seemingly innocuous manner.

15. See https://www.youtube.com/watch?v=riCzQwp0Nr8 for an example of Eino Baskin's work.

16. This threat was underlined one year later, during the New Year's Eve show on ETV in 2016/2017, depicting the aforementioned mock suicide of Estonian comedians.

REFERENCES

Ahmed, Sara. 2004. *Cultural Politics of Emotion*. London: Routledge.

Alfred, Charlotte. 2015. "What History Can Teach Us about the Worst Refugee Crisis since WWII." *Huffington Post*, December 9, 2015. https://www.huffpost.com/entry/alex ander-betts-refugees-wwii_n_55f30f7ce4b077ca094edaec.

Bell, Nancy. 2015. *We Are Not Amused: Failed Humor in Interaction*. Berlin: Mouton de Gruyter.

Billig, Michael. 2005. *Laughter and Ridicule: Toward a Social Critique of Humor*. London: Sage.

Blank, Trevor. 2013. *The Last Laugh. Folk Humor, Celebrity Culture, and Mass-Mediated Disasters in the Digital Age*. Madison: University of Wisconsin Press.

Blank, Trevor. 2016. "Giving the 'Big Ten' a Whole New Meaning: Tasteless Humor and the Response to the Penn State Sexual Abuse Scandal." In *The Folkloresque: Reframing Folklore in a Popular Culture World*, edited by Michael Dylan Foster and Jeffrey A. Tolbert, 179–204. Logan: Utah State University Press.

Boldane, Ilze, and Aleksejs Šņitņikovs. 2006. "Is Cultural Trauma an Impediment to Society Integration?" Providus. June 8, 2006. http://providus.lv/article/is-cultural -trauma-an-impediment-to-society-integration.

Crystal, David. 2001. *Language and the Internet*. Cambridge: Cambridge University Press.

Dal, Vladimir. 1863–1866. = Даль, Владимир 1863–1866. *Толковый словарь живого великорусского языка. I–IV* [A glossary of the spoken Russian language]. Moscow, St Petersburg: О-во любителей российской словесности. http://slovardalja.net/word.php?wordid=26158.

Danet, Brenda, Lucia Ruedenberg-Wright, and Yehudit Rosenbaum-Tamari. 1997. "'Hmmm . . . Where's That Smoke Coming From?' Writing, Play and Performance on Internet Relay Chat." *Journal of Computer-Mediated Communication* 2 (4): n.p.

da Silva, Patrícia Dias, and José Luís Garcia. 2012. "YouTubers as Satirists: Humor and Remix in Online Video." *Journal of Democracy and Open Government JeDEM* 4 (1): 89–114.

Denith, Simon. 2000. *Parody: The New Critical Idiom*. London: Routledge.

Estonian World. 2018. "Estonia Celebrates the Independence Day," February 24, 2018. http://estonianworld.com/life/estonia-celebrates-independence-day/.

Faure, Gunter, and Teresa Mensing. 2012. *The Estonians: The Long Road to Independence*. London: Lulu.com.

Goldstein, Donna. 2003. *Laughter out of Place: Race, Class, Violence and Sexuality in a Rio Shantytown*. Berkeley: University of California Press.

Hancock, Jeffrey T. 2004. "Verbal Irony Use in Face-to-Face and Computer-Mediated Conversations." *Journal of Language and Social Psychology* 23 (4): 447–463.

Hay, Jennifer. 2001. "The Pragmatics of Humor Support." *Humor: International Journal of Humor Research* 14 (1): 55–82.

Howard, Robert Glenn 2008. "Electronic Hybridity: The Persistent Process of the Vernacular Web." *Journal of American Folklore* 121 (480): 192–218.

Jamieson, Kathleen Hall, and Joseph Cappella. 2008. *Echo Chamber: Rush Limbaugh and the Conservative Media Establishment*. Oxford: Oxford University Press.

Jõesalu, Kirsti. 2010. "The Meaning of 'Late Socialism': Analyzing Estonians' Post-Communist Memory Culture." *Asia Europe Journal* 8 (3): 293–303.
Kuipers, Giselinde. 2006. *Good Humor, Bad Taste: A Sociology of the Joke*. Berlin: Mouton de Gruyter.
Kuipers, Giselinde. 2008. "The Sociology of Humor." In *The Primer of Humor Research*, edited by Victor Raskin, 361–398. Berlin: Mouton de Gruyter.
Kuipers, Giselinde. 2015. "Satire and Dignity." In *The Power of Satire*, edited by Marijke Meijer Drees and Sonja de Leeuw, 19–32. Amsterdam: John Benjamins.
Külmoja, Inga. 2016. "No Country Stands Alone—Except Maybe Syria!" *UT (University of Tartu) Blog*, January 15, 2016. http://blog.ut.ee/no-country-stands-alone-except-maybe-syria/.
Laineste, Liisi. 2008. *Post-Socialist Jokes in Estonia: Continuity and Change*. Tartu, Estonia: Tartu University Press.
Laineste, Liisi. 2013. "Funny or Aggressive? Failed Humor in Internet Comments." *Folklore: Electronic Journal of Folklore* 53: 29–46.
Laineste, Liisi. 2016. "Laughing across Borders: Intertextuality of Internet Memes." *European Journal of Humour Research* 4 (4): 26–49. https://doi.org/10.7592/EJHR2016.4.4.laineste.
Laineste, Liisi. 2017. "Othering in Estonian Online Discussion about Refugees." In *Representing the Other in European Media Discourses*, edited by Jan Chovanec and Katarzyna Molek-Kozakowska, 281–305. Amsterdam: John Benjamins.
Lewis, Paul, Christie Davies, Giselinde Kuipers, Rod Martin, Elliott Oring, and Victor Raskin. 2008. "The Mohammad Cartoons and Humor Research." *HUMOR: International Journal of Humor Research* 21 (1): 1–46.
Lotman, Juri. 2018. *George Soros ja Euroopa Liit* [George Soros and EU]. Mikhail Lotman's blog page, June 14, 2018. http://www.lotman.ee/blogi/george-soros-ja-euroopa-liit.
Makarychev, Andrey, and Alexandra Yatsyk. 2017. "Estonia and the Refugees: Political Discourses and Artistic Representations." *Global Affairs* 3 (1): 45–57.
Malmqvist, Karl. 2015. "Satire, Racist Humor and the Power of (Un)Laughter: On the Restrained Nature of Swedish Online Racist Discourse Targeting EU-Migrants Begging for Money." *Discourse and Society* 26 (6): 733–753.
Marsh, Moira. 2016. "Unlaughter, the Unfunny, and the Dreadnought." Keynote address presented at the Australasian Humor Studies Netwrok Conference, Women's College, University of Sydney, Australia, February 6–8, 2016. https://sydney.edu.au/content/dam/corporate/documents/faculty-of-arts-and-social-sciences/research/research-centres-institutes-groups/ahsn/AHSN-2016-Program-Final-Rev.pdf.
Miles, Tom. 2015. "EU Gets One Million Migrants in 2015, Smugglers Seen Making $1 Billion." *Reuters*, December 22, 2015. https://www.reuters.com/article/us-europe-migrants-idUSKBN0U50WI20151222.
Miljan, Toivo. 2004. *Historical Dictionary of Estonia*. Lanham, MD: Scarecrow.
Milner, Ryan. 2013. "Hacking the Social: Internet Memes, Identity Antagonism, and the Logic of Lulz." *Fibreculture Journal* 22: 62–92. http://fibreculturejournal.org/wp-content/pdfs/FCJ-156Ryan%20Milner.pdf.
Pagulasuuring (Refugee Survey). 2014. *Eesti elanike teadlikkus ja hoiakud pagulasküsimustes* [Awareness and attitudes of Estonians toward refugee issues]. Saar Poll survey ordered by Ministry of Internal Affairs. Accessed July 6, 2018. https://www.siseministeerium.ee/sites/default/files/dokumendid/Uuringud/Kodakondsus_ja_r2nne/2014_pagulasuuring_aruanne.pdf.
Palmer, Jerry. 2005. "Parody and Decorum: Permission to Mock." In *Beyond a Joke: The Limits of Humour*, edited by Sharon Lockyer and Michael Pickering, 79–97. Basingstoke: Palgrave Macmillan.

Phillips, Whitney, and Ryan M. Milner. 2017. *The Ambivalent Internet: Mischief, Oddity, and Antagonism Online*. Cambridge: Polity.

Pickering, Michael, and Sharon Lockyer. 2005. "Introduction: The Ethics and Aesthetics of Humour and Comedy." In *Beyond a Joke: The Limits of Humour*, edited by Sharon Lockyer and Michael Pickering, 1–24. Basingstoke: Palgrave Macmillan.

Reitsak, Agnia. 1975. *Valimik vene fraseologisme eesti vastetega* [A selection of Russian phrases with Estonian counterparts]. Tallinn: Valgus.

Roberts, Richard M., and Roger J. Kreuz. 1994. "Why Do People Use Figurative Language?" *Psychological Science* 5 (3): 159–163.

Rost, Katja, Lea Stahel, and Bruno S. Frey. 2016. "Digital Social Norm Enforcement: Online Firestorms in Social Media." *PLoS ONE* 11 (6). https://doi.org/10.1371/journal.pone.0155923.

Ruch, Willibald. 2008. "Psychology of Humor." In *The Primer of Humor Research*, edited by Willibald Ruch, 17–100. Berlin: Mouton de Gruyter.

Sandell, Karin. 2018. "Gay Clowns, Pigs and Traitors: An Emotion Analysis of Online Hate Speech Directed at the Swedish-Speaking Population in Finland." *Folklore: Electronic Journal of Folklore* 74: 25–50.

Shifman, Limor. 2014. *Memes in Digital Culture*. Cambridge, MA: MIT Press.

Šmidchens, Guntis. 2014. *The Power of Song: Nonviolent National Culture in the Baltic Singing Revolution*. Seattle: University of Washington Press.

Smith, Moira. 2009. "Humor, Unlaughter, and Boundary Maintenance." *Journal of American Folklore* 122 (484): 148–171.

Smith, Paul. 1991. "The Joke Machine: Communicating Traditional Humor Using Computers." In *Spoken in Jest*, edited by Gillian Bennett, 257–278. Sheffield: Sheffield Academic Press.

Taaniel, Reet. 2015. *Tujurikkuja––eesti huumor?* [Mood Spoiler––Estonian humor?]. BA thesis, University of Tartu, Estonia. http://dspace.ut.ee/bitstream/handle/10062/38732/bakalaureus_reet_taniel.pdf.

Tay, Geniesa. 2012. *Embracing LOLitics: Popular Culture, Online Political Humor, and Play*. PhD diss., University of Canterbury. http://hdl.handle.net/10092/7091.

Tsakona, Villy. 2018. "Online Joint Fictionalization." In *The Dynamics of Interactional Humor*, edited by Villy Tsakona and Jan Chovanec, 229–256. Amsterdam: John Benjamins.

Tuch, Andrei. 2019. "Welcome to Estonia's New Far-Right Government." *Estonian World*, March 12, 2019. http://estonianworld.com/opinion/andrei-tuch-welcome-to-estonias-new-far-right-government/.

Vakk, Feliks. 1970. *Suured ninad murdsid päid: Pea ja selle osad rahvalike ütluste peeglis* [Big noses racked their brains: Head in the mirror of folk sayings]. Tallinn: Valgus.

Vandergriff, Ilona, and Carolin Fuchs. 2009. "Does CMC Promote Language Play? Exploring Humor in Two Modalities." *CALICO Journal* 27 (1): 26–47.

Veebel, Viljar. 2015. "Balancing between Solidarity and Responsibility: Estonia in the EU Refugee Crisis." *Journal on Baltic Security* 1 (2): 28–61.

Warner, Jamie. 2008. "Tyranny of the Dichotomy: Prophetic Dualism, Irony, and *The Onion*." *Electronic Journal of Communication* 18 (2–4): n.p.

6

Trickster Remakes This White House
Booby Traps and Bawdy/Body Humor in Post-Election Prankster Biden Memes

Jeana Jorgensen and Linda J. Lee

IN THE AFTERMATH OF THE 2016 US presidential election, the popular "Prankster Biden" meme cycle cast the soon-to-be-former Democratic vice president as a comedic foil to his unwitting accomplice and straight man, President Barack Obama.[1] By 2016 Joe Biden, known for a shoot-from-the-hip speaking style that has led to numerous public gaffes in his more than forty years as a prominent figure in American politics, had been a fixture of parodic internet culture for nearly a decade. These post-election memes showed Biden in various settings proposing pranks on incoming president Donald Trump with childish yet incisive humor. These memes frequently contained themes of amorality, disguise, hunger, and childishness—giving the Biden character an odd similarity to trickster figures and culture heroes (Radin 1956; Kerényi 1969; Roberts 1990; Hynes and Doty 1993; Hyde 1998; Mills 2001). By drawing on trickster tropes, bodily humor, and intertextual references from popular culture this meme cycle enabled users to engage in a form of participatory protest on social media.

In this chapter, we argue that this form of digital folklore allowed disappointed citizens to publicly and playfully deal with feelings of grief as well as fears of illegitimacy and chaos following the 2016 US election. By positioning Biden as a trickster operating within an intertextual popular culture framework, this prominent meme cycle conveyed the dissatisfaction that many people had with the incoming administration. Drawing on a "cultural inventory" (Blank 2013) grounded in nerdy and geeky pop culture references, the Prankster Joe Biden meme cycle positioned an idealized version of the outgoing Obama administration against the perceived inadequacy of the incoming Trump administration. These memes use vernacular culture as a resource, albeit a highly remixed one, to posit that Donald Trump was not suitable for the presidency. As a form of participatory digital culture (Shifman 2014; Milner 2016; Wiggins 2018), these memes offer a way for individuals to socially and playfully convey anxiety about the 2016 election results as well as its broader implications for American politics and culture.

To make this argument, we begin by positioning Joe Biden's public life in the context of the memes that play off his mass media persona and his reputation for being both gaffe-prone and mildly "creepy" around women (see Biddle 2015; Petri 2015; Ryan 2017). Next, we establish Biden as a trickster figure within the post-election Prankster Biden memes. We document this meme cycle's main motifs and themes that demonstrate Biden's trickster characteristics. This case study offers contrasting perspectives on the Obama and Trump administrations, primarily through the bodies of Joe Biden and Donald Trump and their performance of masculinity. We argue that the Prankster Biden meme cycle frequently uses language and images of the body to make a two-pronged critique of Trump's perceived unsuitability for the presidency. First, Biden's pranks will make the White House inhospitable to Trump's body. Second, through his failure to perform hegemonic masculinity correctly, Trump's body is *already* unsuited for the White House. Finally, we conclude by asserting that the political and pop culture content of this meme cycle comprises a cultural inventory that critiques Trump's failed performance of hegemonic masculinity and positions Biden as a cultural hero.

BIDEN AS TRICKSTER FIGURE

Many of the trickster qualities that appear in the Prankster Biden meme cycle are also present in Biden's mass media persona, which was well developed prior to the meme cycle of the November 2016 elections, fostered by coverage in mainstream new sources as well as satirical sources like the *Onion* and Comedy Central's *The Daily Show with Jon Stewart*. The *Onion* had run dozens of humorous stories featuring almost-believable Biden gaffes, while *The Daily Show* aired a segment on February 24, 2015, called "The Audacity of Grope" highlighting Vice President Biden's tendency to invade women's personal space and touch them without their consent. These segments depict Biden as impulsive, transgressive, and insatiable—in short, as a political figure already showing trickster-like qualities.

The trickster is an archetypal figure that appears in mythology, folktales, and legends from cultures across the world. In the United States, the trickster is most closely associated with Native Americans, where he often appears as Coyote, Raven, Hare, or Spider. Mischievous and clever, tricksters can appear in many guises and are often responsible for paradoxical or ambiguous actions. In his classic work on tricksters, Paul Radin identifies the trickster's central features: "a hero who is always wandering, who is always hungry, who is not guided by normal conceptions of good or evil, who is either playing tricks on people or having them played on him and who is highly sexed" (1956, 155). Radin describes the trickster as contradictory—a "creator and destroyer, giver and negator, he who dupes others and is always duped himself" (ix). Tricksters are characterized by paradox and ambiguity. Simultaneously a clever hero and a selfish buffoon, the trickster may be a deceiver with an insatiable appetite for food or sex (Carroll 1984), or he may take action to benefit others, as when Prometheus gifted humans with fire stolen from the gods. Tricksters are also sometimes liminal figures (Turner 1969; Babcock-Abrahams 1975). According to Hynes and Doty, "The liminal trickster, the court jester, and the clown are related . . . in that they possess marginal status and bring into the social institution new possibilities for action and self-understanding" (1993, 20).

In many ways, Biden embraced this mass media persona, repeatedly demonstrating his ability to move between the real world and fictional ones through cameos on popular television shows. He made two acclaimed surprise cameos in the television series *Parks and Recreation* (2009–2015), a satirical sitcom that followed the lives and political careers of a group of local government workers in the fictional town of Pawnee, Indiana (Holter 2015). In seasons 5 and 7, Biden interacted with the show's lead protagonist Leslie Knope, an unabashed Biden fan who regularly proclaims her profound affection for him. Prior to Knope's meeting Biden at the White House, she had remarked on his sex appeal, and in the season 5 episode where they meet for the first time, Knope comes dangerously close to sexually harassing Biden.

This is a reversal of the "creepy" image of Biden that many have remarked on; according to Erin Gloria Ryan, writing for the *Daily Beast*, "While Joe Biden has been jokingly depicted as a kooky uncle or Obama's wacky sidekick or Leslie Knope's grin-flashing celebrity crush, he's also got a troubling history of acting weird in public around women who don't seem entirely on board. This isn't just based on whispers or rumors; there are so many photos and clips of Biden looming over, or massaging, or gently nuzzling, or whispering to, or kissing women and girls who don't seem all that into it" (2017). While in his *Parks and Recreation* cameos Biden appeared ruffled by Knope's adoring attention, this take on Biden hints at a man who ruffles others. Either he is blithely unaware of his boundary-transgressing behavior, or he is aware and does not care. Biden also made a cameo appearance on *Law and Order: Special Victims Unit*. In the cold open of "Making a Rapist" (season 18, episode 2), Biden addressed the long-standing backlog of rape kits at police stations nationwide. This appearance is also notable because the message of this appearance and of Biden's championship of the Violence against Women Act is at odds with the implication that perhaps he does not respect women's boundaries (Jensen 2016).

As these examples suggest, Biden's public persona occupied a liminal space between serious politician and the trickster image he developed through this satirical mass media coverage and his own winking cameos. This demonstrates that even before Biden was a meme, his image (both public and satirized) conveyed many classic characteristics of tricksters. This supports Lewis Hyde's statement that tricksters create boundaries as well as break them: "Trickster isn't a run-of-the-mill liar and thief. When he lies and steals, it isn't so much to get away with something or get rich as to disturb the established categories of truth and property and, by so doing, open the road to possibly new worlds" (1998, 13). Karl Kerényi calls trickster "the spirit of disorder, the enemy of boundaries" (1969, 185). In this role of boundary breaker, tricksters often move between the realms of the living and the dead, and they function as destabilizing forces in the many myths, folktales, and legends in which they appear. Biden, like the trickster, eludes boundaries and easy categorization. For instance, Mills distinguishes between tricksters who transform the world, those who trick to fulfill compulsive desires, those who trick for the sake of trickery itself, and tricksters of occasion, often humans who have learned how to trick from a divine donor figure (2013, 111).

In the sections that follow, we argue that this liminality of Biden's trickster-attuned public persona allowed internet users to easily turn him into a meme that could be readily modified, remixed, and reshared for a variety of ideological purposes. To make this argument, we began collecting Biden memes after the 2016 election and continued to document them throughout 2017 and 2018. In total, we collected nearly 150 distinct images. We searched for them using Google and informed friends and colleagues about the project on social media. Consequently, people across the United States sent us memes or links to articles about the memes. We downloaded individual examples as images (as .jpg or .png files), and where possible, recorded the context (such as which social network they appeared on). Our goal was to build an archive of Prankster Joe Biden images in order to focus our analysis on the content of these memetic texts—their motifs, themes, and potential meanings.

Many of the texts we collected—photos of Obama, Biden, and other relevant political figures with words layered over or situated alongside the images—were shared on one social media site as screenshots from another site. This makes the memes akin to Xeroxlore or photocopylore (Dundes and Pagter 1978; see also Blank 2013, 34), in that fixed images were being transmitted with minimal variation. In other cases, different texts were clearly variants on the same theme or image, such as with multiple memes making essentially the same jokes: such as Obama being a good candidate for Batman, or Biden being concerned about Santa finding him once he moved out of the White House. Thus, being attuned to text, texture, and context (Dundes 1980) helps demonstrate that these memes follow folkloric conventions of tradition and variation.

TRICKSTERS, BODIES, AND HEGEMONIC MASCULINITY IN THE PRANKSTER BIDEN MEME CYCLE

The crux of the Prankster Joe Biden cycle revolves around the outgoing vice president's desire to play tricks on incoming president Donald Trump as the political shift of power occurs and the new administration begins to reside in the White House. In many image macros circulating in the immediate aftermath of the 2016 election, Biden suggests various booby traps and pranks in order to mess with the incoming president in chaotic but usually not actually dangerous ways. Outgoing president Barack Obama appears as a regular character in this meme cycle, as the person off whom Biden bounces ideas and whose calls for restraint are usually rebuffed. The vast majority of these memes place only Biden and Obama within the frame, though they explicitly or implicitly reference Trump and incoming Vice President Mike Pence. Examples of pranks suggested in these memes include removing the batteries from the TV remotes, recommending a Samsung Galaxy Note 7 phone (which was recalled due to exploding batteries) for Trump, and replacing doorknobs with cats (so that Trump will have to "grab [the doors] by their pussy" to open them).

These memes demonstrate several trickster characteristics. The narrative places these proposed pranks at a point of transition, with trickster Biden conceptually crossing boundaries from the Obama White House to the Trump White House. The "punch lines" of these memes depend upon an implied or imagined bodily humor: Trump struggling with a nonfunctioning remote control and an inability to fix it because he doesn't know where the batteries are kept at the White House; the surprise at (and possible injury from) an exploding phone; and the humorous image of Trump

Figure 6.1. "Grindr," collected December 29, 2016.

grabbing a (pussy) cat instead of a doorknob. And the variation demonstrates Prankster Biden's insatiability for pranking.

In a variation on this pranking theme, another image suggests that Biden has signed Trump up for Grindr, a phone app that helps gay men find sexual partners, without his consent or knowledge (figure 6.1). This "Grindr" image represents a recurring motif in these memes and suggests a point of correspondence to tricksters and their complex relationship to bodies.[2] Tricksters themselves may be shapeshifters, and their antics correspond to bodylore, as Barre Toelken documented with the multiple levels of meaning in Navajo Coyote tales (1987). Similarly, there are multiple levels of meaning present in this image macro. At the level of plot, Biden as trickster potentially causes problems for Trump by signing him up for an unwanted service. Because that (presumably) unwanted service connects Trump to gay men looking for sex, this image suggests an insatiable craving for sex that is consistent with some trickster figures, as discussed above. Additionally, because this opportunity for (gay) sex is a prank on Trump, it also implies that Trump is homophobic. Given the role Biden played in shifting the Obama administration's position on marriage equality, this image could be read as suggesting the Trump's homophobia is part of what makes him unfit to occupy the Oval Office.[3]

In addition to plotting to make the White House inhospitable to the incoming president Trump, Prankster Biden also schemes to rid the White House of the newly elected president. Figure 6.2, for instance, is one of several Prankster Biden memes that refer to J. K. Rowling's Harry Potter universe. The surface plot suggests that Biden will physically attack Trump, remove his wig (hair), and destroy it with fire (a traditional method for killing certain monsters). The punch line reveals the connection to the Harry Potter franchise by referring to Trump's wig (hair) as a "Horcrux"—a word drawn from insider knowledge of the books' terminology for a talisman that grants extended life to

Figure 6.2. "Horcrux," collected November 19, 2016, from Instagram.

the antagonist Voldemort. Creating a Horcrux involves dark magic, murder, and a spell that endangers the wizard who casts it. Creating seven Horcruxes damages Voldemort's body and soul, leaving him disfigured and bald. Though the term *Horcrux* is unique to Harry Potter, the concept of a villain storing his heart, life power, or soul in an external object to evade death appears in folk narratives from across Europe, Scandinavia, Russia, and elsewhere (Uther 2004, 180–181).[4] Biden's scheme to destroy Trump's (alleged) wig involves crossing (personal) boundaries, violating expected norms, and highlighting Trump's transgressive body, and in doing so Biden as trickster crosses and recrosses conceptual boundaries between the real world and the Harry Potter universe.

Our collection includes several versions of this meme, and the version in figure 6.2 invites multiple possible readings of how Trump's body fails to perform hegemonic masculinity appropriately.[5] By suggesting that Trump's hair is a Horcrux, the meme implies that Trump's source of power has been externalized and relocated to his hair, an iconic part of his body that is a frequent target of negative commentary (Handy 2015; Aggeler 2018;

Lyons 2019). His comb-over hairstyle is often unkempt and unconstrained, moving as a whole rather than as individual strands, suggesting an excessive use of feminine-coded hair product. His hair generates speculation about whether it is real or a toupee (Victor 2018). This excessive focus on Trump's hair compromises his ability to perform masculinity appropriately, emphasizing how inappropriate his body is for the White House.

Further, by suggesting that Trump's hair is a Horcrux, this meme also implies that Trump is an inept villain. The Horcrux is not hidden in a safe place; it is stored on his very body in an easily accessible and—if his hair is actually a wig—easily removable way. This text also suggests who might be part of the folk group making, sharing, and appreciating these memes: nerdy, intellectual people who project their hobbies onto political figures. The dialogue between Biden and Obama suggests that both men are familiar with Rowling's work. Biden references the Horcrux directly, and Obama's reaction (partially covering his face in a gesture suggesting exasperation) makes sense only if he understands the intertextual reference. This use of specific pop culture references suggests populations who might be most interested in and likely to respond to the message or ideas communicated through the meme (see Wiggins 2018, 100–112 for a discussion of imagined audiences of memes). This example is one of many Prankster Biden memes that directly engage with various popular culture properties and franchises, which include films, comic books, and assorted media sequels of *Star Wars*, *Titanic*, *Dr. Strange*, *The Green Lantern*, and the card game Yu-gi-oh.

Tricksters have insatiable appetites for either food or sex, and Biden as trickster is no exception. In one variation of the meme where Obama awards Biden with the Presidential Medal of Freedom, Obama tell Biden that he has something for him. Biden's response is to ask if it is ice cream—a treat that real-life Joe Biden is well known for enjoying. Obama corrects Biden and tells him what he is receiving, and Biden responds with emotional silence (figure 6.3). The ice cream variant suggests the inherent contradictions of Biden's body—both the fictional body of trickster Biden, who has an unlimited capacity to consume ice cream, and the real-world body of Joe Biden, who also loves ice cream.

This image is just one of the many variations of the Prankster Biden meme cycle that references ice cream. There are many other examples depicting Biden as a depressed or petulant child who is forced to wait before enjoying ice cream or who has been denied ice cream. Radin considers "voracious appetite" (1956, 167) one of the primary traits of North American tricksters, also characterizing them as "ageless" (167). Thus, these depictions of Prankster Biden as both immature and voracious reinforce his

Figure 6.3. "Ice Cream," collected January 20, 2017, from a UC Berkeley student.

status as a trickster figure. In contemporary American advertising, movies, and television women are frequently shown consuming excessive amounts of ice cream during times of emotional distress or depression, such as after romantic relationships end. Similarly, this image (and others like it) use hunger and denial of comfort food as a way of expressing deeper feelings of insecurity, depression, and chaos following the unexpected (and for many, unwanted) results of the 2016 election.

The trickster's insatiable appetite for sex is suggested in an image of Obama and Biden speaking on the phone (figure 6.4). In this image Biden brags to Obama about trying to use his big, manly hands to woo soon-to-be–First Lady Melania Trump. Obama responds by asking why Biden is breathing heavily, hinting that there may be inappropriate sexual activity happening on Biden's side of the call. However, the image clarifies Obama's misinterpretation for the audience; Biden is doing repetitions with a hand-held dumbbell, presumably to improve his physical fitness, strength, and—by extension—manliness.

Biden's boast in this meme references both the popular culture belief that Trump has smaller than average hands, and Trump's own oddly sexual defense of his hand size during a March 2016 Republican primary debate.[6] Trickster Biden is staking his reputation on his ability to access an objectively beautiful woman (a former model) who is married to another man (a political rival). Because Joe Biden is married, this meme implicitly suggests that his wife is not enough to satisfy his sexual desires, reinforcing his

Figure 6.4. "Big Hands," collected January 17, 2017.

sexual appetite as insatiable. Overall, this image draws a clear distinction between what kind of body is manly enough to be in the White House, and what body sizes are excluded from participation. As sociologist Michelle Smirnova has argued regarding a Prankster Biden image where Biden replaces White House toiletries with travel-sized ones to accommodate Trump's allegedly tiny hands, these memes often "focused on how [Trump] will 'measure up' in the White House in terms of masculinity and competence" and thus "these critiques unintentionally reaffirm the centrality of essentialist masculinity to presidential ideals" (2018, 6).

In an election that resulted in the loss of the first woman from a major political party to run for president, this image's portrayal of fitness to lead in terms of hegemonic masculinity is troubling. Such acts of braggadocio are rarely about a woman's pleasure and more about the objectification and sexualization of women as a means of proving one's masculinity via sexual prowess.[7]

Hegemonic masculinity in contemporary American society is based upon a number of premises, including homophobia, misogyny, and other forms of domination and hierarchy, such as by social class and ethnicity (Kane 2010). Tom Mould, for example, details the kinds of African American collegiate masculinity performed in step shows, noting that ideals include being physically strong, "cool," "bad," "nasty," and sexually desirable (in a heterosexual context) (2005, 83–87). Masculinity is deployed threateningly in memes created during the 2014 military conflict in Gaza, according to Tsafi Sebba-Elran and Haya Milo, who document the shadowy hidden face and strong arms of "masculine aggression that may represent a threat in the framework of the war's unofficial rules" (2016, 219).[8] Seeing games and wars on a continuum, with masculinity being the main link, makes sense in light of the memes Sebba-Elran and Milo analyze, but we do not perceive the same bids for hegemonic masculinity in the Biden memes.

However, the Prankster Biden meme cycle may also offer users a space for subverting or reinterpreting hegemonic masculinity. For instance, a different reading of the "Big Hands" image is that Biden and Obama are being emotionally intimate with each other over the phone, thereby forestalling the emotional distance between men required of hegemonic masculinity. Similarly, many variations of the meme where Obama awards Biden the Presidential Medal of Freedom suggest emotional intimacy between the men. Alternatively, Biden's occasional violent outbursts might be read more as a result of a chaotic inner child let loose than as an attempt to strategically terrorize an opponent, wielding masculine sexuality as a weapon.

In this light, Biden as trickster is more aligned with aspects of the female tricksters Margaret Mills has studied, particularly with respect to how they operate within the domestic sphere. In analyzing a particular Afghan telling of a humorous folktale, Mills explains that "the woman trickster reactively and opportunistically maneuvers her adversary onto turf that she does control" (2012, 283), which is to say, the domestic sphere. Many of Biden's pranks are about access to and control of domestic amenities, from cable television to the Wi-Fi password, which Biden either withholds from Trump or programs in Spanish or Arabic.

Based on our research, we believe that Biden's mode of trickery is not, for the most part, about enacting hegemonic masculinity over Trump and Pence. His childish pranks usually do not emasculate those men (the hints of cuckoldry in the "Big Hands" image being a notable exception). Instead, Biden as trickster—like his relationship with Obama—seems to offer an alternative masculinity, one based on emotional involvement with other men and caring for the country. This Biden may be immature, but he is neither a bully nor a bigot—in marked contrast to President-elect Trump. In other words, the joke here is not that Biden is hypermasculine; instead, it is that Trump's masculinity is so toxic and fragile that any nonhegemonic interpretation of his sexuality becomes deeply threatening to his sense of well-being.

CULTURAL INVENTORY AND META-COMMENTARY

While tricksters generally resist easy categorization, Biden as a trickster figure serves several important functions. The creation and sharing of pop culture references in the memes afforded users an opportunity to construct group identity, engage in acts of remix and personal expression, and link with others in public discussions on social media (Shifman 2014, 119–122). This was made possible by drawing on a particular cultural inventory of politics and popular culture. As Trevor Blank explains: "Cultural inventories vividly convey the patterns of media consumption and dissemination of traditional knowledge in contemporary vernacular discourse" and "are comprised of images that symbolically encapsulate an idea or an event; these images are drawn from individuals' interactions with mass-mediated information and visual data" (2016, 152). The Prankster Biden meme cycle shows obnoxious but not ultimately pernicious ways of resisting Trump's vision for America. While this meme cycle might offer more comfort than call to action, Prankster Biden hints at a lesson of resilience, joy in simple things, and judiciously selecting opportunities for resistance. As Haase notes of the use of fairy tales since the 2016 US election: "The media's post-election reflections on political humor and satire reaffirm their potential as weapons of resistance" (2018, 307).

One important function of joke cycles also applies to this meme cycle—as Blank notes regarding the Penn State sexual abuse scandal, a joke cycle serves as meta-commentary on current events: "Parodic jokes about the Sandusky saga reflect popular knowledge about the case and function as a meta-commentary on the scandal, how it has been reported, and the corpus of humor that has framed the story" (2016, 165). In the instance of the Biden meme cycle, the people making and sharing the memes from November 2016 and into 2017 reflected on contemporary political events—including the outcome of the election, the transition to a new administration, and shifts in American domestic and foreign policy—as well as imagined tie-ins with popular culture. Those sharing these texts on social media demonstrated their political and pop culture knowledge by electing to pass along certain texts over others, in an act that delivered not only commentary but also meta-commentary. The Prankster Biden meme cycle suggests that Joe Biden retains access to power even after he is no longer in power. This comes not only from his decades as a senator, his status as a presidential candidate, and his association with Obama's legacy but also because power in America is meant to be crowdsourced—it comes from the people. Even if, sometimes, it comes at the expense of others, such as those who have accused Joe Biden of inappropriate physical contact, including touching and kissing. Like his trickster doppelgänger in the meme cycle, Biden seems to resist significant consequences for his boundary-transgressing actions.

Prankster Joe Biden memes offered a sustained critique of the incoming Trump presidency and allowed important meta-commentary to be made and shared. The makers and sharers of the memes on social media used popular culture references to create an imagined parasocial link with Biden based on shared group identity. The question of whether our leaders are like us, and on which grounds it is acceptable to critique them, remains a pressing one in times of political turmoil, with questions of free speech frequently in the air. The Biden memes, with their trickster protagonist, pop culture motifs, and critique of the president's body, make a relevant statement about the relationship of everyday citizens and the American government. By taking a folkloristic approach to social media, our analysis arrives at a vision of Donald Trump performing both hegemonic masculinity and villainy—but badly—while Biden as culture hero remains poised to vanquish the threat and save the average American from the bumbling body occupying the White House.

ACKNOWLEDGMENTS

The authors wish to thank Trevor J. Blank and Andrew Peck for their editorial guidance and engagement. Additionally, Jeana thanks her community of friends and colleagues (both online and offline) who showed immense support and enthusiasm for this project. Linda thanks the students in her American Folklore classes in 2016, 2017, and 2018 who shared, discussed, and debated these and other post-election digital folklore examples.

NOTES

1. More specifically, the images discussed in this chapter represent a subgenre of internet memes known as image macros (digital photos with text—usually in the form of a caption or quotation—superimposed on them). For the purpose of clarity, we have chosen to draw on the popular emic term for these artifacts and refer to the Biden images studied here as a meme cycle. For discussions of the use of *meme* as inspired by Richard Dawkins's concept of memetics (as well as how internet memes might depart from Dawkins's original formulation), see Foote 2007; Shifman 2014; Milner 2016; Wiggins 2018; and Andrew Peck's chapter 4 in this volume.

2. Though Michelle Smirnova's analysis of the Prankster Biden memes alongside other political cartoons and media from 2016 did not focus on trickster figures, she reached a similar conclusion about the importance of bodies in the overall meanings of the over 200 texts she analyzed: "This analysis revealed recurrent themes of the body, virility, (sexual)

dominance, control, gender conformity, heteronormativity, and whiteness within political cartoons, memes, and tweets that critiqued the two frontrunners, Hillary Clinton and Donald Trump" (2018, 13).

3. Biden publicly announced his support for same-sex marriage during a May 6, 2012, appearance on *Meet the Press*. This put pressure on President Barack Obama to declare support for marriage equality rather than civil unions, which he did on May 9, 2012 (Daly 2012).

4. This motif is integral to tale type ATU 302, "The Ogre's (Devil's) Heart in the Egg." Uther identifies several types of objects used to store the ogre or devil's soul, including animals (motif E710.1), eggs (E711.1), boxes (E712.4), and swords (E711.10) (2004, 180). Stith Thompson identifies dozens of variations of the "External soul" motif (E710), including multiple separable souls (E718) (1955, 2:493–496).

5. Other variants of the "Horcrux" Prankster Biden meme feature alternate images of Biden and Obama, while the text includes Biden speculating whether Trump's hair is a Horcrux, and Obama forbidding Biden to ask Trump if his hair is a Horcrux.

6. At a campaign event in Salem, Virginia, on February 29, 2016, Florida senator and candidate for the Republican presidential nomination Marco Rubio joked about the size of Donald Trump's "little hands" in retaliation for Trump's pejorative moniker "Little Marco." Though Rubio alluded to the folk idea that there is a relationship between the size of a man's hands and of his penis, he shifted the punch line to a comment about trustworthiness. ("And you know what they say about men with small hands? You can't trust them.") Trump responded to this insult during the FOX News Republication presidential debate on March 3, 2016, stating directly what Rubio had left unsaid: "[H]e referred to my hands, saying if they're small, something else must be small. I guarantee you there's no problem. I guarantee it."

7. It is also ironic that this text suggests the possibility of cuckolding, given the resurgence of "cuck" as an insult in alt-right circles, to which Trump's presidency seems to have given greater license to engage in bigoted discourse in public spaces.

8. The association of threatening masculinity with war is not new; as Dundes (1978) argued in his psychoanalytic consideration of American football, the sport is a form of ritual male combat in which sexual threats are only thinly disguised.

REFERENCES

Aggeler, Madeleine. 2018. "We Finally Know the Secret to Donald Trump's Hair." *The Cut*, January 4, 2018. https://www.thecut.com/2018/01/we-finally-know-the-secret-to-donald-trumps-hair.html.

Babcock-Abrahams, Barbara. 1975. "'A Tolerated Margin of Mess': The Trickster and His Tales Reconsidered." *Journal of the Folklore Institute* 11 (3): 147–186.

Biddle, Sam. 2015. "Joe Biden, We Need to Talk about the Way You Touch Women." *Gawker*, February 19, 2015. https://gawker.com/joe-biden-we-need-to-talk-about-the-way-you-touch-wome-1686648038.

Blank, Trevor J. 2013. *The Last Laugh: Folk Humor, Celebrity Culture, and Mass-Mediated Disasters in the Digital Age*. Madison: University of Wisconsin Press.

Blank, Trevor J. 2016. "Giving the 'Big Ten' a Whole New Meaning: Tasteless Humor and the Response to the Penn State Sexual Abuse Scandal." In *The Folkloresque: Reframing Folklore in a Popular Culture World*, edited by Michael Dylan Foster and Jeffrey A. Tolbert, 179–204. Logan: Utah State University Press.

Carroll, Michael P. 1984. "The Trickster as Selfish-Buffoon and Culture Hero." *Ethos* 12 (2): 105–131.
Daly, Corbett. 2012. "Obama: Biden Forced Hand on Same-Sex Marriage, but 'All's Well.'" *CBS News*, May 10, 2012. https://www.cbsnews.com/news/obama-biden-forced-hand-on-same-sex-marriage-but-alls-well/.
Dundes, Alan. 1978. "Into the Endzone for a Touchdown: A Psychoanalytic Consideration of American Football." *Western Folklore* 37 (2): 75–88.
Dundes, Alan. 1980. "Text, Texture, and Context." In *Interpreting Folklore*, 20–32. Bloomington: Indiana University Press.
Dundes, Alan, and Carl R. Pagter. 1978. *Work Hard and You Shall Be Rewarded: Urban Folklore from the Paperwork Empire*. Bloomington: Indiana University Press.
Foote, Monica. 2007. "Userpicks: Cyber Folk Art in the Early 21st Century." *Folklore Forum* 37 (1): 27–38.
Haase, Donald. 2018. "No Laughing Matter: Fairy Tales and the 2016 US Presidential Election." In *Terra Ridens—Terra Narrans: Festschrift zum 65. Geburtstag von Ulrich Marzolph*, edited by Regina Bendix and Dorothy Noyes, 282–313. Dortmund: Verlag für Orientkunde.
Handy, Bruce. 2015. "An Illustrated History of Donald Trump's Hair. Warning! Don't Read Before Lunch!" *Vanity Fair*, September 8, 2015. https://www.vanityfair.com/news/photos/2015/09/an-illustrated-history-of-donald-trumps-hair.
Holter, Lauren. 2015. "Joe Biden's *Parks and Recreation* Cameos Will Seriously Psyche You Up for His *Late Show* Appearance." *Bustle*, September 10, 2015. https://www.bustle.com/articles/109678-joe-bidens-parks-and-recreation-cameos-will-seriously-psych-you-up-for-his-late-show-appearance.
Hyde, Lewis. 1998. *Trickster Makes This World: Mischief, Myth, and Art*. New York: Farrar, Straus, and Giroux.
Hynes, William J., and William G. Doty. 1993. "Historical Overview of Theoretical Issues: The Problem of the Trickster." In *Mythical Trickster Figures: Contours, Contexts, and Criticisms*, edited by William J. Hynes and William G. Doty, 13–32. Tuscaloosa: University of Alabama Press.
Jensen, Erin. 2016. "The Internet Is Here for Joe Biden's Cameo on *Law & Order: SVU*." *USA Today*, September 29, 2016. https://www.usatoday.com/story/life/entertainthis/2016/09/29/joe-biden-law--order-svu-cameo/91261270/.
Kane, Emily W. 2010. "'No Way My Boys Are Going to Be Like That!' Parents' Responses to Children's Gender Nonconformity." In *Men's Lives*, edited by Michael S. Kimmel and Michael A. Messner, 52–69. New York: Allyn and Bacon.
Kerényi, Karl. 1969. "The Trickster in Relation to Greek Mythology." In *The Trickster: A Study in American Indian Mythology*, edited by Paul Radin, 173–191. New York: Greenwood.
Law & Order: Special Victims Unit. "Making a Rapist." Season 18, episode 2. Directed by Michael Pressman. Written by Kevin Fox. NBC, September 28, 2016.
Lyons, Kate. 2019. "Comb Over? Donald Trump Sports New Hairstyle After Golf Trip." *Guardian*, June 3, 2019. https://www.theguardian.com/us-news/2019/jun/03/donald-trump-sports-new-hairstyle-after-golf-trip.
Mills, Margaret A. 2001. "The Gender of the Trick: Female Tricksters and Male Narrators." *Asian Folklore Studies* 60 (2): 237–258.
Mills, Margaret A. 2012. "Destroying Patriarchy to Save It: Safdar Tawakkoli's Afghan Boxwoman." In *Transgressive Tales: Queering the Grimms*, edited by Kay Turner and Pauline Greenhill, 277–293. Detroit: Wayne State University Press.
Mills, Margaret A. 2013. "Trickster between Myth and Tale." In *Folklore: New Challenges; The Proceedings of the International Folklore Conference, Dhaka, Bangladesh, 13–15 April*

2013, edited by Firoze Mahmud and Shahida Khatun, 105–114. Dhaka, Bangladesh: Folklore Museum and Archive Division, Bangla Academy.

Milner, Ryan M. 2016. *The World Made Meme: Public Conversations and Participatory Media*. Cambridge, MA: MIT Press.

Mould, Tom. 2005. "'Running the Yard': The Negotiation of Masculinities in African American Stepping." In *Manly Traditions: The Folk Roots of American Masculinities*, edited by Simon J. Bronner, 77–115. Bloomington: Indiana University Press.

"Parks and Recreation." *IMDb*. Accessed June 6, 2018. https://www.imdb.com/title/tt1266020/.

Petri, Alexandra. 2015. "What Are We Going to Do about Creepy Uncle Joe Biden?" *Washington Post*, February 15, 2015. https://www.washingtonpost.com/blogs/compost/wp/2015/02/18/what-are-we-going-to-do-about-creepy-uncle-joe-biden/.

Radin, Paul. 1956. *The Trickster: A Study in American Indian Mythology*. New York: Shocken Books.

Roberts, John. 1990. *From Trickster to Bad Man: The Black Folk Hero in Slavery and Freedom*. Philadelphia: University of Pennsylvania Press.

Ryan, Erin Gloria. 2017. "Dear Lord Joe Biden Would Be a Terrible Candidate for These Times." *Daily Beast*, November 15, 2017. https://www.thedailybeast.com/dear-lord-would-joe-biden-be-a-terrible-candidate-for-these-times.

Sebba-Elran, Tsafi, and Haya Milo. 2016. "The Struggle over Locality in Israeli Humoristic Memes from the 2014 Military Conflict in Gaza." *Narrative Culture* 3 (2): 206–230.

Shifman, Limor. 2014. *Memes in Digital Culture*. Cambridge, MA: MIT Press.

Smirnova, Michelle. 2018. "Small Hands, Nasty Women, and Bad Hombres: Hegemonic Masculinity and Humor in the 2016 Presidential Election." *Socius: Sociological Research for a Dynamic World* 4: 1–16.

Thompson, Stith. 1955. *Motifx-Index of Folk-Literature: A Classification of Narrative Elements in Folktales, Ballads, Myths, Fables, Mediaeval Romances, Exempla, Fabliaux, Jest-Books, and Local Legends*. Bloomington: Indiana University Press.

Toelken, Barre. 1987. "Life and Death in the Navajo Coyote Tales." In *Recovering the Word: Essays on Native American Literature*, edited by Arnold Krupat and Brian Swann, 388–401. Berkeley: University of California Press.

Turner, Victor. 1969. *The Ritual Process: Structure and Anti-structure*. New York: Schocken Books.

Uther, Hans-Jörg. 2004. *The Types of International Folktales: A Classification and Bibliography*. Helsinki: Academia Scientiarum Fennica.

Victor, Daniel. 2018. "Trump on His Hair: 'I Try Like Hell to Hide That Bald Spot, Folks.'" *New York Times*, February 23, 2018. https://www.nytimes.com/2018/02/23/us/politics/trump-hair-bald.html.

Wiggins, Bradley E. 2018. *The Discursive Power of Memes in Digital Culture: Ideology, Semiotics, and Intertextuality*. New York: Routledge.

7

Dear David
Affect and Belief in Twitter Horror

Kristiana Willsey

IN AUGUST 2017, WEB CARTOONIST Adam Ellis began telling a ghost story on Twitter, detailing his haunting experiences with a dead child he called "Dear David." Over the next few months, relying on a combination of text, photographs, artist's renderings, and video and audio clips, Ellis updated an ever-growing audience on his encounters with the supernatural. At the height of the story's popularity, each new post generated thousands of likes and retweets and was reported and debated by various news outlets and popular websites. Between August and the following July, Ellis's follower count grew from 73,000 to 1.02 million. The record of feedback on a performance unfolding over months permits a rare granular analysis of a community of belief.

This chapter examines the viral life of a ghost story through the emotional engagement of its audience: how does the audience response to Dear David scaffold the mediated performance, and what is the relationship between affect and belief? Like affect, belief is not located in individual bodies or passed off like a static object but emerges only within social relationships—belief in fact creates those social relationships. Applying the model of affect theory to the study of belief, we can see the circulation of affect and belief operating separately, as overlapping but not synonymous online communities. This slippage between emotional engagement and belief reflects the tension between online texts as folkloric (collaboratively created, open-ended, and "free") and commercial (single-authored, closed, copyrighted).[1] Memorates and legends are believed or believable, while commercial supernatural fiction is not, but online these frameworks overlap, so whoever has the power to determine a story's genre dictates

DOI: 10.7330/9781646420599.c007

the terms of belief. Dear David is a memorate, a supernatural personal experience narrative, that can't get free of its originator and become a more abstract, depersonalized legend (see Mullen 1971) because our social media platforms are always already commodified.

GHOST IN THE MACHINE

Ellis begins his story with this blunt and arresting narrative abstract: "So, my apartment is currently being haunted by the ghost of a dead child and he's trying to kill me" (figure 7.1). He meets his ghost—a small boy with an oversized, misshapen head—in eerie dreams he has while experiencing sleep paralysis (see Hufford 1982). In a pithy combination of classic folk narrative functions and motifs (three-part structure, interdiction and violation, power of names, contact at liminal time periods), he dreams that the ghost will appear at midnight and, if Ellis knows his name, he can ask David questions, but only two. Inevitably, in the final dream Ellis forgets and violates the interdiction, asking David not just where and how he died, but who killed him. He awakes terrified and begins to experience strange events in his apartment: odd behavior from his cats, strange noises and shadows, objects moving on their own, uncanny coincidences. The story unfolds sporadically, in long, near-daily Twitter threads between August 7 and August 17, then every few days through September, then every few weeks from October through January, finally ending on something of a cliffhanger in early February 2018. In July 2018, Ellis announced a movie was in the works from Buzzfeed Studios and the production company behind the 2017 *It* remake (Verhoeven 2018). Ellis's audience generally took this announcement as confirmation that Dear David was a work of fiction, though Ellis maintains everything he posted is true.[2]

Journalists and Ellis's Twitter followers have treated Dear David as a work of creepypasta: "an emergent genre of Internet folklore that ... draws on the disturbing, monstrous, strange, grotesque, and/or unknown while invoking the thematic and structural qualities of legendary narratives" (Blank and McNeill 2018, 6). Appropriately for a web-born genre, creepypasta straddles the line between sincere scares and ironic detachment—explicitly composed as fiction yet also adopting the told-for-true stance of legends. In a 2013 article for *Aeon* magazine, Will Wiles points out that creepypasta texts aim for authenticity by adopting the informal, conversational tone of their medium: "Since these stories are shared on forums, why not use the direct and unliterary vernacular of the everyuser to tell your story, putting it as an anecdote?" The most viral monsters are the most versatile, and

Figure 7.1.

creepypasta leans into the open-ended, crowdsourced nature of storytelling for some of its most famous creations. As Andrew Peck writes of the Slender Man, "The ability of users to tap into the ideas of others while also supplying their own helped inspire the collaborative culture that arose surrounding the Slender Man . . . In effect, the Slender Man's popularity derives from being seen as a shared public resource" (2015, 344).

Like many creepypasta, Dear David does not just rely on social media platforms to tell the story but also meta-discursively comments on the affordances and vulnerabilities of changing technology—the medium is the message (McLuhan 1964). In a skeptical essay on the *Awl*, Rick Paulas calls the story "too tidy" for its convenient escalation, not just of scares but of technology: "Ellis is quickly going through every potential storytelling medium available to use on Twitter, and he's doing it in the *right storytelling order*" (2017). The majority of David's haunting interfaces with technology in some way: mysterious electronic humming, crank phone calls, the backlight on Ellis's TV flickering and burning out. One of the earliest updates, on August 9, involves a series of photographs Ellis takes of his well-lit hallway that mysteriously appear pitch black when developed. Ellis exhaustively attempts to demonstrate the ghostly nature of these photographs by comparing them to undeveloped film and apparently normal photos taken with his phone.

Old media is more secure than new media, it would seem, since David seems to have an allergy to the traditional film but ultimately infiltrates the mediated story itself. One of the last Dear David updates before the announcement of the film came via Ellis's Instagram: a brunch selfie he claimed had been an ordinary image on his cell phone, but had uploaded with a digital glitch: an apparently corrupted file that appeared to merge Ellis's image with an image of David, giving Ellis himself a distended, dented head (figure 7.2).

Ellis's Instagram followers interpreted this image as a confirmation of a fan theory that Ellis was now possessed and that some of his online activity was coming from David himself (Peters 2018). For highly invested audience members following Ellis across multiple social media platforms, this eerie glitch played out in real time, with followers seemingly aware of it even before Ellis himself. This put them in the exciting position of completing or resolving the story, furiously commenting or tweeting at Ellis to warn him of his supernatural stalker.

Ghosts are virally transmitted—you catch them through stories. Wiles (2013) argues that creepypasta as a form of horror literature gives shape to our technological anxieties: fears of corrupted data, spyware, and unstable identities, the uncanny blurring of offline selves and our digital doppel-

Figure 7.2. A "glitched" image Ellis uploaded to Instagram.

gängers: "What if something dark is able to breach that all-important final firewall, the gap between the central processing unit and the person sitting at the keyboard? What if it already has?" In physically co-present storytelling, the joint experience of fear feeds into the folk belief "Speak of the devil and he'll appear." Devils, monsters, and bad luck are listening, and the shared somatic state of communal storytelling acts as a summoning ritual. The internet, which distributes the experience of collaborative, communal storytelling across space and time, allows for networked monsters that can find you wherever your phone can.

COLLABORATIVE STORYTELLING ON TWITTER

Social media reshapes the possibilities for communication and creates new spaces for folklore to thrive. As Anthony Bak Buccitelli notes, "Folklorists must stop thinking of digital technologies as simply media that record or transmit offline folklore. Instead, we must think of them as places of performance" (2012, 73). The lively public chat room of Twitter is a natural venue for storytelling, allowing users to thread individual tweets into extended performances that can (like offline storytelling) be formal and highly structured narratives or energetic, off-the-cuff rants. Since audiences can enter the story at any point in its performance, the teller need not fear losing her claim to the conversational floor by deliberating too long between tweets, and the medium sidesteps the offline problem of needing to repeat or summarize the story thus far for interested latecomers. Storytelling on Twitter is collaborative and multi-modal, responding to and incorporating audience responses and relying on a variety of media.

Stories travel because they are open-ended—finishing or fleshing out a story with our own experiences and interpretations gives us a stake in it and a feeling of ownership over it as co-authors. Ellis's tweets include embedded photographs, sketches, and video and audio clips; his followers respond by interpreting the images, using photo-editing tools to highlight strange faces or shadowy figures, and posting time links for videos in the comments to call attention to moments that Ellis seems to miss. Especially in the early stages of the story, Ellis actively invites this collaboration and critique and often incorporates it back into the main canonical thread. "Folks have been urging me to get some sage, so I did," Ellis posts on August 14 with accompanying photographs, affirming the companionable dialogue between himself and his readers. On August 12 he posts a selfie in his apartment, then retweets a comment that zoomed in on a blurry shadow that might be a face, with the caption "I . . . have no explanation for this." Alternatively, some visual elements of the haunting that are caught and called out by the audience never make it into the explicit narrative. For example, a video uploaded on September 5 shows Ellis's cat jumping over empty air. Ellis remarks only on the cat's strange behavior. He appears not to notice that a green jar on a nearby table visibly slides several inches sideways—he has the restraint to let the audience catch this uncanny escalation.[3]

Belief is not located in individual texts or audience members but in the social context of telling; legends are an implicitly more contested and collaborative genre than other forms of oral narrative. Legends are opportunities to hammer out the contours and nuances of belief itself; "the legend is more controversial than other genres, and a true legend-telling event is not therefore the solo performance . . . It is a dispute, a dialectic duel of ideas, principles, beliefs, and passions" (Dégh and Vázsonyi 1978, 253). Contemporary legends do not need to be believed to be retold; they can be spread by skeptics seeking to reassure themselves of their rational convictions, retold as evidence of fraud or to mock the credulous (Dégh and Vázsonyi 1973; Brunvand 2012; Willsey 2016). Open-ended storytelling leaves the audience to draw its own conclusions, creating space in the margins (or the comments) for belief to be debated.

By building participation and co-construction into the narrative, Ellis gives the work of instilling belief to his audience; he doesn't need to convince his readers if they are busy convincing one another. When Ellis posts the first clear images of David, a series of "pitch black photos" he finds on his phone, he tells readers, "It's better to just show you. Turn up your brightness, because they're pretty dark." Since it would be simple for Ellis to manipulate the light levels of the photos himself, this do-it-yourself touch adds to the engagement and consequent investment his followers have in the ongoing narrative. Posts with enigmatic images generate significantly more engagement and particularly discussion. As Simon Bronner observes, "When images are broadcast from peer to peer in a play frame, the Internet becomes folklorized through the discourse of belief involved. The perceptions that every picture tells a story and that it attracts unseen viewers only add to the Internet's folkloric dimension" (2009, 30).

Belief and disbelief can exist simultaneously because they are both forms of social knowledge; the question isn't whether or not something is real but when is it real and for whom. The intersubjective nature of shared narrative breaks down the distinction between author and audience. "Live" storytelling requires audiences to imagine themselves as tellers in order to anticipate the next step of the story, just as it requires storytellers to imagine their audience in order to decide what will hold its attention. Online, even more so than in in-person communication, users must invent their interlocutors. The storyteller shudders at the story he is artfully constructing, and the audience members who work out the plot twist ahead of the reveal enjoy the superiority of the trickster. Playing both parts allows for the potential of engaging with the story from different positionalities, even slipping between them at our pleasure or as social situations require. To possess the story is to be possessed by it—if you believe a ghost story, it's because you have some control over it, because you have the power to personalize or interpret the tale on your terms.

BUILDING AUDIENCES THROUGH AFFECTIVE FEEDBACK

Readers contribute to the ongoing narrative in two ways: by directly offering advice and interpretations that feed into the emerging plot, and by building suspense through their virtual emotional responses. The psychologist Silvan Tomkins, credited as the originator of affect theory, describes the way humans fall into step with one another's emotional states as "affective resonance" or "contagion"—gestures, expressions, and tone of voice are catching, we connect with one another through unconscious imitation (1962; see also Gibbs 2001; Young 2011). Affect theorist Sara Ahmed summarizes centuries of scholarship on emotion as, in simple terms, disputes over the primacy of sensation or cognition, body or mind (2013). What comes first, the somatic experience of fear or the social relations that inform the fear? Ahmed sets aside this debate to define affect as process rather than product, fluid and relational rather than biologically bounded. It is a form of communication that is located not in individual bodies but in networks. She argues, "Emotions are not simply something 'I' or 'we' have. Rather, it is through emotions, or how we respond to objects and others, that surfaces or boundaries are made" (11). Communities are created and reinforced by shared emotions—like the feelings of horror and fear experienced while reading ghost stories on Twitter.

Through the networked sociality of Twitter, commitment to the narrative (which is not synonymous with belief) builds through the companionable thrill of virtually performing fear, uncertainty, and suspense. "Networked" affect extends beyond our real-life family and friend groups; the imitative processes that lead us to emotionally align with members of a group do not require co-presence. Recent high-profile discussions of affective or emotional contagion have focused on the commercial and political potential of manipulating moods on Facebook and Twitter (Kramer et al. 2014; Ferrara and Yang 2015). After all, texts and images are as good or better than oral performance at engaging audience emotions. As media theorist James Ash observes, "Affects do not simply germinate at a point of encounter between two bodies but are intimately tied to the sensations, which travel via human, technical, and nonhuman means" (2015, 131). Reaction GIFs function as quotable affect, lifting moments of heightened, heavily marked feeling from popular culture and allowing them to stand in for the gestures, postures, and facial expressions lost through the disembodiment of text-based storytelling (see Newman 2017; Huber 2015). If your interlocutor cannot see your face or hear your voice, you can convey your emotional state via Raven Simone's wide-eyed, frantic gum chewing (figure 7.3, top middle), or Jesse Ferguson's panicked flailing (figure 7.3, bottom left).[4]

Tonally, Ellis's tweets tend to be emotionally understated, anticipating and undercutting skepticism with a reasoned explanation and a compellingly

Figure 7.3. A sampling of GIF comment responses to a ghostly image Ellis posts, captured August 14, 2017.

ambiguous photograph or video. He reports being afraid but does not emote much himself, favoring short, declarative sentences over exclamation points, stream-of-consciousness realism, or literary language.[5] Instead, he lets his followers model the appropriate emotional response—capitalized strings of vowels to indicate screams of horror, wide-eyed or crying emoji, animated GIFs quoting scenes of terror or revulsion. YouTube vloggers convert the Twitter thread to the medium of oral storytelling, dramatically reading the tweets aloud while facing the camera and modeling the appropriate emotional response (figure 7.4).

Particularly in the beginning, Ellis does not so much tell as tease—"This could be nothing," he repeats, as he posts enigmatic photos and videos for the consumption and interrogation of his growing fan base. "There could be a totally logical explanation for it," he says of the bruises he finds on his arm after a dream of David dragging him through an abandoned warehouse. "Tell me this doesn't look like him," he challenges his readers, posting a photograph of a shadowy figure that resembles later images he

Figure 7.4. A screengrab of popular YouTube gamer Alia Shelesh/"SSSniperWolf" reading and reacting to Dear David, captured July 18, 2018.

captures of David (figure 7.5). The story thrives via this slightly detached approach, because readers eagerly fill in the gaps, providing the requisite virtual shudders and screams.

BELIEF ON THE MARKET

To frame the story as believable and true, it has to be open-ended and debatable—yet to control and eventually market the story Ellis also has to be the sole arbiter of its ending and meaning. Folklore online must reconcile the tension between the audience involvement that makes a story marketable and the individual authorship that markets require. Though the early virality of the ghost story benefited from a high degree of audience involvement, as the story develops and the narrative arc solidifies, Dear David necessarily becomes less open to new spins or digressions. Ellis is no longer engaging with the audience so much as negotiating with it, struggling to enforce a particular interpretation without appearing to have authorial knowledge. On December 12 he writes, "People tweet at me at lot that

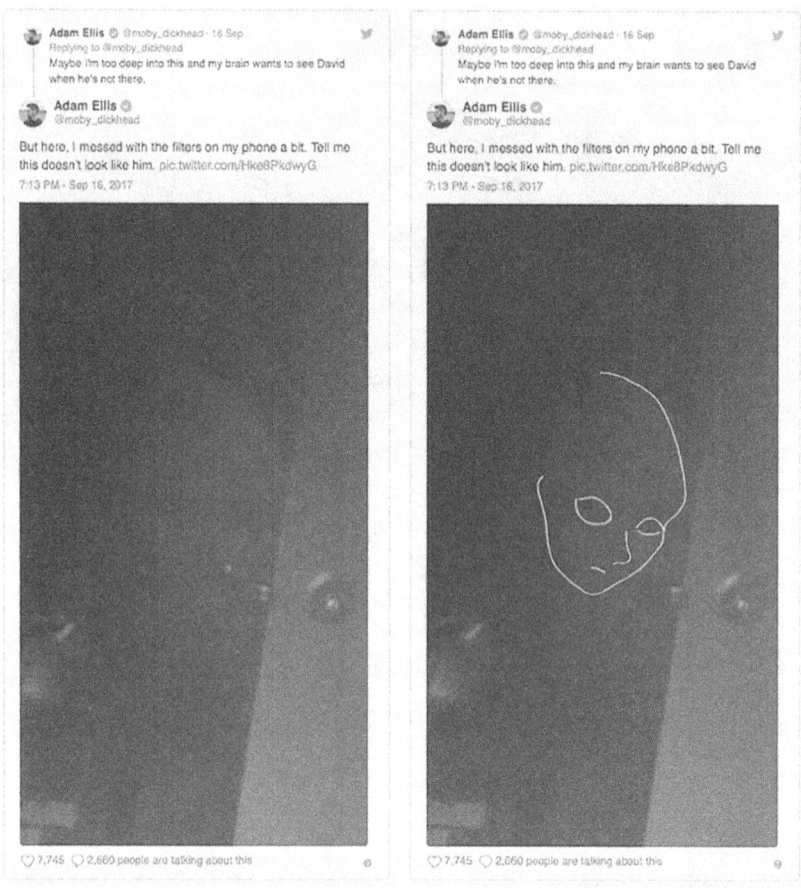

Figure 7.5. Photo of a ghostly shadow posted on social media by Ellis on August 14, 2017 (*left*); author's illustration of ghostly figure's location in image (*right*).

he might just need help, but I'm certain that's not the case. Every time he shows up I feel a palpable sense of malice." Using an app that takes photos automatically on a timer, Ellis captures seven photos of David coming progressively closer to the camera until he appears to be standing directly in front of it. For many readers these images, clearer and more detailed and impossible to mistake for anything other than a child or a doll, tipped the scales on the side of "fake."

A headline of the British tabloid the *Sun* read: "Is This Proof 'Dear David' is Fake? Fans of Bloke Who's Shared Videos of the 'Ghost' in His Home Are Convinced the Latest Clip Went Too Far" (Allen 2017). The website Elite Daily asks, "Does David look fake AF?" (Rosenberg 2017).

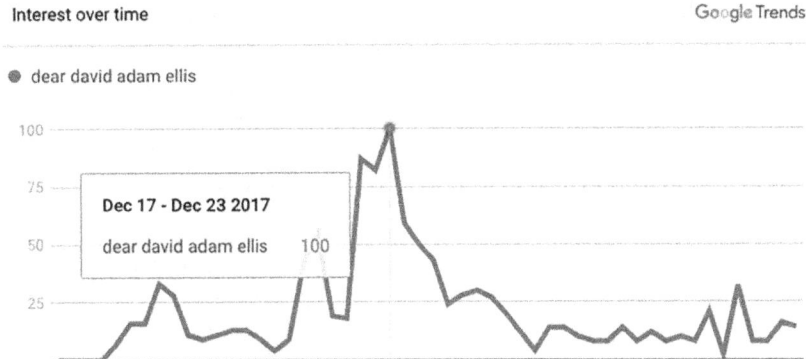

Figure 7.6. Popularity of "dear david adam ellis" between July 2017 and July 2018, captured July 8, 2018, via Google Trends.

Numerous comments on the Twitter images ask why a ghost is casting a shadow. Followers who were overcome with terror at a smudge that might be a face rolled their eyes at a blond manikin in a striped shirt. Earlier tweets in the story require more interpretative work, entrusting readers with higher orders of meaning making. The more Ellis fleshes out his experience with realistic imagery, the more his audience pulls back.

Belief is inherently disputed, and disputes are what drive web traffic. As seen in figure 7.6, Dear David was never more frequently discussed than immediately after the more obvious images were posted. Yet after this no new updates (tiny footsteps in the snow outside his window in January, then an image of David falling onto—or into—Ellis's body from above, the glitching Instagram story, the film announcement) generated as much discussion as anything had before. Like a rush of oxygen to a fire, the story leapt up, then dimmed. Evidence suffocates belief, which requires gray areas for interpretive work.

FOLK CULTURE, CORPORATE MEDIA PLATFORMS

The circulation of shared affect creates communities of feeling but not necessarily communities of belief. Fear doesn't require belief; even a dubious reader may greet new installments of the unfolding narrative with clammy hands or quickened heartbeat.[6] Rather, belief acts to *frame* and *interpret* affect; changing the genre changes readers' relationship to that fear. When Ellis announces the film adaptation of Dear David with New Line Cinema, it recontextualizes his audience's affective experience—the horror remains, but the frame changes. As Ahmed writes, "Emotions in their very intensity involve miscommunication, such that even when we feel we have the same feeling, we don't necessarily have the same relationship to the feeling" (2013, 10). Some followers feel angry or betrayed, believing that they have been made to look foolish, whereas others are happy to enjoy their fear, congratulating Ellis on his storytelling skills. Those who reframe the narrative as fiction engage it with more ironic detachment. When, on February 13, Ellis posts "please dont worry about me. I'm ok and everything will be like it was before :)" a popular reply is "david you aren't even old enough to use twitter please consult the terms of service." Since the tweet comes after the glitching Instagram post, followers interpret Ellis's post (syntactically different from Ellis's usual style and posted around midnight, with an uncharacteristic emoticon) as coming from David himself, digitally "possessing" Ellis. With the narrative arc now decided, followers are disconnected from the earlier co-performance and instead perform belief humorously.

Though Ellis maintains the authenticity of his haunting experience, for many followers the film announcement marked a shift from a folkloric narrative (collaborative, believable, natural/unscripted) to a commercial narrative (individually owned, explicitly fictional, artfully composed).[7] Follower response was mixed—genuine excitement about the adaptation tempered with cynicism about the inevitable commodification of storytelling on social media. The top comment on the film announcement tweet is "Ohhhh everything was marketing." This is the particular paradox of social media as sites of folk performance—no matter how much they might operate like oral culture offline, communication is taking place on corporate platforms like Facebook, Twitter, and Gchat that monitor and monetize our emotions. Though the story is unquestionably Ellis's to sell, the commercial potential of the narrative is a direct result of the audience's emotional investment: "The generation of affect becomes a measure of market effectivity. To generate affective responses is to generate the churn that makes markets function" (Jarrett 2015, 214). If the story was a hoax or a stunt, the emotional score provided by followers has added significant value that those followers will never profit from themselves. If the story is true, the story as corporate property still does not belong to them, and they must now buy a ticket to see the ending in theaters.

The film announcement gave many readers the impression there is a definitive ending that Ellis is waiting to reveal, one that he is withholding from his audience as a form of narrative control. As one follower says, "I get he doesn't want to let on when the film's not even out yet. Wait for that fat check to roll in first! ;D." But Dear David's final enigmatic posts, which imply Ellis is now possessed by David, are typical of ghost stories in oral tradition. Folklorist Bill Ellis says a legend is the kind of story that "leaves itself suspended, relying for closure on each individual's response" (2001, 60). Traditional ghost stories like "The Golden Arm," "The Stolen Liver," and other variants of ATU 366 play with the connection between fear and belief by incorporating a "catch" element—the story does not wind down with a coda that restates the moral, like personal narratives do, nor it is not bracketed off with a closing formula like "and they all lived happily ever after," as in fairy tales. Instead, the story ends with a pivot to theater, by grabbing and startling the listener, shouting, or (as is often the case in camp stories) by a third party leaping out in disguise—a playful intrusion of the taleworld into the storyrealm (Young 2006). The story ends on a peak feeling and lacks formal closure, which encourages both the story and the ghost to "follow you home," like the holographic hitchhikers of Disney's Haunted Mansion. But audiences expect more closure and resolution from fiction than they do from life, and the repeated requests for the "ending" to Dear David reflect how the end of belief reframes generic expectations.

It is the folkloric (collaboratively created, open-ended, and "free") quality of the web that makes a story believable, and paradoxically also what must be discarded for a story to be commercially viable (single-authored, closed, copyrighted). Because folk culture online necessarily takes place on commercial media platforms like Facebook and Twitter, the boundary between what is "told for true" and what is "told to sell" is not well defined. Is Dear David meant to represent one individual's experience or to be open-source creepypasta? Ellis treads a difficult line, orchestrating a dialogic and collaborative viral ghost story that thrives on uncertainty, while still holding the reins on what eventually becomes a commercial project. As the narrative arc is locked down and controlled, the relationship between Ellis and his followers changes: they move from being collaborators, generating a market, to spectators, the target market themselves. Social media creates new contexts for the performance of folk narratives, but the commodification of our digital commons also shapes the possibilities for stories we tell there.

NOTES

1. I do not mean that folk culture necessarily operates outside of market economies, only that it is not a good fit for contemporary copyright laws (see Hafstein 2004).

2. According to the *Wrap*, Ellis claims, "I've never been interested in convincing anyone that ghosts are real—I just wanted to tell my story. If it was all fiction, I probably would've

updated more than once every couple weeks." Essentially, his argument is that the emotional understatement and erratic pacing of his narrative are evidence of its authenticity, rather than part of a deliberate production of authenticity.

3. Since the rocking chair where Ellis first sees David is green, many followers seize on the color as particularly significant or potentially haunted.

4. Ash sees the endlessly renewable appeal of the GIF as a counterargument to the idea that social media is drained of affect, that emotion online (empathy being brought up the most) is a shadow of face-to-face interaction. The intensification of feeling found in GIFs, he writes, "contest[s] a narrative in which digital grammatization is about the creation of disaffection through repetition and cognitive saturation" (2015, 131). I would argue that GIFs are sites of *both* intense feeling and disaffection, and this ambivalence is what makes them such popular vehicles for online commentary. The most frequently used GIFs no longer strike with the sharp charge of pure affect, but they carry the intertextual burden of previous uses—emotion in the second degree. A popular GIF of Michael Jackson eating popcorn is meant not to be a literal representation of the poster's current expression or actions, but to convey ironic detachment from a contentious topic, a spectator's anticipation: "I don't care who wins or loses this argument, I'm just here for the drama." A GIF of David Tennant looking forlorn in the rain is not purely tragic; it is shopworn enough to convey humorous self-deprecation about one's sadness. The endlessly looping recursions of the GIF play, like belief, with the simultaneous layers of irony and sincerity.

5. The most literary passages describe David's dream visits—in these liminal spaces that need not be proven, Ellis takes a freer hand with descriptive prose: the ghost "shamble[es]" "mumbles," and "mutters." In a more menacing dream, David "crawled down off the chair and began shuffling toward me. He moved slowly, like it was a struggle for him." Ellis himself emotes more as a character in his story than as the narrator; in one vivid dream, he awakes to find a severed head and bloody spinal column on the pillow beside him: "Horrified, I screamed, 'What happened to you?!' The head smiled even bigger. 'It feels great,' the head groaned."

6. Intellectually, I don't believe in Ellis's ghost, but when I watch the Polaroid develop black, I get goosebumps, my scalp prickles. When he describes a dream of a grinning severed head and bloody spinal column on the pillow beside him, my breath stops, my eyes fill with tears. This is a somatic experience of horror that isn't commensurable with critical reason.

7. Journalist Amanda Tait compares Dear David to Spanish cartoonist Manuel Bartual's weeklong viral pseudo-autobiographical horror story, in which Bartual spends his vacation seemingly stalked by an eerie doppelgänger. Ironically, Tait notes, when at the end of the week Bartual declared his posts had been fiction, "hundreds of people refused to believe him, instead claiming that the 'other Manuel' had got hold of his Twitter account and was lying" (2017). Unlike Ellis, by formally ending and disavowing the story, Bartual frees up his ghost story for public consumption and reinvention—he names his story a fiction, and immediately becomes fictional himself (2017).

REFERENCES

Ahmed, Sara. 2013. *The Cultural Politics of Emotion*. 2nd ed. Edinburgh: Edinburgh University Press. First published 2004.

Allen, Felix. 2017. "Night-Scare Before Christmas: Is This Proof 'Dear David' is Fake?" *Sun*, December 14, 2017. https://www.thesun.co.uk/news/5140286/dear-david-fake-ghost-fans-adam-ellis/.

Ash, James. 2015. "Sensation, Networks, and the GIF: Toward an Allotropic Account of Affect." In *Networked Affect*, edited by Ken Hillis, Susanna Paasonen, and Michael Petit, 119–134. Cambridge, MA: MIT Press.

Bartual, Manuel. 2017. "Everything Is Fine: An English Translation of Manuel Bartual's Vacation." *Storify* (no longer available; Twitter thread available at https://twitter.com/BartualEnglish/status/911258915018551297).

Blank, Trevor J., and Lynne S. McNeill. 2018. "Introduction: Fear Has No Face: Creepypasta as Digital Legendry." In *Slender Man Is Coming: Creepypasta and Contemporary Legends on the Internet*, edited by Trevor J. Blank and Lynne S. McNeill, 3–24. Logan: Utah State University Press.

Bronner, Simon. 2009. "Digitizing and Virtualizing Folklore." In *Folklore and the Internet*, edited by Trevor Blank, 21–67. Logan: Utah State University Press.

Brunvand, Jan. 2012. *Encyclopedia of Urban Legends*. 2nd ed. Santa Barbara: ABC-CLIO.

Buccitelli, Anthony Bak. 2012. "Performance 2.0: Observations toward a Theory of the Digital Performance of Folklore." In *Folklore in the Digital Age*, edited by Trevor Blank, 60–84. Logan: Utah State University Press.

Dégh, Linda, and Andrew Vázsonyi. 1973. *The Dialectics of the Legend*. Bloomington, IN: Folklore Preprints Series (1) 6.

Dégh, Linda, and Andrew Vázsonyi 1978. "The Crack on the Red Goblet or Truth and Modern Legend." In *Folklore in the Modern World*, edited by Richard Dorson, 253–272. The Hague: Mouton.

Ellis, Bill. 2001. *Aliens, Ghosts, and Cults: Legends We Live*. Jackson: University Press of Mississippi.

Ferrara, Emilio, and Zeyao Yang. 2015. "Measuring Emotional Contagion in Social Media." *PLoS ONE* 10 (11): e0142390.

Gibbs, Anna. 2001. "Contagious Feelings: Pauline Hansen and the Epidemiology of Affect." *Australian Humanities Review* 24. http://australianhumanitiesreview.org/2001/12/01/contagious-feelings-pauline-hanson-and-the-epidemiology-of-affect/.

Hafstein, Valdimar. 2004. "The Politics of Origins: Collective Creation Revisited." *Journal of American Folklore* 17 (465): 300–315.

Huber, Linda. 2015. "Remix Culture and the Reaction GIF." *Gnovis*, February 25, 2015. http://www.gnovisjournal.org/2015/02/25/remix-culture-the-reaction-gif/.

Hufford, David. 1982. *The Terror That Comes in the Night*. Philadelphia: University of Pennsylvania Press.

Jarret, Kylie. 2015. "Let's Express Our Friendship by Sending Each Other Funny Links instead of Actually Talking: Gifts, Commodities, and Social Reproduction in Facebook." In *Networked Affect*, edited by Ken Hillis, Susanna Paasonen, and Michael Petit, 203–220. Cambridge, MA: MIT Press.

Kramer, Adam D. I., Jamie E. Guillory, and Jeffrey T. Hancock. 2014. "Experimental Evidence of Massive-Scale Emotional Contagion through Social Networks." *PNAS* 111 (24): 8788–8790.

McLuhan, Marshall. 1964. *Understanding Media*. New York: McGraw-Hill.

Mullen, Patrick B. 1971. "The Relationship of Legend and Folk Belief." *Journal of American Folklore* 84 (334): 406–413.

Newman, Michael. 2017. "In the GiF Space." *Flow*, October 2, 2017. https://www.flowjournal.org/2017/10/in-the-gif-space/#identifier_5_32882.

Paulas, Rick. 2017. "The Bit Too Tidy Ghost Story of 'Dear David.'" *Awl*, October 11, 2017. https://www.theawl.com/2017/10/the-bit-too-tidy-ghost-story-of-dear-david/.

Peck, Andrew. 2015. "Tall, Dark, and Loathsome: The Emergence of a Legend Cycle in the Digital Age." *Journal of American Folklore*, 128 (209): 333–348.

Peters, Lucia. 2018. "'Dear David Appeared in Adam Ellis' Instagram Feed & Now People Are Worried He May Be Possessed." *Bustle*, January 17, 2018. https://www.bustle.com/p/dear-david-appeared-in-adam-ellis-instagram-stories-now-people-are-worried-he-may-be-possessed-7930018.

Rosenberg, Lizzie. 2017. "These 'Dear David' Reddit Threads Will Turn You into a Complete Nonbeliever." *Elite Daily*, December 22, 2017. https://www.elitedaily.com/p/these-dear-david-reddit-threads-will-turn-you-into-a-complete-nonbeliever-7672776.

Tait, Amelia. 2017. "'Dear David Found Me, I Think': The Lure (and Ethics) of Twitter Ghost Stories." *New Statesman*, October 24, 2017. www.newstatesman.com/science-tech/social-media/2017/10/dear-david-found-me-i-think-lure-and-ethics-twitter-ghost-stories.

Tomkins, Silvan S. 1962. *Affect, Imagery, Consciousness: The Positive Affects*. New York: Springer.

Verhoeven, Beatrice. 2018. "'Dear David': 'It' Producer, Buzzfeed to Develop Horror Film Based on Viral Ghost Story." *The Wrap*, June 6, 2018. https://www.thewrap.com/dear-david-it-producer-buzzfeed-to-develop-horror-film-based-on-viral-ghost-story-exclusive/.

Wiles, Will. 2013. "Creepypasta Is How the Internet Learns Our Fears." *Aeon*, December 20, 2013. https://aeon.co/essays/creepypasta-is-how-the-internet-learns-our-fears.

Willsey, Kristiana. 2016. "Ted Cruz Is the Zodiac Killer: Contemporary Legends on Twitter." *CaMP Anthropology*. May 9, 2016. https://campanthropology.wordpress.com/2016/03/09/ted-cruz-is-the-zodiac-killer.

Young, Katharine. 2006. *Taleworlds and Storyrealms*. New York: Springer. First published 1986.

Young, Katharine. 2011. "Gestures, Incorporeity, and the Fate of Phenomenology in Folklore." *Journal of American Folklore* 124 (492): 55–87.

8

The Beauty, the Beast, and the Fanon
The Vernacularization of the Literary Canon and an Epilogue to Modernity

Tok Thompson

THE FANON AND THE END OF MODERNITY

IN 1991, DISNEY RELEASED A LAVISH ANIMATED musical entitled *Beauty and the Beast* to great commercial and popular acclaim. Fan fiction online stemming from this movie quickly developed a fanon, a community-held tradition, that the Beast's human name was Adam. Eventually, Disney came to support this fan-established move, and, six years later, its 1997 live-action musical remake used the name "Adam" in its production. This new name began as fanon, then became canon: "ascended fanon," in the parlance of fan fiction. Given that *Beauty and the Beast* has so many sources of authorship, including that of the folk tradition, this short example can serve as a useful introduction to the topic of this chapter: the fanon and the role it plays in navigating the complex and changing traditions of authorship in the digital age.

The *fanon* is a term emanating from the realm of fan fiction, a genre resting uneasily between authored literature and vernacular participatory practices. Fan fiction is an immensely popular yet somewhat liminal cultural production: neither authored literature nor folk tradition, fan fiction has often been derided as derivative or amateurish by literary scholars, while at the same time, because of its frequent reliance on copyrighted material, for most folklorists it seems far removed from the traditional purview of the discipline. Often excluded from both disciplines, fan fiction nevertheless remains a vibrant genre: many stories and writing processes are shared online, creating vast webs of social groups working on various narrative worlds, all enjoined in the wider creative community that fan fiction affords. My own interest in fan fiction focuses on an analysis of the *fanon* as a term and a practice.

The fanon is etymologically derived from "fan canon," creating something analogous to a canon yet without the canon's singular (and often copyrighted) status. The fanon is a folk practice of establishing vernacular authority (as per Howard 2013), guiding the production of new stories in the wider narrative world shared by the participants. The fanon emerges from literary canons in order to invert the usual process in authorship, instituting a vernacular authority in shaping guidelines for creative copying and further storytelling.

In this light, the fanon can be seen as a bookend to the "Gutenberg parenthesis" (as per Professor Lars Ole Sauerberg of the University of Southern Denmark—see Pettitt 2010), which is to say, as an epitaph—or perhaps an epilogue—to modernity.

FAN FICTION AS ART AND COMMUNITY

Currently there are millions of works of fan fiction available online spread across many different sites and online communities. Fan fiction is a vibrant cultural production involving millions of people in creative and appreciative endeavors, enmeshed in online communities.

Fan fiction communities have created a sizable vocabulary to discuss themselves and their practices. Some of the lore is known throughout the entire fan fiction community, including widely used general terms. For example, "shipping" refers to putting together two characters in a romantic (and usually heterosexual) relationship, while "slashing" refers to altering the sexual orientation of characters, usually remaking heterosexual male characters into homosexual characters (see, e.g., Tosenberger 2008a, 2008b).

Other lore can be found in more specific communities. Within the realm of fan fiction, there are many smaller subcategories and communities, differing in terms of their subject matter, websites, and generic approaches and very often organized around a canonical title. The fanon serves as an organizing rhetoric for the multiplicitous voices of worldwide fan fiction communities. It is the lore of the group that must be learned, thes traditions respected, if one wants to be a successful participant in any given fan fiction community. In this way, the fanon specifies and defines the particular community.

Despite its popularity and productivity, fan fiction has been often underappreciated, both as an art form and as a nexus of community building. In large part, this may be due to its strange, liminal position in terms of cultural production: fan fiction is often held to be derivative of a particular authored work, and indeed this is often explicitly the case. "Derivative" has negative connotations, as it seems to imply the opposite of "original." In our social system, which privileges originality, the very form of fan fiction works against its acceptance as a serious cultural force.

While this is somewhat understandable given the literary traditions in Europe, it is also true that fan fiction has not been investigated as "folklore" since it often proceeds on the assumption that it is indeed derived from literature, thus giving precedence to the canonicity of the copyrighted piece. Fan fiction, therefore, sits uneasily between the disciplines of folklore and literature, pleasing neither, perhaps, but nevertheless remaining immensely popular in our society.

Sheenagh Pugh, in her 2005 book on fan fiction, labeled it a "democratic genre," while Henry Jenkins (one of the first scholars to take fan fiction seriously) likened the practice to "textual poaching," as concerns about copyright and ownership are an inherent part of fan fiction practice because of its ambivalent relationship to authored works (see Jenkins 1992). The idea of textual poaching, borrowed from Michel de Certeau (1984), is primarily concerned with the ways people enact creative, fulfilling lives within a highly controlled society. De Certeau takes Foucault's view of the modern disciplined society as a starting point, but then focuses his attention on the individual's agency *within* such a system. Textual poaching, for de Certeau, is reminiscent of the medieval practice of poaching game on the "king's land." Now, rather than woodlands and game, the issue becomes literature and copyright. Who is allowed to participate? The question is by necessity one of the overriding concerns of any stratified system.

Jenkins (1992) pointed out that fan fiction overlaps with fandom generally, and the individuals involved can in many ways form a generative, productive community, taking part in conventions, sharing exchanges online, or otherwise involving themselves with the other fans of the product. For example, the *Star Trek* fan community ("fandom" in the parlance) coalesces in various ways, including face-to-face at conventions and online in various fan communities, one of which is the fan fiction community. Jenkins's work on *Star Trek* fandom, for which he conducted extensive participant observation, is perhaps most often cited, but in terms of the fanon, more important may be another fan fiction community that he covered in his pioneering text *Textual Poachers*—that of the burgeoning *Beauty and Beast* fan fiction communities that arose after the 1991 film, those that first bestowed the name of Adam on the Beast.

THE LIVELY TALE TYPE OF ATU 425C

Beauty and the Beast is an old tale, variously authored, with a history stretching all the way back to, ultimately, the folk tradition, where it has been catalogued as ATU 425c (see Uther 2004). The history of the story is illuminating, displaying the changing roles of authorship and indeed of the very nature of the story. What is examined here is not really the ATU 425c itself—not the plot, the symbolic meanings, the permutations, or the ongoing cultural appreciation of all this: rather, this chapter examines the life history, in terms of authorship, of the tale.

As ATU 425c, the story is folklore: told with a loose (or completely absent) sense of authorship, the tale varied widely in many permutations and was referred to under a plethora of titles. While storytelling was a refined art in premodern Europe, the telling of the story was not restricted to any one social class or individual. No one had a monopoly on the story. Nevertheless, the basic plot line remained remarkably similar, similar enough that the various folklore collectors working in many parts of Europe could all agree that they were working with essentially the same tale. Similar enough that Anti Aarne, and later Stith Thompson, and later still Han-Jorg Uther, all saw fit to label the tradition within the larger 425 category as 425c. The idea that a story could be at the same time so remarkably varied and widely spread, yet so internally consistent as to its major plot line and characters, might seem puzzling to people used to the idea of a singular printed text providing canonicity.

The Estonian folklorist Walter Anderson tried to address this issue with his famous "Law of Self-Correction" (1951). According to Anderson's theory, the reason for the coherence of the overall plot was the tale's ubiquity in wider cultural settings: a storyteller did not hear the tale in one telling; rather, the tale was already well known and widely spread throughout the overall culture. Therefore, the storyteller was limited in the changes that he or she might be tempted to make. Further, the audience was also already used to the story, and so would object to any radical changes. As explored by Elo-Hanna Seljamaa, Anderson introduced his theory to buttress support for the historic-geographic school and the belief that folktales are "autonomous entities governed by their own inherent laws" (Seljamaa 2007, 888), rather than products of people with agency. Such views were in line with the times, which valorized the folk tradition while sidelining the agency of individuals. In this view, the coherence of the tale is provided by its social ubiquity, as opposed to the literary idea that authorship and canonicity provide coherence. The fanon, as we shall see, combines elements of both.

ENTER THE AUTHOR AND THE BIRTH OF FAN FICTION

The introduction of the printing press in Europe (c. 1450) contributed to widespread literacy and the rising importance of "authored literature" as the main venue for storytelling. As has been explored numerous times (see, e.g., Ong 1982), early printed literature drew heavily from folk tradition for its source of stories. Yet this development was more than a change of storytellers or media: this was a wholesale change of how storytelling was considered. The emerging printed literature was now "authored," and "authored works" were supposed to be "original," which is to say, authors were the sole originators of the stories. Such a move into modernity further sidelined the folk, and in its place gave us the notion of the individual genius, the Nietzschean *übermensch*. This conflict can be viewed in the genre of fairy tales, in competing ideas of the authorship of Hans Christian Andersen versus that of the Grimms, with Andersen presenting himself as an author and the Grimms as collectors, both somewhat erroneously (see Hafstein 2014). Fairy tales became (and remain) a very liminal genre, existing in both the oral and literary realms.

We can see this in the story of the Beauty and the Beast. Although clearly deriving from the oral tradition, Beauty and the Beast became "canonized" not as folklore (as in the case of the Grimms' fairy tales) but rather as a literary production by a singular author. The literary view of Beauty and the Beast commonly traces its origins to the French novelist Suzanne Barbot de Villeneuve's version, first published in 1740 in *La jeune américaine et les contes marins* (The Young American and Marine Tales). This long and meandering version was abridged and rewritten by Jeanne-Marie Leprince de Beaumont in 1756 in *Magasin des enfants* (Children's Collection), from which many of the canonical elements are derived. Yet, before de Beaumont's version was published, a play, *Amour pour amour* (Love for Love), was written by Nivelle de la Chaussée and published in 1742. This version was the basis for a wildly popular operatic version, *Zémire et Azor*, which premiered in 1771 and remained popular for decades. (See, e.g., the account in Hearn 1989). Even in these early days, the story was clearly intertextual.

Although these dates were firmly entrenched in the era of modernity and the notion of single authorship, such conceptions had not yet been given the legal status of copyright. Authors often felt free to lift plots and devices from other authors, and the question of whether a story was essentially folkloric or whether it actually originated with the author was of no particular legal consequence: the first "author-centered" copyright in France was not granted until 1761. This grant gave the ownership of Jean de La Fontaine's celebrated *Fables* to his granddaughters—somewhat ironically, as the work was, once more, a recitation of already well-known stories. In 1777, subsequent court decisions in France further limited the publisher's monopoly to the lifetime of the author (see Latournerie 2001).

Multiple authored origins can be seen in the histories of Beauty and the Beast: in the literary view, it is clear that de Villeneuve's version was influenced by earlier stories, such as Apuleius's "Cupid and Psyche" version in the second-century *Golden Ass* (perhaps via the rendition published by Jean de La Fontaine in 1669), as well as the Venetian Viovanni Francesco Straparola's "Pig King," published in his *Facetious Nights of Straparola* (1555). Apuleius was clearly inspired by earlier Greek myths, such as the rape of Europa by Zeus in the form of a bull (see Tatar 2017), while Straparola declared himself to be reworking tales rather than producing original works. Straparola wrote that the tales "written and collected in this volume are none of mine, but goods which I have feloniously taken from this man and that. Of a truth I confess they are not mine, and if I said otherwise I should lie, but nevertheless I have faithfully set them down according to the manner in which they were told by the ladies, nobles, learned men and gentlemen who gathered together for recreation" (Straparola 1901, vi–vii).

Straparola's account of the provenance of his stories provides a view of this early state of literary writing: much of the early "authored literature" was simply reworked folk tales, often told in a framing device. Frame stories were common ways of "setting the stage" for a literary retelling of folk tales. Examples of this include *One Thousand and One Arabian Nights*, Chaucer's *Canterbury Tales*, and Boccaccio's *Decameron*. Frame tales created a fictional "frame," such as a pilgrimage to Canterbury, for the retelling of folk stories: the text is largely comprised of the stories told by the pilgrims to enliven the journey. Likewise, the *Decameron* describes a group of aristocrats who attempt to escape the plague by residing in the country, where theypass the time by telling stories. Such literary productions were not quite authored literature but not quite folklore, either. Rather, they sat between these two genres, fictionalizing settings for the retellings of traditional narratives (a popular entertainment, as Straparola's quote indicates). De Villeneuve's version of Beauty and the Beast was similarly presented as part of a larger frame tale.

Some of the early scholars of folklore (e.g., Hans Naumann) tended to believe that all culture originated with the aristocracy and only later spread among the peasant population, the *gesunkeness Kulturgut* approach (see Bendix 1997) This approach has been thoroughly discredited, as the data from international folklore studies has shown that the ubiquity of tales such as ATU 425c must have long predated the spread of aristocratic works.

In a decided turnabout, the gesunkeness Kulturgut approach is now more appreciated as revealing the prevailing sentiments of the time: that peasants were not able create culture, merely replicate it, badly. Instead, much of what passes for authored literature and music can be traced to the vernacular realm, beyond the reaches of single authorship (examples include *Hamlet*, "Ode to Joy," and "Auld Lang Syne"). The scholarly understanding of the authorship of folklore has, therefore, been largely inverted, and with this, an appreciation of the creative potential of the vernacular realm has been increasingly emphasized. Nonetheless, the view of elite production of culture remains in many literary scholars' views of folk literature: for example, Ruth Bottigheimer has published repeated claims that Straparola was the single origin for *all* fairy tales (1986, 2002), claims that have been savaged in folkloric scholarship (Zipes 2010b; Vaz da Silva 2010; Ziolkowski 2009, 2010), as well as contraindicated by the writing of Straparola himself. In a more limited approach, Swahn (1955) argued that the specific forms of 425c (as opposed to the other parts of the 425 category) all derive from the literary version of de Villeneuve, claims that have been severely critiqued by later writers (see, particularly, DeVries in Hearn 1989), who have been able to demonstrate that all key motifs and plot functions existed widely in European and Russian folk traditions.

Yet it is true that the frame tale, among other influences, helped the rise of the modern notion of the author as the origin of stories. Along with the frame tale, the impact of the printing press can hardly be overstated in this regard: the printing press allowed for widespread literacy and widespread dissemination of published works (Ong 1982). This combination created literary "stars" whose works were read by many, many people. Storytelling became increasingly connected with the "cult of the author," a revealing aspect of much of modernity. It also allowed for new forms of writing to emerge, such as serialized works, which became a popular feature in journals and magazines. Even with these changing genres and changing expectations of authored literature, folk and fairy tales continued to inform a great deal of Victorian literature, particularly works for children (see, for an extended discussion, Ostry 2002).

Charles Dickens (1812–1870), for example, made ample use of fairy tales in his works as well as frame tales. In *Social Dreaming: Dickens and the Fairy Tale*, Ostry displays the many debts to fairy tale traditions evident in Dickens's work. "Throughout his career, Dickens engaged in fairy tales on every level: he wrote them, defended them, alluded to them and used techniques of the genre in his essays and novels" (2002, 10). As Maria Tatar put it, "The myth of fairy tales as a kind of holy scripture was energetically propagated by Charles Dickens, who brought to the literature of childhood the same devout reverence he accorded children" (1999, xi). Dickens made a career of protesting what he saw as the ugly aspects of modernity: "In an utilitarian age, of all other times, it is a matter of grave importance that Fairy tales should be respected" (Dickens 1854, 97). In his attachment to past-oriented aspects of culture (Christmas and ghosts being among his favorite themes), he echoed the common view of oral provenance of fairy tales and specifically acknowledged his debt to his childhood nurse, Mary Weller, who introduced him to vivid storytelling and the fairy tale genre (see Ostry 2002, 1, 3). Dickens also inveighed against bowdlerizing fairy tales (literally, it was Thomas Bowdler who produced "moral" versions of the classics, particularly in his 1854 "Frauds on the Fairies" article, published in his own journal *Household Words*, which printed many fairy tales).

Folklorists Katherine M. Briggs (1970) and Jacqueline Simpson (1984) have both written on Dickens's use of fairy tales as well, while Harry Stone (1979) investigated how the fairy tale was integral to Dickens's work (see also Grob 1964). Jessica Campbell (2015) has argued that Dickens's *Great Expectations* was profoundly influenced by de Villeneuve's 1740 version of "Beauty and the Beast," tracing the essential similarities of much of the plot and characters. *Great Expectations* reads in many ways like a fairy tale: a young impoverished man leaves home, receives goods from a mysterious donor, and after many adventures finally finds his way back to domesticity.

Dickens was one of the very first literary celebrities of the modern era. While some of his works were eventually published as novels, most of them first appeared as series of installments in popular journals. Dickens also often gave live readings of works in progress as well as completed works. Both the live performances and the serialized episodic publications allowed for a wide variety of audience feedback on the story line as it developed, and occasionally Dickens invited friends and literary colleagues to contribute episodes as well. Thus, although we often look back at Dickens's works as examples of the authored novel par excellence, this is not how they were produced or received at the time—a significant degree of audience participation aided the development of the stories (see, e.g., Patten 2002).

At the same time, Charles Dickens was also an early passionate advocate for the international copyright system in order to protect and promote the work of individual authors, increasingly seen as the single origin for stories. He repeatedly characterized the uncopyrighted reprinting of his work (for example, in the United States), for which he was paid nothing, as theft, an idea that has largely been accepted in the realm of copyright and the culture industries of modernity (see the account in Hudson 1964).

If Charles Dickens makes an ironic example of someone who "crowd-sourced" writings and yet passionately argued for copyright protection for individual writers, then the birth of fan fiction and the idea of the "literary canon," from which the fanon is derived, can be dated from the only slightly later career of Sir Arthur Conan Doyle (1859–1930), and, in particular, from the highly popular Sherlock Holmes series of fifty-six short stories and four novellas.

Sherlock Holmes has been remade into countless plays, films, TV shows and, of course, literature not written by Conan Doyle. The earliest "fan fiction" version was produced in 1893—long before the death of the author.[1] The immense popularity of fan fiction works inspired by Sherlock Holmes even gave rise to the first fan fiction community, which tasked itself with the "Great Game" of trying to make sense of the irregularities in the overall story line, both in terms of fan fiction authors and in the works of Conan Doyle, who wrote quickly with little concern for internal cross-story consistency. In 1911, Ronald Knox published the essay "Studies in the Literature of Sherlock Holmes," which borrowed from theological terminology to talk of the Sherlock Holmes "canon," in humorous analogy to theological debates regarding the Bible (see Knox 1928, 2011).

The life and works of Sir Arthur Conan Doyle, therefore, bring us firmly to the subjects of the role of copyrights, fan fiction, and the idea of the literary canon, all wrapped up together. Sherlock Holmes tales continue to be retold as literary productions with the longest-ever claim to a canon of authorship but also with a long history of fan adaptations—and now freed from the restrictions of copyright. The numerous cinematic reinterpretations of Sherlock Holmes have also ensured the continuance of the fan fiction community centered on the perceptive detective.[2]

BEYOND THE AUTHOR

During the early part of the twentieth century, the culture industries, including cinema, appropriated more and more culture from the past *Great Expectations*, Sherlock Holmes stories, and *Beauty and the Beast* were all remade numerous times, to great success. Each of these was an adaptation, partly original and partly copied, occupying the space of "creative copying" (Hafstein 2004). Yet in the age of modernity, industrial structures favored the essential recognition of the single copyright, held by a single legal person, which could be placed on the market, bought and sold, and ultimately controlled and commodified. Presses were not (and are not) allowed to print material in copyright violation—which is to say, for the most part, large institutions (governments, corporations, etc.) controlled the official discourse, which overlapped with the society's discourses in general. Folklore, not held to stem from a single author, was (and largely is) conspicuously free from these strictures. There is a great irony here, in that much early copyrighted literature drew heavily from folklore and received copyright, while fan fiction, which draws heavily from authored stories, is neither copyrighted nor free from copyright, occupying a liminal space in our cultural productions.

Law scholar Lawrence Lessig (2004) makes the historical case that the rise in copyright parallels the growth of the industrial, mechanical culture of modernity. Further, he sees the introduction of digital technology and digital means of communication as fundamentally challenging the previous legal order, which was predicated on the ownership of ideas, stories, and much of culture. As he points out, early copyright, even when established, was a much smaller piece of the cultural pie. Lessig's *Free Culture* traces the growth of copyright: from protecting the author during his life to extending far beyond his life—currently seventy years after the death of the author.[3] To trace the development of the rise of the "critical moment" in copyright studies, he focuses on the growth and influence of the Disney Corporation and its iconic character Mickey Mouse, which has emerged as a symbol of stringent copyright protection.

Mickey first appeared as "Steamboat Willie" in the first-ever cartoon with synchronized sound. The cartoon was a huge hit and Mickey became the central icon for the corporation. As Lessig points out (2004, 22), "Steamboat Willie" was a parody of *Steamboat Bill*, a popular movie starring Buster Keaton—which is to say, Mickey, now a symbol of copyright protection, began as a knockoff of someone else's work. But Disney also traffics in fairy tales, and these are, by definition, noncopyrightable. One is not free to publish a story with Mickey Mouse without permission from the Disney Corporation, but one is free to remake *Snow White and the Seven Dwarfs* (1937), *Cinderella* (1950), and other works based on folk traditions. Disney reaped great rewards retelling folk classics, so much so that the company has been deeply associated with fairy tales for much of its history (see, e.g., Zipes 2010a).

In between those two folk-based Disney films, in 1946, Jean Cocteau released his celebrated film *La Belle et la Bête* (Beauty and the Beast) to great and lasting critical acclaim. Cocteau's version owes a great deal to that of de Beaumont (1756) and, by extension, to that of de Villeneuve (1740). Cocteau's version was a major inspiration for the next major cinematic reworking: Disney's wildly successful 1991 version of the same tale.

Disney's 1991 *Beauty and Beast* was an astonishing success, becoming the highest-grossing animated musical ever (Mentel 2013). Due in large part to the success of the animated film, Disney decided to produce a Broadway musical version, first presented publically in 1994. The massive and sustained popularity of this version transformed Broadway, initiating a series of "family-friendly" theatrical adaptations of Disney films: *The Lion King* (1997), *Mary Poppins* (2004), *The Little Mermaid* (2008), and *Aladdin* (2014).

Based largely on this astonishing success, Disney created a live-action adaptation of the Broadway musical for its 2017 live-action film *Beauty and the Beast*. The film was a global hit, becoming the highest-grossing live-action musical in cinematic history. It is no surprise, then, that a rich fan fiction community should be formed around the realm of *Beauty and the Beast*.

Or should I say, ATU 425c? Returning to the nomenclature of ATU 425c allows us fresh perspectives as well as old ones. The primary advantage of the Aarne-Thompson-Uther cataloguing system is the recognition that the same tale, the same plot, might occur with different names and with different characters. Therefore, in terms of modern renditions of the tale, we might look beyond the words "Beauty and the Beast" to see the essential tale being retold in other forms.[4]

The *Twilight* series of books is, in many ways, another variation on ATU 425c. The best-selling series for young teens deals with a young girl named Bella ("Beauty") who falls in love with a vampire, portrayed here in a "beastly manner" (living in the forest, drinking the blood of animals), yet with a good heart. In the end, the love they share is enough to conquer the "beastliness" of the man. At the end of *Beauty and the Beast*, the beast is transformed into a human, while in *Twilight*, Bella is transformed into a vampire. The ATU defines 425c as having four distinct elements: a monster as husband, disenchantment of the monster, loss of the husband, and recovery of the husband: essentially the plot of the story of *Twilight*, with the exception that it is rather Bella Swan who is transformed rather than her husband. In any case, the "enchantment" of Bella achieves the same effect as the "disenchantment" of the husband would—it removes obstacles to their marriage. Love, once again, conquers all. Due to its widespread popularity, it is little surprise to see the *Twilight* series also spawn vigorous fan fiction communities.

One of the *Twilight* fan fiction works, initially called "Master of the Universe," took the *Twilight* story line and characters into sexually explicit and sexually charged territory. In direct opposition to the *Twilight* series, which avoided sexuality (often seeming to replace sexual lust with the "lust for blood" of the vampire), "Master of the Universe" swung the pendulum hard to the other extreme, with the vampire/beast now represented as interested in sexual sadism and with Bella being introduced to a life of extreme masochism.

"Master of the Universe" exploded in popularity in the fan fiction world, prompting its creator, E. L. James, to publish the work as a piece of original fiction. In the process, the supernatural elements were carefully removed to avoid the obvious connection to the *Twilight* series. Left in its place was essentially the same plot once more, in which the protagonist falls in love with a mortal sadist—not a true beast, although a beastly sort of mortal. The character's names were also changed, and the book was released to vast commercial success as *Fifty Shades of Grey*.

The plot of *Fifty Shades of Grey* is even *more* similar to 425c than the *Twilight* series, in that the "beast" is transformed, by love, into a less beastly state. Further, the role of the "fairy" is reintroduced, as from the de Villeneuve version, in the character of Elena, an older woman who seduced the protagonist at a young age, corrupting his sexuality into that of the "beastly" variety. *Fifty Shades of Grey* became an international best seller, selling over 125 million copies, and translated into fifty-two languages. As of 2012, Amazon UK announced that it had sold more copies of *Fifty Shades of Grey* than the entire *Harry Potter* series combined. Which is also to say, one of the best-selling works in recent times is another reiteration of ATU 425c and was originally composed as fan fiction.

Unsurprisingly, *Fifty Shades of Grey* has inspired a tremendous amount of fan fiction material. As of this writing, fanfiction.net boasts holdings of over 3,678 fan fiction pieces elaborating the world of *Fifty Shades of Grey*.[5] Meanwhile, the same site also hosts over 2,034 stories dedicated to *Beauty and the Beast*. Neither, however, comes anywhere near the staggering amount of *Twilight* fan fiction hosted on the same site: 219,109, second on this site only to fan fiction dedicated to *Harry Potter* (795,000). Meanwhile, Archive of Our Own, another popular site, lists over 4 million works altogether, with nearly 5,000 inspired by *Beauty and the Beast*, 12,639 by *Twilight*, 484 by *Fifty Shades of Grey*, and a whopping 1,116,764 works using the character of Sherlock Holmes (as of September 21, 2018). Many *Beauty and the Beast* fan fiction communities center on the Disney story (as retold in the three versions) as the canon, yet, as is common in fan fiction, very often other elements, characters, and stories are brought in as well (there is, of course, even a Sherlock Holmes version).[6] Some writers draw from "both the movie and the original fairy tale," displaying an authorial process that freely acknowledges the borrowing of plots, characters, and style. Some extend the plotline into unique areas, while others rework the stories using the same plot or general plot elements. Overall, these approaches tie together the community in a joint world-building project, the most elemental connective tissue being the traditions upheld, both the canon and the fanon.

CONCLUSIONS

The temporal arc of Beauty and the Beast bears testament to the transformations of the cultural practices of storytelling. The story has been performed live for millennia, and we see the portrait of such social events in the early literary works, such as Straparola's, which sought to capture the storytelling sessions of the day. From there the story worked its way into the literary realm of modernity, authorship, and copyright (the "Gutenberg parenthesis"), and now, finally, all the way into the cyber realm and the muddied confluence of folklore and authorship found in fan fiction, guided by the fanon.

The digital is quite new, to be sure, but we already see the "usual suspects" of traditional plots: ATU 452c seems to have lost none of its vitality in the various mutations. Rather, it has remained a cultural juggernaut. In fan fiction, we can further witness the reemergence of the involved audience and the reblurring of production between audience and performer, between fan and creator, and between originality and traditionality as part and parcel of the fanon. As per Hafstein's work on collective creations (2004), these performative acts can be viewed as somewhat creative and somewhat derivative: and, in the case of the fanon, purposefully so.

While fan fiction may be "textual poaching," in accordance with Jenkins's interpretations of de Certeau, there is another aspect of de Certeau's writings that also might find fertile ground for thought. De Certeau wrote that he wanted to understand how collective action can be undertaken in a seemingly unconscious way, not directed by official forces, and not solely from individual agency or cultural traditions, but by something a bit more mysterious: "Increasingly contained, yet less and less concerned with these vast frameworks, the individual detaches himself from them without being able to escape them and can henceforth only try to outwit them, to pull tricks on them, to rediscover, within an electronicized and computerized megalopolis, the 'art' of the hunters and rural folk of earlier days" (1984, xxiii–xxiv).

De Certeau displaces the usual foci by concentrating not on the overarching systems themselves (as did Foucault), nor on the individuals within the systems, but rather on the connections that create the plurality of society and provide for meaningful actions stemming from both individuals and systems. As he puts it: "Each individual is a locus in which an incoherent (and often contradictory) plurality of such relational determinations interact. Moreover, the question at hand concerns modes of operation or schemata of action, and not directly the subject (or persons) who are their authors or vehicles. It concerns an operational logic whose models may go as far back as the age-old ruses of fishes and insects that disguise or transform themselves in order to survive" (1984, xi).

The fanon, then, might be taken as an example of "how fish swim together," to paraphrase de Certeau, moving beyond the realm of individual poachers and toward a wholesale change in ways of constructing authorship and storytelling. Poaching, in theory, acknowledges the legal ownership, while fan fiction seems to move impatiently beyond such concepts.

Yet fanon is not simply rejecting the notions of authorship and copyright: a breakdown of texts shows the enduring aura of the "authentic" (as per Benjamin 1969), with great weight given to the notion of the authored canon. Indeed, it is usually the canonical piece that provides the common ground for these communities of storytelling. Rather, I believe that the fanon can be seen as a folk practice of asserting vernacular authority while maintaining clear formative links to the realm of authored literature. The fanon, at its most basic level, is any tradition of telling a particular story held in common by two or more people, echoing Dundes's definition of a minimal folk group (1965). Like folklore generally, the fanon has cultural weight and vernacular authority when it is accepted and performed by large swaths of people, creating, in terms at least of this singular definition, a folk community built around a literary creation.

This is not to discount the individual: rather, fan fiction easily displays individuals in terms of their contributions, whether in writing stories, responding to them, or engaging in other community work (such as discussing and establishing the accepted fanon). Communities and traditions are made up of individuals. Here Walter Anderson's "Law of Self-Correction" (1951) can be revisited (stories can maintain consistent form), yet now with the missing *agency* added into the mix (it is not the case that the fanon demands adherence to tradition, but rather that people, and their own social processes, establish, enforce, and perform such guidelines). The results, however, may be very similar: the traditions remain. Cultural traditions of practice help establish the ethical background considerations: why something is or is not acceptable. Respect for the canon of authored literature and published works implies some lasting moral and ethical views regarding recognition of cultural contributions, if not "ownership" in the way that copyright law indicates, as the fanon uses the canon as its basis. Yet copyright law itself tends to be at its least helpful in cases like fan fiction:

the contribution of a story inspired by "the most recent film and the original fairy tale" invokes complex ideas about authorship and traditionality, rather than a binary of "folk traditions vs. authored literature" on which the copyright regime is built (see Hafstein 2018; Bendix 2018). Rather, the gray areas between these two binaries are increasingly being explored and utilized by vernacular social media–based communities.

Modernity, it seems, still has its relevance, even if perhaps this might be more of an exercise in community building or even nostalgia than any particular power given to the author. Authorial intent itself is not held to have much weight in establishing or even altering the fanon, and indeed is routinely ignored. Nonetheless, a nostalgia for modernity would scarcely seem out of place, considering the nostalgia for premodernity so visible in our society (and so evident in Disney's *Beauty and the Beast*).

Yet even as the very nature of fan fiction continues to provide homage to the realm of authored literature, it inverts the process of authorial control, instituting a vernacular authority that shapes guidelines for creative copying and further storytelling. It is in many ways a genre for our times: blurring the legal, political configurations of modernity and postmodernity, relying on modernity for new imaginings of our collective culture. The fanon is a vernacular production, both in concept and in the performance of the genre. It is also hybrid in its digital text: neither "fixed print" nor "oral ephemerality," the fanon points to possible future ways of thinking about establishing protocol and decorum in social media groups.

The fanon exhibits the complex character often characteristic of online communities, as the new digital epoch of production emerges from the traditions of the literary canons and the sacredness of the original. Further, the "folkishness" of the practice points to the very social nature of the fan fiction community and the establishment of the fanon.

Storytelling is a social activity, whose contours are shaped by the medium through which the story is told and received. From the parlor rooms of the 1800s to the bookshops, libraries, classrooms, and cinemas of modernity and now to social media sites, ATU 425c has been told again and again and again, providing hours of entertainment and sociability for generations upon generations of people.

If the frame tale provided a bridge from the folk forms of storytelling toward new regimes of authorship, spurred on by the development of the printing press and modernity, then the fanon can be seen as a similar process, but in reverse, providing a bridge between the realms of the printing press and modernity toward an essential folk practice, relying on the digital revolution and the quickly emerging postmodernity. The fanon, in this light, is far from trivial: rather, it represents how online communities have crafted a form of storytelling that reflects the nature of communications in the postmodern digital age. The contentious relationship that fan fiction has with the world of the copyright also reflects this schism of the epochs, between the modern and the postmodern. The notion that fan fiction, and the fanon, is dependent on an authored original is rendered inherently problematic when looking at the recurrent tales that have traversed this entire story line, such as ATU 425c. ATU 425c was with us before, during, and after modernity and likely will continue to be with us, regardless of the future of authorship. The fanon, it is argued, can thus be seen as a bookend to the "Gutenberg parenthesis," a nostalgic epitaph for modernity and the printing press, as its own internal rhetoric points toward new ways of authoring narratives in the folk traditions of social media.

NOTES

1. "The Late Sherlock Holmes," written by Conan Doyle's good friend J. M. Barrie.

2. A keyword search for *Sherlock Holmes* on the Internet Movie Database (IMDb) returns 306 titles as of October 8, 2020.

3. Lessig also documents the growth of cultural products covered by copyright: originally aimed only at novels, copyright in the US is now taken to cover *all creative acts*; an opera and a piece of bathroom graffiti are equally protected (2004, 138).

4. This point is made similarly at the end of Hearn's 1989 *Beauty and the Beast*, where she examines some examples of recent literature that seem to conform to the 425c tale type. Hearn concludes, "'Beauty and the Beast' has been told many times, with many intentions. It represents aspects of the worst and best in society, story, and self. It is shaped for survival" (1989, 154).

5. https://www.fanfiction.net/book/Fifty-Shades-Trilogy/ (accessed October 8, 2019).

6. Viewable at https://www.fanfiction.net/s/10445467/1/Beauty-and-the-Beast (accessed October 8, 2019).

REFERENCES

Anderson, Walter. 1951. *Ein Volkskundliches Experiment*. FFC 141. Helsinki: Suoma-lainen Tiedeakatemia.

Bendix, Regina. 1997. *In Search of Authenticity: The Formation of Folklore Studies*. Madison: University of Wicsonsin Press.

Bendix, Regina. 2018. *Culture and Value: Tourism, Heritage and Property*. Bloomington: University of Indiana Press.

Benjamin, Walter. (1936) 1969. "The Work of Art in the Age of Mechanical Reproduction." In *Illuminations*, edited by Hannah Arendt, 217–251. New York: Schocken.

Bottigheimer, Ruth. 1986. *Fairy Tales and Society: Illusion, Allusion, and Paradigm*. Philadelphia: University of Pennsylvania Press.

Bottigheimer, Ruth. 2002. *Fairy Godfather: Straparola, Venice, and the Fairy Tale Tradition.* Philadelphia: University of Pennsylvania Press.
Briggs, Katherine M. 1970. "The Folklore of Charles Dickens." *Journal of the Folklore Institute* 7: 3–20.
Campbell, Jessica. 2015. "Tradition and Transformation: Fairy Tales in the Victorian Novel." PhD diss., University of Washington.
De Certeau, Michel. 1984. *The Practice of Everyday Life.* Berkeley: University of California Press. First published 1980.
DeVries, Larry. 1989. "Literary Beauties and Folk Beasts: Folktale Issues in 'Beauty and the Beast.'" In *Beauty and the Beast*, edited by Betsy Hearn, 155–188. Chicago: University of Chicago Press.
Dickens, Charles. 1854. "Frauds on the Fairies." In *Household Words: A Weekly Journal.* New York: McElrath and Barker.
Dundes, Alan. 1965. "What Is Folklore?" In *The Study of Folklore*, edited by Alan Dundes, 1–3. Englewood Cliffs, NJ: Prentice-Hall.
Grob, Shirley. 1964. "Dickens and Some Motifs of the Fairy Tale." *Texas Studies in Literature and Language* 5: 567–579.
Hafstein, Valdimar Tr. 2004. "The Politics of Origins: Collective Creation Revisited." *Journal of American Folklore* 117: 300–315.
Hafstein, Valdimar Tr. 2014. "The Constant Muse: Copyright and Creative Agency." *Narrative Culture* 1: 9–48.
Hafstein, Valdimar Tr. 2018. *Making Intangible Heritage: El Condor Pasa and Other Stories from UNESCO.* Bloomington: Indiana University Press.
Hearn, Betsy. 1989. *Beauty and the Beast.* Chicago: University of Chicago Press.
Howard, Robert Glenn. 2013. "Vernacular Authority: Critically Engaging Tradition." In *Tradition in the Twenty-First Century*, edited by Trevor J. Blank and Robert Glenn Howard, 72–99. Logan: Utah State University Press.
Hudson, Edward. 1964. "Literary Piracy, Charles Dickens and the American Copyright Law." *American Bar Association Journal* 50 (12): 1157–1160.
Jenkins, Henry. 1992. *Textual Poachers: Television Fans and Participatory Culture.* London: Routledge.
Knox, Ronald. 1928. "Studies in the Literature of Sherlock Holmes." In *Essays in Satire*, 98–120. London: Sheed and Ward.
Knox, Ronald. 2011. *Ronald Knox and Sherlock Holmes: The Origin of Sherlockian Studies.* Edited by Michael J Crowe. Indianapolis: Gasogene Books.
Latournerie, Anne. 2001. "Petite histoire des batailles du droit d'auteur." *Multitudes* 2 (5): 37–62.
Lessig, Lawrence. 2004. *Free Culture: How Big Media Uses Technology and the Law to Lock Down Culture and Control Creativity.* New York: Penguin.
Mentel, Thomas. 2013. "The 5 Highest Grossing Disney Animated Musicals." *Cheatsheet*, November 7, 2013. https://www.cheatsheet.com/entertainment/movies/the-5-highest-grossing-disney-animated-musicals.html/.
Ong, Walter. 1982. *Orality and Literacy: The Technologizing of the Word.* London: Methuen, Ltd.
Ostry, Elaine. 2002. *Social Dreaming: Dickens and the Fairy Tale.* Routledge: New York.
Patten, Robert L. 2002. *Charles Dickens and 'Boz': The Birth of the Industrial-Age Author.* Cambridge: Cambridge University Press.
Pettitt, Thomas. 2010. "The Gutenberg Parenthesis: Oral Tradition and Digital Technologies." *MIT Communications Forum.* http://techtv.mit.edu/videos/16645-the-gutenbergparenthesis-oral-tradition-and-digital-technologies.
Pugh, Sheenagh, 2005. *The Democratic Genre: Fan Fiction in a Literary Context.* Bridgend, Wales: Seren.

Seljamaa, Elo-Hanna. 2007. "Täiustatud tõde ehk Walter Andersoni rahvajuttude enesekontrolli seadus" [Perfected truth: Walter Anderson's Law of Self-Correction]. *Keel ja Kirjandus* 11: 888–906.
Simpson, Jacqueline. 1984. "Urban Legends in the Pickwick Papers." *Journal of American Folklore* 96: 462–470.
Stone, Harry. 1979. *Dickens and the Invisible World: Fairy Tales, Fantasy, and Novel-Making*. Bloomington: Indiana University Press.
Straparola, Viovanni Francesco. 1901. *The Facetious Nights of Straparola*. Translated by Girolamo Morlini. Boston: Burton Ethnological Society. First published 1555.
Swahn, Jan-Öjvind. 1955. *The Tale of Cupid and Psyche*. Lund: Gleerup.
Tatar, Maria, ed. 1999. *The Classic Fairy Tales*. New York: W. W. Norton & Co.
Tatar, Maria. 2017. *Beauty and the Beast: Classic Tales about Animal Brides and Grooms from around the World*. New York: Penguin.
Tosenberger, Catherine. 2008a. "Homosexuality at the Online Hogwarts: Harry Potter Slash Fan Fiction." *Children's Literature* 36: =185–207.
Tosenberger, Catherine. 2008b. "'Oh My God, the Fan Fiction!' Dumbledore's Outing and the Online Harry Potter Fandom." *Children's Literature Association Quarterly* 33: 200–206.
Uther, Hans-Jörg. 2004. *The Types of International Folktales: A Classification and Bibliography*. 3 vols. FF Communications, 284–286. Helsinki: Academia Scientiarum Fennica/ Suomalainen Tiedeakatemia.
Vaz da Silva, Francisco. 2010. "The Invention of Fairy Tales." *Journal of American Folklore* 123 (490): 398–425.
Ziolkowski, Jan. 2009. *Fairy Tales from Before Fairy Tales: The Medieval Latin Past of Wonderful Lies*. Ann Arbor: University of Michigan Press.
Ziolkowski, Jan. 2010. "Straparola and the Fairy Tale: Between Literary and Oral Traditions." *Journal of American Folklore* 123 (490): 377–397.
Zipes, Jack. 2010a. "Grounding the Spell: The Fairy Tale Film and Transformation." In *Fairy Tale Films: Visions of Ambiguity*, edited by Pauline Greenhill and Sidney Eve Matriz, ix–viii. Logan: Utah State University Press.
Zipes, Jack. 2010b. "Sensationalist Scholarship: A Putative 'New' History of Fairy Tales." *Cultural Analysis* 10: 129–145.

9

Classifying #BlackLivesMatter
Genre and Form in Digital Folklore

Lynne S. McNeill

THE DIGITAL FOLKLORE PROJECT

IN 2014, THE HASHTAG #BLACKLIVESMATTER was the winner of the Digital Folklore Project's first ever Digital Trend of the Year award. The Digital Folklore Project (DFP) is a virtual research and tracking center co-hosted by Utah State University's Folklore Program, Department of English, and the Fife Folklore Archives. Folklorist Jeannie Thomas, who also serves as the head of the English department, proposed the idea as a way to promote Utah State's folklore program and to encourage greater awareness among the general public of the cultural and communicative value of digital folklore. Dr. Thomas and I became the project's co-founders. The project's aim is to follow and document folkloric digital trends, such as internet memes, contemporary legends, visual art, hashtags, participatory customs like challenges and poses, and short videos. The project tracks and archives these trends on a month-by-month basis, and at the end of the year, the DFP research team prepares a ballot of contenders for the "Digital Trend of the Year," which is voted on by a panel of folklorists from across the country.

The DFP research team's ongoing ethnographic work is aided by crowdsourcing efforts using the hashtag #DigitalTrendOfTheYear. The team encourages all who are interested in participating to tweet emerging trends that they spot in their own online experiences; in this way, we hope to reach beyond our own limited experiences of the internet (largely an academic, female, middle-class, white internet) to represent other experiences and manifestations of the internet from a diverse range of perspectives.

The DFP is unique among folkloristic endeavors in that it requires the folklorists who work on the project to apply the abstract concepts of the discipline in concrete ways. Folklorists regularly offer interpretations of traditional narratives, for example, but are rarely required then to make policy out of those interpretations (a burden that falls to other disciplines that study culture, such as economics or political science). With the advent of the Digital Folklore Project in 2014, the initial research team was tasked with determining exactly *what* makes something a piece of digital folklore. This determination wouldn't simply end in a presentation of the abstracted idea; the criteria would actually have to work. Panelists would be using those criteria to vote for the most significant trend of the year, meaning that the criteria would actually have to produce a viable set of candidates from the mass of digital content that emerges every year. The criteria must not only produce a recognizably folkloric outcome, they also have to be reasonable; panelists (as feedback from early years has shown) do not have the time or the interest to consider more than a handful of criteria for a given trend. As a result, any more than four or five criteria become unsustainable for the project.

In the end, the DFP settled on five criteria to determine its top contenders from the wealth of ethnographic data collected over the year. A successful example of digital folklore must (1) exhibit *dynamic variation* (not simply be viral; see Shifman 2013); (2) appear in a *folkloric form* (there must be a clear genre, so it can't simply be a popular theme or topic); (3) be *grassroots*, emerging from the bottom up rather than the top down (generated predominantly by everyday people rather than by institutions or publications—or at least perpetuated or taken over by everyday people); (4) *persist* to some degree as part of an ongoing process (it can't be a single, static "thing" that happens once); and, most important (this is our tie-breaking criterion), (5) be *culturally meaningful or significant* (it must be saying something for and/or about the culture that shares it).

The panelists use these criteria to vote on a winner in two categories: social justice and serious fun. The DFP learned early on that comparing two popular digital trends against each other can be decidedly imbalanced; for example, how could our voters be expected to reasonably compare the #MeToo movement to the "distracted boyfriend" meme? Both are wildly popular, but they exist in two different realms. The DFP risks diminishing a serious social movement by comparing it to a funny meme and risks overlooking the genuinely meaningful manifestations of what may seem to be a silly meme if we toss it out on the grounds that it's not serious enough. The two categories allow us to acknowledge that digital folklore moves in multiple spheres, which has been a revealing issue to contend with—sometimes we're surprised by the significance of something we initially believed to be purely humorous.[1] The contenders are put into a ballot with examples, a brief overview of the trend, and short explanations of how each criterion is met, and after voting is complete, the winning trends are publicized in a press release.

The Digital Folklore Project has three main goals in tracking trends and promoting their results to mass and digital media gatekeepers. The first is knowledge mobilization. There is an ongoing need to get information out of the university and into the public sphere. Utah State University, as a land grant institution, is especially dedicated to this endeavor, and digital folklore as a subject of study is ripe for sparking public interest. When Jeannie Thomas first conceived of #DigitalTrendOfTheYear, she was inspired by the *Oxford English Dictionary*'s annual Word of the Year announcement, which is a lighthearted (and sometimes enjoyably contentious) way to bring a discussion of the evolution of accepted language to the general public. The DFP hopes to do the same with digital folklore. Most members of the general public don't think of folklore as emerging on the internet (if they think of folklore as contemporary at all), and they often don't think of user-generated, bottom-up internet content as culturally significant or valuable; the DFP hopes to change those perceptions.

The DFP's second main goal is the documentation and preservation of digital folklore for study by future generations. The internet has been described as self-archiving, in that typically ephemeral content (conversations and interactions) created and shared online are often incidentally preserved by websites as artifacts that can be revisited. But there are two obvious dangers in relying on this unintentional archive. First is the fact that the web isn't nearly as stable as users tend to think it is. As Jill Lepore, writing for the *New Yorker*, notes, "No one believes any longer, if anyone ever did, that 'if it's on the Web it must be true,' but a lot of people do believe that if it's on the Web it will *stay* on the Web. Chances are, though, that it actually won't" (2015). Between link rot, content drift, and the rise and fall of social media companies, the average life of a web page is only 100 days or so. Second, while information may still be *preserved* through the efforts of organizations like archive.org, it is not necessarily *differentiated*. The internet is self-archiving the way a landfill is self-archiving; it may all be in there, but it's hard to dig through, and it's deteriorating fast. As such, the DFP works to identify specifically folkloric content on the web and to gather it folkloristically, noting and preserving meta-textual elements like context, texture, and community.

The project's third—and most important—goal is to highlight the incredibly important expressive and communicative role that digital folklore can play in a variety of contemporary contexts, which brings us back to our first Digital Trend of the Year award winner, #BlackLivesMatter. #BlackLivesMatter (BLM) is a Twitter hashtag originally initiated by Alicia Garza, Patrisse Cullors, and Opal Tometi in 2013 after the fatal shooting of Trayvon Martin. The hashtag gained increased visibility and use after Michael Brown, an unarmed black teen, was fatally shot by a white police officer in August 2014 in Ferguson, Missouri. Michael Brown's death was not the only racially charged incident between police and civilians in 2014; after a Staten Island grand jury's decision to acquit a white police officer accused of using a chokehold on Eric Garner, another unarmed black man who later died from his injuries, the BLM hashtag became ubiquitous online, galvanizing protests and "die-ins" nationwide, and spawning related hashtags such as #IfTheyGunnedMeDown, #HandsUpDontShoot, and #ICantBreathe.

Jeannie Thomas (2017) has written an excellent study of the BLM hashtag and its history as a focal point for collective storytelling. My goal in this chapter is to consider a different aspect of the hashtag, the pragmatic question of the classification of hashtags as a form of folklore.[2] The impetus for this consideration is that the Digital Trend of the Year award was not the only honorific that BLM received in 2014. One month after the DFP announced its winning trend, the American Dialect Society named #BlackLivesMatter the 2014 "Word of the Year."[3]

The American Dialect Society's decision was met with immediate pushback from some linguists. These linguists claimed that a hashtag, especially one made up of three distinct words, was an inappropriate choice for Word of the Year, as it not a word per se. The experts quoted in the *New York Times* expressed frustration, saying things like, "By what manner of well-meaning legerdemain . . . does a three-word Most Notable Hashtag become Word of the Year?" and "So I guess there is no real distinction between 'word of the year' and 'quotation of the year'?" (Bennett 2015).

In a press release, Ben Zimmer, chair of the society's new words committee, addressed the criticism head-on: "While #blacklivesmatter may not fit the traditional definition of a word, it demonstrates how powerfully a hashtag can convey a succinct social message. Language scholars are paying attention to the innovative linguistic force of hashtags, and *#blacklivesmatter* was certainly a forceful example of this in 2014" (American Dialect Society 2015). The competition, of course, is not "innovative linguistic force of the year," but it seems definitions are changing. What is clear is that many fields want to claim the hashtag as their domain; linguists want them to be words and folklorists want them to be folklore.[4]

Almost all the runners-up for the 2014 Digital Trend of the Year were hashtags or were expressed via hashtags. Another runner-up was the ALS Ice Bucket Challenge, which we classified predominantly as a custom, but which also manifested a number of related forms, including folk art, narrative and, yes, hashtag. I cannot begrudge the American Dialect Society its recognition of the same trend, but it is noteworthy that "competitions" like these almost always serve as advertising for their professional organizations. Folklore studies, as an academic discipline, has struggled to gain the recognition among the general public that English or linguistics has, and allowing a hashtag to be an example of folklore stands to help the public better recognize folklore in its often unexpected contemporary forms. But if a hashtag isn't only a word, which a folklorist might classify as folk speech, what kind of folklore is it?

Hashtags have been described as folksonomies (grassroots systems of organization and categorization), games, topic markers, meta-commentary, parenthetical explanations, emotion indicators, scare quotes, humor, memes, "searchable talk," and affiliative markers (Zappavigna 2011). Folklorist Sheila Bock has suggested that in the context of Black Twitter, hashtags can serve as a form of "signifyin(g)" (2017, 144), a broad form of symbolic discourse, and as boundary construction between different social identities (160). All of these definitions highlight the communicative *function* of a hashtag, one of the four modes by which Dan Ben-Amos (1976) has suggested that folklore genres are often defined, and they all seem to pitch a hashtag more as a component of a speech *act* than as an utterance in itself. Considering Dell Hymes's (1974) model for the analysis of speech events and acts, hashtags appear to be eligible for several roles within the speech act that is a tweet or other social networked post: they can set the scene, providing the psychological or cultural definition of the setting; or they can provide the key, indicating tone, manner, or spirit. They can even serve to indicate ends and to determine participants.

So as a framing device (see Goffman 1974), setting the scene or providing the key for the communication that is taking place, the hashtag takes on the air of customary folklore. To use William Wilson's (1986) simple breakdown of folkloric forms, hashtags appear to be *something we do*, not *something we say*; they are behaviors more than words. Offline corollaries would be traditionally learned performative elements such as gesture, stance, and facial expression, or the use of a meta-folkloristic construct such as, "knock knock," or "once upon a time," or "did you hear what happened to my cousin's friend's hairdresser?" to cue expectations for how listeners should comprehend the information that follows. Understanding predominantly textual genres as behavioral is nothing new for folklorists. Bill Ellis has suggested that legends, a form of folklore consistently classified as narrative, "are not folk literature but folk behavior" (2001, 10). Hashtags, similarly, are not folk speech but a form of folk practice. It may not be a stretch to consider their use a form of ostension—the acting out of a traditional narrative that serves to perpetuate that narrative as much if not more than the verbal or textual sharing of stories. Andrew Peck's concept of ostensive practice—highlighting the aggregation of individual actions into a larger, communally shaped concept of traditional competence—may fit even better in that the action of keying or framing a micro-narrative with a traditional hashtag "[guides] and [delimits] the potential for further action" (2018, 54) from future users. The performative nature of a hashtag is evident.

A hashtag is not only an act more than a word, it's also a *call to* action for others, a suggestion at least to *receive*, to actively listen to, if not actively collaborate with, an ongoing performance or event. As Anthony Bak Buccitelli has noted: "The reactions of audience members are themselves a kind of performance . . . If the reactions in a face-to-face setting are communicative fronts constructed by audience members in accordance with their accepted social and performative roles, then response postings on the Internet, themselves a kind of communicative display, must also be examined as socially governed forms of expression that can be profitably thought of in similar terms to audience reactions in f2f settings" (2012, 82). In other words, the performative nature of hashtags, especially when used artfully in their functions as games, meta-commentary, or humor, implies the familiar concept of "feedback" in face-to-face folkloric interaction. Rather than a static item, a hashtag in its full meaning is an emergent concept, each iteration simply a manifestation of a larger discursive process of constructing a shared sense of meaning and communicative competency within the form.

But the call to action of a hashtag goes beyond the basic performative demands of appropriate audience response as well. As sociolinguist Michele Zappavigna puts it, all hashtags, in their function as "searchable talk," are implicitly saying, "Search for me and affiliate with my value!" Zappavigna defines searchable talk as "online discourse where the primary function appears to be affiliation via findability," a process that she sees as inherently community building (2011, 789). So, unlike the comment posts that Buccitelli considers, hashtags in tweets are often specifically linking to a larger ambient context that potential audience members are expected to pursue. Zappavigna explains: "Users can *choose to mean* in an explicitly searchable manner by integrating metadata into their talk through typographic conventions, like the hashtag, that increase the 'loudness' of their discourse by increasing the likelihood that their words will be found" (2011, 800). In other words, hashtags correspond to a change in the *texture* of the tweet, the equivalent of modulating one's voice to garner greater attention.

The idea of searchable talk is made even more interesting by the fact that BLM has, as have many hashtags, transcended both its original form and context, regularly appearing offline, where its hyper-linked nature is technically disabled, but where its role as searchable talk is still intriguingly possible. Mobile devices are increasingly bringing online culture to offline spaces, providing us with digital portals to our hyper-linked lives that mesh seamlessly into our analog experiences. More than ever, a sense of real virtuality—the social and cultural impact of online networks brought to bear on the lived experience of the offline world—is achieved via mobile technology, and it's easy to see that a handheld sign offline with a hashtag indicator on it is asking observers to seek them out online and affiliate with the movement's value. The online experience of a hashtag as an affiliative marker extends offline as well—we see a familiar hashtag out in the world and the community-building effects of that emergent process are brought to bear on our analog perceptions. Zappavigna explains, "The affiliation is ambient in the sense that the users may not have interacted directly and likely do not know each other, and may not interact again" (2011, 801). Taking that affiliation offline, where affiliation is less ambient and more specific, the community-identifying power of a hashtag is more directed. The people involved in the ambient online discussion become real and tangible, as does the shared ostensive convention that identifies that larger discussion.

So does it matter whether a hashtag is a word or a form of folklore, as long as people are recognizing the power of this form of grassroots community building? I think it does, and not just because I don't want the American Dialect Society stepping on the Digital Folklore Project's turf. We've seen that a hashtag plays the role of behavioral folklore, expressing the key, frame, or texture of a given speech act in a traditionally understood way. But the benefit of identifying a hashtag as folklore goes beyond that basic idea.

Calling an individual hashtag folklore highlights that it's part of larger process of cultural communication rather than a single static utterance.

This isn't simply to say that folklore is used expressively in ongoing cultural movements or exchanges, which would be true for words as well; it's to highlight that *the thing itself*, the hashtag, is a grassroots emergent process, constantly evolving and generating a complex of forms and meanings that allow it to adapt to the performative and communicative needs of a massive amount of people in a variety of contexts.

This evolution, the tension between the form one receives and the adjusted, adapted, renegotiated form that one hands back into circulation, is central to identifying any given form as folklore. BLM does not exist in an expressive vacuum. It has spawned related and sometimes contentious hashtags such as "#PoliceLivesMatter," "#BlueLivesMatter," and "#AllLivesMatter"—forms that require an understanding of BLM in order to make sense. Other forms join in the complex that is BLM as well: customary die-ins, legends and rumors about the police and their victims, videos of police encounters, the self-consciously selfie-based folk art of "#IfTheyGunnedMeDown." If BLM is a word, then these expressions are not a part of it; they're separate, if not unrelated, artifacts. But if it's folklore, then these diverse forms of repetition and variation are a central part of the phenomenon itself, and we gain a much better understanding of the cultural significance of #BlackLivesMatter.

The Digital Folklore Project works hard to capture the emergent and discursive nature of digital folklore. While our public output highlights a single winner, the more important (as least to folkloristics) aspect of the project is the archive of the research team's collected folklore and field notes, which are gathered and preserved by the Fife Folklore Archives. Month by month, the research team builds a database of ongoing trends, noting the evolution and adaptation of specific forms, so that while the final press release may simplify the matter for the general public, the information that goes into constructing the ballot preserves the nature of the material in a much more realistic way (not to mention driving our archivists crazy—figuring out how best to input metadata for a bunch of cyclical, recursive, and nascent digital trends has proven to be one of the biggest hurdles to overcome).

The classification of forms of folklore is an ongoing challenge, one that remains largely abstract for most of us who don't work in archives; those who do will know that the categorization of a given piece of folklore is a necessary fact of preservation. I am hopeful that the efforts of the DFP will help others recognize both the significance and the complexity of digital forms of folklore, as well as folklore's need to be at the forefront of these preservation efforts.

NOTES

1. For one year the DFP had a third category, the "animal mascot," in honor of the many animals that stand out online in a given year, but it was eventually deemed too distracting for the panel of voters.

2. As always, the DFP pushes us into considerations that we might otherwise be able to set aside in favor of deep interpretation or analysis. As any archivist—digital or analog—knows, determining exactly what kind of folklore one is dealing with is the first step in knowing where to put it, but initial classification also risks preemptively interpreting the material.

3. The word *hashtag* was the 2012 winner, and the competitive subcategory of "most notable hashtag" was introduced in 2014, which BLM also won.

4. In 2015 Black Lives Matter was a runner-up for *Time* magazine's Person of the Year, adding yet another perception to the mix: hashtags representing the people behind them.

REFERENCES

American Dialect Society. 2015. "2014 Word of the Year Is '#blacklivesmatter.'" *American Dialect Society*, January 10, 2015. https://www.americandialect.org/2014-word-of-the-year-is-blacklivesmatter.

Ben-Amos, Dan. 1976. "Analytical Categories and Ethnic Genres." In *Folklore Genres*, edited by Dan Ben-Amos, 215–42. Austin: University of Texas Press.

Bennett, Jessica. 2017. "At the Super Bowl of Linguistics, May the Best Word Win." *New York Times*, December 21, 2017. https://www.nytimes.com/2015/01/18/style/at-the-super-bowl-of-linguistics-may-the-best-word-win.html.

Bock, Sheila. 2017. "Ku Klux Kasserole and Strange Fruit Pies: A Shouting Match at the Border in Cyberspace." *Journal of American Folklore* 130 (516): 142–165.

Buccitelli, Anthony Bak. 2012. "Performance 2.0: Observations toward a Theory of the Digital Performance of Folklore." In *Folk Culture in the Digital Age: The Emergent Dynamics of Human Interaction*, edited by Trevor J. Blank, 60–84. Logan: Utah State University Press.

Ellis, Bill. 2001. *Aliens, Ghosts, and Cults: Legends We Live*. Jackson: University Press of Mississippi.

Goffman, Erving. 1974. *Frame Analysis: An Essay on the Organization of Experience*. Boston: Northeastern University Press.

Hymes, Dell. 1974. *Foundations in Sociolinguistics: An Ethnographic Approach*. Philadelphia: University of Pennsylvania Press.

Lepore, Jill. 2015. "What the Web Said Yesterday." *New Yorker*, January 19, 2015. https://www.newyorker.com/magazine/2015/01/26/cobweb.

Peck, Andrew. 2018. "The Cowl of Cthulhu: Ostensive Practice in the Digital Age." In *Slender Man Is Coming: Creepypasta and Contemporary Legends on the Internet*, edited by Trevor J. Blank and Lynne S. McNeill, 51–76. Logan: Utah State University Press.

Shifman, Limor. 2013. *Memes in Digital Culture*. Cambridge, MA: MIT Press.

Thomas, Jeannie Banks. 2017. "#BlackLivesMatter: Galvanizing and Oppositional Narratives." In *Race and Ethnicity in Digital Culture: Our Changing Traditions, Impressions, and Expressions in a Mediated World*, edited by Anthony Bak Buccitelli, 95–114. Santa Barbara: Praeger.

Wilson, William. 1986. "Documenting Folklore." In *Folk Groups and Folklore Genres*, edited by Elliott Oring, 225–254. Logan: Utah State University Press.

Zappavigna, Michele. 2011. "Ambient Affiliation: A Linguistic Perspective on Twitter." *New Media & Society* 13 (5): 788–806. http://nms.sagepub.com/content/13/5/788.

10

The Clown Legend Cascade of 2016

John Laudun

SINCE THE 1980S, LEGENDS ABOUT CREEPY CLOWNS HAVE arisen in the weeks and days leading up to Halloween and subsided shortly thereafter, usually only a day or two after the holiday passes. In 2016, however, the furor over clowns was not only much greater than it had been in the last half dozen years, it also started much earlier.[1] The change in intensity, timing, duration, and spread of this annual legend cycle can be traced to two distinct yet increasingly connected media environments: mass media and social media. As the 2016 clown legend cascade moved back and forth across these two domains, it eventually began to express deeper anxieties about the status and nature of social media itself—a legend consumed, like an ouroboros, by its own place in the world.

Most studies of cascades in information and computer sciences assume a consistent, if not uniform, substrate (Bikchandani et al. 1992; Sadikov et al. 2011). But, as Trevor J. Blank (2015), Andrew Peck (2015), and Robert Glenn Howard (2011) have made quite clear, the relationship between folk culture, mass media, and social media infrastructures is complex. Social media does more than simply expand informal and formal communication networks: it can extend, refute, amplify, and comment on them, among many other possibilities.[2] In the case of the clown legends of 2016, we have a hybrid cascade: there appeared to be legend performances (of various kinds) on the ground, followed by reports of such performances in both mass and social media.[3] These reports fed back into the legend cycle, forming the basis for further legend performances, ongoing discussions on social media, and subsequent mass media coverage. In other words, the clown legends of 2016 occurred locally, in mass media, and in social media, and all three domains were aware of, and informed by, the others.

The idea of following an idea as it moves through a particular medium is not a new one, of course. It is the touchstone of the study of folk culture. What is new, and what folklorists are trying to grapple with, is the speed and spread of information like legends and rumors in the age of networked devices that are always on, always with us, and seemingly always in our faces. As in previous eras, all information has an origin, and as in previous eras, that which we call folklore becomes such by its widespread diffusion with little to no regard for its origins. Folklorists have long assumed that legends had a fairly even and/or random distribution through communities, but the rise of online communities has given folklorists the opportunity to reexamine some of their founding assumptions and to attend to matters of affinity, as Linda Dégh and Andrew Vázsonyi set out in their consideration of the legend conduit, and which they later realized could be generalized as the folklore conduit.[4]

This chapter examines 180 instances of the 2016 clown legend cascade, attending to the first instances closely, then treating subsequent texts in aggregate with occasional texts profiled as indices of larger trends. Of these texts, 162 were drawn from mass media sources, which, as noted above, often cyclically drew not only on oral instances but also on social media instances.[5] In this work, as in others, the nature of the network is understood in terms of text reuse: who likes, shares, retweets, quotes, forwards, or replies.[6] While a more comprehensive study would trace the lines of social and institutional networks with the texts as evidence of linkages, the current study attends only to the texts themselves, tracing how the legend changes as it transits through the various networks.

ORIGINS

The clown legend cascade of 2016 seems to have as its "event zero" the dissatisfaction felt by residents of an apartment complex in Greenville, South Carolina. There is no way to determine if the residents' lack of safety concretized into clown sightings, but a search for news about clowns ahead of the first legend report reveals the following chronology: On July 22, a local television station reported that people living in the Fleetwood Manor apartment complex had filed complaints about what they believed were unsafe living conditions (Cedrone 2016). There was no mention of clowns. Two weeks later and several states away, a viral marketing campaign for an independent film became a national news item when the film's creator started circulating "real" photos of a creepy clown lurking around Green Bay, Wisconsin, on social media (Le Duc 2016). On August 4, for example, *USA Today* reported that "Wisconsin residents are calling police, asking about a disheveled clown walking through Green Bay with four black balloons." Three weeks afterward, on August 26, matters seem to have converged, with a South Carolina Fox affiliate reporting that "multiple law enforcement agencies are investigating a rash of incidents involving clown sightings at apartment complexes and other areas of Greenville and Spartanburg counties." The report further detailed:

> Greenville County deputies were called to investigate a clown sighting on Rutherford Road Friday afternoon, emergency dispatchers confirmed. Dispatchers said they received a call from the 1700 block of Rutherford Road about a man dressed as a clown who was last seen running into the woods. Both the Greenville Police Department and Greenville County Sheriff's Office have open cases and the Spartanburg Police Department confirmed Thursday that a clown sighting had been reported at an apartment complex there. Deputies in Greenville County said the clowns were initially seen in wooded areas, where they reportedly tried to encourage children to join them, but the situation escalated to reports that clowns were also knocking on the doors of homes. Investigators said no conclusive photo or video evidence has surfaced and no suspects have been named in any of the incidents. Officer Gilberto Franco with the Greenville Police Department said the biggest obstacle investigators are facing is lack of detail in the descriptions they are receiving of the clowns. Franco said that of the three reports his agency is investigating, not enough information was received about the costumes, hair colors, and whether or not the suspects had on masks or painted faces. (Shaw et al. 2016)

In a moment where material evidence was otherwise in short supply, the report also included reference to a letter sent out by the heretofore-mute Fleetwood Manor Apartments management. As local news outlets began reporting on the clown sightings at the complex, residents shared a letter they said they found on their apartment doors. The published images are all of tri-folded pieces of paper with a company logo at the top and the complex's address at the bottom and typically include a portion of a hand holding the letter, a graphical representation that acts to authenticate the letter both through the seeming realism of a person holding it as well as through the implied presence of an apartment complex resident in whose hand the letter resides. The letter in the images is dated August 24 and states that the complex's management has received complaints of a person dressed as a clown trying to "lure children into the woods." It concludes by reminding its readers, who are now also readers of the photographed image of the letter around the world, that "to ensure your childrens [*sic*] safety please keep them in the house duing [*sic*] night hours."

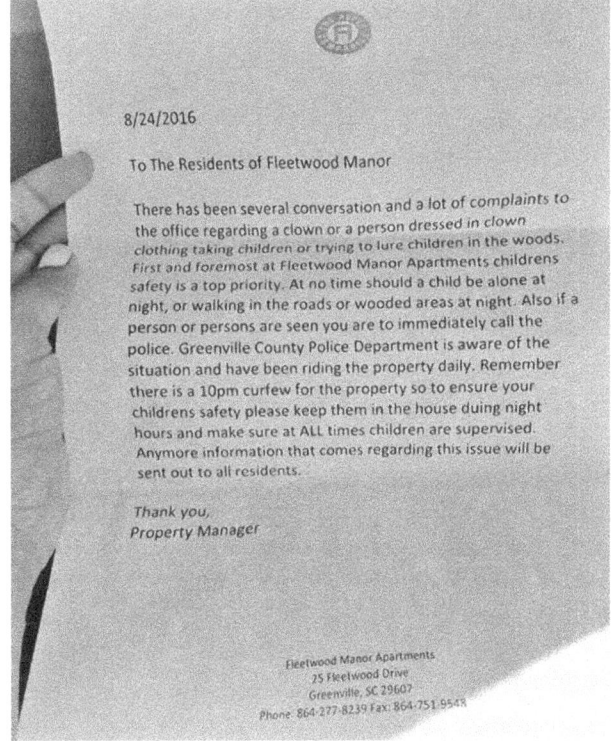

Figure 10.1. A local warning letter shared on social media.

On the same day, a Facebook post of the photo appeared with the caption: "Greenville Area Alert: This came from one of the residents of Fleetwood Manor apartments, over behind Waffle House on South Pleasantburg." The accompanying photo is of the letter sent out by the Fleetwood Manor apartment management and is again held by a hand that presumably belongs to a complex resident (figure 10.1). The text of the letter notes that clowns have been seen "trying to lure children in the woods" and that management takes safety seriously. It also advises that police patrols have increased, and there is a curfew.

Three days later the local NBC affiliate, WYFF, returned to the scene and captured additional information: according to residents, the clowns were whispering and making strange noises in the woods; they offered children cash; they lived in a house near a pond in the woods. Other sources seemed to quote other residents, some (not all) of whom had reported what they had seen or heard from children to the police: the clowns were hanging out in the woods near the basketball courts; they were flashing "laser lights" in the woods. While these variations are compelling, their overarching nature is of clowns in the woods luring or threatening children, who then report this to adults. That same day, August 29, the story, still focused on Greenville, appeared in the *New York Daily News*, on another Fox affiliate, WPMT, in Harrisburg, Pennsylvania, as well as in *People* magazine and on *CNN*.

PATHS

The story continued to spread and, as more and more outlets attended to the clowns, the reported nature of them became part of the story. On August 30 the *Atlantic* observed, in a somewhat self-serving fashion, that the virality of the clown legend was a product of mass media attention: "The story has garnered national media attention—the *Washington Post*, *USA Today*, and *BuzzFeed* all reported on the alleged sightings. It's not surprising, considering scary clowns are, after all, one of pop culture's favorite tropes, as *The Atlantic*'s Sophie Gilbert wrote in 2014" (Wagner 2016).

Even in these early reports, several features that would become standard in the 2016 cascade were present. These include: "a suspicious character . . . dressed in circus clown attire and white face paint, enticing kids to follow him/her into the woods"; "clowns in the woods whispering and making strange noises"; "clowns . . . flashing green laser lights before they ran away into the woods"; "chains and banging on the front door"; "large-figured clown with a blinking nose, standing under a post light near the garbage dumpster area"; "clowns had displayed large amounts of money in an attempt to lure [children] into the woods"; "the clowns lived in a house located near a pond at the end of a man-made trail in the woods"; "a teenage girl . . . saw a man taking pictures of kids, and shortly after, saw a man wearing a black jacket and a clown mask coming out of the woods."

While the features above are all from just one text (Shaw et al. 2016), they are repeated in other reports, with some features clearly repeated and others a blend of features added by later reports, allowing the legend to tune itself to spread more widely. In an effort to understand a similar collection of texts, Tim Tangherlini (2017) has used tiered, or scaled, structures to understand how vaccine legends, among others, circulate, actualizing certain ideas through focusing on particular kinds of stories featuring particular kinds of agents. In order to move from the legend as a device that structures the essential sequence (or sequences) of texts, through the narrative frameworks available to populate the sequences with agents and actions, to the discourse where actual instances of stories are performed, Tangherlini relies upon a set of algorithmic methods that discern the relevant features for each level. In the case of the 2016 clown legend cascade, one concern is to determine what features of the legend tend to cohere with other features.

In this case, our features are words, and one method for understanding how words stick together across/within a collection of texts is to use a technique known as topic modeling, which seeks to understand which words regularly occur with other words, a measure known as co-occurrence in corpus linguistics, natural language processing, and machine learning. Working with the current collection of 180 news reports and social media posts (which is relatively small for these kinds of approaches), a couple of trials suggested that twenty topics were analytically useful.[7] The results of the model can be seen in table 10.1, which has limited the number of words associated with each topic to the top ten. *Clown* or *clowns* feature in all but two of the topics wherein *police* also appears and, perhaps not surprisingly given the basis for the legend's reproduction based on quotative authorization, both those topics feature either a speaking verb or a reporting agenda: topic 6 has "said police" as its top two words and topic 10 has "news add police" as three of its four top words. Interestingly, *said* features in half the topics, underlining that the legend, as it is reproduced in mass media, is about reported events.

Such a set of topics, developed for exploration and not for precision, contains a great deal of overlap. Our concern here is to discern which topics occur most frequently in news media reports and in social media reports as well as to determine which topics are common to both. By compiling a list of the top three topics for each of our 180 news reports and social media posts, we can count the number of times a topic occurs in the first, second, or third position in terms of frequency. The results are compiled in table 10.2, which reveals that the topics common to all the texts are, principally, 4, 6, and 17, with 5 and 14 having significant but not dominant roles. Topic 4 clearly expresses the sentiment most regularly, and alliteratively, associated with the clowns: creepiness. Topics 6 and 17 are keyword clusters that combine both authoritative figures and quotative verbs. Topic 6 in particular focuses on the reportings by police, featuring *said* and *police* as the top words and then a number of terms drawn from police vocabulary, including both *victim* and *incident* as well as the precision of days of the week.

The two kinds of texts, news reports and social media posts, also distinguish themselves in terms of topics, though, given the overwhelming number of news reports in the collection, it is not surprising that it is difficult to distinguish common elements from those particular to the news. Nevertheless, some collating suggests that the dominant topics for news

Table 10.1. The top 10 words for 20 topics in the clown legends

Topic	Keywords
Topic 0	just like didn clown let don time going wasn did
Topic 1	clown clowns police children sightings reports evil oct local pennywise
Topic 2	ago months clown point people just school comments clowns video
Topic 3	greenville clown said clowns children deputies county apartments police woods
Topic 4	clowns people creepy like fear really time creepiness said don
Topic 5	clown police reports reported wearing sept woman dressed person mask
Topic 6	said police monday reading mask street victim wearing tuesday incident
Topic 7	aid henry house clown just dude ronald fucking party parents
Topic 8	clown clowns state penn people students campus twitter reports said
Topic 9	ago months clown machete just point deleted good kids like
Topic 10	news county add police office sheriff com sponsored site facebook
Topic 11	clown said 2016 police clowns threats october children sightings girl
Topic 12	woods clowns report told deputy saw children said according clown
Topic 13	clown said event threats march matter lives creepy tucson canceled
Topic 14	clown says people sightings scary year hysteria creepy media just
Topic 15	clowns clown circus people king jester clowning anxiety trump hysteria
Topic 16	school threats schools threat media social county students said clown
Topic 17	said clowns clown people school flomo police woods told old
Topic 18	people clowns reports uk clown sightings 10 police including trend
Topic 19	clown town night like school clowns wasn got eyes wanted

Table 10.2. The top 3 topics as they appeared in news reports and social media posts

News Reports			Social Media		
T1	T2	T3	T1	T2	T3
6	17	6	4	17	17
4	4	5	9	14	19
17	5	4	11	4	9
16	6	14	6	0	5
5	14	17	19	19	14
14	12	1	16	16	10
12	16	10	14	15	7
3	3	19	10	8	6
8	1	15	8	7	4
15	2	16	7	6	3
9	19	12	2	2	2

reports are 17, 5, and 12. The latter two topics, 5 and 12, feature people who are not police officers: women and children, with women being associated with dressing and masking and children associated with woods. The dominant topics for social media posts appear to be 9, 11, and 19, which feature two novelties: weapons in the form of machetes and schools.

In fact, on August 31, the *Columbus Dispatch* in Ohio reported that a teenaged boy said he had been chased as he walked to a school bus stop, which is the first instance of schools in the 2016 cascade. The passage below is representative of the larger text, which uses the police as authorities upon which the veracity of the report can be based, deferring responsibility to the police in such a way that the report suggests that neither itself, as reporting agent, nor the police, as receivers of the originating report, can afford to do anything but take matters at face value: "A knife-wielding clown reported in the Northland area might prove a hoax, but Columbus police say they aren't taking any chances. A 14-year-old boy told police that a 6-foot-tall man in dark clothing and a clown mask chased him a short distance as he walked to a school bus stop at about 6:15 a.m. Tuesday, said police spokesman Sgt. Rich Weiner" (Widman 2016). Later in the report we encounter more details about the clown, described as a tall man dressed in dark clothing and wearing a clown mask, as well as the boy's successful defense (throwing a rock at the clown) and his eventual safe arrival at school. The story ends somewhat ominously, however, noting that school security personnel and police will remain vigilant: "They haven't seen anything suspicious since. Forest Park Elementary School is located just down the road." This story was subsequently picked up by *NBC News* and the *New York Daily News*.

It's quite possible that the introduction of the school motif was polygenetic, or that the news traveled more quickly than this discussion can treat, but on September 1 the police in a second community in Greenville County received a call from a concerned parent whose daughter had allegedly seen a clown in the woods while walking home from school. Included in the article are additional sightings, again, of clowns taking photographs: "The girl stated that she saw a man taking pictures of kids, and shortly after, saw a man dressed as a clown and coming out of the woods. She said the man taking pictures of kids was riding a blue bike, and the other man was wearing a black jacket and a clown mask" (Kates 2016).

Within a few days, on September 5, Fox News reported an instance of the legend in Winston-Salem, North Carolina, in which "two children reported seeing a clown trying to lure kids into the woods with treats" (Fox News 2016). This instance of the legend included a detailed inventory of how the clown was dressed: "The 'clown' was described as wearing white overalls, white gloves, red shoes with red bushy hair, a white face and a red nose." The quotation marks serve a double purpose, marking the word *clown* as used by others and, as a result, marking it as dubious. Two days later, on September 7, *People* magazine combined several reports of clown sightings, including one that stated "a man brandishing a machete chased a clown into the woods" and another telling of a delivery driver noticing a clown who then ran into the woods. In both cases, the clown's garb is a focus of the legend text: the man who brandished a machete reported that the person he chased wore "a scary clown mask, red curly wig, yellow dotted shirt, blue clown pants and clown shoes" (Pelisek 2016). The delivery driver said the man he saw wore "a clown mask [and] a clear poncho." The last two reports in *People*'s compilation simply repeat reports of people seeing someone dressed in a "clown costume."

At this point the multiple incidents began to coalesce into a full-blown panic. There are many clowns in many places, reports began to warn, and they are threatening children. On September 6, one headline read: "Another Clown Was Spotted in the Woods and Police Say This Needs to Stop" (Van Dyke 2016). It was followed the next day by "Three More Creepy Clown Sightings Reported in North Carolina" (Tribune Media Wire 2016); "North Carolina Residents on Edge After Multiple Clown Sightings"; and "Reports of Creepy Clowns Spread to More Cities: 'It Is Not Funny,' Police Say" (Pelisek 2016). As the headlines reveal, the police assume increasing agency in the legends, as do other adults. With so many news outlets reporting, and it not being entirely clear which reports are of new events and which are repetitions of previous reports, the overall effect likely gives those following the news the impression of increased activity by clowns. With the police almost omnipresent in reports, the legend's authority also grows—that is, the textual effect of the police as "the authorities" is to authorize the legend, to legitimate it. The takeaway is simple and direct: a larger national craze creates a milieu within which certain kinds of behavior are made imaginable and thus possible.

As September drew to a close, a steady stream of analyses began to appear alongside the individual clown sightings. Published in national media like the *Washington Post, USA Today*, and *Rolling Stone*, these analyses variously sought to debunk or bust the clown stories or attribute them to foolish pranksters unaware of, or indifferent to, the havoc they were causing. They featured authorities of various kinds to objectify the trend: the president of the World Clown Association appeared in one, and in another the work of cryptozoologist Loren Coleman was quoted in addition to analysis of the phenomenon by a child psychiatrist. But that would not be enough to quell the immanent explosion that began at the very end of September when Ohio schools were reported closed due to clown threats and gangs of clowns terrorized Nova Scotian drivers. More than one serious report attempted to point out that these things happened every year, but none noticed that the cycles tend to play out later in the year, closer to Halloween.

SOCIAL TRANSFORMATIONS

As Andrew Peck (2020) observes about the relationship between mass media and social media, reporters are increasingly aware of the role social media can play in disseminating information, not only as part of their public service but also to increase their standings by various measures. A week after the Fleetwood Manor letter photo was posted to Facebook, a reporter with a local NBC news affiliate, Sarah Krueger, posted the following to her Twitter feed: "This is where clown sighting was reported. @cityofwspolice say he used treats to try & lure kids into woods @myfox8" (2016). The accompanying photo (figure 10.2) is composed of a street intersection sign, apparently in the middle of the woods because no road is visible. Just behind the street sign is a large "No Trespassing" sign with quite a bit of writing anchored by "By Order of the City of Winston-Salem." There is another sign below that one. To the right of the signs, tucked just inside the lower-right corner of the photo, is a guard rail. The entire scene appears to be illumined not by the camera's flash but by a light coming in from the right, as if by a pair of headlights. This motif of road signs became a part of the visual language of clown legends as they progressed across social media networks.

Back on Facebook, on September 13, a user from Roanoke, Virginia, posted a collection of images and a video in which the status of the legend as possibly ostensive in nature is confirmed. Within the collection of images there is a bit of text that reads: "Everyone in poor moiuntain please stay inside.[8] This isn't a joke. STAY SAFE." If the news reports are composites of children and of people reporting to police, then the legend on social media is now a hybrid of both the original reality and these news reports, with the latter providing an additional semantic layer. In addition, like the news reports, which often required some sort of image (even if it's little more than a street sign), to mark an "on the scene" imprimatur of veracity, some of the digitally mediated legend texts now come with images as either a subsidiary or principle focus. The Roanoke Facebook post also mirrors news reports in ostensibly not offering any answers in order to let readers and viewers decide for themselves: "I don't know if this is real or fake. I

Figure 10.2. A clown sighting reported on Twitter by a reporter for a local NBC news station.

didn't take this video or the pictures. A friend of my son sent these to him. I am not saying this is real. I don't know if this is a creepy man or woman or teen. I don't know if this is a person playing a prank. All I'm saying is there are news reports everywhere warning about this. I am simply saying to be careful and be cautious and lookout. That's all."[9]

In the comment thread, the original poster adds, "This was in the glenvar area at the back of one of Josh's friends." What follows are various reactions from other users, ranging from fear to claims that someone will get shot. Three early comments (out of the total of 157) are indexical of the larger dialogue that ensues: "This is happening all over"; "I'm not afraid of clowns but I am a little intimidated by a grown man in a clown costume stalking people"; and "Just a warning, some people [are] firm believers in the second amendment. And believe in private property, so a clown could be held at gun point until proper authorities can determine what a psychopath is doin dressed like a clown on private property." The overall sense such comments produce is the inescapability of the moment. The first comment emphasizes that this has happened before, which is indeed true, as we have already seen in the discussion of origins, while the second comment addresses anxiety—although the underlying legend about clowns themselves is not true or "real," we must still be concerned about people acting upon ideas that the legend suggests. As Bill Ellis notes: "Legends can help the folk relieve themselves of contemporary fears, but they may also serve as patterns for psychotics—or even sane but cunning criminals—for provoking the same fears" (1989, 203). Added to the fear that people will act ostensively upon the legend is the concern, often articulated angrily or with bravado, that someone is going to get shot, either by police or by an armed individual.

After the initial comments several users begin to question why the police had not been called as well as query the overall status of the legend: "Anyone know what the 'story' is behind all these clown incidents???" Some commenters ask about the location, and some of the responses challenge people to "see for yourself." The central tension remains "now a days you don't know what anybody will do." Inevitably someone "mythbusting" intercedes. Sometimes the comment addresses the legend from a global perspective: "It's a hoax that teens all over the US are participating in. This same video has been spread across three states and whoever is sharing it as being filmed in VA is not telling the truth. Hysteria spreads like wildfire when ignorance is abundant. Don't share and spread the hype, people!" Other comments offer insider knowledge that video is not real.[10] This dampens the feverish pitch of the comment thread a bit, but discussion continues to pursue the dangers of ostension, warning that individuals may get shot as a result of ostensive actions. Thus, no matter what, the clown legend endangers the lives of children, or at least of adolescents, who do not know when a prank has gone too far.

This transformation of the legend as it moved onto social media can be glimpsed in the shift in language itself. As Tangherlini notes: "Every story performance, be it in whole or in part, offers information about a knowledge domain. Through the repeated telling of stories, a narrative framework, which comprises a relatively stable group of actants (people, places, objects) drawn from a culturally determined pool of potential actants and relationships for that domain, emerges" (2017, 2). There are a variety of ways to approach this task, and while Tangherlini used facets of NLP to compile a list of actants and their relationships (perhaps using SVO [subject-verb-object] triplets), a somewhat simpler, if also a little less granular, technique is used here: word collocation networks.[11]

The idea behind collocation networks is that a text, or a genre of texts, is organized into lexical patterns that can be understood as networks of

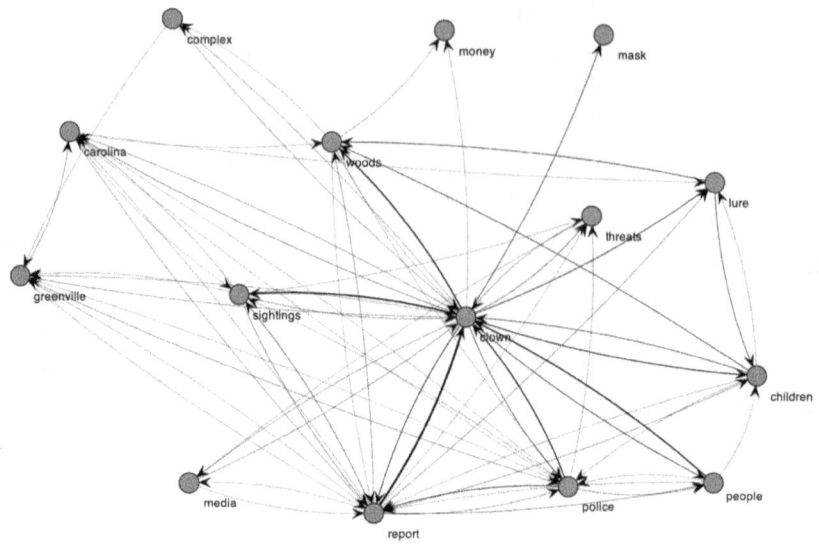

Figure 10.3. A collocation network of the news reports.

words that are located near each other in the discourse that makes up the text (Brezina et al. 2015, 142). They are useful for highlighting "syntagmatic lexical sets" (Phillips 1989, 52), or sets of words that co-occur in sentences or, as Tangherlini describes it, the microlevel of discourse itself (2017). The networks were compiled using a three-word window for both the news reports and the social media posts. The same set of words was dropped from both sets of texts, and each set was then lemmatized by hand so that words like *clown* and *clowns* converged, as did *report, reports, reported* or *police, officer, deputy*.

The first graph (figure 10.3) is drawn from the 162 news reports and only the 20 most prominent nodes of the 2,660 possible nodes (each representing a word) remain. As is also the case in figure 10.4, *clown* is central, but here there are significant enough relationships between *report, police, children, lure,* and *woods* that even should *clown* disappear, there would still be a relationship between them. The same is not the case for the second graph (figure 10.4), drawn from the eighteen social media posts, with the seventeen most prominent words presented here. In that graph, should *clown* be removed, the network itself would hang together only by the relationship between *sightings*, which carries over from the news reports, and *months*, which is a novelty found in the social media dimensions of the legend. Not only does it appear to represent a durative sense that the legend has about

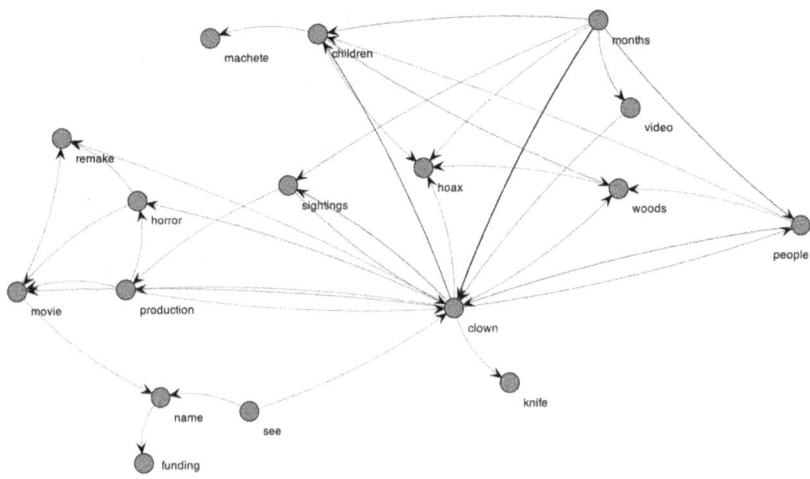

Figure 10.4. A collocation network of the social media posts.

itself, it also underlines the theme of inevitability that seems to permeate the social media versions: someone somewhere is going to go too far and either they or an innocent bystander will get hurt. This facet of the social media versions of the legend is underlined by the regular presence of *hoax* in the discourse, here featured fairly centrally in the graph.

In the shift from mass media to social media the reported nature of the legend, especially with the police as a source for authorizing the reports, drops out of the legend complex. Instead, in the transition to social media the legend picks up a bit more reflexivity, with references to the remake of the movie version of *It* being a component loosely attached to the legend, perhaps again underlining the dangers of ostension. To Facebook users, children are no longer in danger of being lured into the woods so much as at risk of being chased by clowns wielding weapons like knives or machetes.

The convergence of social media and mass media, alongside a variety of ostensive activities, can perhaps be best glimpsed in a report published on October 5 in the New Orleans newspaper the *Times-Picayune*, which was picked up from the *Washington Post*:

> It was just after midnight Tuesday at James Madison University when the clown calls started pouring in. Phones beeped and buzzed. There was no official alert at the Harrisonburg, Virginia, school, but on Yik Yak, Twitter and GroupMe, students learned of a possible intruder on campus. A grainy Snapchat video purported to show a menacing clown outside of one of the residence halls. Freakout ensued. Some students panicked; others were

just wary. No one really thought it was funny. In minutes, undergrad posses carrying flashlights and pepper spray roamed the Quad, seeking to capture the clown or at least chase it off. (Heim and Shapiro 2016)

Multiple social media platforms are cited as sources for the legend's circulation, with Snapchat being the one responsible for transmitting the video. This makes a certain amount of sense, given the high anxiety many users, especially adults, have about the purposefully ephemeral, and thus possibly secret, nature of Snapchat posts.

In the transition from mass media to social media, the legend morphed from clowns lurking in the woods attempting to lure children away to clowns lurking in social media (itself) threatening schools with Columbine-like events. The range of schools was rather wide, with the preponderance of legends focused on or mentioning middle schools and local universities. Not unlike the escalation of poisoned candy legends, these legends similarly escalated to include the idea that schools had been locked down. Across the United States, in report after report, local authorities were at great pains to clarify that no schools in their jurisdiction had been locked down or closed.[12]

TRENDS

The clown legend cascade of 2016 arose out of a tense social situation in which apartment dwellers felt that their needs were being ignored, or even dismissed, by their complex's management. Thanks in no small part to coverage by local media that got picked up by the national media, despite the presidential election dominating American news, the clown legend spread quickly not only to areas where we have seen legends flower before but also to other, less established ones.[13] It might very well be that the clown legends did, in fact, address an otherwise unarticulated complaint about neglect or some other anxiety that allowed the idea of clowns lurking at the edges of civilized places, threatening children, to spread so quickly across the United States, even leaping to other parts of the world.

As Sylvia Grider notes, most contemporary Halloween legends focus on the danger of strangers, or the estranged, among us (1984, 132). Anxiety lurks at the heart of the 2016 cascade as well, but such an explanation does not address why this phenomenon started much earlier, almost two months ahead of schedule. A closer examination of the five months of web searches focused around the 2016 cascade reinforces the conclusion suggested by the current analysis: the cascade occurred six weeks ahead of the usual timing and, in addition to the early start,

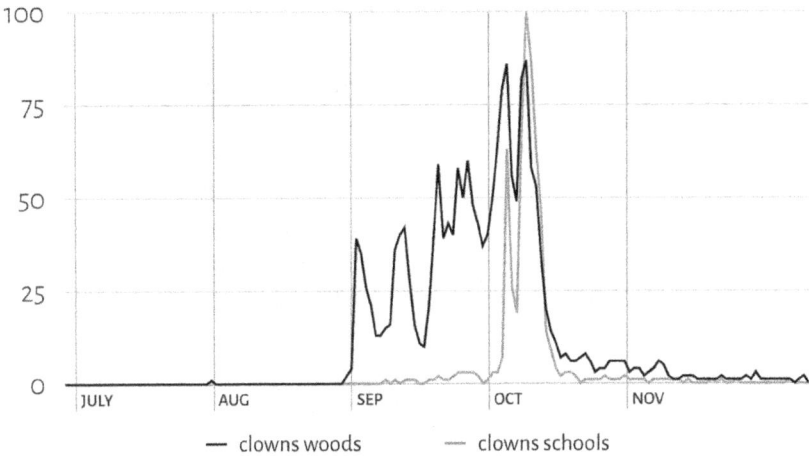

Figure 10.5. Searches for *clowns* and *woods* alongside *clowns* and *schools*. (Data source: Google Trends, https://www.google.com/trends.)

there is a pronounced surge in pairings of *clowns* with *schools* that in fact eclipses previous concerns with *clowns* and *woods* (figure 10.5). Curiously, as if eschewing its expected relationship with Halloween, the 2016 cascade diminished significantly in the second half of October, the moment in which clown legends have usually peaked in other years. Moreover, as noted at the beginning of this examination, the 2016 cascade exhibited ten times the usual volume of web activity.

What began as anxiety about masked figures lurking at the edge of civilization ended with a much more troubling consideration of the masks we all wear, and a certain morbid fascination with the thought that there are those among us who might, under the right circumstances, be compelled to do terrible things. A legend that began with clowns luring children into the woods either with treats or money in one locale spread rapidly across the United States—regularly featuring clowns glimpsed at roadsides or playgrounds. Sometimes the clowns chased adults, and sometimes they were themselves chased. Always the clowns got away. But as coverage in mass media ran its course, the legend shifted to social media, where the focus became a concern with pranks going too far. As the cascade continued on social media, almost all the versions of the legend focused on clowns threatening schools (on or through social media). In this way, perhaps, the 2016 cascade articulated the emergent anxiety Americans, in particular, have about mass shootings that too often take place on school campuses, be the schools primary, secondary, or higher education facilities.

Such a broad conclusion must be subject to a broader investigation than the one offered here. The current study is limited in scope by the materials it draws on, but the methods upon which it is founded are open to an expansion of the corpus. For folklorists, computational methods offer a way not only to repeat work we have done before with expansions, refinements, or reconsiderations of the materials at hand, but also to seize the opportunity that the internet offers as the infrastructure through which legends cascade, whether the legend is transmitted by a mass media report or a social media post. Moreover, as other studies of social networks in other disciplines have revealed, we can begin to understand how legends change as they pass through select communities of mass media or social media sites. With the rise of fake news as a topic of popular interest, folklorists face the possibility not only of demonstrating the effervescent power of the legend conduit, as Dégh and Vázsonyi once termed it, but also begin to trace the outlines of the conduit itself as it is instantiated, one legend at a time.

NOTES

1. According to Google Trends data, the 2016 clown legend cascade outpaced those of previous years by a factor of ten. (For a popular history of clown scares, see Faraci 2016, which it should be noted was published in January, a full seven months ahead of the start of the 2016 cascade.)

2. In an exploration of vulnerability to disease spread, Campbell and Salathé found that when ideas from overlapping social groups coincided, those ideas were more likely to form an individual's own response. They termed this complex "contagion" and described it as "[t]he density of potential social reinforcement is determined by how structured or random the contact network's topology is prior to the period of opinion formation" (2013, 4).

3. Much of legend scholarship assumes this hybrid nature, but it still helps, I think, to articulate it up front in order to foreground, if only for analytical purposes, that the "social" of social media is not purely online. In many cases, posts are, depending upon the platform involved (and email still counts as social media here), shared, liked, commented, forwarded, quoted, and/or retweeted solely online—and we do not yet have a clear discussion of cross-platform diffusion. But in one experience of the clown legends, I witnessed a group of middle school soccer players discuss the legend's various manifestations online as well as a particular localized version that reported the closure of a school because of an online threat.

4. By turning to the conduit, Dégh and Vázsonyi refocus folklore studies from our usual objects of examination, the things themselves and the people who say/use them, to the act of procession: how and why objects pass through people and how people transform them in their passing. Whereas others regularly imagined homogeneity, a sameness we still project with notions of "culture" or "society" or "community," Dégh and Vázsonyi focused our attention on the matter of message velocity and distortion through a course of variable individuals. The problem, as they understood it, was the impossibility of studying the conduit itself. "There is," they observed, "no way to follow the progress of oral transmission in society" (1975, 214). While oral transmission remains difficult to document, digital

transmission practically documents itself. This focus on the conduit and how it affects the nature and meaning of a given form have proved to be quite prescient, where Dégh and Vázsonyi had to be somewhat speculative when they later noted: "The legend might, for example, be developed into another genre; it might be shaped into a *Marchen* or a joke; it might be reduced to a rumor. Wandering from conduit to conduit, eventually the legend may retrieve its lost track as likely as it might become mutilated and distorted or wither away into nothingness" (1976, 96). We can now track the transformation of legends into jokes as they pass from one network into another.

5. The complete corpus, as well as the computational notebooks referenced in the discussion, is available as a GitHub repository (http://github.com/johnlaudun/CLC2016). In addition to the 180 news reports and social media posts discussed above, there are also two fictions—there are many more such texts, but for the current project I decided to focus on the nonfictional texts.

6. Regarding retweet networks, see Brady et al. 2017; for text reuse, see Smith et al. 2014a; for Twitter topic networks shares, see Smith et al. 2014b.

7. There are a number of approaches to topic modeling. Here, nonnegative matrix factorization (NMF) was chosen because of the quality of its results when treating small corpora. Readers may also be familiar with the more widely known and used topic-modeling algorithm LDA. Both approaches assume that any given document is simply a product of a set of topics, and that the likelihood of one word occurring with another is a function of them being a part of the same topic. Both approaches also take a document to be simply a "bag of words," such that a word's position within a text or in relationship to other words is not considered. There are ways around this lack of concern with word position—by breaking documents into smaller sections so that a document's beginning, middle, and end, for example, may be taken as different in nature—but such an approach was not used here: given the size of the texts and my interest in discovering word associations, the documents, both news reports and social media posts, were taken as the units of analysis. The top three topics for each of the 180 texts is outlined in a CSV file in the GitHub repository. Finally, it should be noted, for those less familiar with topic modeling, that the number of topics is something the analyst provides to the algorithm. The number chosen here, twenty, reflects a number of trials as well as prior experience with corpora of various sizes: it is an outsized number for a corpus this small, but the model of analysis used here was that first demonstrated by Ben Schmidt (2015) in his work on plot arcs and then further explored by Archer and Jockers (2016) in their examination of best sellers.

8. Poor Mountain is a location within Roanoke County, Virginia.

9. https://www.facebook.com/melissa.dooley.397/posts/10210653052873261. The complete post with comments is available as an image in the repository.

10. One lengthy comment offers the following rebuttal: "This is not real. My nephew shot the video. I called him out on it Sunday after I saw it. The costume belonged to my son. We still have the package it came in from spirit halloween 2 years ago. They took it from my in-laws house. Aaron sent me a message telling me it was a prank wanting me to go along with it. He has taken this way to far. I can tell you exactly where it was recorded. That is his brother in the costume. I nor my son had anything to do with this. This is completely ridiculous what Aaron has done. All to get attention. He blocked me and from what I can tell he has now deleted his Facebook. I do not uphold what he has done."

11. NLP, or Natural Language Processing, is an outgrowth of corpus linguistics and an integral part of machine learning in particular and artificial intelligence in general when

it comes to handling actual discourse, which tends to be, from the point of computation, extraordinarily disorderly and messy. The most successful uses of NLP in the current moment assume larger data sets, or corpora, such that an algorithm can be trained or the larger semantic matrix can be discerned. Tangherlini and colleagues' approach uses thousands of instances to discover a generalized narrative kernel which largely holds true for their corpus. Individual examples, however, may or may not agree with that generalization. (For a more detailed description of the methods involved in Tangherlini's studies, see Tangherlini et al. 2016.)

12. This legend struck close to my own home in Louisiana, with the girls on my daughter's soccer team claiming that this or that school had been closed or that students had been huddled into a gym or some other communal space, while deputies came to search the school.

13. Some sense of the geography of American legendry is captured by Bill Ellis in his examination of the Satanic cult legends of the late 1970s and early 1980s (1989), which featured southeastern and midwestern states that were also active in the 2016 clown legend cascade—and, interestingly, the history of Satanic panics has also become part of conventional wisdom (Romano 2016).

REFERENCES

Archer, Jodie, and Matthew Jockers. 2016. *The Bestseller Code: Anatomy of the Blockbuster Novel.* New York: St. Martin's.

Bikhchandani, S., D. Hirshleifer, and I. Welch. 1992. "A Theory of Fads, Fashion, Custom, and Cultural Change as Informational Cascades." *Journal of Political Economy* 100 (5): 992–1026.

Blank, Trevor J. 2015. "Faux Your Entertainment: Amazon.com Product Reviews as a Locus of Digital Performance." *Journal of American Folklore* 128 (509): 286–297.

Brady, William J., Julian A. Wills, John T. Jost, Joshua A. Tucker, and Jay J. Van Bavel. 2017. "Moral Contagion in Social Networks." *Proceedings of the National Academy of Sciences* 114 (28): 7313–7318. https://doi.org/10.1073/pnas.1618923114.

Brezina, Vaclav, Tony McEnery, and Stephen Wattam. 2015. "Collocations in Context: A New Perspective on Collocation Networks." *International Journal of Corpus Linguistics* 20 (2): 139–173. https://doi.org/10.1075/ijcl.20.2.01bre.

Campbell, E., and M. Salathé. 2013. "Complex Social Contagion Makes Networks More Vulnerable to Disease Outbreaks." *Scientific Reports* 3: 1905.

Cedrone, Tony. 2016. "Fleetwood Manor Residents Claim Poor Living Conditions." *WSPA/7News*, July 22, 2016. http://wspa.com/2016/07/22/fleetwood-manor-residents-claim-poor-living-conditions/.

Dégh, Linda, and Andrew Vázsonyi. 1975. "The Hypothesis of Multi-Conduit Transmission in Folklore." In *Folklore: Performance and Communication*, edited by Dan Ben-Amos and Kenneth S. Goldstein, 207–252. The Hague: Mouton.

Dégh, Linda, and Andrew Vázsonyi. 1976. "Legend and Belief." In *Folklore Genres*, edited by Dan Ben-Amos, 93–123. Austin: University of Texas Press.

Ellis, Bill. 1989. "Death by Folklore: Ostension, Contemporary Legend, and Murder." *Western Folklore* 48 (3): 201–220.

Faraci, Derek. 2016. "When Pennywise Was Real: The Phantom Clown Scare of 1981." *Blumhouse.com,* January 4, 2016. http://www.blumhouse.com/2016/01/04/when-pennywise-was-real-the-phantom-clown-scare-of-1981/.

Fox News. 2016. "Creepy Clown Sightings Expand to Second South Carolina City." September 5, 2016. http://www.foxnews.com/us/2016/09/05/creepy-clown-sightings-expand-to-second-south-carolina-city.html.

Geoghegan, Jemma L., Alistair M. Senior, Francesca Di Giallonardo, and Edward C. Holmes. 2016. "Virological Factors That Increase the Transmissibility of Emerging Human Viruses." *PNAS* 113 (15): 4170–4175. https://doi.org/10.1073/pnas.1521582113.

Grider, Sylvia. 1984. "The Razor Blades in the Apples Syndrome." In *Perspectives on Contemporary Legend: Proceedings of the Conference of Contemporary Legend*, edited by Paul Smith, 128–140. Sheffield: CECTAL.

Heim, Joe, and T. Rees Shapiro. 2016. "Scary Clown Rumors, Threats Feed Hysteria, Leading to School Lockdowns, Arrests." *Washington Post*. October 5, 2016. https://www.washingtonpost.com/local/education/scary-clown-rumors-threats-feed-hysteria-leading-to-school-lockdowns-arrests/2016/10/05/1adf27c4-8b0b-11e6-bff0-d53f592f176e_story.html.

Howard, Robert Glenn, ed. 2011. *Network Apocalypse: Visions of the End in an Age of Internet Media*. London: Sheffield University Press.

Jakobson, Roman, and Petr Bogatyrev. 1980. "Folklore as a Special Form of Creation." *Folklore Forum* 13 (1): 1–21.

Kates, Graham. 2016. "Creepy Details Released in South Carolina Clown Sightings." *CBS News*. August 31. http://www.cbsnews.com/news/clown-sightings-south-carolina-creepy-details-released/.

Krueger, Sarah. 2016. "This Is Where Clown Sighting Was Reported." @WRALSarah. September 5, 2016. https://twitter.com/WRALSarah/status/772706941034459137.

Le Duc, Shelby. 2016. "Creepy Clown Was Marketing Ploy." *Green Bay Press Gazette*, August 10, 2016. https://www.greenbaypressgazette.com/story/news/2016/08/10/green-bays-creepy-clown-marketing-ploy/88527696/.

Peck, Andrew. 2015. "Tall, Dark, and Loathsome: The Emergence of a Legend Cycle in the Digital Age." *Journal of American Folklore* 128 (509): 333–348. www.jstor.org/stable/10.5406/jamerfolk.128.509.0333.

Peck, Andrew. 2020. "A Problem of Amplification: Folklore and Fake News in the Age of Social Media." *Journal of American Folklore* 133 (529): 329–351.

Pelisek, Christine. 2016. "Reports of Creepy Clowns Spread to More Cities: 'It Is Not Funny,' Police Say." *People*. September 7, 2016. http://people.com/crime/creepy-clowns-reported-in-more-cities-in-north-carolina-south-carolina/.

Phillips, Martin. 1989. *Lexical Structure of Text: Discourse Analysis Monograph 12*. Birmingham, UK: University of Birmingham.

Romano, Aja. 2016. "The History of Satanic Panic in the US—And Why It's Not Over Yet." *Vox*, October 30, 2016. https://www.vox.com/2016/10/30/13413864/satanic-panic-ritual-abuse-history-explained.

Sadikov, Eldar, Montserrat Medina, Jure Leskovec, and Hector Garcia-Molina. 2011. "Correcting for Missing Data in Information Cascades." *WSDM 11: Fourth ACM International Conference on Web Search and Data Mining*, 9–12. New York and Hong Kong: Association for Computing Machinery.

Schmidt, Benjamin M. 2015. "Plot Arceology: A Vector-Space Model of Narrative Structure." *2015 IEEE International Conference on Big Data (Big Data)*, 1667–1672.

Shaw, Amanda, Sierra Hancock, Shale Remien, and Dal Kalsi. 2016. "Deputies Called to Investigate Another Clown Sighting." *Fox Carolina*, August 26, 2016. http://www.foxcarolina.com/story/32852558/residents-anxious-after-clown-sightings-letters-received-at-greenville-co-apartments.

Smith, David A., Ryan Cordell, Elizabeth Maddock Dillon, Nick Stramp, and John Wilkerson. 2014a. "Detecting and Modeling Local Text Reuse." *Proceedings of the 14th ACM/IEEE-CS Joint Conference on Digital Libraries*, 183–192.

Smith, Marc A., Lee Rainie, Ben Shneiderman, and Itai Himelboim. 2014b. "Mapping Twitter Topic Networks: From Polarized Crowds to Community Clusters." *Pew Research Center* 20: 1–56.

Tangherlini, Timothy. 2017. "Toward a Generative Model of Legend: Pizzas, Bridges, Vaccines, and Witches." *Humanities* 7 (1): 1.

Tangherlini, T. R., V. Roychowdhury, B. Glenn, C. M. Crespi, R. Bandari, A. Wadia, M. Falahi, E. Ebrahimzadeh, and R. Bastani. 2016. "'Mommy Blogs' and the Vaccination Exemption Narrative: Results from a Machine-Learning Approach for Story Aggregation on Parenting Social Media Sites." *JMIR Public Health and Surveillance* 2 (2): e166. http://publichealth.jmir.org/2016/2/e166/.

Tribune Media Wire. 2016. "Three More Creepy Clown Sightings Reported in North Carolina." Tribune Media Wire. September 7, 2016. http://fox8.com/2016/09/07/three-more-creepy-clown-sightings-reported-in-north-carolina/.

Van Dyke, Michelle Broder. 2016. "Another Clown Was Spotted in the Woods and Police Say This Needs to Stop." *Buzzfeed*. September 6. https://www.buzzfeed.com/mbvd/stop-clowning-around-police-say.

Wagner, Laura. 2016. "Are the Clown Sightings in South Carolina Real?" *Atlantic*, August 30, 2016. https://www.theatlantic.com/news/archive/2016/08/are-the-clown-sightings-in-south-carolina-real/498059/.

Widman, Alissa. 2016. "Teen Reports He Was Chased by Clown with Knife." *The Columbus Dispatch*. August 31, 2016. http://www.dispatch.com/content/stories/local/2016/08/31/Police-investigate-clown-scare.html.

11

The Blue Whale Suicide Challenge
Hypermodern Ostension on a Global Scale

Elizabeth Tucker

DURING THE ELEVEN YEARS SINCE Trevor J. Blank's *Folklore and the Internet* was published, we have gained more understanding of the "paradoxically familiar . . . and simultaneously foreign" digital world (2009, 10). Analysis of creepypasta, an emergent genre of internet folklore in the form of fictional short horror stories shared online, has shown how well the online medium works as a site for legend dissemination (see Blank and McNeill 2018). An understudied aspect of legends' appearance online is the performance of pranks by adolescents. In one popular kind of prank, teenagers assume the role of perhaps the most (in)famous figure of creepypasta fandom, Slender Man, to torment their younger brothers and sisters (Tucker 2018).

Other pranks have arisen from the recent Blue Whale Suicide Challenge, a rumor panic alleging that curators or administrators of social networks give teenagers fifty upsetting and dangerous tasks. The first tasks are relatively easy: waking up at 4:20 a.m. to watch a horror video, listening to troubling music, or drawing a whale on a piece of paper. Gradually the demands become more disturbing and painful: standing on the edge of a roof, climbing a crane, or cutting "yes" on one's leg. The final task is to commit suicide by jumping off a building or following another fatal demand from the curator or administrator (Dwilson 2017).

The idea of cruel adult administrators making adolescents kill themselves is certainly alarming, but manipulative behavior of this kind is more compatible with youth culture than with adult culture. The fifty-task Blue Whale Challenge fits a larger pattern of dangerous challenges that has become well known on the internet in recent years. The Cinnamon Challenge mandates eating a teaspoonful of dry cinnamon; the Tide Pod Challenge calls for eating

DOI: 10.7330/9781646420599.c011

a plastic container of laundry detergent, and the Condom Snorting Challenge suggests inhaling a condom, then pulling it out. Teen-produced videos of all three of these challenges have become extremely popular on YouTube, but there is more to this phenomenon than the desire to impress and entertain an audience. As Iona and Peter Opie explain in their classic study of children's and adolescents' games, young people frequently test each other's courage through dares, some of which seem outrageous and dangerous to adults (1969, 263–274). For young people, dares and other dangerous games serve as rites of passage toward maturity. Some recipients of dares, however, do not survive this process. Dares and other aspects of bullying have resulted in victims' suicides (Tucker 2002). Internet communication has made it possible for kids to challenge and bully each other online, sometimes with tragic results.

How much can adult researchers learn about teenagers' behavior online? It can be extraordinarily difficult to penetrate what folklorists of childhood call the childhood/adolescent underground. Fearing punishment, kids tend to exclude parents and other adults from dares, bullying, and other kinds of behavior that may get them in trouble. It is, however, possible to learn about young people's behavior through posts that are available to the public. This chapter explores adolescents' interpretation of Blue Whale rumors and legends in YouTube videos and comments and their expression of moral messages through outrageous pranks that victimize fellow teenagers and irritate adults. Adolescents' pranks, which do not usually get much attention from adults, offer important insights into youth culture and social problems. For twelve months, from the spring of 2017 to the spring of 2018, I watched Blue Whale videos that I found through Google alerts and YouTube searches. This chapter analyzes videos that are characteristic of adolescent behavior during that year of research.

Some pranks happen because of ostension, which brings legends to life. In their introduction of the term *ostension* for legend study, Linda Dégh and Andrew Vázsonyi (1983) explain that enactment of legends takes a number of forms. One of these is pseudo-ostension, which can also be called a hoax or a prank. Dégh and Vázsonyi worried about criminal ostension, which can result in people being charged with such crimes as property damage and personal injury; they did not express concern about people killing themselves as a result of ostension, but such behavior fits their paradigm of legend enactment. Indeed, ostension has both serious and humorous elements. Blue Whale pranks express *hypermodern* ostension: legend enactment that makes extensive use of digital technology (Tucker 2016). As Jeannie Banks Thomas explains, hypermodern folklore "emerges from, deals with, or is significantly marked by contemporary technology and media (including the omnipresent

Internet) or consumerism (with all its accessible excesses and its ability to generate pleasure mixed with anxiety)" (2015, 8). Ostension based on hypermodern behavior has developed on a global scale because access to computers and smartphones has become so common around the world.

Although the Blue Whale Suicide Challenge is a recent phenomenon grounded in internet behavior, it has roots in earlier patterns of imitative behavior based on knowledge of famous people's and fictional characters' suicides. Stories of the suicides of the Roman general Mark Antony and the Egyptian queen Cleopatra, both in 30 BCE, make listeners think about self-destruction. The medieval Japanese samurai warriors' code of honor includes *hara kiri*: choice of self-inflicted death rather than a dishonorable life. In Johann Wolfgang von Goethe's semi-autobiographical novel *The Sorrows of Young Werther* (1774), a young man (who habitually wears a blue jacket and yellow pants) kills himself with a friend's pistol after finding that he cannot extricate himself from a romantic triangle. For some time after this book was published, police in a number of northern European countries found the bodies of young men wearing clothing of the same colors who had committed suicide with pistols; some of the young men were holding Goethe's novel. This spate of suicides resulted in the novel being banned in Denmark, Italy, and parts of Germany. Sociologist David P. Phillips (1974), coined the term "the Werther effect" for this kind of self-destruction, which has also become known as copycat suicide.

The Blue Whale Challenge is a newer, faster-moving version of the kind of imitative behavior that became familiar to the public in eighteenth-century Germany. While the "Werther effect" is well known, teenagers' responses to contemporary expressions of this phenomenon deserve more attention. Pranks or practical jokes, which tend to be a favorite genre of the adolescent years, victimize peers and may also criticize people's behavior (see Marsh 2015, 57–71). Close examination of the Blue Whale Challenge's movement around the world and its resultant rumors, legends, and pranks helps us understand how young people amuse, scare, and manipulate each other online.

GLOBAL MORAL PANIC

First, we should consider what we can learn from studies of the "Satanic panic" of the 1980s (Ellis 1990, 1991; Victor 1993). Like the Blue Whale Suicide Challenge, this earlier moral panic began with alarming stories about endangerment of young people by evil adults. Rumors and legends about Satanic cults' activities spread rather slowly from one part of the United States to another and eventually reached the British Isles and parts of Scandinavia. In those pre-internet days, rumors and legends traveled through oral transmission and print and broadcast media. The legend scholar Bill Ellis (1990, 1991) argues that teenagers' ostensive behavior convinced adults that Satanic rituals were actually taking place. Ellis's argument, based on examination of legends, artifacts, and community histories, is very persuasive, but he did not find teenagers who admitted to engaging in pseudo-Satanic behavior. That was probably because, as in the more recent case of the Blue Whale Suicide Challenge, adolescents don't like to tell adults what they are doing if there is a possibility that they will be punished.

When Slender Man was created on the internet in 2009, the stage was set for rumors and legends to travel much more quickly. The story of two twelve-year-old girls who stabbed a friend in Waukesha, Wisconsin, in 2014 was rapidly disseminated around the world. Because the girls claimed to be proxies of Slender Man, worry about Slender Man's possible influence on young people spread quickly across the United States. This did not become a global rumor panic, however. People outside the United States found Slender Man legends interesting but did not seem to view them as a threat to public safety in their own countries. However, this was not the case with the Blue Whale phenomenon.

The Blue Whale Challenge first came to international attention in February 2017, when websites in English reported that an online game had resulted in at least 130 deaths in Russia. In an article in the Russian *Novaya Gazeta* in May 2016, a reporter linked child/adolescent suicides to a group called F57 on the social network VKontakte in Russia. According to Snopes.com, which has investigated the claim these suicides and found it "unproven," this linkage was a misinterpretation; although some of the young people belonged to the same online game community on VKontakte, their decisions to take their own lives did not necessarily come from the Blue Whale Challenge itself (Evon 2017).

Further notoriety came to the Blue Whale Challenge when international news reported that half sisters Yulia Konstantinova, fifteen, and Veronika Kolkova, sixteen, had jumped to their deaths from the upper floor of an apartment building in Irkutsk, Siberia, on March 12, 2017. Although there was no evidence that the Blue Whale Challenge had caused their deaths, a BBC reporter noted that authorities had "said that the girls may have been influenced by conversations with others on social media" (*BBC News* 2017a). The same reporter mentioned that young people were discussing Blue Whale in closed groups on VKontakte and that journalists who had tried to become part of one of the groups had received the task of cutting "F58" on their arms. A different BBC report quoted VKontakte as saying that Blue Whale hashtags came from "tens of thousands of bots" (Alluri 2017). Considered together, these journalistic statements strangely combine secrecy with evil intent and mechanical artificial intelligence chaos: an ideal blend for stimulating rumors and legends.

Another part of the journalistic record from Russia caused consternation in other countries in May 2017. Philipp Budeikin, an expelled university student who had been identified as a Blue Whale administrator, pleaded guilty to encouraging at least fifteen teenagers to commit suicide. Budeikin told Russian reporters that those teenagers were "biological waste" and he needed to "cleans[e] society" (*BBC News* 2017b). This harsh statement made people worry that sardonic elitists might be manipulating vulnerable teens into taking their own lives.

At this point, an important revelation occurred through folklore research. Concern about harm to young people from the Blue Whale Challenge became so intense in Russia that police asked scholars to help them understand what was going on. A team of Russian folklorists—Alexandra Arkhipova, Daria Radchenko, Maria Volkova, and Anna Kirzyuk—investigated "death groups" through participant observation; Volkova joined some groups and participated in conversations online, expressing interest in Blue Whale tasks (2017). Through this experience, the research team learned that current leaders of "death groups" were teenagers, not adults. Their analysis showed that both ostension and pseudo-ostension took place in the groups and that adults in Russia viewed the internet as a source of danger because the Blue Whale Suicide Challenge had become a moral panic (Arkhipova et al. 2018).

The Blue Whale Challenge became news in the United States in July 2017, when members of two families in the South expressed concern that the challenge had induced their teenagers to commit suicide. The brother of a teenaged girl who had committed suicide in Atlanta, Georgia, told reporters that his sister had painted and displayed pictures of blue whales in her bedroom; in addition, she had drawn a sketch of a Russian girl, Rina Palenkova, who had committed suicide in 2015 (Kutner 2017). Her behavior seems to have been an ostensive expression of the Blue Whale Challenge but was not clearly linked to a manipulative source. Another grieving relative was the father of fifteen-year-old Isaiah Gonzalez, who hanged himself July 8, 2017, in San Antonio, Texas, after propping his smartphone up nearby to record the hanging. Gonzalez's father told a reporter that his son had participated in the Blue Whale Challenge, which "talks about satanic stuff and stuff like that" (Ferguson and Swenson 2017). His mention of Satanism provides significant information about people's fears at that time. No definitive proof of Blue Whale involvement was found in either suicide case, but dissemination of details on radio, television, and the internet caused considerable alarm.

Fear of Satanic elements in the Blue Whale Challenge has also been expressed in Arab countries. In the religion of Islam, Iblis or Eblis is the fallen angel who was, like Lucifer, banished from heaven. On September 7, 2017, Mohammad Javad Azari Jahromi, Iran's information and communications technology minister, wrote in a post to Instagram that his ministry would try to protect Iranian young people from "satanic ideas" in the Blue Whale Challenge. Twitter, Facebook, and the Russian VK network are blocked in Iran, but a recent survey showed that more than 69 percent of the country's young people bypass filters to gain access to banned websites (Karimov 2017). Concern about harm from the challenge has also arisen in other Arab countries, including Algeria and Tunisia (Khlifi 2018; *Ansamed* 2018). The extent of these reports shows that fear of Satanism—more specifically, fear of evil adults who want to kill children—is very much alive in global rumors and legendry.

In India, the first suicide attributed to Blue Whale took place on July 30, 2017, when a fourteen-year-old boy leaped to his death from the seventh floor of a Mumbai apartment building. Less than two weeks later, on August 10, a boy in the seventh grade almost succeeded in jumping from a building; according to a reporter, he "apparently recorded all 50 stages [of the challenge] in his school diary." A male in the tenth grade in West Bengal who was "allegedly playing the game," was discovered dead in a bathroom with a plastic bag over his face and a cord encircling his neck (Baruah 2017). This tragic loss and others motivated the Indian government's Ministry of Electronics and Information Technology to insist that Facebook, Google, Yahoo, and other internet companies remove all forms of access to Blue Whale. Impassioned debate ensued, with commentators accusing the government of instigating a moral panic based upon a "game" for which there was almost no evidence (Worley 2017). Later, in January 2018, the Indian government announced that involvement of the Blue Whale Challenge in recent suicides could not be proven, but assertions of its validity continued to arise. In this impassioned exchange, as in the "Satanic panic" of the 1980s, the power of rumors and legends became clear.

BLUE WHALE RUMORS AND LEGENDS IN YOUTUBE COMMENTS

Although the journalistic record of Blue Whale's spread is richly detailed and intriguing, it does not tell us much about what teenagers are actually thinking and doing; instead, it applies adults' judgment to available evidence. When I did research on choking and fainting games (Tucker 2008–2009, 2014), I found that children and adolescents were reluctant to talk about this clandestine subject because their parents would not approve. YouTube offers researchers a chance to read young people's comments on videos without asking them questions that may cause discomfort. Now that YouTube is more commonly used and better established around the world, it offers a good index of what children and adolescents are thinking and feeling, as well as their creation of videos with a foundation in folk tradition.

Since the Blue Whale Challenge has been avidly discussed around the world, people have posted many videos about it on YouTube. YouTube has invoked its community policy to remove videos that seem overly graphic or offensive, but images of blue whales inscribed on arms are still viewable. In order to explore young people's comments, I watched twenty Blue Whale videos and read their comments. One popular video, posted by Scare Theater (Eric Wise) on March 10, 2017, offers a typical example of lively discourse. Titled *Blue Whale Suicide Game*, this video had been viewed 7,311,595 times by March 9, 2018, and had accrued 6,638 comments. The video names suicide victims in Russia, repeatedly shows images of whales and hangman's nooses, and mentions a Radio Free Europe reporter who supposedly infiltrated the VKontakte social media network. Although it is impossible to do justice to all of the comments here, we can assess their patterns in relation to Blue Whale rumors and legends. The main subjects on which people comment are whether the challenge actually exists, whether or not people should accept it, what adults are doing to help, and why suicide might seem desirable. In relation to those subjects, rumors and legends arise.

Those who comment on YouTube's Blue Whale videos are numerous and diverse. Most of them seem to be teenagers or young adults, with more males participating than females. All of the commenters on Scare Theater's Blue Whale video speak English, but not all of them live in the United States, the United Kingdom, and other English-speaking countries; many commenters live in Asia, the Middle East, or Africa. This diversity gives their discussion of the challenge's possible reality a global perspective. When an American asks, "O m g that's not real yes?" a North African replies, "Hello scare theater big fan I watched this video like a year ago but the blue wale is a hot topic in North Africa over dozen of kids killed them selfs then, they even talked about it on tv and teachers are also advising kids to not play the game." With these details, he suggests that Blue Whale is real, not just a rumor. Similarly, a young Iranian affirms the challenge's existence: "Its real somebody died of my land in dis game ITS IN NEWS STAY AWAY day put a logo whale on your arm to[o]." One especially intriguing comment seems to come from a young Russian: "All girls had whales cutted on theyr Arms and admins created group to clear 'biological vaist' i can link vidio where police arrested all currators and they anser questions but its in Russian language." Comments like this one disseminate a legend about Blue Whale's origin in Russia that can be shared with others online.

As the group gathers details about Blue Whale's existence, participants talk about whether or not they want to accept the challenge. Two typical statements are "Can you plzzz send me a link of this game plzzzz plzzz I can't find it" and "This game looks awesome. I am trying it now. See you guys after 50 days." Objections usually follow such eager statements: "Please don't download the game!" "This game is wrong," and "A boy just killed himself two weeks [ago] in Algeria just because of this shitty game," for example. An American asks, "What is wrong with the old games like jigsaws, dominoes, Monopoly, and table tennis with your friends?!" Many commenters express contempt for people who choose to accept the challenge in comments such as "this is sooo dumb, how could you fall for this shiz" and "how stupid are these people?" These divergent opinions resemble the comments on YouTube choking game videos that I found in my previous research (Tucker 2008–2009, 2014). After watching videos about choking games, some commenters insist they want to play; others argue that the game is too dangerous, and others deride the stupidity of anyone who wants to accept such a risk. Videos about both choking games and the Blue Whale Challenge generate expressions of excitement, horror, and disdain that come together with dramatic opposition.

Some commenters tell legends about Blue Whale's strange and/or supernatural effects. One comment expresses a fear of demonic influence: "this is not a game. That's a demon controlling you and telling you what to do" (see Howard 2009, 2011). Another comment emphasizes control without mention of a demon: "This is actually a dangerous game, if you download it: IT WILL STAY IN YOUR PHONE and if you don't do what it says it will go around your phone and sent bad pictures to your mother or something bad you did to your mother, how? I don't know." Other interesting comments describe a video game called *Mariam* that originated in Saudi Arabia and is popular in the Arab world. According to online news reports, this game, which urges players to help a lost child get home, has been rumored to collect personal information from players and hack into their computers (Khalaf 2017). One comment warns, "don't download it, and I've h[e]ard if you play it over 15 minutes your device will break." Another variant suggests, "[*Mariam*] has subliminal messages/suggestions (kind of hypnosis) and been designed in such a way that leaves the obstruction between reality & surreal." These comments and others warn that video games can have terrifying consequences, damaging a person's life. The *Mariam* game and the Blue Whale Challenge are just two of many digital phenomena that evoke this kind of worry.

Besides legends about machines taking control, rumors about an administrator coming to get players or their families arise repeatedly in the comments on this video. A female commenter asks, "Can it be a real aspect that they will surely find u n harm ur family? I think its for just terrifying n fooling the people." Nineteen replies quickly follow. The first sounds comforting: "they won't actually harm your family. It's just a game." A later reply, however, matter-of-factly predicts horror: "they do hack your device and know all about you." What is "real" in this electronic age? As the young people's discussion demonstrates, the boundary between real and unreal can be hard to determine.

The saddest comments tell of suicide attempts. For example, "I actually tried to kill myself 2 times but it was hard because i was thinking about my mother that she will feel so sad and i wanted to help her and my father is already dead when i was just 4 yrs old." This heartbreaking account reminds the reader that vulnerable teens need attention and nurture. It is also important to note that some comments describe tragic self-hangings that may have happened because of choking games: "A kid from my town just hung himself inside his closet after finishing this game and I'm actually so freaked out after watching this video because the information that he's giving us are accurate." During my previous research on choking games, I found many descriptions of the games' aftermath that resembled this one. Since choking games have had a strong appeal for adolescents in the twentieth and twenty-first centuries, it is possible that this kind of game playing explains some of the deaths that friends and family members have interpreted as results of the Blue Whale Challenge.

It is not surprising that curious adolescents and young adults try to understand why Blue Whale has gotten so many young people's attention. A long comment from Random Guy, who seems to be an older adolescent or young adult, states:

> I know it's obvious and fake but for a suicidal 14 year old who legitimately thinks the "administrator" actually can follow through with the threats and may not even realize they just pull info from their facebook page, they might actually get scared into continuing with the game And for others

it might be an easy way out—an excuse to act on their suicidal thoughts, HELL, it even gives you a comfortable way to work yourself up to it. This game is terrible, and should be taken seriously.

This comment insightfully interprets Blue Whale's potential for harming vulnerable adolescents who have already thought about suicide. Reading about a self-destructive challenge can be disturbing, but enactment of frightening rumors and legends on this subject can make the challenge seem more credible and upsetting.

PRANK VIDEOS

Pranks related to the Blue Whale Challenge have taken place in a number of countries, but the largest number of Blue Whale prank videos has come from India. From the summer of 2017 to January 2018, Indian adults argued about the impact of the Blue Whale Challenge. An intense moral panic culminated in an attempt to ban the game and an admission that there was no evidence children had died because of it. Teenagers closely observed their parents' arguments and came up with their own folkloric correctives.

According to a scientific study, India has the highest rate of youth suicide in the world (Patel et al. 2012). Changes in family norms and values, inadequate support systems, mental health problems, and other issues have made young people more vulnerable to despair (Lodha 2017). Since suicide was already such a source of concern in India in 2016 when the Blue Whale moral panic began, it is not surprising that the panic escalated rapidly there.

In India, pranksters vie for attention in short videos posted on YouTube. Since 2014, the Pranks in India series has presented videos from young video makers who want to outdo each other in making viewers laugh. These video makers come from different parts of India and post in different languages—though primarily in Hindi or English—and most of them are males in their late teens or early twenties. Their pranks range from internationally known classic pranks (stink bombs, ghosts, fake corpses, and invisible ropes) to more specifically Indian pranks related to Holi and other festivals. Many of the most popular pranks are those boys play on girls: farting on girls, peeing near girls, and doing other embarrassing things to get girls' attention. Some pranks show awareness of social and political trends. As people have become more fearful of terrorism, bomb pranks have grown in popularity. In this regard and others, pranksters seize upon current topics of concern and use them to victimize the unwary.

The morality of pranks is a crucial issue to consider. According to Moira Marsh, pranks "satisfy our thirst for poetic justice on small-time wrongdoers" (2015, 60). In the course of everyday life, pranks can attempt to correct inappropriate or mildly illegal behavior. Of course, Blue Whale rumors and legends suggest something much worse: predation upon vulnerable teenagers that makes them hurt themselves and think about committing suicide. Pranks about the Blue Whale Challenge act out dangerously destructive behavior that alarms and angers people. Whether or not curators actually make teenagers commit suicide in real life, the Blue Whale Challenge violates moral standards for appropriate nurture of young people. Through prank playing, tricksters can try to restore a better moral balance to the realm of social media. In addition, they can express skepticism about adults' worries and enjoy making people laugh (see Marsh 2015, 53–56).

Pranks are such serious business on YouTube that people compete for the honor of posting first in certain key categories. Thus, it is easy to determine that the first Blue Whale prank video in India was *India's First Blue Whale Prank / Prank in India 2017 / Prank by Chandu*, which was posted on August 21 (Freak Prank 2017). Chandu, a young man in his late teens or early twenties who lives in Mumbai, enjoys playing pranks for the Holi and Gudi Padwa holidays and actively pursues subscriptions to his YouTube channel. His video begins with a serious statement: "Blue Whale Challenge is a business game which was build [*sic*] in Russia." At the video's beginning, he asks, "What's up, guys?" and waves one of his arms, covered with red scratches, in front of the camera. Then he begins a rapid series of encounters with passersby in which he shows them his arm, points at his phone, and tries to engage them in conversation about Blue Whale. When Chandu victimizes schoolboys with backpacks, they pull back and push him away; some of the boys run away from him. His smartphone provides more of a focal point than his scratched arm does. After each potential dupe's refusal to look at his phone, a *boing* sound shows that he has not succeeded. It would, however, be simplistic to say that his prank is a failure. He shocks young people so effectively that they run from him, pushing his phone away, so his prank gets a high level of attention. At the end, Chandu cheerfully states, "Hope you guys enjoy your videos. Like, share, subscribe. Here is Chandu signing out"—a typical request for recognition, applause, and fame on YouTube.

A similar video, *Blue Whale Prank on Girls*, was posted by the Garv Jaiswal Team on September 2, 2017. Viewed 10,640 times by March 17, 2018, this is a moderately successful video in the hugely popular Pranks in India series. In this video one phone is used to make a request, while a second phone held by a team member records the prank: a clear case of hypermodern ostension.

Garv and his team members live in Kolkata and record most of their pranks on city streets. They post videos on Facebook and Instagram as well as their own YouTube channel, trying to attract as many subscribers as possible. *Blue Whale Prank on Girls* begins with a few words of welcome from a boy in his late teens, possibly Garv himself. Brandishing his smartphone, this teenager walks down a busy street, asking passersby in Hindi if they will download the Blue Whale game for him. First he accosts several male teenagers; then he approaches two older men and two teenaged girls. None of them show any interest in helping with a download; a laugh track plays after each unsuccessful request. The next person who goes by, a friendly-looking woman, pauses when he asks, "Excuse me, can you help me? Can you download Blue Whale game for me?" Replying, "No, no, better not," she rapidly moves on. Lastly, three teenaged boys wearing Batman shirts and hats come up to the prankster and start chatting in Hindi. The prankster points toward the videographer; one member of the group makes a "thumbs-up" gesture, and all of them laugh. The video's last message is "Thanks for watching ☺."

Like other videos in the Pranks in India series, this one does not seem to shock or amaze the people it targets. Only one of the people the prankster stops in the street—the woman who speaks English—takes the time to explain kindly, though briefly, that it would not be wise to download Blue Whale. Playing a laugh track after each unsuccessful attempt, Garv's team identifies the prankster as a fool. At the end, the prankster laughs with three boys dressed in Batman clothing, who seem to be his team members. The video's most obvious message is that no one should download Blue Whale, but there is a subtext: teenagers should not try to get attention from peers and adults by brandishing a smartphone. This prank entertains its viewers and also serves as a moral corrective, making fun of dangerous behavior that has alarmed many adults and adolescents.

Another Blue Whale prank, *Blue Whale Suicide Game*, tries to fool YouTube's viewers rather than those who are present at the time it was recorded. A group of four friends known as Humorous Gang recorded this video in Delhi on August 17, 2017; it had accrued a modest 1,052 viewers by March 17, 2018. Its summary on YouTube explains, "Our friend played this Blue Whale Game, and see what happen with him." As the video begins, three friends fool around with their smartphones as they sit on a concrete wall. One of them, Sanjay, teeters and falls over the wall's edge.

Somber music plays; the two remaining friends seem to be overwhelmed by grief. Then music from the film *The Pink Panther* (1963) starts to play, and Sanjay's fingers appear on the edge of the wall. His friends shriek. He is alive! Sanjay's reappearance and the *Pink Panther* music change the video from a tragic enactment of social media–induced suicide to a comic performance that celebrates teenagers' cleverness: an amusing shift that diminishes the impact of the Blue Whale Challenge. The last part of the video, "Making of the Blue Whale Suicide Video," shows how Sanjay pretends to suffer a fatal fall from a very low wall, and the last frame dictates, "Please like, share and subscribe." Both the comedic tone and the emphasis on social media fame correct the video's moral balance, replacing the horror of suicide with the joy of irreverent prank playing.

In contrast to these three prank videos produced by young Indian men, *BLUE WHALE PRANK (Gone Wrong!!)* is a professionally edited video by Sham Idrees, a young Canadian man who spends much of his time in Dubai. Posted on September 19, 2017, Idrees's video had had 1,037,825 views by March 24, 2018. Idrees has a large, multinational audience. In the realm of YouTube, he is a celebrity. His Blue Whale video deserves consideration because it delivers a more explicit version of the moral conveyed by simpler Blue Whale prank videos. First, Idrees shows viewers bloody cuts on one arm that "a professional makeup artist" has created. Then he shows his arm to Froggy, his female partner, explaining that he has cut himself and asking her to "be my Blue Whale." She objects and makes fun of him. When he tries to take the makeup off, he screams in pain; Froggy shouts, "It's gone wrong, because look what Allah did to him!" Following the classic legend pattern of "The Surpriser Surprised" (Jansen 1975), this video ends with the moral that those who victimize others through prank playing deserve to become victims themselves.

CONCLUSIONS

Tracing the progress of the Blue Whale Challenge helps us realize how much impact rumors and legends can have through rapid dissemination online. Since the spring of 2017, people around the world have grappled with the allegation that evil Russian curators have caused vulnerable teenagers to hurt themselves and/or commit suicide. Is it possible that thousands of Russians or Russian bots have served as curators, causing the deaths of many innocent young people? Putting this question in the context of the Satanic panic that started in the 1980s, we can conclude that such an elaborate conspiracy is highly unlikely. Just as no evidence of Satanic cults was found in the 1980s, no evidence of a worldwide effort by Russians to kill teenagers has surfaced since the challenge began, and it seems improbable that any will appear in the future.

However, revelations in Russia have helped us understand what has really been happening. In May 2017, the expelled university student Philipp Budeikin admitted to encouraging fifteen teenagers to kill themselves through online activity. Also in 2017, Alexandra Arkhipova, Daria Radchenko, Maria Volkova, and Anna Kirzyuk published the results of their research on "death groups" on the internet: those who were trying to get young people to kill themselves were teenagers, not adults. In both the Budeikin court case and the publication by four folklorists, it became clear that young people were attempting to manipulate each other. Although no such clear evidence exists in other countries, it seems likely that the Blue Whale Challenge is a product of global youth culture, in which bullying, dares, and dangerous games have been prominent. Access to the internet has given young people opportunities to intimidate, entertain, and scare each other more quickly and easily than they could before.

Through hypermodern ostension, rumors and legends spread across the world very rapidly. The accessibility of computers and smartphones makes it possible for people to watch videos, post comments, and then post videos of their own. Videos about young people's suicides raise viewers' awareness of suffering and may increase the likelihood of copycat suicides. Young people who act out aspects of the Blue Whale Challenge may make the challenge seem real and alarming, but they may also make it the subject of a prank that restores moral balance. Showing the prankster's failure to get a rise out of passersby when pointing to a Blue Whale image on a phone's screen reminds viewers that this is not a socially acceptable form of behavior. A video that seems at first to be a suicide leap but proves to be a spoof drains tension from the Blue Whale scenario, turning what appears to be a tragedy into a playful interaction that fools viewers.

In spite of the unprecedented rise of technology, some things have not changed much since the late eighteenth century. The sorrows of young Werther, who commits suicide while wearing a blue jacket and yellow pants, may not be very different from the sorrows of a teenager today who is contemplating the image of a blue whale on a computer screen, but ostension has evolved substantially since Werther's time. Filming pranks with their smartphones, teenagers can create humorous videos that delight audiences online. As long as teenagers keep playing imaginative pranks, laughter will enliven this strange but familiar digital world.

REFERENCES

Alluri, Aparna. 2017. "Why Is 'Blue Whale' Gripping India?" *BBC News*, Delhi. September 19, 2017. http://www.bbc.com/news/world-asia-india-40960593.

American Association of Suicidology. 2020. "Warning Signs of Acute Suicide Risk." Accessed July 13, 2020. https://suicidology.org/resources/warning-signs/.

Ansamed. 2018. "'Blue Whale' Game Banned." March 8, 2018. http://www.ansamed.info/ansamed/en/news/sections/generalnews/2018/03/08/tunisia-blue-whale-game-banned_6e125485-4add-426a-b20b-f90dc1fbb982.html.

Arkhipova, Alexandra, Daria Radchenko, Maria Volkova, and Anna Kirzyuk. 2017. *"Death Groups": From a Game to Moral Panic*. Moscow: Ranepa.

Arkhipova, Alexandra, Maria Volkova, Anna Kirzyuk, Daria Radchenko, Leta Yugay, and Josef Zislin. 2018. "'Death Groups': From Urban Legend to Moral Panic." Paper presented at the annual meeting of the International Society for Contemporary Legend Research, Brussels, June 5, 2018.

Baruah, Joyshree. 2017. "Blue Whale Challenge and Other 'Games' of Death." *Economic Times*, August 20, 2017. https://economictimes.indiatimes.com/magazines/panache/blue-whale-challenge-and-other-games-of-death/articleshow/60135835.cms.

BBC News. 2017a. "Are Teenagers Killing Themselves in Russia as Part of a Social Media Game?" March 16, 2017. http://www.bbc.co.uk/bbcthree/item/f4db7d77-3a2f-441e-9104-38513e43c295.

BBC News. 2017b. "Blue Whale Challenge Administrator Pleads Guilty to Inciting Suicide." May 11, 2017. http://www.bbc.co.uk/newsbeat/article/39882664/blue-whale-challenge-administrator-pleads-guilty-to-inciting-suicide.

Blank, Trevor J. 2009. "Toward a Conceptual Framework for the Study of Folklore and the Internet." In *Folklore and the Internet: Vernacular Expression in a Digital World*, edited by Trevor J Blank, 1–20. Logan: Utah State University Press.

Blank, Trevor J., and Lynne S. McNeill, eds. 2018. *Slender Man Is Coming: Creepypastas and Contemporary Legends on the Internet*. Logan: Utah State University Press.

Dégh, Linda, and Andrew Vázsonyi. 1983. "Does the Word 'Dog' Bite? Ostensive Action: A Means of Legend-Telling." *Journal of Folklore Research* 20 (1): 5–34.

Dwilson, Stephanie Dube. 2017. "Blue Whale Challenge: List of All 50 Tasks." *Heavy.com*, July 12, 2017. https://heavy.com/news/2017/07/blue-whale-challenge-game-what-are-the-50-challenges-tasks/.

Ellis, Bill. 1990. "The Devil-Worshippers at the Prom: Rumor-Panic as Therapeutic Magic." *Western Folklore* 49: 27–49.

Ellis, Bill. 1991. "Legend-Trips and Satanism: Adolescents' Ostensive Traditions as 'Cult' Activity." In *The Satanism Scare*, edited by James I. Richardson, Joel Best, and David G. Bromley, 279–295. New York: Aldine de Gruyter.

Evon, Dan. 2017. "'Blue Whale' Games Responsible for Dozens of Suicides in Russia?" *Snopes.com*, February 27, 2017. https://www.snopes.com/fact-check/blue-whale-game-suicides-russia/.

Ferguson, Amber, and Kyle Swenson. 2017. "Texas Family Says Teen Killed Himself in Macabre 'Blue Whale' Online Challenge That's Alarming Schools." *Washington Post*, July 11, 2017. https://www.washingtonpost.com/news/morning-mix/wp/2017/07/11/texas-family-says-teen-killed-himself-in-macabre-blue-whale-online-challenge-thats-alarming-schools/?utm_term=.ca30a331a59e.

Freak Prank & Entertainment. 2017. *India's First Blue Whale Prank /Prank in India2017 / Prank by Chandu. YouTube*, August 21, 2017. https://www.youtube.com/watch?v=iF1zqSxQH6Q.

Garv Jaiswal Team. 2017. *Blue Whale Prank on Girls / Blue Whale Prank / Pranks in India.* *YouTube*, September 2, 2017. https://www.youtube.com/watch?v=0xQBjiWEttM.

Goethe, Johann Wolfgang von. 1774. *Die Leiden des jungen Werthers* [The sorrows of young Werther]. Leipzig: Weygandsche Buchhandlung.

Howard, Robert Glenn. 2009. "Crusading on the Vernacular Web: The Folk Beliefs and Practices of Online Spiritual Warfare." In *Folklore and the Internet*, edited by Trevor J. Blank, 159–174. Logan: Utah State University Press.

Howard, Robert Glenn. 2011. *Digital Jesus: The Making of a New Christian Fundamentalist Community on the Internet.* New York: New York University Press.

Humorous Gang. 2017. *Blue Whale Suicide Game. YouTube*, August 17, 2017. https://www.youtube.com/watch?v=0xQBjiWEttM.

Jansen, William Hugh. 1975. "'The Surpriser Surprised': A Modern Legend." *Folklore Forum* 6 (1): 1–24.

Karimov, Faith. 2017. "Iran Challenges 'Killer Game' Blue Whale Challenge." *Trend*, September 9, 2017. https://en.trend.az/iran/society/2794694.html.

Khalaf, Rayana. 2017. "Police and Experts Warn against *Mariam* Game." *StepFeed*, August 11, 2017. https://heavy.com/news/2017/07/blue-whale-challenge-game-what-are-the-50-challenges-tasks/.

Khlifi, Roua. 2018. "Blue Whale Challenge Claims Lives of More Teens in Magreb." *Arab Weekly*, March 4, 2018. https://thearabweekly.com/blue-whale-challenge-claims-lives-more-teens-maghreb.

Kutner, Max. 2017. "What Is the Blue Whale Game, the Russian 'Challenge' Blamed for Suicides?" *Newsweek*, July 18, 2017. http://www.newsweek.com/what-blue-whale-game-russia-suicides-637798.

Lodha, Pragha. 2017. "India Has the Highest Suicide Rate among Youth." *Better India*, July 17, 2017. https://www.thebetterindia.com/108700/suicide-prevention-a-growing-public-health-concern-in-india/.

Marsh, Moira. 2015. *Practically Joking.* Logan: Utah State University Press.

Opie, Iona, and Peter Opie. 1969. *Children's Games in Street and Playground.* New York: Oxford University Press.

Patel, Vikram, Chinthanie Ramasundarahettige, Lakshmi Vijayakumar, J. S. Thakur, Vendhan Gajalakshmi, Gopakrishnan Gururaj, Wilson Suraweera, and Prabhat Jha. 2012. "Suicide Mortality in India: A Nationally Representative Survey." *Lancet.* Accessed March 8, 2018. http://www.thelancet.com/journals/lancet/article/PIIS0140-6736(12)60606-0.

Phillips, David P. 1974. "The Influence of Suggestion on Suicide: Substantive Theoretical Implications of the Werther Effect." *American Sociological Review* 39 (3): 340–354.

The Pink Panther. 1963. Dir. Blake Edwards. MGM.

Sham Idrees Vlogs. 2017. *BLUE WHALE PRANK (Gone Wrong!!). YouTube*, September 19, 2017. https://www.youtube.com/watch?v=5oRo-0-xJzM.

Thomas, Jeannie B. 2015. *Putting the Supernatural in Its Place: Folklore, the Hypermodern, and the Ethereal.* Salt Lake City: University of Utah Press.

Tucker, Elizabeth. 2002. "'Mean Girls': The Reclassification of Children's and Adolescents' Folklore." *Children's Folklore Review* 25 (3/4): 7–22.

Tucker, Elizabeth. 2008–2009. "'Go to Bed, Now You're Dead': Suffocation Songs and Breath Control Games." *Children's Folklore Review* 31: 45–58.

Tucker, Elizabeth. 2014. "The Endangered Child: Choking and Fainting Games in the Online Underground of YouTube." *Children's Folklore Review* 36: 19–34.

Tucker, Elizabeth. 2016. "There's an App for That: Ghost Hunting with Smartphones." *Children's Folklore Review* 38: 27–38.

Tucker, Elizabeth. 2018. "Slender Man Is Coming to Get Your Younger Brother or Sister: Teenagers' Pranks Posted on YouTube." In *Slender Man Is Coming: Creepypastas and Contemporary Legends on the Internet*, edited by Trevor J. Blank and Lynne S. McNeill, 141–154. Logan: Utah State University Press.

Victor, Jeffrey S. 1993. *Satanic Panic: The Creation of a Contemporary Legend*. New York: Open Court.

Worley, Will. 2017. "Blue Whale: Fears in India over 'Viral Suicide Game' Mount as 'Government Calls for Internet Giants to Ban Links to It.'" *The Independent*. September, 19, 2017. Accessed October 20, 2017. https://www.independent.co.uk/news/world/asia/blue-whale-suicide-game-latest-news-india-online-viral-internet-google-ban-links-a7954786.html/.

12

Overt and Covert Aspects of Virtual Play

Bill Ellis

ON MARCH 17, 2018, THE *NEW YORK TIMES* REPORTED that Facebook had been exploited by Cambridge Analytica (CA), a data-mining firm used by a variety of conservative candidates in the 2016 American election to identify and influence voters. After Facebook created a platform allowing third parties to gain access to users' private and public information, CA released an app in 2013, titled "This Is Your Digital Life," which asked a series of apparently innocuous questions about users' online habits. Typical of these online quizzes, the app provided a digitally generated psychological profile. But users were not aware that their answers, as well as their user data (and the user data of their friends) continued to be stored in an online database that could subsequently be exploited to predict their personality types and political preferences (Rosenberg et al. 2018; Chappell 2018). In 2015 this database was used by Ted Cruz in his primary battle with Donald Trump. After Trump won the Republican nomination, his campaign would go on to use the database even more intensively during the 2016 US presidential election (Meredith 2018). In 2018, the *New York Times* exposed the extent of this covert use of Facebook data during the election, sparking a firestorm and making Facebook executives scramble to patch up loopholes and reassure users that data they had entered would no longer be exploited without their consent. Tim Cook, head of Facebook's rival, Apple, was scathing in his reply to these patch-up measures: "The ability of anyone to know what you've been browsing about for years, who your contacts are, who their contacts are, things you like and dislike and every intimate detail of your life," Cook told reporters, "from my own point of view it shouldn't exist" (*Bloomberg News* 2018).

The affair fleetingly made visible a social factor that Brian Sutton-Smith (1970) called the "triviality barrier." The scandal focused on the consequences of unproductive play, engaged in purely for "fun" with no victory or problem solving involved. Survey apps like "This Is Your Digital Life" invite users to engage in a formless pastime, which, Sutton-Smith noted, has long been dismissed as unworthy of academic analysis. By contrast, games, particularly those that foster physical skills or mental strategy, carry status and economic power in American culture. Competitive games have been recognized as having valid functions in society, particularly teaching and mastering physical and mental skills that are central to social success.[1] However, Sutton-Smith found that choices made by children in unproductive forms of play tracked significant psychological features in their personalities. Sutton-Smith proposed that all forms of play are "orderly expressive sequences with [their] own historical and developmental characteristics." They are hardly trivial because they reveal and clarify the emotional makeup of participants (8).

The Facebook scandal similarly seems to be based on a trivial pursuit: online play is by nature an idle pastime that becomes controversial only when bosses discover employees engaging in it covertly during work hours. Yet Sutton-Smith's challenge remains valid: can any widespread form of human behavior really be trivial by nature, even if it appears self-consuming and unproductive?

This chapter looks more closely at forms of play that have emerged online, particularly those that appear to be purely "for fun." In doing so, I intend to show that such pastimes in fact have complex and significant functions, particularly by encouraging participants to share personal information with others and reflect on the social significance of what has been revealed. These forms of play include a number of Facebook activities that resemble the app that caused the Cambridge Analytica scandal. I focus on six common indicators of playfulness: three that are overt or objectively observable from the texts that constitute the playful activity, and three that are covert or expressed in participants' subjective response to the entertainment. These aspects reduce to three dyads, each containing an overt and a covert aspect of the same issue. First, an activity objectively must result from an *invitation*, which is accepted when it is subjectively seen as *sociable*. Second, the rules of play must be kept *simple*, and participants expect that the group will be *inclusive* of their responses. And third, playfulness embodies a commitment to reciprocity, seen objectively as *restitution* (the player publicly gives up something in return for the chance to play) and subjectively as *reflexivity* (the player privately gains something by doing so).

When these aspects are in action, the resulting activities pull together traditional themes and tactics into a form of play that draws on participants' wish to learn more about themselves. The pleasure of receiving an answer that "feels right" is the result of reflexivity, and the urge to publicize the outcome of one's personal insight leads to public discussion, which perpetuates the chain of play. Even if it appears to be formless and unproductive, this kind of play proves to be, as Sutton-Smith proposed, integral to the "personality and culture patterns in which the player participates" (1970, 8). This essay applies Sutton-Smith's insight to the realm of social media, which has proved to be a vital setting for generating and preserving traditions of play.

THE INTERNET AS A PLAYGROUND: STEPPING IN AND STEPPING OUT

Organized games matching players or teams against each other in a real-time, real-space competition enjoy a higher status than games without clear stakes or victory conditions. Likewise, games involving mental strategy to solve puzzles or deal with problems have obvious practical functions and likewise enjoy a place of pride. But play in its purer forms, as Sutton-Smith (1999) noted, has proved difficult for academics to discuss. Much of the anthropological and folkloristic research dealing with virtual play thus has focused on role-playing games (RPGs), in which participants imaginatively enter a fantasy frame, assuming the identity of a mythical or nonhuman character (wizard, dragon, elf, halfling, etc.).[2] A growing number of ethnographers argue that such gaming allows participants to distance themselves from real-world issues, improvise and enact a narrative using shared traditional motives, and subjectively reflect on their imaginative experience.[3] This scholarly theme, as Tom Boellstorff (2008) observes, harks back to John Huizinga's influential 1938 work *Homo Ludens*, in which the Dutch scholar argued that play is defined by its voluntary nature and by the specific time and place its participants use for the activity. Most important, Huizinga argued, play is a "stepping out" from consensus reality into a temporary "magic circle" with its own rules and conventions. Thus, Boellstorff finds, many scholars have assumed that an activity that involves a virtual world is, by definition, a form of play.

However, Boellstorff found that residents in virtual RPGs such as Linden Lab's *Second Life* strongly disagreed that they were engaged in any "game."[4] It was misleading, they maintained, to characterize the entirety of their activities in such a platform as "play." While users conceded that some participants engaged in games and other playful activities while spending time on this platform, calling *Second Life* itself a form of play disparaged serious endeavors such as social discourse, community building, and politics as mere "entertainment" (2008, 22–23). A virtual world was a *venue*, one contended, in which one *could* play, but it was not in itself a form of play. Boellstorff supports this perspective, noting that the social sciences' various definitions and theories of play are notoriously vague and permeable. Even so, by emphasizing that virtual worlds are not intrinsically goal-oriented and so do not focus on "winning" or "losing," Boellstorff affirms Sutton-Smith's key point about pure, unconstructive play. For the notion that "play" is "just" a form of entertainment seems precisely the fallacy presented by a "triviality barrier," implicit or explicit.

Bonnie A. Nardi, on the other hand, argues that *World of Warcraft*, an internationally popular virtual world platform released by Blizzard Entertainment, "is of course a form of play" (2010, 94). At the same time, she observes that residents do not understand virtual worlds as play-oriented realms distinct from the real social worlds in which they live. Play is by no means a trivial pursuit; rather, she shows, the act of stepping out of a world governed by "work" into one dedicated to "play" is a means of using worklike activities for individual and social results that are felt to be socially rewarding. Thus play and the real world coexist in a dynamic relationship, she concludes (108). Like Boellstorff, she acknowledges that residents may interpret their actions in the virtual world as self-evidently playful and pleasurable or as relatively serious, repetitive chores necessary for the health of the overall game that constitute a form of "work." And not all RPGs generate the same kinds of play spaces, nor do all players adopt the same playing roles. Games involving responses to challenges and gaining (or losing) virtual assets are often tightly controlled by the rules and limitations of proprietary software algorithms, making them more a form of virtual "work." But even in platforms that put less stress on achievement and competition, Nardi observes, some residents freely choose to spend most of their time performing necessary game-enhancing tasks rather than engaging in adventures for their social benefits alone.[5] For that reason, she concludes, play may either affirm or critique the serious world's cultural norms, and its special power is that "it affords grounding through a capacity to reproduce the familiar while simultaneously yielding the potential for transformative activity" (113).

Other observers have found that the residents of less structured virtual worlds were more apt to use these platforms to project elements of their real social worlds and to reflect on them. Katryn Stam and Michael Scialdone found a similar "work/play" contrast between residents who engaged in *Runescape*, a highly structured game with complex rules, and others who chose *Furcadia*, a more socially interactive fantasy-based activity. The first group, they found, focused more on worklike activities leading to "leveling up" (i.e., gaining status through success in competition). Furcadians, by contrast, stressed "meeting new friends and the joy and satisfaction of the role-playing aspects," adding that "entertainment and companionship" were their key reasons for choosing to play (2008, 88–89). Such dynamics entered the RPG community early on: Milspaw and Evans, discussing a virtual-world activity conducted in face-to-face sessions rather than through web links noted that such platforms often approach a "true interactive narrative," in which players make "dramatically interesting choices" to maintain a satisfying story line. Such a dynamic, their informants stressed, was not always available in achievement-based video games, but was "absolutely central and richly possible" in imaginative worlds (2010, 232–233). Turkle, another early ethnographer of such imaginative activities, summed up this complex dynamic concisely: "Virtual reality is not 'real,' but it has a relationship to the real. By being betwixt and between, it becomes a play space for thinking about the real world" (1994, 165).

In summary, role-playing games are more complex in structure than the pastimes discussed by Sutton-Smith, and the communities they invite are also more diverse in their modes and motives for playing. Even so, we see that they often show the same dynamics as pure play: projection of real-life issues onto a playground defined as separate from consensus reality, negotiating these issues with others in a socially safe way, and engaging in conscious self-reflection on real-world issues. And so it is all the more essential that folklorists study such "unproductive" play as thoroughly as competitive and puzzle-solving forms of play, which have a more obvious function in training participants in skills that society believes are economically productive. A bias toward "productive" play, after all, presumes that such activities must by definition support socially sanctioned goals.

In fact, the main attraction of "unproductive" play may be precisely that it challenges hegemony. Sutton-Smith observes that pure play has an additional rarely discussed feature: "[In] the highly repetitive, ritualized, even compulsive character of much play . . . the players seem driven from within by impulse or from without by the motifs of the game." The tactical or social rationale for engaging in play, Sutton-Smith adds, is not as important as the activity's key rationale: "passionate idiosyncratic pleasure" (1999, 65). Rhetorician Richard Lanham agreed, citing authorities who suggest that play is rooted in some neurological need from humans' evolutionary past. There is no need to find any social rationale, he argues: humans have an innate need for pure play. The so-called practical world, Lanham suggests, may instead be based on patterns of thought and action first learned through play (1993, 110). One of the first critics to predict that digital media would be founded in play, Lanham argued that this mode of communication encouraged the brain to focus simultaneously on the meaning of the message *and* on the medium through which it is being said. When a text can be read both ways, as medium and message, Lanham concludes, this creates ample room for verbal play, and "where the verbal creative spirit has room to play, play it will" (4–5).

Scarlett et al. (2005) likewise admit that there is no definitive academic way to characterize play; they suggest that perhaps the only truly empirical solution is to pay attention to what participants *feel* is "play." Indeed, the authors suggest that we stop considering "play" as a noun, a thing-in-itself to be analyzed, and understand the phenomenon as "playing," a process experienced rather than defined. Its most important element, for this reason, is not formal but subjective—that is, the pleasure experienced during it. "When we actually play," they explain, "even when we play at explaining play, we notice that something freeing and refreshing happens. The grains of truth in our playing are interesting and important, but by playing with them and not taking themselves too seriously, we open ourselves to the process of knowing" (2–3). This process-focused understanding likewise seems present in Sutton-Smith's final comment on play: that it in some way "catapults . . . from reflexive behavior into enactive contemplation" (1999, 69). It is, in short, a practical means of thinking about thinking, in a mode that lets the brain observe its own functioning and, in a pleasure-driven way, learn something about how thinking takes place, perhaps with an option to reprogram oneself in productive ways.

Sutton-Smith had remarked on the extraordinary rise of "solitary play" in the late twentieth century, with growing numbers of affluent children becoming more attached to televisions and other electronic devices rather than engaging in physical face-to-face games (1999, 68). But the emerging computer-mediated playground was far from solitary. Brenda Danet applied Sutton-Smith's theories to a variety of interactive activities in the first decade of widespread internet use. The absence of physical bodies and reduced accountability, she reasoned, generated a play space that was "anarchic, playful, and even carnivalesque" (2001, 8), with participants more freely able to mask identity and engage in fantasy-based group activities. Since then the prevalence of playful discourse in cyberspace has been discussed by a number of ethnographers, notably Ana Deumert (2014), who describes such a dynamic as creating a "ludic self" central to the way in which many users construct identity in virtual spaces.

So play (including games) has a double nature. Formally, it generates a "magic circle" and fills it with motifs and challenges that motivate players to "step in" and promises them some reward for doing so. Subjectively, this reward could include a spectrum of emotions, ranging from the satisfaction of doing a job well or winning a competition to the more ludic enjoyment of play itself. So play might attract minds who thrive on personal challenges, but also those who passionately enjoy engaging in disorder. This latter invitation encourages participants to "step out" of their normal modes of thinking, finding pleasure in learning something about how they and others think. And so, analysis must include both play's overt (formal, public) elements and its covert (subjective, private) aspects.

OBSERVING OVERT AND COVERT FEATURES OF PLAY

To carry out this analytical task, we first need to negotiate a tricky methodological pitfall that Danet has identified: academic descriptions of such traditions often combine *formal* features of play—those that an observer can view and objectively identify as "playful"—with *informal* features that participants register subjectively (2001, 10). In conventional ethnography, observation is normally restricted to social behavior that explicitly "keys" or publicly designates an activity as "playful."[6] And yet much of the research on play, Danet observes, puts equal stress on participants' subjective reactions to such activity. When behavior is characterized as "lighthearted," "frolicsome," "quirky," "spontaneous," or marked by "manifest joy," the observer seems to be making a subjective characterization of players' behavior or, at best, recording participants' own subjective reactions while engaging in play.

An analysis of the *overt* aspects of virtual play would focus exclusively on the way in which the activity is started and structured, rather than trying to assess and categorize the emotions that such activity provokes as it unfolds. Nevertheless, such an objective examination of agreed-upon rules and explicitly stated responses provides only a partial view of this folk tradition—indeed, of any folk tradition. Japanese folklorist Kunio Yanagita famously instructed his students to pay attention to three significant aspects of customs: (1) things seen, (2) things heard, and (3) things felt.[7] The third of these he considered central, encouraging ethnographers not just to stand aloof and record but to register the "feeling" that is central in the traditions they studied. Such an "art of listening," he argued, gave observers access to deep structures that cannot be readily abstracted from visible or audible signs alone (see Iwasaka and Toelken 1994, 56). In a similar way, Danet argues that a complete study of virtual play needs to move past overt features of play and confirm that play occurred by considering *covert* signs of playful behavior: joy, humor, or insights gained as a result of the activity (2001, 10).

Such evidence is best gained not through formal analysis of observed data but directly, by investigators agreeing to engage in acts of play and reflecting on their subjective experiences. So this essay will use two different modes of discourse, one that is quite formal, relying on disciplinary concepts and methods, and another that is seemingly quite informal, based on my subjective self-awareness of moods and insights gained during moments of virtual play. Both modes, Yanagita and Danet agree, are essential to a complete understanding of this tradition.

Accordingly, I argue that much virtual play on social media has six common aspects that scholars need to consider to grasp this ubiquitous form of traditional pastime. Some derive from existing scholarship on play, particularly that found in computer-based discourse, and others are culled from my previous observation of virtual communities. The first three are *overt* aspects that are objectively observable from the texts that structure the playful activity.

1. The activity is *invited*. It does not occur spontaneously, but results from the circulation of an opportunity for play. On the other hand, the invitation does not require participation, and there is no tangible reward for doing so—it is, as Sutton-Smith stated, "fun" (1970, 2). Or, adapting Goffman's more objective description of such activities, the actions do not fulfill their ordinary functions and are tactically exaggerated to make it clear to participants that they are interacting in a state of play. This state is voluntary and participants can withdraw at will (1974, 41–42).

2. The activity is *simple* to enact. If a complex system of rules and directions is needed to fulfill the activity's structure, it becomes a game, and as we have seen, this shifts the focus of the activity toward competition and gaining status. Therefore, the most widespread forms of virtual play are built on actions that participants can enact immediately and without much investment of time. The text that invites participation often emphasizes how little is expected of players: only responding to yes/no or multiple-choice questions, or one-word answers based on personal history.

3. The structure of the activity expects *restitution*. The term is borrowed from literary critic George Steiner (1975), who in turn had adapted it from anthropologist Claude Lévi-Strauss: it refers to the social duty to balance any self-centered action with a counteraction that benefits the community.[8] In a previous study, I used this concept to understand a virtual community of collectors of Japanese animation art. Restitution, I concluded, was the

principle that allowed collectors to be competitive in seeking and capturing high-status objects, but then reimburse the community in an equitable way: "A potential 'hoarder' becomes a valued 'sharer' by becoming tactful in acquiring art and generous in sharing information, by being ruthless in auctions and polite in public discussions, and by being willing to value other collectors' collections as highly as one's own" (Ellis 2012, 202). One effect of restitution is to keep the community in a pleasurable turmoil, with members constantly claiming status and giving something back (194–195). In the case of the forms of play studied here, participants are urged not just to play but to perpetuate the fun by responding to others' posts and recruiting new players.

These three overt indicators of playfulness in virtual spaces are closely linked to three *covert* indicators, each of which represents a subjective rationale for the three overt aspects. In some cases, these are easily inferred from reactions posted by the players, but in others one has to enter the melee and trust to one's own ensuing experiences. In any case, they are the subjective analogs to the three directly observable aspects just named.

4. The invitation is *sociable*. It identifies an audience of co-players whom participants recognize as sharing one or more of their interests. That is, the fun is not random but proceeds along conduits that suggest a folk group. A common definition of "folklore" is "artistic communication in small groups" (Ben-Amos 1971, 13), and so the request to participate implicitly defines an opportunity to engage in such discourse, using traditional structures and motifs that will be (equally implicitly) understood by a limited circle of people whom one already knows well. And indeed, as we have seen, virtual play has been seen subjectively as a means of meeting new friends and socializing with them in an unstructured way. Stam and Scialdone noted, for instance, that "random chat" was seen as an attractive feature of the RPG *Furcadia* (2008, 88), and in my study of the virtual community Anime-Beta, I too discovered that many members found that a certain amount of random goofiness kept the forum interesting and active (2012, 186).

5. The activity is *inclusive*. That is, there are rules for participation, but not for winning, and so every player's contribution is taken as valid, whether conventional or offbeat. This does not mean that all such posts are considered equal, for it is common for some to receive a chorus of congratulations, often in the form of emojis or acronyms like "LOL" (laugh out loud). But it is uncommon for posts made in an overt context of virtual play to be called out as trite or inadequate.[9] Participation is its own reward. Stam and Scialdone likewise noted this distinction in the virtual-play-focused RPG

Furcadia, where interactions were brief, random, and "were seen as having few consequences," while in the more competition-focused *Runecraft*, random chat was discouraged, game-related talk was given priority, and a message to a player with higher status "could easily result in a rude dismissal" (2008, 88). In a different (but, I believe, closely related) form of discourse, women meeting to read their fortunes in Tarot cards valued their right to discuss intimate topics "without concern about judgment or envy" (Baldwin 2018, 149).

6. The activity involves *reflexivity*. If virtual communication fosters self-awareness of language and our linguistic choices, then virtual play is based on an intuitive process of learning something about the way we communicate. Many invitations openly promise the opportunity to see oneself in a new way. In any case, players participate in order to learn more about themselves, the community they share, and/or the language they use. This too has been suggested by a range of scholars as a basic function of play and as a key focus of computer-mediated discourse. By creating a luminal context for discourse, the research we have surveyed suggests, participants generate a "play space for thinking about the real world" (Turkle 1994, 165) or a process in which, through playing with elements drawn from the real world, in a consciously non-seriously way, "we open ourselves to the process of knowing" (Scarlett et al. 2005, 2–3).

So there are three key issues in virtual play that are visible in the play itself and palpable in the emotional responses of the players. First, virtual play is a social activity, enacted by friends (*invitation*) and affirming their friendship (*sociable*). Second, it generates an easy (*simple*) and safe (*inclusive*) way for participants to share something about themselves. And third, it encourages pleasurable activity among the group (*restitution*) and kindles personal insights (*reflexivity*). In a nutshell, the activity is engaging, comfortable, and fun. It takes only a modest effort to become involved, and players find value in participating. The reward may vary in kind depending on the mood and personality of the player. One might enjoy being the center of attention and receiving a chorus of kudos, while another might enjoy reading and reacting to others' posts. The most durable threads display a balanced give-and-take between these impulses and, as Sutton-Smith notes, "a considerable degree of license may ensue, as well as venturesome and novel combinations of thought and behavior" (1999, 68).

This study looks at typical examples of virtual play from social media, beginning with frequently forwarded emails and playful threads in online forums that derive from earlier playful activities carried on through photocopying or faxing. Then the chapter surveys a range of threads generated on Facebook that invited and received playful responses from the participants' "friend lists." In doing so, this study identifies and reflects on the aspects of these activities that link them as allied traditions of play.

VIRTUAL PLAY BEFORE SOCIAL MEDIA

The first widely popular form of peer-to-peer digital communication, email was developed in 1971 from early experiments in creating linked networks of computers. Originally used in military and contracting contexts, it became more widely adopted in academic settings in the late 1980s and by the early 1990s penetrated into general use. Within a short time it became a common conduit for all kinds of folklore, notably contemporary legends and topical humor (Ellis 2002; Frank 2009; Howard 2012). The development of email groups, driven by programs that directed messages to all subscribers, contributed to the medium's use in creating and maintaining folk groups in cyberspace. However, emails' format as self-contained messages limited their ability to function in interactive play: to participate, a recipient needed to open, read, and then respond to the message.

The Travel Scrabble email is a typical example of such play. My personal copy is dated January 13, 2011, but a search of email messages archived by Google Groups shows that it circulated as early as June 2009.[10] The body of the email contains this invitation: "O.K. . . . the game is on! Travel Scrabble. Keep it going! Change one letter of the bottom word posted and let's see who gets stuck and can't continue! Rules: You cannot add letters. You can only use English. You can only change one letter. Send it back to the person who sent it to you, plus 10 new people . . . To make it even more interesting, include your location and the date to see how far this goes and how long it's been out." My copy included a list of 347 four-letter words, each varying by only one letter, beginning with "toot" (January 13, 2010, Carmel, California) and ending with "maps" (January 13, 2011, Worcester, UK)—an unbroken chain lasting exactly one year.

The play activity is triggered by receiving an overt invitation. The rules of the play were simple: make a new word by changing just one letter of the last word. The directions also included the traditional request for restitution: return your solution to the sender and also pass the entire chain on to ten additional people who might be willing to continue the chain. This element is identical to that of the classic "Good Luck Chain Letter" (Ellis 2004, 64–68; Blank 2007, 19; VanArsdale 2016), which evolved as an ideal strategy to ensure that, even though most recipients will not play along, chances are that one out of the ten will comply, and so the chain will live on.

These directions indicate one potential way in which the play might be reflexive by suggesting that the thread, if it continues, may well "come back to you in a week or a month or a year!" However, in a way Danet finds typical of cyberplay, it does call the player's attention to the physical letters that make up a word, causing participants to deconstruct the work and find a way to make a new word. This effort could mean simply changing a first letter and forming a rhyme, or looking for deviant and possibly witty ways of adding a word that clashes with the previous one. While these rules seemed restrictive, the results were inclusive: in several instances participants carried on the game by changing more than one letter (e.g., tool → lout; tape → mate; mare → tame).

This example is interesting in showing how verbal play adapted to a virtual context. The "chain letter" format, openly asking recipients to forward the message on to a wider circle of friends, looks back to older models that asked participants to copy the contents of the message or, as technology advanced, to photocopy or fax the message onward. And Travel Scrabble would have been cumbersome to circulate in these media. Part of the appeal of the game is viewing how long and widely the chain has circulated. My version, if printed out, would run to seventeen pages, much too long for easy copying and circulation. Thus, while these sorts of emails are clearly related to earlier examples of graphic folklore such as those studied by Dundes and Pagter (1978), it would have been much more difficult to circulate them in a pre-virtual age, and the game wouldn't have spread as widely or as successfully.

When it comes to facilitating virtual play, online forums have several advantages over email. First, ongoing interactions between users in a familiar virtual space often allows users to develop a focused sense of group identity (Baym 2015, 118ff.), and frequent posters become widely known for their distinctive expertise and personalities. Messages are displayed in the form of linear discussion threads in which all responses to a given topic are shown together. In addition, these are normally archived on the forum site, allowing members to refer back to earlier discussions. Thus, the community has a stronger sense of history, and discussions can be more specific because all aspects of a subject are addressed in one place.

Take, for example, interactions among anime fans on a forum called Anime-Beta (see also Ellis 2012). Founded in April 2002, the forum is dedicated to sharing information on collecting production art from Japanese anime. Passion for the objects they collect and the larger imaginative world these represent, Danet and Katriel found, set participants apart from ordinary people as more prone to engage in "celebration of the irrational" (1994, 43–44). Accordingly, the most appealing threads that developed on the Anime-Beta forum were those that were unpredictable and chaotic, within acceptable limits.

To promote sociability, members of the Anime-Beta forum regularly circulated invitations for random virtual play. One typical example, started in June 2003 by a longtime member, was titled simply "Something fun." The invitation reads: "I love looking at others galleries, and i really like it when people look at mine. I thought this might be kind of a cool thing to do. [Smiley emoji] Anyway—I think we should do a thread where you look at the person who posted before you's gallery, and then post what is your favorite cel or sketch or genga set—whatever—and what you like the most about it. Then the next person will post what cel they like most in your gallery and why." This thread is still active over fifteen years later, having received 10,920 responses and 219,218 individual visits by July 2020.[11] This is an eternity on a forum, where a discussion that lasts for a month is considered an exceptionally durable one.

One reason for this thread's longevity has to do with its overt aspects. When Beta members logged in, they routinely searched for new topics, so this thread and its *invitation* turned up in this list over and over. The directions were *simple*: participation involved only visiting the last poster's website, then copying and pasting a URL into a new message, enacting *restitution*.

But the real key to this thread's immortality is that this overt pattern was predictable in one way and endlessly quirky in another. It honored the *restitution* principle, as it expected members to give a compliment in return for receiving one. The capricious part of the activity is that it demanded that participants "play it forward" by visiting others' galleries and calling out special items *before* they could expect to receive accolades on their own possessions. Thus the act of accepting the invitation relied on a desire to be *inclusive*, visiting fellow collectors' galleries. Participating ensured that the players' galleries would be searched and commented on in short order, and the *inclusive* principle allowed new members just starting their collections to play on the same level as more established forum members with more impressive holdings. A check of 100 recent posts in the thread confirmed this dynamic: while most of the individual posts came from a group of fifteen central members, nearly half of the overall participants were new arrivals to the forum. Finally, learning which items others would select to share often provided users with insight into what collectables were actually popular among one's friends, thus ensuring *reflexivity*. Overall, the game's unpredictable course did encourage contacts among different groups and factions of the forum and honored the activity's sociability function.[12]

Both forums and email remain strong forces for the remediation of traditional folklore and play in cyberspace. But, by 2010, social media had overtaken email as the top internet activity among young Americans (Heimlich 2010). Forums persist but have seen a drop in popularity as more and more of the web becomes centered around a few large social networks. However, much as in the transition from chain letters to chain emails, the expressive behaviors remain similar even if the locations and fine details adapt to the distinctive possibilities of each virtual medium. And, as I argue in the next section of this chapter, we continue to see these six distinctive aspects of virtual play expressed in new ways on social media.

VIRTUAL PLAY ON FACEBOOK

The creation of social media spaces where folk groups could form and easily share communications using a wide range of media, as Peck (2015a) has noted, enabled the flourishing of many forms of virtual play. Ana Deumert (2014) has also observed that participation in Facebook itself has become a form of social play, often conducted in niches of time secretly snatched between workplace duties or in otherwise empty moments, such as waiting for a bus or an appointment. Typical of Facebook's liminal contexts, Deumert finds that its users adopt identities customary in play activities, in which facetiousness and illogic prevail. "In much digital communication," she observes, "obscurity and ambiguity are licensed, relevance a matter of choice, and truthfulness at times unnecessary. What matters is amusement, laughter, and creative enjoyment" (2014, 27). From December 2017 to June 2018, I watched for examples of virtual play on Facebook that had the overt and covert aspects familiar from my previous research, or else demonstrated their "staying power" by generating lengthy strings of responses or imitations. Most of the time I merely observed, but, following Yanagita's emphasis on "things felt," at times I accepted the invitations and engaged in play.

In the end, I saved thirty-one threads that exhibited characteristic virtual play dynamics. Some were close variations of each other: five asked participants to share their answers to a list of "odd facts about themselves," while two asked for a memory (or a "meme") about how readers met the person posting the thread. In one thread, the game asked the participant to make posts on ten consecutive days, naming movies that were influential to the poster's life. On each day the poster tagged a specific friend and challenged that person to continue the thread. I participated in one such thread, but changed the theme to another topic. Other threads I observed showed that this was a common variation: similar threads listed books, music albums, beers, TV series, and so on. Two asked readers to post a random photograph, often the eleventh (or some other number) from their "camera roll" (a common name for a cell phone's directory of digital photographs). Some games made references to traditional behavior such as foodways or pranks.

The invitations and topics were quite diverse in nature, but I found that the course of play that followed was relatively consistent. It would therefore be repetitious to discuss each of these examples, or even a representative sampling, one by one. Therefore, I focus this section on the three aspect dyads, explaining how each of these functions was fulfilled in the threads I observed as part of my participant ethnography.

Invited/sociable. In all cases, the opening post passed on directions for engaging in a playful thread. In some cases the rules were explicit, as in one actively circulating activity that began, "Let's play #FamilyFeud![13] You CAN-NOT use my answers. Your answers must be different" (posted December 21, 2017). Ten questions about common topics followed, typical of this popular game show's format, along with the poster's answers (e.g., "Something you use in the bathroom? Toilet Paper."). The last question prompted the player to tag six friends to play the next round. Another prevalent post began, "Post the 17th picture in your [cell phone's] camera roll, no matter what! Have fun & play along. Then copy and paste this post on your timeline using the number I give you in reply to your photo!" (posted January 20, 2018). The friend-based dynamic of Facebook ensured sociability: the poster was someone whom the viewer had "friended," and many already showed "like" designations and responses from other familiar names. One especially direct invitation came from a folklorist who "nominated" me in a post and challenged me to generate a "Top Ten" list of films I'd seen. In this case, I did continue the activity, duly tagging ten more friends, at least two of whom later developed "Top Ten" lists, thus perpetuating the activity.

Simple/inclusive. Most play activities involved sharing private but seemingly random information about participants' lives or current activities. A seventeenth picture on the camera roll of one's cell phone would naturally reveal a place visited recently, a favorite activity, or a close companion. A list of "odd facts about yourself" disclosed minute but revealing details of participants' personal lives: a favorite subject in school, choice of music, a "guilty pleasure," belief in aliens, and the like. A number of activities dealt with recent purchases. One simply said, "You just won a lifetime supply of the last thing you bought!!" (collected May 15, 2018). Within two weeks, this thread had received 250 responses, inclusively calling out purchases that were mundane (gasoline, coffee), esoteric (car window paint, horse feed), or confessional (condoms, a handgun). A wittier variation on this "your present moment" theme began "THE ZOMBIE APOCALYPSE HAS BEGUN!" and asked players to take the nearest thing on their left as a weapon, bring the main character of the last film/miniseries they watched along as their buddy, and assume that they have an endless supply of the last thing they ate. The results were often fanciful—I ended up with a Bible, Richard Burton playing Dr. Faustus, and cara cara oranges; my daughter, by contrast, ended up with a box of tissues, the Japanese anime android detective Heat Guy J, and pizza.

Other games required use of an external "app," or online application. For example, on February 22, 2018, a friend posted a link titled "What Would You Look Like As The Opposite Gender?" The directions made the answer look simple to know and to share: "Click here and see YOUR opposite version!" The site used a facial recognition program to scan users' image (using the camera included above the screen in most laptops). The site then generated an algorithm and next carried out an online search for a similar image in Google's visual database. In this case it led to a cubist portrait "à la manière de Picasso," which provoked a cascade of amused reactions from other folklorists. The process was hardly "simple," as it involved the use of a complex paradigm employing sophisticated software. But this effort was carried out behind the scenes, and so long as players were willing to click through a series of websites, giving consent when asked, displaying results required no special skills or effort.

None of these threads were competitive, and rules were, as Peck would say, "concealed and mutable" (2015b, 337). Some contained directions not to copy or repeat answers, but since Facebook displays only a brief selection of responses made so far, it is easy for a player to contribute an answer that has already been given without realizing it. If the directions were supposed to be objectively easy and participation assumed to be inclusive, then all answers, legal or illegal, would be accepted. And I found that such was the case. One invitation to play read, "You're a burglar and you break into a house, except instead of stealing, you do things to mildly inconvenience the owners. What did you do?" (posted February 9, 2018). I came in about halfway and offered, "Switch the sugar and salt" (a traditional April Fool's Day prank that my sister actually carried out when we were children).[14] The same answer, I later found, had been given twenty-seven posts earlier. Nevertheless, my post got two "likes," a typical inclusive reception, and when the same answer was subsequently given two more times, each of these posts likewise received no criticism but instead a "like."

Restitution/reflexive. Many of the play activities promised (sometimes facetiously) to provide players with a "deep truth" about themselves. The responses to seemingly inconsequential answers, in short, gave participants the chance to see themselves in a different light. This often set up an actively reciprocal situation, in which friends shared information and compared it with that offered by others. For instance, I responded to the "Odd facts about yourself" (on January 15, 2018) and found my response to whether I believed in aliens ("I think they are fairies and boggarts updating their images for the times") publicly applauded by other folklorists and included in their own "Odd facts" list. On May 31, 2018, my daughter filled out a very similar list, and I was struck that while most of our answers were, understandably, different, we had given verbatim identical answers to the question "Do you talk to yourself?" ("Yup, I'm good company.")

A second example of this sort began with an offer to identify one's "Alternative Patronus," which would embody the key personality traits of the player. This especially engaging invitation plays on the viewer's familiarity with the Harry Potter fictional world. At the climax of *The Prisoner of Azkaban* (2004), the hero is beset by "dementors," magical creatures who suck positive feelings from those they beset. Drawing on his inner strengths, Potter summons a "patronus" in the form of a mystical animal, which is able to dispel the wraiths. The idea that one has a psychic "spirit animal" is a common one in fantasy and New Age thinking, and identifying this entity is a common element in fortune telling, which we have already seen as having important elements in common with virtual play.[15]

The Facebook app's invitation to reveal my alternative patronus, appealed to my familiarity with J. K. Rowling's fantasy and also to my past experience with "spirit animals." It had been posted by a folklorist whom I respected as an authority on the spiritual role of animal figures in religion and ritual. She had already posted an image of her own alternative patronus, further whetting my curiosity. In addition, the others in the group already playing were acquaintances whom I recognized as having become comfortable with the ludic give-and-take of Facebook, "not only as someone who is fun, playful and creative," as virtual ethnographer Ana Deumert observed, "but also as someone who is familiar with the genre and the potential freedoms such informal spaces can offer to the expression of the self" (2014, 42).

I visited the app, clicked through the tabs (consenting to the use of my private data when necessary), and accessed the questions, each of which was pleasantly linked to the Harry Potter world.[16] In short order I was surprised and pleased when the Facebook app identified my alternative patronus as a fennec fox, explaining, "You're brave, but also not afraid to be silly." I honored my restitution duties by posting the result on my timeline (complete with the link to the app so others could join the play). It earned thirteen "likes" and a comment from a folklore colleague who had taken the test and received the same answer. Other friends' posts about this quiz revealed different alternative patronuses, often quirky ones, with sometimes pointed and perceptive personality explanations. It was good play, I felt: I got to see myself in a slightly new way, talk about this in the company of friends who were doing the same thing for themselves, and have an interesting long think about what fennec foxes and I have in common.

Returning to the objective vein, I learned something about the holistic way in which virtual play works. Literally, it involves an invitation and a sense that I will be playing in the company of people I know well and trust as colleagues and friends. But in a more esoteric sense, my decision to play was based on a common familiarity with the popular culture of J. K. Rowling's fantasy world. Using this app was an affirmation of my membership in a broader fan culture, as well as a token that I, like others in the group playing, had investigated the many ways in which the Harry Potter story referenced living folk cultures (see Ellis 2004, 13–15 and passim). Taking the "personality quiz" and posting the results took only a few minutes, and the rewards were gratifying: I'd created an interesting discussion with close friends about how they saw me as a distinctive personality and how they found new ways to see themselves. Restitution and reciprocity worked together. Playfulness enabled insight. Illogic bred community. Overtly and covertly, as Steiner might have said, the books balanced.[17]

ONE MORE COVERT ASPECT: DATA MINERS' ALGORITHMS

The "Alternative Patronus" was not the only app that I was tempted to try out during my participant ethnography. For a number of reasons (notably my interest in how animation calls traditional gender identity into question), I was tempted to try out "What Would You Look Like As The Opposite Gender?" But something about the directions spooked me. When I clicked on the link to the remote website, a screen opened where I was prompted to "Login with Facebook." The site reassured users that it was intended to generate fun material and did not store or share users' information. Nonetheless, this raised red flags in my thinking. Clicking on the "Login" site produced another screen that told me that I was in fact consenting to share the contents of my entire public profile with the proprietors of the website. At yet another screen, I was prompted to allow the site access to my timeline, so that it could post the resulting image however it saw fit. Demur (as I did at this point) and the website's bot peevishly refused to let the process go further.

Clearly such apps demand a more stringent level of restitution: in order for the virtual play to remain *simple*, I was being asked to provide quite a bit of information to strangers, which I would normally share only with people I trust. This exposes a vulnerability in this mode of virtual play. As I have argued, some integral aspects are by nature *covert*—that is, part of the intuitive mental mode of the persons playing. This novel aspect, however, is "covert" in a different and more portentous way: it is consciously concealed from the participant, much as the success of a prank or practical joke relies on misrepresenting to one of the players the social frame being enacted. There is a show of *sociability*—an invitation to share private information with members of a folk group. But the information offered is also being observed silently by interested parties who are not part of the players' social circles. My vulpine alternative patronus (i.e., the personality traits that the animal image made tangible) warned me that playing in this particular app-driven arena meant exposing personal data to a much larger and less well-defined group. The level of *restitution* was no longer limited to my folk group. I was giving more than I was getting. For me, the books no longer balanced. I backed out of the game.

My survey of Facebook games included other incidents in which participants declined invitations, warning others that the information requested could be covertly data mined by criminals seeking to commit identity theft. This occurred most visibly in non-app forms of play, such as the invitation (posted May 19, 2018) that celebrated the wedding of Prince Harry to Meghan Markle by asking viewers to make up a "royal wedding guest name." The directions said to combine a grandparent's name, the name of a first pet, and the street the player grew up on. The first person to respond cautioned that answering these questions gave away the answers to common security questions used by banks and other online accounts to confirm that a login is legitimate. A second poster added, "May as well say, your seat assignment is the expiration date of your debit card. Haha." (This drew two "laughing" emojis from viewers.) Similarly, a "What's your Star Wars name" invitation (posted May 27, 2018) asked for the first three letters of your last name, the first two letters of your first name, plus the first two letters of your mother's maiden name and the first three letters of the city where you were born. This too was quickly flagged as a security risk: "Great way for them to find the answer to 2 standard security questions." In these cases, however, the person who posted the invitation observed that posters should feel free to use the name of other relatives and make up names of nonexistent pets and streets. But that seemed to add an unnecessary level of complexity: rather than using answers that were simple to give (and simple for data-mining readers to exploit) one needed to pause and make up a convincing lie. Again, for many players, the books no longer balanced.

Nevertheless, these threads and others like them continue to be patronized on Facebook. After all, the invitations are enticing, and the invisible algorithm makes them simple to perform. However, as Nancy Baym (2015) has noted, these algorithms are also designed for the benefit of people outside of the group that uses the platforms they generate. Facebook itself operates through algorithms, and while its users keenly read and respond to posts on their friends' profiles and on their timelines, they are typically unaware of the digital programs that filter what posts they see and (more ominously) what they are prevented from seeing (Baym 2015, 73). In 2014, a brief controversy erupted when it was revealed that a group of experimenters had altered the Facebook algorithms for two study groups, blocking (for one group) stories with positive news and blocking (for the other) stories with a negative slant. None of the participants were informed that they were taking part in the study, which some critics (e.g., Shaw 2015) considered a serious violation of the expectation of informed consent. Facebook countered that its privacy agreement with users allowed it to share information posted by its users for scholarly purposes.

To be sure, most users routinely and rapidly click through such waivers and agreements to play app-driven games and indeed to register on Facebook itself. These terms of service are thus theoretically overt to Facebook residents, but data miners rely on the likelihood that few participants actually *read* such provisions. That is, they are designed to be covert in actual practice. In fact, a survey of such privacy agreements (Litman-Navarro 2019) recently found that the vast majority were couched in readability levels that exceeded those expected for college students. They were written not to inform consumers of the risks they were taking on, but to shield firms from litigation in case consumers believed their rights (or their computers) had been compromised. They are "documents created by lawyers for lawyers," one critic commented. In other words, the author concluded, "a significant chunk of the data collection economy is based on consenting to complicated documents that many Americans can't understand" (Litman-Navarro 2019). Baym agrees that the social media experience is driven by feeds, and these feeds are shaped by algorithms generated by programmers with interests quite different from those of the folk groups resident on platforms like Facebook (2015, 73).

The additional covert aspect added by the algorithm and its corporate designers affirms that virtual play is by no means trivial; instead, it is immensely valuable for mercantile and political purposes. Well-designed apps, add-ons, and play invitations honor the three dyads of virtual play discussed above while also using these aspects to hail an ample supply of players and, subsequently, user data. If answers like "fennec fox" and "brave but not afraid to be silly" feel right to me, it is probably because they derive from a web-based algorithm that makes good predictions about my personality, my choices in popular culture, my intellectual interests, and, ultimately, my purchasing and voting preferences. One might argue, as Tim Cook did (*Bloomberg News* 2018) that such algorithms perhaps should not even exist, if their sole purpose is to harvest personal information for the purposes of covert manipulation.

These practices are effective in engaging users because on the folk level virtual play exists for many other nontrivial reasons. As I have argued above, virtual play has surprisingly complex social and psychological functions, in which honest real-world issues are projected onto a platform that allows them to be viewed and discussed in a lucid way. It is a ubiquitous social means for verbalizing intensely personal insights and sharing them with select groups of friends. Sharing and discussing these insights with others in a virtual frame involves participants intensely, sometimes more so than in their face-to-face interactions. And this act of negotiation, as ethnographers of RPGs have agreed, creates a playground for reflecting on the non-virtual world and an opportunity for transformational changes in self-identity. Admittedly, involvement in a specific form of virtual play is short-lived, compared with long-term residency in a virtual world. Still, I argue, the two are based on identical mental processes and have similar functions, and the sheer number of forms of play (and the ubiquity of participants) is in itself proof that this tradition is a significant and influential force in the folklore of social media.

So there are excellent reasons why virtual play exists and has, as we have seen, moved from the face-to-face forms documented by Sutton-Smith and his colleagues into the earliest prevalent forms of digital communication (email, forums) and now into social media. What doesn't exist is nuanced observation and description of how such play influences culture, providing millions of people opportunities for personal introspection and pleasurable exchange with others. Analysts of play agree that such activities are hardly random, never trivial, and represent a deeply compelling human activity. Based on robust neural pathways, they represent a subtle means of understanding who we are and what we want our culture to become.

If we choose not to study such a "trivial" pursuit, however, there are many other interest groups that already understand its value to individuals and are ready to observe and covertly exploit it for their own purposes.

NOTES

1. At the same time, digitally enhanced versions of such pastimes, particularly video games, have long been stereotyped by conservative observers as socially dangerous, preparing its participants for a life of criminal activity, involvement in Satanism, and/or acts of mass murder (see Laycock 2015). For this reason, I've resisted using the term *game* to describe the virtual traditions of unproductive play, though "internet game" is the usual emic term among participants.

2. The fantasy frame was originally named a "MUD," or Multi-User Dimension (originally, "Dungeon"), i.e., a computer-mediated virtual social setting in which participants adopt an alternative identity and interact with other players, usually through typed text.

3. These scholars include Fine (1983), Boellstorff (2008), Nardi (2010), Milspaw and Evans (2010), and Laycock (2015). Boellstorf et al. (2012) provide a useful history of virtual worlds and a methodology for anthropological study of the communities that evolve around them.

4. A "resident" is a participant in a virtual-reality platform. Boellstorff (2008) prefers this etic term to others commonly used to refer to informants in computer-enhanced social worlds such as these, including "user," "player," and "gamer," as they suggest false characterizations of these worlds as necessarily a form of "play."

5. Ben Gillis (2011), however, notes that residents of *World of Warcraft* often treat adventures as a form of virtual "work," actively preparing for difficult dungeons or battles by making spreadsheets and using other occupational strategies.

6. See Goffman (1974, 41–43) for an extensive list of the implicit social rules involved in framing social behavior as "playful."

7. Yanagita's important theoretical work *Minkan Denshō Ron* (A Study of Popular Oral Transmission, 1933), sadly, remains unavailable in English. I have used the detailed paraphrase by Leith Morton (2003, 79) here. Iwasaka and Toelken also reference this work, but render the third aspect as "things believed" (1994, 55). I've followed Morton's rendering here as it seems truer to the Japanese ethnographer's belief that some traditions needed to be experienced to be fully understood.

8. Steiner credits Lévi-Strauss's formative work *Anthropologie structurale* (1958) but without providing a specific page reference (see Ellis 2012, 194).

9. This by no means suggests that all playful interaction in social media is welcomed or understood as mutually inclusive. Obviously in many contexts "trolling" (deliberately inciting a public quarrel) or "flaming" (attacking a group member publicly) are seen as play by the perpetrators and as a serious matter by the victims and by moderators. See, for instance, Phillips and Milner (2017), who argue that one-sided criticism of such behavior fails to grasp the full ambivalent spectrum of playful purposes and perspectives that "trolling" can include (10).

10. The earliest example I found is archived on the Google Group Fuzz Users Unite, dated July 1, 2009. It contains message headers dating back to June 25, 2009. The list of words offered by players begins "1/02/09," i.e., February 1, 2009, in British dating conventions. An earlier version, with the same directions but not calling the activity "Scrabble,"

existed as early as June 7, 2006, when a version (with an already substantial list of word transformations) was archived on the Google Group CPCS Friends. This earlier version gave players' first names but not dates or locations.

11. The thread, still live, is available in the Anime-Beta forum's archive: Board index > Anime and Production Art > General Production Art > Something Fun.

12. A second thread, begun on February 23, 2012, likewise proved immortal. The starting member introduced it by saying, "Some of the old old collectors may remember on the animanga forums we would sometimes have [a] Show me thread where one person would propose a theme (ex. show me wings, show me couples) and people would respond with cels that met the theme. I thought it might be fun to do something similar here, but where the person responding gets to pick a new theme for the next person." This likewise adds the "restitution" element by allowing the person who fulfills the "show me" request to control the next move in the play activity. While less active than "Something fun," the newer thread also remains active in July 2020, having gathered 739 posts and 24,632 individual visits.

13. *Family Feud* is the name of a syndicated game show created in 1976 by Mark Goodson and still in the lineup of American daytime broadcasting. The "Let's Play!" invitation in the header is itself a traditional element in internet folklore, as it appears in the title of a 2008 YouTube video, *ROCK PAPER SCISSORS!! (Lets play!!)*. This homemade video explained the rules of the common gestural competitive game and invited viewers to add their own answering gestures as comments on the video (see Buccitelli 2012, 71–72).

14. Googling "April Fool's" + "switch salt and sugar" returned about 2,060,000 results (September 3, 2018), including a number of websites giving lists of "great" or "best" April Fool's Day pranks.

15. The link between animals and spiritual beings is a deep one in world religions and surprisingly strong among contemporary Americans as well. See Magliocco (2018) for a discussion of these contemporary traditions.

16. My Hogwarts house? Hufflepuff, of course.

17. The phrase adapts Steiner's discussion of restitution as part of a "dynamic equilibrium" that unifies communities. A self-centered act, he argued, requires an equal but opposite action that benefits the group; "both formally and morally the books must balance" (1975, 303). See also my own adaptation of Steiner's phrase expressing the communal dialectic (2014, 201).

REFERENCES

Baldwin, Karen. 2018. "Reading Tarot: Telling Fortunes, Telling Friends, and Retelling Everyday Life." In *The Supernatural in Society, Culture, and History*, edited by Dennis D. Waskul and Marc Eaton, 136–51. Philadelphia: Temple University Press.

Baym, Nancy K. 2015. *Personal Connections in the Digital Age*. 2nd ed. Cambridge: Polity. https://www.hs-heilbronn.de/16580627/2015-baym-nancy-personal-connections-in-a-digital-age-pdf.pdf.

Ben-Amos, Dan. 1971. "Toward a Definition of Folklore in Context." *Journal of American Folklore* 84 (331): 3–15.

Blank, Trevor J. 2007. "Examining the Transmission of Urban Legends: Making the Case for Folklore Fieldwork on the Internet." *Folklore Forum* 37 (1): 15–26.

Bloomberg News. 2018. "Apple's Tim Cook Calls for More Regulations on Data Privacy." March 24, 2018. https://www.bloomberg.com/news/articles/2018-03-24/apple-s-tim-cook-calls-for-more-regulations-on-data-privacy.

Boellstorff, Tom. 2008. *Coming of Age in Second Life: An Anthropologist Explores the Virtually Human*. Princeton: Princeton University Press.
Boellstorff, Tom, Bonnie Nardi, Celia Pearce, and T. L. Taylor. 2012. *Ethnography and Virtual Worlds: A Handbook of Method*. Princeton: Princeton University Press.
Buccitelli, Anthony Bak. 2012. "Performance 2.0: Observations toward a Theory of the Digital Performance of Folklore." In *Folk Culture in the Digital Age*, edited by Trevor J. Blank, 60–84. Logan: Utah State University Press.
Chappell, Bill. 2018. "How to Check If Your Facebook Data Was Used by Cambridge Analytica." *The Two Way*, April 10, 2018. National Public Radio. https://www.npr.org/sections/thetwo-way/2018/04/10/601163176/how-to-check-if-your-facebook-data-was-used-by-cambridge-analytica.
Danet, Brenda. 2001. *Cyberpl@y: Communicating Online*. New York: Berg.
Danet, Brenda, and Tamar Katriel. 1994. "Glorious Obsessions, Passionate Lovers, and Hidden Treasures: Collecting, Metaphor, and the Romantic Ethic." In *The Socialness of Things: Essays on the Socio-Semiotics of Objects*, edited by Stephen Harold Riggins, 23–61. New York: Mouton de Gruyter.
Deumert, Ana. 2014. "The Performance of a Ludic Self on Social Network(ing) Sites." In *The Language of Social Media*, edited by Philip Seargeant and Caroline Tagg, 23–45. London: Palgrave Macmillan.
Dundes, Alan, and Carl R. Pagter. 1978. *Work Hard and You Shall Be Rewarded: Urban Folklore from the Paperwork Empire*. Bloomington: Indiana University Press.
Ellis, Bill. 2002. *Making a Big Apple Crumble: The Role of Humor in Constructing a Global Response to Disaster. New Directions in Folklore* 6 (June). https://scholarworks.iu.edu/journals/index.php/ndif/article/view/19883/25953.
Ellis, Bill. 2004. *Lucifer Ascending: The Occult in Folklore and Popular Culture*. Lexington: University Press of Kentucky.
Ellis, Bill. 2012. "Love and War and Anime Art: An Ethnographic Look at a Virtual Community of Collectors." In *Folk Culture in the Digital Age*, edited by Trevor J. Blank, 166–211. Logan: Utah State University Press.
Fine, Gary Alan. 1983. *Shared Fantasy: Role-Playing Games as Social Worlds*. Chicago: University of Chicago Press.
Frank, Russell. 2009. "The *Forward* as Folklore: Studying E-mailed Humor." In *Folklore and the Internet: Vernacular Expression in a Digital World*, edited by Trevor J. Blank, 98–122. Logan: Utah State University Press.
Gillis, Ben. 2011. "An Unexpected Font of Folklore: Online Gaming as Occupational Lore." *Western Folklore* 70 (2): 147–170.
Goffman, Erving. 1974. *Frame Analysis*. New York: Harper.
Heimlich, Russell. 2010. "Email vs. Social Networks." *Pew Research Center, Factank*, September 13, 2010. http://pewrsr.ch/UMOa84.
Howard, Robert Glenn. 2012. "How Counterculture Helped Put the 'Vernacular' in Vernacular Webs." In *Folk Culture in the Digital Age*, edited by Trevor J. Blank, 25–45. Logan: Utah State University Press.
Iwasaka, Michiko, and Barre Toelken. 1994. *Ghosts and the Japanese: Cultural Experience in Japanese Death Legends*. Logan: Utah State University Press.
Lanham, Richard. 1993. *The Electronic World: Democracy, Technology, and the Arts*. Chicago: University of Chicago Press.
Laycock, Joseph P. 2015. *Dangerous Games: What the Moral Panic over Role-Playing Games Says about Play, Religion, and Imagined Worlds*. Berkeley: University of California Press.
Litman-Navarro, Kevin. 2019. "We Read 150 Privacy Policies. They Were an Incomprehensible Disaster." *New York Times*, June 12, 2019. https://www.nytimes.com/interactive/2019/06/12/opinion/facebook-google-privacy-policies.html.

Magliocco, Sabina. 2018. "Beyond the Rainbow Bridge: Vernacular Ontologies of Animal Afterlives." *Journal of Folklore Research* 55 (2): 39–67.
Meredith, Sam. 2018. "Facebook–Cambridge Analytica: A Timeline of the Data Hijacking Scandal." *CNBC*, April 10, 2018. https://www.cnbc.com/2018/04/10/facebook-cambridge-analytica-a-timeline-of-the-data-hijacking-scandal.html.
Milspaw, Yvonne J., and Wesley K. Evans. 2010. "Variations on Vampires: Live Action Role Playing, Fantasy, and the Revival of Traditional Beliefs." *Western Folklore* 69 (2): 211–250.
Morton, Leith. 2003. *Modern Japanese Culture: The Insider View*. New York: Oxford University Press.
Nardi, Bonnie A. 2010. *My Life as a Night Elf Priest: An Anthropological Account of "World of Warcraft."* Ann Arbor: University of Michigan Press.
Peck, Andrew. 2015a. "At the Modems of Madness: The Slender Man, Ostension, and the Digital Age." *Contemporary Legend* (3) 5: 14–37.
Peck, Andrew. 2015b. "Tall, Dark, and Loathsome: The Emergence of a Legend Cycle in the Digital Age." *Journal of American Folklore* 128 (509): 333–348.
Phillips, Whitney, and Ryan M. Milner. 2017. *The Ambivalent Internet: Mischief, Oddity, and Antagonism Online*. Cambridge: Polity.
Rosenberg, Matthew, Nicholas Confessore, and Carole Cadwalladr. 2018. "How Trump Consultants Exploited the Facebook Data of Millions." *New York Times*, March 17, 2018. https://www.nytimes.com/2018/03/17/us/politics/cambridge-analytica-trump-campaign.html.
Scarlett, W. George, Sophie C. Naudeau, Dorothy Salonius-Pasternak, and Iris Chin Ponte. 2005. *Children's Play*. Thousand Oaks, CA: Sage.
Shaw, David. 2015. "Facebook's Flawed Emotion Experiment: Antisocial Research on Social Networkusers." *Research Ethics*, May 15, 2015. Sage Journals. https://journals.sagepub.com/doi/full/10.1177/1747016115579535.
Stam, Kathryn, and Michael Scialdone. 2008. "Where Dreams and Dragons Meet: An Ethnographic Analysis of Two Examples of Massive Multiplayer Online Role-Playing Games (MMORPGs)." *Online—Heidelberg Journal of Religions on the Internet* 3 (1): 61–95.
Steiner, George. 1975. *After Babel: Aspects of Language and Translation*. New York: Oxford University Press.
Sutton-Smith, Brian. 1970. "Psychology of Childlore: The Triviality Barrier." *Western Folklore* 29 (1): 1–8.
Sutton-Smith, Brian. 1999. "Overview: Methods in Children's Folklore." In *Children's Folklore: A Source Book*, edited by Brian Sutton-Smith, Jay Mechling, Thomas W. Johnson, and Felicia R. McMahon, 63–72. Logan: Utah State University Press.
Turkle, Sherry. 1994. "Constructions and Reconstructions of Self in Virtual Reality: Playing in the MUDs." *Mind, Culture, and Activity* 1 (3): 158–167.
VanArsdale, Daniel W. 2016. *Chain Letter Evolution*. http://www.silcom.com/~barnowl/chain-letter/evolution.html#s2-1predecessors.

About the Contributors

TREVOR J. BLANK is an associate professor of communication at the State University of New York at Potsdam. He specializes in the study of digital expression, pop culture, humor, public health, and urban legends, and is the author or editor of nine books, including *Folklore and the Internet*, *Folk Culture in the Digital Age*, and *The Last Laugh: Folk Humor, Celebrity Culture, and Mass-Mediated Disasters in the Digital Age*.

SHEILA BOCK is associate professor in the Department of Interdisciplinary, Gender, and Ethnic Studies at the University of Nevada, Las Vegas. Her diverse research interests include material and digital enactments of personal and community identities, the intersections between folklore and popular culture, and the contested domains of illness experience. Her work has been published in *Journal of American Folklore*; *Journal of Folklore Research*; *Western Folklore*; *Journal of Folklore and Education*; *Western Journal of Black Studies*; *Journal of Medical Humanities*; *Health, Culture, and Society*; *Diagnosing Folklore: Perspectives on Disability, Health, and Trauma*; *Comfort Food: Meanings and Memories*; and *The Oxford Handbook of American Folklore and Folklife Studies*.

PETER M. BROADWELL is a digital scholarship research developer at the Center for Interdisciplinary Digital Research in the Stanford University Libraries. His research applies machine learning and other methods of computational analysis to complex cultural data. Recently, he has contributed to studies involving automatic translation and indexing of folklore collections in multiple languages, as well as choreography detection in online video collections. He also has contributed to studies investigating the relationships between social media, television news, and web content.

BILL ELLIS is professor emeritus of English and American studies at Penn State University. He is a fellow of the American Folklore Society and past president of the International Society for Contemporary Legend Research. He has published on many forms of emergent folklore, including legends and legend tripping, topical jokes and humorous anti-legends, the use of Western fairy tales in Japanese anime, the formation and maintenance of virtual communities, and digital folklore generated by fan cultures such as Bronies (adult fans of *My Little Pony*).

JEANA JORGENSEN is a feminist folklorist, alt-ac scholar, blogger, sex educator, and dancer. She currently teaches at Butler University and has taught at Indiana University and the University of California, Berkeley, in recent years. Her research focuses on gender and sexuality in fairy tales and folk narrative more broadly, the intersections of folklore and pop culture, body art, dance, digital humanities, feminist and queer theory, and the history of sex education. Her research has been published in *Marvels and Tales, Journal of American Folklore, Cultural Analysis, Literary and Linguistic Computing, Journal of Ethnology and Folkloristics*, and elsewhere.

LIISI LAINESTE is a senior researcher in the Department of Folkloristics of the Estonian Literary Museum and the Center for Excellence in Estonian Studies. Her main research interests are folk humor and its online manifestations. She has published articles on ethnic humor, internet folklore, and caricatures. She has co-authored studies that deal with ethnic jokes and their globalization (with A. Fiadotava) and online rumors (with E. Kalmre), and, with Sharon Lockyer, she is the editor of a special issue of *HUMOR: International Journal of Humor Research*, entitled "Jokes, Targets and Spontaneous Order."

JOHN LAUDUN is professor of English at the University of Louisiana, where his research focuses on computational models of discourse, especially narratives, and how they cascade through sociocultural networks both online and off. In addition to his work on folk narrative and the intellectual history of folklore studies, he has published a monograph on material folk culture, *The Amazing Crawfish Boat*, one of the first folklore studies to make a case for the application of network theory to creativity and tradition. He has been a Jacob K. Javits Fellow with the US Department of Education, a MacArthur Scholar, a fellow at the EVIA Digital Archive, a fellow with the NEH Institute on Network Studies in the Humanities, and a senior researcher in culture analytics at UCLA's Institute for Pure and Applied Mathematics. For more information, please see http://johnlaudun.net/.

LINDA J. LEE is the director of instructional design at the Wharton School of the University of Pennsylvania and a part-time lecturer at Penn, where she teaches online and face-to-face courses in folklore. Her research focuses on gender issues in folk and fairy tales, and on the transformation of traditional narratives in contemporary media and popular culture. Her research has been published in *Marvels and Tales* and *Channeling Wonder: Fairy Tales on Television*, and she co-curated the "Grimms' Anatomy: Magic and Medicine" exhibit for the Mütter Museum of the College of Physicians of Philadelphia.

LYNNE S. MCNEILL holds a PhD in folklore from Memorial University of Newfoundland and serves as chair of the folklore program at Utah State University. Her research interests include contemporary legends, the supernatural, and digital culture, among other diverse subjects. She is the co-editor of *Slender Man Is Coming: Creepypasta and Contemporary Legends on the Internet* and the author of the popular textbook *Folklore Rules*. She has made many appearances on national television and radio, in productions for Animal Planet, the Food Network, the Travel Channel, and Public Radio International.

About the Contributors

RYAN M. MILNER is an associate professor of communication at the College of Charleston. He studies internet culture, which means he studies everything from funny GIFs to Twitter debates to large-scale propaganda campaigns. Throughout this work, he assesses how online interaction matters socially, politically, and culturally. He's the author of *The World Made Meme: Public Conversations and Participatory Media* and the co-author, with Whitney Phillips, of *The Ambivalent Internet: Mischief, Oddity, and Antagonism Online*. Ryan has also contributed commentary to outlets like *Time*, *Slate*, the *Los Angeles Review of Books*, *NBC News*, and the *New York Times*.

ANDREW PECK is assistant professor of strategic communication in the Department of Media, Journalism, and Film at Miami University. His research focuses on how digital media offers new possibilities for the practice of everyday communication and frequently deals with topics such as humor, play, internet memes, fake news, vernacular authority, and contemporary legends. His work has appeared in the *International Journal of Communication*, the *Journal of American Folklore*, and in the edited collection *Slender Man Is Coming*.

WHITNEY PHILLIPS is an assistant professor of communication and rhetorical studies at Syracuse University. She's the author of *This Is Why We Can't Have Nice Things: Mapping the Relationship between Online Trolling and Mainstream Culture* and coauthor of *The Ambivalent Internet: Mischief, Oddity, and Antagonism Online* and *You Are Here: A Field Guide for Navigating Network Manipulation*, both with Ryan Milner. In addition to a dozen journal articles and book chapters on a range of media studies topics, Phillips has written numerous pieces for publications such as the *Atlantic*, the *New York Times*, and *Slate*.

VWANI ROYCHOWDHURY is a professor of electrical and computer engineering at the University of California, Los Angeles. His research focuses on machine learning, artifical intelligence, computational social science and culture analytics, complex networks, and quantum and bio-inspired computing. Roychowdhury received a PhD in electrical engineering from Stanford University. Contact him at vwani@ee.ucla.edu.

TIMOTHY R. TANGHERLINI is professor in the Department of Scandinavian and the graduate advisor for the graduate program in folklore at the University of California, Berkeley. He is the author of *Danish Folktales, Legends and Other Stories; Interpreting Legend* and *Talking Trauma*. His research focuses on the political dimensions of storytelling, and how legends and rumors circulate on and across social networks. He was the co-director of the NSF program on culture analytics at the sInstitute for Pure and Applied Mathematics. His research has been funded by NEH, NSF, NIH, the American Council of Learned Societies, the John Simon Guggenheim Foundation, and Google Books.

Tok Thompson received his bachelor's degree in anthropology from Harvard College, his master's degree in folklore from the University of California, Berkeley, and a PhD in anthropology from the same institution, studying under the late great folklorist Alan Dundes. He has taught at Trinity College (Dublin), the University of Ulster (Northern Ireland), Addis Ababa University (Ethiopia), and the University of Iceland, in addition to his post at USC, where he is now a professor of anthropology and communications. He co-founded the journal *Cultural Analysis: An Interdisciplinary Forum on Folklore and Popular Culture*, which he co-edited for fifteen years. From 2013 to 2017 he was the editor of *Western Folklore*. He is a well-known author of a number of scholarly articles, chapters, and books on a variety of folkloric topics, including his most recent book, *Posthuman Folklore*.

Elizabeth Tucker, Distinguished Service Professor of English at Binghamton University, specializes in children's and adolescents' folklore, supernatural narratives, and legends. Her books include *Campus Legends, Haunted Halls: Ghostlore of American College Campuses, Children's Folklore, Haunted Southern Tier*, and *New York State Folklife Reader*, co-edited with Ellen McHale. With Lynne S. McNeill, she co-authored *Legend Trips: A Contemporary Legend Handbook*. She has edited *Children's Folklore Review*, served as president of the International Society for Contemporary Legend Research and the Children's Folklore section of the American Folklore Society, and been a fellow of the American Folklore Society.

Kristiana Willsey has a PhD in folklore from Indiana University, and currently teaches in the anthropology department at the University of Southern California. Her research focuses on the intersection of folk narrative with popular culture and mass media. She has published work in the *Journal of American Folklore, Humanities*, and *Children's Folklore Review*, as well as chapters in several edited volumes.

Index

adolescents, adolescence, 7–8, 199, 209–18
anxiety, 41, 130, 148, 199, 202–3
appropriation, 83–87, 89, 92–93, 98–102, 102n2
audience, audiences, 25, 35, 70, 90–91, 111–14, 122–24, 136–37, 145–46, 148–53, 155–57, 168, 173, 184–85, 234
authenticity, 93, 97–102, 102n2, 146, 156, 157–58n2, 174

belief, 43, 54–56, 61, 89, 91–92, 117–18, 124, 145–46, 148–51, 153–57
Biden, Joe, 129–41
Black Lives Matter, #BlackLivesMatter, 179, 182–83, 186, 187n4
Blank, Trevor J., 4–5, 70, 140, 209
Bock, Sheila, 71
bodylore, the body, 130, 134–36, 138, 141, 141–42n2

cable news. *See* mass media
children, 3–4, 190–92, 203, 210, 214–15, 218, 227, 231. *See also* adolescents
Clinton, Hillary, 49–50, 52–53, 56
clowns, 123, 131, 188–204. *See also* Trump, Donald
collaboration, 95, 145, 147–50, 157, 184
commenting. *See* forums
community, communities, 7–9, 27, 35, 59–61, 88, 91, 100, 108, 151, 155, 161–63, 171, 174–76, 185, 230, 233–37
contemporary legends. *See* legends
conspiracy/conspiracy theories, 39–63, 119. *See also* legends; rumors
copyright, 157n1, 161–63, 165, 168–70, 174–76, 176n3, 209
creepypasta, 146–48, 157, 209
cultural inventory, 89–90, 129–30, 140–41

Dégh, Linda, 87, 89–91; and Vázsonyi Andrew, 69, 189, 204, 204–5n4, 210
discussion boards, forums, groups. *See* forums

Digital Folklore Project, 179–82, 186, 187n1–2
Disney, 161, 170–72

email, 204n3, 236–37, 239
Ellis, Bill, 43, 69, 157, 184, 199, 206n13, 212
Estonia, 109–21, 125n3,7–8,12,14

Facebook, 5, 7–9, 25, 93, 95–98, 197, 220, 226–27, 239–45
"fake news." *See* news
fairy tales, 140, 165, 167–68, 170, 172
fandom/fans, 148, 152, 161–78
folk tales, 164–67, 171, 173. *See also* fairy tales; storytelling
folkloresque, 91, 103n5
forums, 42, 45, 55, 110, 114–23, 146, 234–39

gender, 25–26, 36n4, 243

hashtags, 11–12, 25–26, 28–35, 36n6, 39, 50–52, 57, 71, 75–77, 94, 179, 182–86, 187n3, 213
hegemonic masculinity, 138–39
Howard, Robert Glenn, 4–5, 90
humor, 84, 91, 95–96, 99, 108–24, 129–42, 142n6, 156, 183–84, 211, 222, 236, 244. *See also* parody
hybridity, 4, 6, 69–71, 87–88, 90, 92, 95–96, 101, 103n4, 175, 188, 197, 204n3

immigrants, immigration, 25–35, 36n6, 72, 113–14, 119, 121. *See also* refugees; xenophobia
India, 214, 218–21
Instagram, 8, 24–25, 29–30, 34, 54, 147–48, 155–56, 214, 220
institutions, institutional authority, institutional communication, 5–6, 11–13, 68–74, 79–80, 83–86, 102, 102n2–3, 103n4,10; memes and, 86–102. *See also* hybridity

Jenkins, Henry, 8, 163, 173
jokes. *See* humor

255

legends, 42–44, 47–49, 63n7, 69, 145–46, 149, 157, 188–206, 209–22
legend tripping. *See* ostension
literature, 161–63, 165–70, 174–75; Dickens, Charles, 167–69; Doyle, Sir Arthur Conan, 169, 176n1; *Fifty Shades of Grey*, 172

material culture, 24, 32–33
memes, 83–107, 129–44; definition, 88–89; Doge, 83–87; Ice Bucket Challenge, 183; Thanks, Obama, 98, 100, 103n11

news, 3–4, 11–12, 39, 43, 45–46, 53, 57, 59, 61, 68–80, 83, 111, 115, 117, 189–98, 200–2, 212–13; "fake news," 59, 76–79, 204

Obama, Barack, 37n10, 83–87, 90, 94, 98, 100, 103n11, 129, 131, 133–34, 136–40, 142n3,5
ostension, 58–59, 69, 184–85, 197, 199, 201, 210–14, 220, 222

parody, 110–23, 129
protest, 24, 36n7, 112, 129, 182

QAnon, 44, 47, 54–62, 63–64n17–21

racism, 31, 34, 71, 77, 80
Reddit, 49–50, 52, 55, 77, 92
refugees, 109–112, 117, 121, 125n13. *See also* immigrants; xenophobia

rumor, rumors, 41, 55, 57, 209–19, 221–22. *See also* conspiracy theories
Russia, 53, 56, 63n14, 68, 73, 112, 125n13, 135, 167, 212–16, 219, 221–22

Satan, Satanism, Satanic activity, 44, 47–50, 52, 54–55, 59, 63n12, 214, 221–22, 247n1
sex, 131, 134, 136–139, 162, 171–72
SnapChat, 201–2
storytelling, 36n6, 41, 49, 59, 62, 147–52, 156, 162, 164–68, 173–76
Sutton-Smith, Brian, 226–31, 233, 235, 246

Tangherlini, Tim, 192–93, 199–200, 205–6n11
teenagers, 7, 104n13, 192, 195, 199, 209–22. *See also* adolescents
transmission, 4, 6, 204–5n4
Trump, Donald, 31–32, 39, 53, 56, 67–69, 71–80, 129–30, 133–41, 142n6,7, 226
Twitter, tweets, (re)tweeting, 10, 39, 50–51, 55–58, 61, 62n1, 67–69, 71–79, 83–84, 86, 145–49, 151–57, 179, 182–85

vernacular authority, 86–101, 162, 174–75
virtual community. *See* community

witches, witchcraft, 47–49, 52–53, 62n3, 63n12

xenophobia, 76, 108–114, 121

YouTube, 9, 92, 114, 152, 210, 214–21

www.ingramcontent.com/pod-product-compliance
Lightning Source LLC
Chambersburg PA
CBHW020249030426
42336CB00010B/689